HTML PUE

ON THE inte… …et

FOR MACINTOSH

Create Great-Looking Documents Online:
Home Pages, Newsletters, Catalogs, Ads & Forms

Brent Heslop & David Holzgang

VENTANA

HTML Publishing on the Internet for Macintosh: Create Great-Looking Documents Online: Home Pages, Newsletters, Catalogs, Ads & Forms

Library of Congress Cataloging-in-Publication Data

Heslop, Brent D.

HTML publishing on the Internet for Macintosh: create great-looking documents online: home pages, newsletters, catalogs, ads & forms / Brent Heslop & David Holzgang. — 1st ed.

p. cm.

Includes bibliographical references and index.

ISBN 1-56604-228-3

1. Hypertext systems. 2. HTML (Document markup language) 3. Internet (Computer network) 4. Macintosh (Computer)

I. Holzgang, David A. II. Title.

QA76.76.H94H48 1995

005.75—dc20 95-652

CIP

Book design: Marcia Webb
Cover illustration: Tom Draper Design
Acquisitions Editor: Cheri Robinson
Art Director: Marcia Webb
Design staff: Bradley King, Charles Overbeck, Dawne Sherman
Editorial Manager: Pam Richardson
Editorial staff: Angela Anderson, Amy Moyers, Beth Snowberger
Developmental Editor: Tim C. Mattson
Project Editor: Jessica Ryan
Print Department: Kristen DeQuattro, Dan Koeller, Wendy Bernhardt
Production Manager: John Cotterman
Production staff: Patrick Berry
Index service: Richard T. Evans, Infodex
Proofreader: Angela Anderson
Technical review: Matthew Saderholm

First Edition 9 8 7 6 5 4 3 2 1
Printed in the United States of America

Ventana Communications Group, Inc.
P.O. Box 13964
Research Triangle Park, NC 27709-3964
919/544-9404
FAX 919/544-9472

Trademarks

About the Authors

Brent Heslop has co-authored over 14 books on a wide range of computer topics. He is a co-author of Ventana's *HTML Publishing on the Internet for Windows*. He is a partner in Bookware, a technical writing firm with offices on the East and West coasts. Brent is a frequent contributor to *PC Magazine* and other computer-related magazines. Currently he is teaching classes on HTML publishing for the University of California, Santa Cruz. He lives in Mountain View, California, with his lovely wife Kim and their devoted dog Cassius.

David A. Holzgang is a recognized authority on automated text and document handling and printing in distributed systems. He is the author of many leading books on programming, desktop publishing and graphics. David is the founder and managing general partner of the Cheshire Group, which is a software development and consulting organization. The Cheshire Group specializes in graphics and graphics programming and has developed programs and presentation material in both the IBM and Macintosh environments. He lives and works in the San Francisco Bay area.

Acknowledgments

No one person can tackle as fast changing a topic as publishing on the Internet. Numerous people supplied us with valuable information and software for which we are extremely grateful. First and foremost we want to thank Elizabeth Woodman at Ventana Communications Group, Inc. and our agent, Matt Wagner, at Waterside Productions for having the foresight to publish this book. One person we want to thank in particular for his research and contributions to this book is David McConville, who wrote Chapter 9, "Adding Scintillating Sound & Vivid Video." His great expertise and writing skill helped make this a better book.

Essential to writing a book on publishing on the Internet is an Internet connection. We are in debt to Rich White at Best Internet Communications for letting us use Best Internet Communication's service to set up the Web site used for examples in this book. Rich helped us by answering many of our questions and kept us on the cutting-edge by sharing up-to-date information about relevant Web publishing technologies throughout this project.

The greatest source of information about the Internet comes, of course, from the Net itself. We used many sites as resources for this book, and have tried to note each one in the text where appropriate. We hope that these listings will give you a head start on building your own list of valuable sites. This community of information is part of what makes the Internet a great resource on so many topics. In that regard, we would like to especially thank Jon Wiederspan for his work in putting together a great site that is a primary resource for anyone who wants to use the Macintosh on the Internet.

His site, at http://www.uwtc.washington.edu/Computing/WWW/Mac/Directory.html, is a great place to get all types of information on Macintosh Internet software, general Macintosh development topics and related goodies.

Many thanks to Cheri Robinson, Max Leach and Colin Soloway at Ventana Communications, who were instrumental in setting up the CD-ROM. We especially want to thank all the companies and individuals that let us include their software on the Companion CD-ROM. Some companies and products were essential to writing this book and deserve special recognition. SoftQuad helped us throughout this project, in particular we want to thank Lucy Ventresca for supplying us with HoTMetaL PRO and HoTMetaL LITE and late-breaking news, Liam Quin for his technical review and Donald Teed for answering our many questions. A special thanks to John Hahn at Netscape Communications for letting us include the commercial version of Netscape Navigator. We were overjoyed that Michael Dawson let us include a full-functioning evaluation version of the WebSTAR Server and Guy Stevens let us include a full-functioning evaluation version of InterServer Publisher and their respective related utilities. We are grateful to Tammy Wing at Image Club Graphics, Inc. for letting us include some impressive clip art and digital photos. Natalie Angelillo at PhotoDisk and Ann Burgraff at CMCD helped by supplying us with some great digital photo samples. Thanks also to Rick Brown for keeping us in the know about Adobe Acrobat products and letting us include Adobe Acrobat Reader.

We also want to express our thanks to John Wiechman at A Clean Well-Lighted Place for Books for letting us use ACWLP as an example throughout the book and John Scott for letting us help write and publish the information for their Web pages.

Additionally we want to thank Cheri Robinson, Pam Richardson, Angela Anderson, Tim Mattson, Patrick Berry and John Cotterman at Ventana Press who helped in the production of this book. We want to thank Jessica Ryan, our editor, who offered valuable insight and guidance to help improve this book. Jessica went beyond the call of duty in order to help us keep the book as up-to-date as possible by making numerous last minute changes.

Dedication

We want to thank our wives Kim Merry and Shirley Grant for supporting us through this entire project.

Contents

Section II: Working With the Pieces

Section III: Putting the Pieces Together

Section IV: Appendices

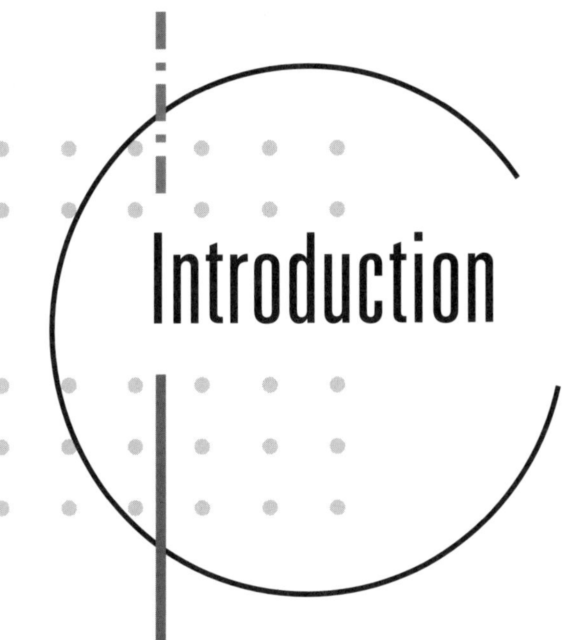

Introduction

Everyone wants to get published on the Internet, and why not? Publishing on the Internet is one of the most important and exciting happenings in computing since the launching of the PC revolution back in the early '80s. This book focuses on the most effective and by far the most popular Internet publishing method, publishing on the World Wide Web using HTML and HTTP.

Who Needs This Book?

Any Macintosh user who is interested in how to publish pages on the World Wide Web will find the answers in this guide. Even if you don't want to create the pages yourself, this book offers helpful information as to what you need to do to have someone publish Web pages for you. Knowing how Web publishing works can save you time and money. Many services charge between $100 to $200 an hour to create Web pages. So if you're interested in creating a presence for yourself or company on the Internet, this book will step you through the entire Web publishing process.

This book is written for the new user as well as the seasoned Net surfer. If you are already familiar with HTML, you'll find it includes numerous Web design tips, powerful Web publishing tools and a valuable HTML reference. If you're not familiar with the Web, the first part of the book gives a concise introduction to the Web and hypermedia publishing.

What's Inside?

The book is divided into four sections: The Elements of Hypermedia Design; Working With the Pieces; Putting the Pieces Together; and four appendices.

Chapter 1, "The World Wide Web & Hypermedia Publishing," introduces you to Internet jargon and provides a broad overview of publishing on the Internet.

Chapter 2, "HTML Editors & Converters," helps familiarize you with the most popular HTML editors and converters that exist to create Web documents.

Chapter 3, "Structuring Information in Web Documents," provides a short introduction to structuring and designing effective hypertext documents.

CD-ROM

Chapter 4, "Getting Started With HoTMetaL PRO," introduces you to the HoTMetaL LITE editor, which is included on the Companion CD-ROM, and shows you how to install and use it to create HTML documents. This chapter forms the basis for the next several chapters, which will lead you through the process of creating Web pages.

Chapter 5, "Creating Your First Web Document," is a hands-on guide to creating a home page, the cornerstone of your Web site.

Chapter 6, "The Art of Linking," shows you how to exploit the power of links to publish complex Web documents and connect to files and other Web documents around the world.

Chapter 7, "Creating Your Text Appeal," introduces you to the many possibilities for creating and formatting text using HTML.

Chapter 8, "Getting Graphic With Images," explains the basic HTML tags for creating Web documents with hyperlinks and explains how to include images. Although the hands-on examples are centered around using HoTMetaL PRO, the standard HTML codes, called tags, are also included for anyone interested in using another HTML editor.

Chapter 9, "Adding Scintillating Sound & Vivid Video," takes a look at publishing multimedia files, both sound and video, on the Internet.

Chapter 10, "Forms, Databases & CGI," gives step-by-step instructions for creating forms and using the Common Gateway Interface to publish interactive documents.

Chapter 11, "Looking Good on the Net," shares examples of unique, professionally designed Web documents that you can use as design examples to help you look good on the Net.

Chapter 12, "Service Providers & Server Services," and Chapter 13, "Servers at Your Service," explain the different Web publishing alternatives, including using a service provider, server service or setting up a Web server and publishing Web documents from your own Mac.

In the Appendices you'll find an annotated HTML reference section that includes HTML tags and Netscape extensions to HTML. Each HTML tag entry includes the standard syntax, an example and cross-references to similar or associated HTML tags and Netscape extensions. Also included is a comprehensive resource listing of Internet publishing-related programs and periodicals.

About the Online Companion

The *HTML Publishing on the Internet Online Companion* is an informative tool as well as an annotated software library. It aids in your understanding of HTML authoring and publishing on the World Wide Web, while at the same time providing you with the resources and utilities you need to accomplish these tasks. The *HTML Publishing on the Internet Online Companion* hyperlinks Chapter 11 of the hard-copy book to the World Wide Web sites it references. So you can just click on the reference name and jump directly to the resource you are interested in.

Perhaps one of the most valuable features of the *Online Companion* is its Software Archive. Here, you'll find and be able to download the latest versions of all the freely available software mentioned in *HTML Publishing on the Internet for Macintosh*. This software ranges from HTML editors, converters and templates, such as HoTMetaL PRO and BBEdit Lite, an outstanding freeware general editor, with the BBEdit HTML Tools package to allow you to add HTML markup to text documents prepared with BBEdit Lite, to many of your essential publishing programs, such as WebMap, a tool for making image maps, and SoundEffects, an editor for audio files. To access the Online Companion, connect via the World Wide Web to http://www.vmedia.com/pim.html.

About the Companion CD-ROM

We are proud to include on the Companion CD-ROM a special version of the highly acclaimed HoTMetaL editor, HoTMetaL PRO 2.0. This version, known as HoTMetaL LITE, is fully functioning, but does not contain some of the advanced import and export features of the full-blown version 2.0. To present Web document examples that can be applied to the real world, we use A Clean Well-Lighted Place for Books, a real bookstore, for most of the book's examples. A Clean Well-Lighted Place for Books is one of the premier general bookstores in the San Francisco Bay area.

Free voice technical support for *HTML Publishing on the Internet* is offered but is limited to installation-related issues and is available for 30 days from the date you register your copy of the book. The number for technical support is 1-919-544-9404. After the initial 30 days and for non-installation-related questions, please send all technical support questions via Internet e-mail to help@vmedia.com. Our technical support staff will research your question and respond promptly via e-mail.

What You Need

Other than an Internet connection, this book includes all you need to get started publishing on the World Wide Web. The Companion CD-ROM includes several of the Web-related applications and Web publishing tools explained in the book, including the newest commercial release of Netscape Navigator. Over twenty graphic image files and an assortment of graphic tools explained in Chapter 8 are also on the Companion CD-ROM. For example, we have included both the GraphicConverter application that allows you to save GIF graphics in interlaced format, for faster display, and the Transparency application that lets you save graphics with a transparent background so the image appears to float on the Web page. On the multimedia front, we have included the shareware application SoundEffects, an impressive sound editor. To help you publish your documents, the CD also includes two demonstration versions of the most popular Macintosh Web server (HTTP) program for publishing Web documents: StarNine's WebSTAR server, the commercial successor to Chuck Shotten's tremendously popular MacHTTP and InterCon' exciting new InterServer. See Appendix B, "About the Companion CD-ROM," for a complete listing of the CD's contents.

The World Wide Web is moving at an incredibly fast pace. Netscape Communications, creator of the popular Netscape Navigator, which is quickly becoming the de facto-standard Web browser, is continually adding powerful extensions to HTML. Many sections in this book were rewritten for the late-breaking Netscape extensions. At the rate things are changing on the Internet, it's nearly impossible to provide information that is 100 percent up-to-date. For that reason, wherever possible, we have also given you the Internet addresses of sites and tools that we have used so you can check them out for yourself. If you find something we've missed or if you have any comments about this book, we would appreciate hearing from you. Please send us e-mail at either of the following addresses.

Brent Heslop
bheslop@isdn.bookware.com

David Holzgang
cheshire@halcyon.com

SECTION I

The Elements of Hypermedia Design

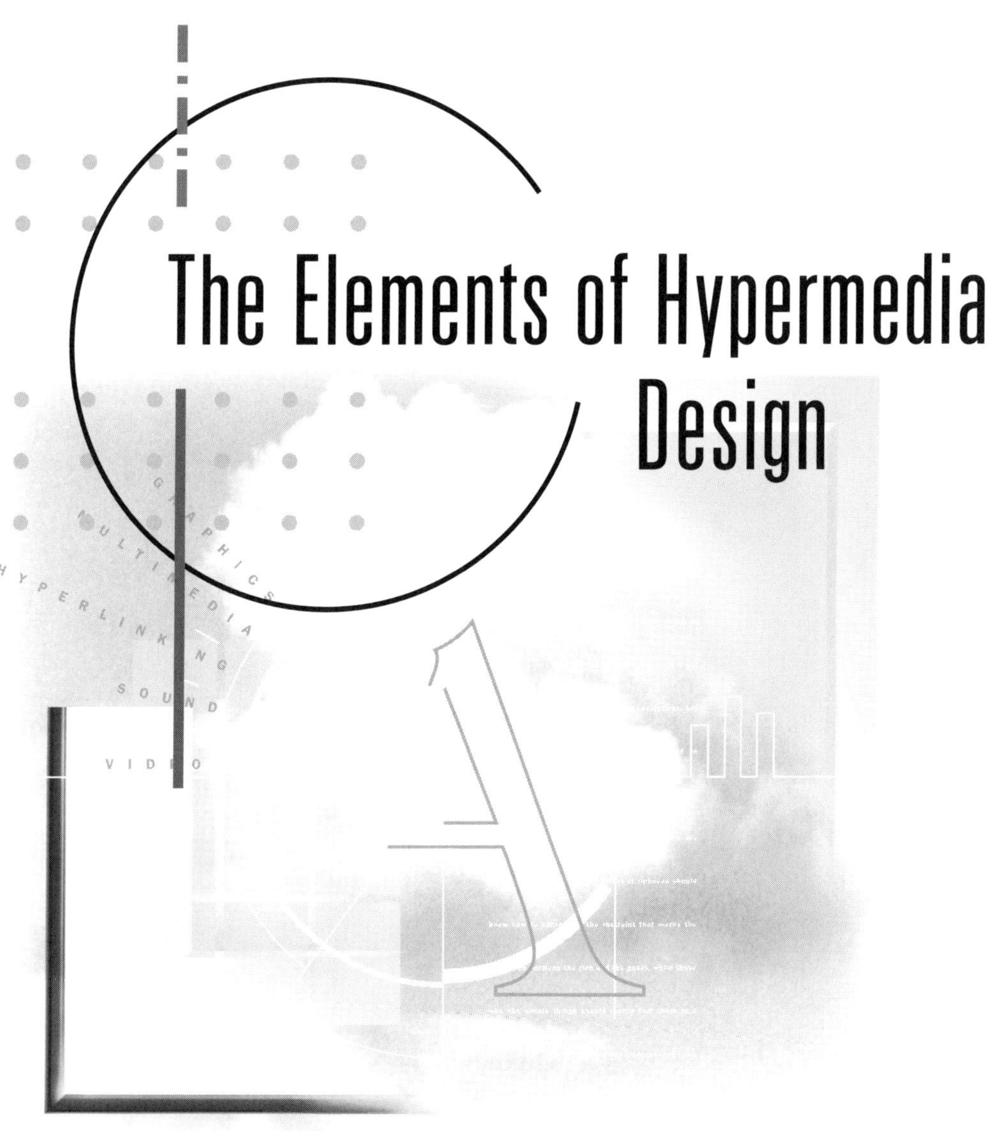

1 The World Wide Web & Hypermedia Publishing

Johannes Gutenberg's invention of the printing press advanced the changes in economy and commerce, politics, society, literature and ultimately in ideology that marked the beginning of the Renaissance. The World Wide Web is ushering in the next generation of publishing, bringing together hypertext, multimedia and global networking. The Web is growing at an astounding rate and is changing the publishing world by making it possible for anyone to publish information to people around the world.

In the fast-moving, global, competitive business environment, it is crucial that current information is available to the consumer who needs it. The World Wide Web lets you quickly publish marketing, customer service and research information from a central location. The Web is also a great forum for personal expression that lets you share ideas and topics of interest with others around the world. This chapter introduces the World Wide Web, explains how Web publishing works and gives an overview of Web publishing options.

What Is the World Wide Web?

The World Wide Web project was started in 1989 by Tim Berners-Lee at the CERN high-energy physics laboratory. The goal of the project was to find a way to share research and ideas with other employees and researchers scattered around the world. In its initial proposal, the Web was called "a hypertext project." *Hypertext* is a term coined by Ted Nelson back in the sixties that refers to text containing connections to other documents, so the reader can click a word or phrase to get additional information about a related topic. *Hypermedia* is a more inclusive term for documents that include information in multimedia formats, such as sound and video.

Technically speaking the World Wide Web refers to the abstract cyberspace of information. The Internet typically refers to the physical side of the network—that is, the hardware consisting of cables and computers. The foundation of the Internet and the World Wide Web is the use of *protocols,* the language and rules by which the computers communicate. For example, TCP/IP (Transmission Control Protocol and Internet Protocol) is a suite of networking protocols that lets different types of computers communicate and is the underlying protocol of the Internet. The World Wide Web is not just one type of protocol. Like a puzzle, the Web connects several protocols together, including FTP (File Transfer Protocol), telnet, WAIS (Wide-Area Information Servers) and more. Figure 1-1 shows the protocols that are used to share information. Because the World Wide Web uses the standard Internet protocols to transmit files and documents, the Web is often used synonymously for the Internet, referring to the collective network of computers as well as the body of information.

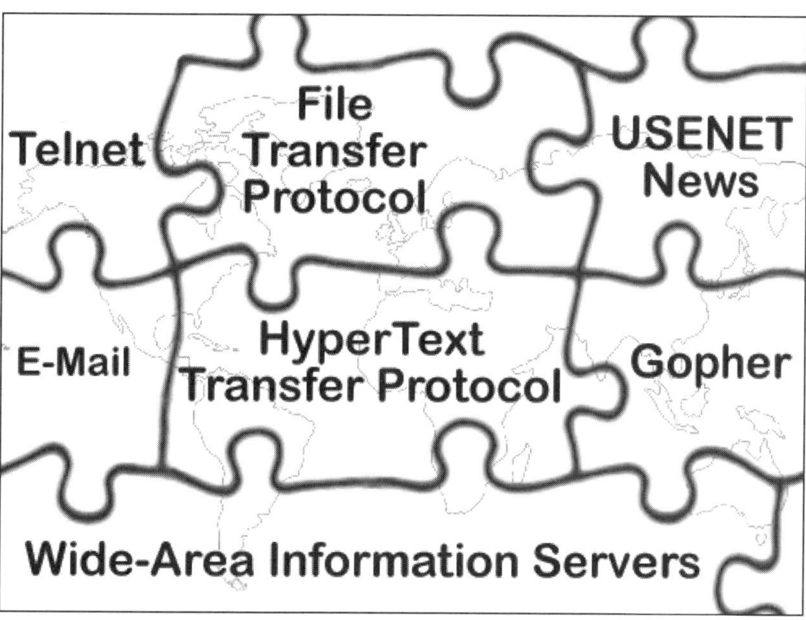

Figure 1-1: *The World Wide Web includes several Internet protocols, including FTP, telnet, WAIS and more.*

How Big Is the World Wide Web?

The release of the Mosaic Web browser by the National Center for Supercomputing (NCSA) in November 1992 marked the beginning of the Web's popularity. At the beginning of 1993, there were only 130 sites, less than half a year after the introduction of Mosaic, there were over 10,000 servers. John Quarterman, who mailed out an Internet demographic survey to over 4,700 sites, estimates that, on the low side, there are more than three-and-a-half-million users.

Since that survey was completed, the Web has been growing exponentially. There are now over 12,000 Web servers worldwide and more than 50 new servers are added daily. This makes the Web community at over 25 million and increasing every day.

How Web Publishing Works

Web publishing works under the client-server model. A *Web server* is a program running on a computer that is set up to serve documents to other computers that send requests for the documents. A *Web client* is a program that lets the user request documents from a server. Because the server only operates when a document is requested, it's an efficient way to share documents because it requires only a small amount of the server's resources.

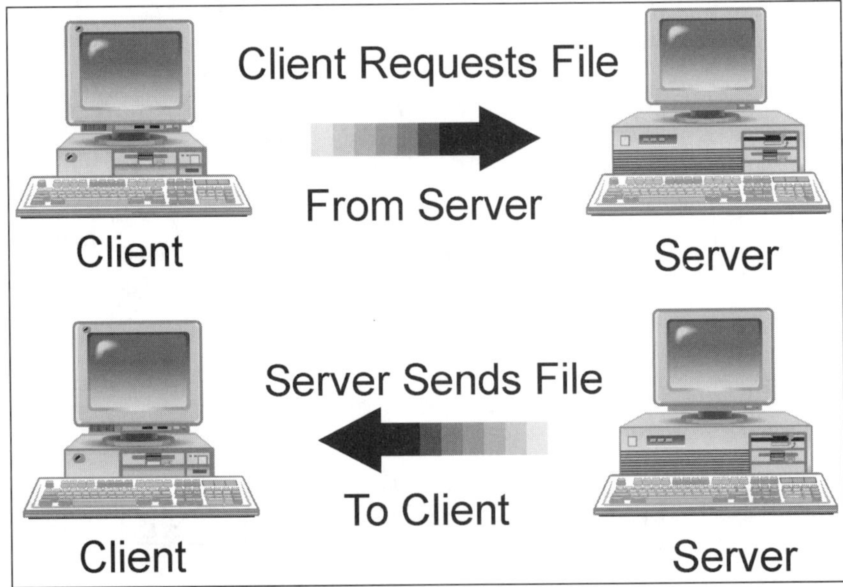

Figure 1-2: *The client and server connection.*

What Is a Web Browser?

Running a Web client, usually called a *Web browser,* the client connects to a computer specified by a network address, called a Uniform Resource Locator (URL), which sends a request to that computer's Web server for the Web document. The server responds by sending the text and any other media referenced by a hyperlink in the text (pictures, sounds or movies) to the user's Mac or PC. The document the server sends is in the HTML (HyperText Markup Language) format. HTML documents, also called *Web documents,* let the reader click on a hypertext word or phrase to access files or jump to other HTML documents. These

hypertext links between files and documents from servers around the world make the system work as if it were one huge web of information.

The best-known browsers are the NCSA Mosaic family of browsers, and the Netscape Communications family of Netscape browsers for UNIX, Windows and Macintosh computers. Text-based browsers, such as Lynx and Emacs-W3, are available for terminals, such as the VT100, which do not support graphics.

Some companies give away a browser and then offer a more powerful version of the browser for sale. Many software vendors are purchasing licenses for browsers, such as Mosaic, and waiving the license fees for users in order to offer freeware implementations of browsers. The logic behind this is to create name recognition and to add value to other products. Netscape Navigator, for example, is licensed from Netscape Communications and is included on the

Companion CD-ROM accompanying this book. Figure 1-3 shows Microsoft's main Web page, called a *home page,* using the Netscape Navigator browser.

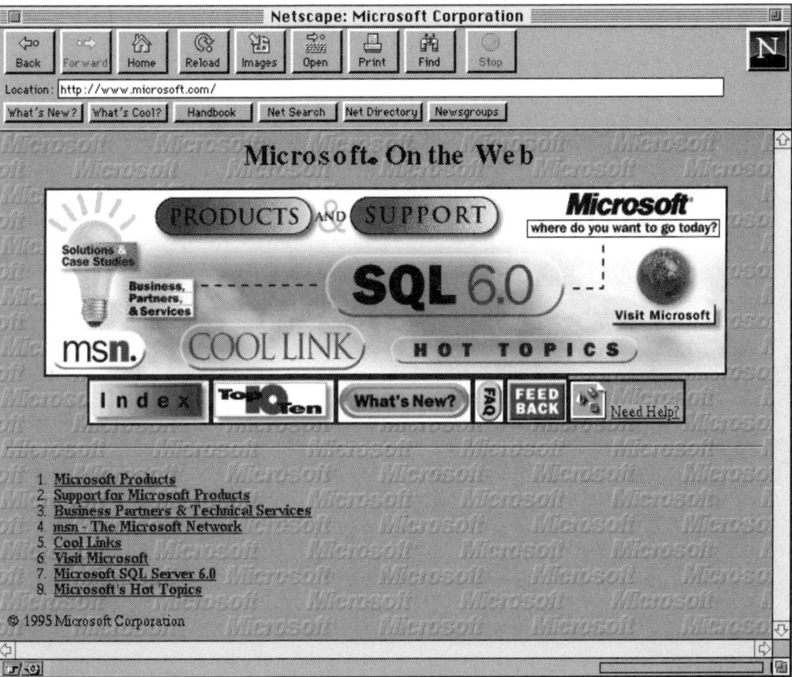

Figure 1-3: *Microsoft's home page in the Netscape Navigator Web browser.*

The appearance of a document will vary from one browser to the next according to the capabilities of each system and the user's preferences. Because there are different browsers, it's important to write and publish documents that will look good on any browser and not just the specific browser you have access to.

What Is a Uniform Resource Locator?

Web browsers allow the user to specify a Uniform Resource Locator (URL) and connect to a document or resource. When selecting hypertext in a Web document, the user is actually sending a request to open a URL. It is possible to represent nearly any file or service on the Internet with a URL. A Web browser can also act as an FTP, Gopher and telnet client. Hyperlinks then can be made not only to other Web documents and media, but also to other network services. Users access different resources by using different types of URLS. Figure 1-4 shows the structure of a URL. Notice that the first part of the URL (before the two slashes) specifies the method of access. The second part is typically the address of the computer where the data or service is located. Further parts may specify the names of files, the port to connect to or the text to search for in a database. Table 1-1 lists some examples of URLs for accessing different resources.

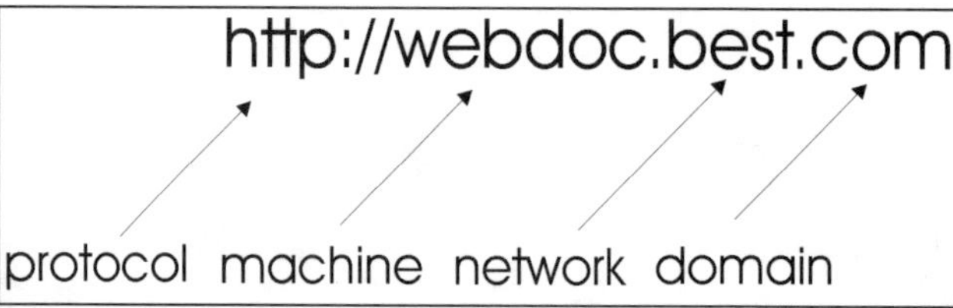

Figure 1-4: *The structure of a URL.*

Resource	URL
HTTP	http://akebono.stanford.edu/
FTP	ftp://mac.archive.umich.edu/mac/
File	file://sumex-aim.stanford.edu/info-mac/help/mirror-list.txt
Gopher	gopher://gopher.micro.umn.edu:70/1
telnet	telnet://rs.internic.net
USENET News	news:comp.infosystems.www.announce

Table 1-1: *URLs for Internet resources.*

What Is an HTTP Server?

The language Web clients and servers use to communicate with each other is called the HyperText Transmission Protocol (HTTP). All Web clients and servers must be able to speak HTTP in order to send and receive hypermedia documents. The success of the Web is due partly to the ability of Web clients to handle multiple application protocols that allow users access to many Internet protocols, such as anonymous FTP, Gopher and WAIS data servers. HTTP also gives the system its multimedia capabilities, supporting the retrieval and display of text, graphics, animation and the playback of sound using helper applications. Because the HTTP protocol is the foundation for most Web transactions, Web servers are often called HTTP servers.

Although World Wide Web servers are primarily run on UNIX servers, they are available for many platforms and environments, including Windows, Windows NT, Macintosh, VM and VMS. The domination of the Internet by UNIX servers is likely to change with the introduction of 32-bit platforms, such as System 7.5, Windows NT, Windows 95 and OS/2.

Which operating system and Web server you use to publish your Web documents depends largely on the audience you want to address. If you want to make your documents available to all the users on the Internet, you'll need to publish your Web documents on a multitasking version of the operating system that can handle more than one user at a time, such as Macintosh System 7.5 (or 7.0 with the Thread Manager extension) or a BSD UNIX or

Linux operating system. Chapter 11 explains how to use a full-time connection offered by a service provider or a server service to publish Web documents. Chapter 12 gives hands-on help for setting up your own server to publish Web documents.

Security & Authentication

Web servers are now including encryption and client authentication services so users can send and receive secure data. A secure server lets you be selective as to who can receive information to ensure that sensitive information is kept private. The advent of secure servers is sure to have a powerful impact on the number of commercial ventures on the Internet. Several companies are already setting up "pay-per-view" hypermedia Web sites. For example, users can subscribe to a service to access the *Encyclopedia Britannica* through the World Wide Web.

Dr. James H. Clark, the founder of Silicon Graphics Inc., and Marc Andreesen, who designed and developed the original Mosaic program, both joined forces to create Mosaic Communications. Shortly after introducing the Netscape Navigator browser, and because of a lawsuit by the University of Illinois who owned the copyright to Mosaic, the company's name was changed to Netscape Communications. Netscape Communications was the first company to introduce a secure server. In December 1994, Netscape Communications announced the Netsite server line, including the Netsite Commerce Server. This secure server is based on RSA Data Security Technology that incorporates Netscape Communications's Secure Sockets Layer (SSL). When combined with Netscape Navigator or other Internet browsers supporting SSL, the Netsite server lets users perform secure transactions to take advantage of commercial services, private online publications, financial services and online shopping. The Netsite Commerce Server was introduced at a whopping $5,000. A nonsecure server was also introduced at $1,495. Following the rule of supply and demand, the price for a secure server is sure to go down as more and more companies compete for the server market.

NCSA Mosaic isn't far behind. Version 2.0 of Mosaic supports

three types of security: basic authentication, enhanced authentication and secure HTTP. Basic authentication was developed by CERN/NCSA and is the least safe, allowing a password to travel unencrypted over the Net. Enhanced authentication uses Data Encryption Standard (DES) private-key encryption to let a business verify customers without sending passwords over the Net. A confirmation challenge is encoded along with the password to ensure that it was not captured from a previous message. Secure HTTP uses public-key technology from RSA Data Security, Inc. Secure HTTP is supplied by Terisa Systems. Terisa Systems is the most secure method, using a variety of public–key-based security schemes to encrypt data, such as a credit card number and expiration date, to perform secure, authenticated transactions. Several companies will be offering secure servers that work with these security standards in the near future. For example, Open Market (http://www.openmarket.com) has announced it will be selling secure servers, and First Virtual Holdings, Inc. (http://www.fv.com) lets you publish a page using a secure server for a nominal fee and small percentage of sales.

HTML, SGML & the Common Gateway Interface

The standard language the Web uses for creating and recognizing hypermedia documents is the HyperText Markup Language, commonly called HTML. Until the advent of Mosaic, the Internet was a multiplatform environment that made interchanging documents somewhat difficult. A special language called Standard Generalized Markup Language (SGML) was invented to solve the problems of sharing documents. SGML focuses on the elements in a document, so the recipient of the information is freed from the proprietary choices of the originator.

SGML documents let you resize windows to make optimal use of your screen and let you print the documents so the printed document retains its layout. HTML was derived from SGML as a simple nonproprietary delivery format for global hypertext. Like SGML it provides a common method of authoring and format conversion.

HTML is fairly new and the language itself is easy to master. Web documents are typically written in HTML and are usually named with the extension ".html" or ".htm." These HTML documents are nothing more than standard ASCII files with formatting codes that contain information about layout, such as text styles, document titles, paragraphs, lists and hyperlinks.

The Three Versions of HTML & HTML Extensions

HTML is called a *markup language,* or simply *markup* for short. The description of the markup is called a "Document Type Definition," or DTD. The current HTML DTD supports basic hypermedia document creation and layout. There are three versions of HTML DTDs. HTML 1.0 was created primarily with specifications for creating hyperlinks. It has recently been replaced by HTML 2.0, the newly ratified standard by the Engineering Task Force. Version 2.0 specifications define features that let users display inline images and use interactive forms.

The Web moves fast, but most Web document authors are currently looking for new possibilities. Dave Raggett of the W3 Organization presented a set of HTML specifications in a white paper that have come to be known as HTML+. Some browser suppliers are adding their own extensions; for example, Netscape is already implementing HTML+ and extensions that are specific to the Netscape browser. The next section takes a look at HTML and the emerging HTML 3.0 standard.

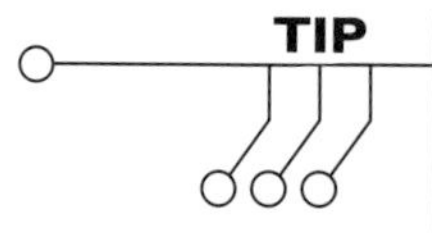

Information on HTML 2.0 is available on the Web at http://www.w3.org/hypertext/WWW/MarkUp/MarkUp.html/html-spec/html-spec_toc.html. The Internet draft for HTML 3.0 is now available in ASCII text format via the Web at http://www.w3.org/hypertext/WWW/MarkUp/html3-dtd.txt. You can also get it at ftp://hplose.hpl.hp.com/pub/WWW/html3.dtd.

HTML Markup

HTML is a fairly limited formatting language. HTML includes markup elements for headers, paragraphs, various types of character highlighting, inline images, hypertext links, lists, preformatted text and simple search facilities.

Although HTML 3.0 is still in its developmental stages, most browsers already support some HTML 3.0 features, such as tables. HTML 3.0 also supports e-mail URLs, so hyperlinks can be made to send e-mail automatically. For instance, selecting an e-mail address in a piece of hypertext would open a mail program, ready to send e-mail to that address. Additional layout and formatting options, such as text flow around floating figures, styles, figures and mathematical equations are also quickly being added. HTML 3.0 also allows arbitrary nesting of the various kinds of lists, and lists items can now include horizontal rules. It also adds additional tags for Web information searching programs. Another interesting feature that is part of the HTML 3.0 specification is the ability to create text and graphics as objects. This allows users to use icons to drag and drop text and graphics from the browser to another application.

The Common Gateway Interface

The unsung hero of Web publishing is the Common Gateway Interface (CGI). CGI is the interface that handles manipulating data generated by fill-in forms. It is also the basis for image mapping, which lets you define "hotspots" in images. Clicking a hotspot is the same as clicking a URL. Chapter 7, "Getting Graphic With Images" and Chapter 9, "Getting Interactive With Forms & Databases" give some examples of creating CGI scripts for creating interactive Web documents.

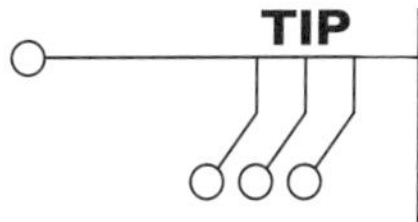

For an online introduction to CGI that includes a list of links to sample CGI programs, guides to creating and handling forms data and the common gateway interface specification, enter the URL: http://hoohoo.ncsa.uiuc.edu/cgi.

Authoring & Publishing Tools

Several programs exist to help you create HTML documents or to convert existing documents into HTML format. Tools also exist that let you create interactive graphics with hotspots that the user can click to move to a specific location. The following section briefly describes some of the authoring and publishing tools that help in the creation of HTML documents.

HTML Authoring & Conversion Tools

A variety of HTML authoring tools save you from having to enter HTML markup elements, called *tags.* An HTML editing program can also ensure that the resulting document complies with the HTML Document Type Definition (DTD). A few programs let you use macros or filters with common word processing packages, such as Microsoft Word, to convert formatted documents to HTML. A few SGML tools let you convert SGML-based document formats to HTML documents. Chapter 2 takes a look at the HTML editors and converters.

Portable Document Programs

One of the hottest areas of publishing on the Internet is creating a portable multiplatform format standard that lets users view files off-line no matter what type of computer they're using. Not everyone wants online information. Many users pay for online time. It makes sense to present large documents, such as detailed reports and online documentation, in a file that can be downloaded and read off-line. Up until recently many document files were stored in the PostScript format, which like UNIX, was a dominant Internet standard. With the advent of portable multiplatform document formats, however, this has changed.

True to form, each company is trying to create its own portable document standard. Adobe Acrobat is a suite of tools for creating and viewing documents in a Portable Document Format (PDF). Virtually any document can be converted into a PDF document

since Adobe (the creator of the widely used PostScript graphics language) provides tools for converting any PostScript file into PDF format. Apple is developing QuickDraw GX, but Apple is known for its proprietary formats and is not making the font format an open standard. Microsoft, the 800-pound gorilla, is developing TrueType Open. WordPerfect is currently shipping Envoy, a program that embeds a runtime viewer with the document. Farallon's Replica for the Macintosh and Windows also embeds a viewer and the document into a single file. BitStream, a formidable font company, has developed a technology called True Doc. The True Doc format is used in the next version of Common Ground, version 2.0, from No Hands Software. Common Ground 2.0 functions as a helper application, but it has the ability to load a mini-viewer on the fly to display documents, so you don't have to wait until the whole document is downloaded to start viewing it.

As of early 1995, Adobe's Portable Document Format is stealing the show with the ability to embed TrueType and Adobe Type I fonts, an Applications Program Interface (API) for plug-ins, and by offering the Adobe Acrobat Reader for free. Adobe Acrobat is one of the first applications to support the Mosaic Software development Interface (SDI) and Netscape's NCAPI, which are two-way interfaces that let other applications automatically work with the browser. This lets you include hyperlinks in a PDF document to a Web page.

Common Ground is the dark horse that is a little late out of the starting gate. The new version's ability to view a file on the fly is a marvelous feature. If, for example, you're downloading a 20-page document, you can see the first page within 30 seconds. The free mini-viewer is scaled down to only 200k so that it can be downloaded with a document. Common Ground version 2.0, like Acrobat Reader, supports Mosaic's SDI and Netscape's NCAPI, so you can also include hyperlinks in a Common Ground document to a Web page.

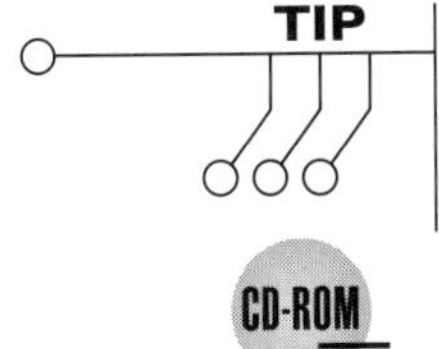

The Adobe Acrobat Reader and the Common Ground mini-viewer are included on the CD-ROM accompanying this book. The Adobe Acrobat Reader is also available for free at http://www.adobe.com. You can find out about Common Ground at http://www.commonground.com.

Web Publishing & Options

In order to publish a Web document, you need to make sure it is located on a server that is constantly available. Paying for a full-time connection is costly and publishing documents at modem speed is an unrealistic way to handle traffic. But relax, you don't have to have a Web server with a full-time connection in order to publish on the Internet.

Many service providers include special options for publishing Web documents as a part of their service or for a *small* fee. How much it costs to publish a Web document depends on the service you're using and what you want to publish. Costs can range from $10 a month for a simple home page to thousands of dollars a month for an interactive storefront.

Server Services & Web Design Services

You don't have to create a Web document on your own. Many server services and Web design services exist that will gladly do it for you—for a price. The resources section at the back of this book lists server services and Web design services that you can use to help you publish Web documents. The following section describes some of the types of Web documents you can publish.

From Home Pages to Virtual Storefronts

Web publishing can be broken down into three categories: a single-page brochure, an information center and a virtual storefront. The main page that most users connect to is called a *home page.* The following types of documents can be published on the Web: advertising, brochures, database, demos, newsletters, press releases, customer support/FAQs (Frequently Asked Questions), interactive storefronts and magazines.

The Future of Web Publishing

As fast as the Web is growing, there are a number of new developments that you may want to keep an eye on. The two largest of these are the issues of additional formatting and styles for Web documents and the automation of Web processing. In the rest of this section, we'll talk about each of these issues and where they may be headed.

Extended Styles for Web Documents

Most Web browsers, such as Mosaic and Netscape, now support simple fill-out forms and tables. SGML Web browsers and portable document viewers are beginning to address the limitations of HTML. SoftQuad has announced Panorama (freeware) and Panorama Pro (commercial version) to address the formatting features that are lacking in HTML. These SGML browsers work in conjunction with browsers, such as Netscape Navigator and NCSA Mosaic. Panorama opens automatically when the browser encounters an SGML file. The formatting features allow you to display interactive tables and basic mathematical equations. A powerful capability of Panorama is that it lets users choose from multiple DTDs to define styles for Web documents.

Styles for Web browsers are a hot topic. It is possible that styles could be identified as part of the document. Using styles, authors could specify aspects of Web documents, such as font families, text color and point size, and the use of white space around text and graphics. The use of images, colors and textures of the background offer further ways of creating a unique Web document. Inline images, images that appear in HTML documents, are currently limited to the GIF and JPEG formats. Work is already underway to support other inline image formats, such as JPEG images and MPEG video and QuickTime movie formats. This will allow images and videos to be displayed from within a document.

At the end of March 1995, Adobe Systems and Netscape Communications took the next logical step for Web publishing. Adobe and Netscape announced they were teaming up to incorporate

Acrobat into a future version of Netscape. The new Web browser would allow you to preserve the layout of the printed page. For example, you could display a two-column document with text that wrapped around an inline graphic in the center of the page. It will also make it possible to include sound and videos in Web documents that don't rely on external applications. Look for Common Ground to either be integrated with an existing stand-alone browser or ultimately include the capability to browse the Web to display formatted documents.

HTML and HTTP are already extended to include workgroup features; for example, Lotus announced in early 1995 the InterNotes Web Server. This server works with the HTTP protocol to publish Notes databases on the Net. Anyone can quickly convert an existing Lotus Notes database into an HTML document. This is only the beginning; it is quite possible that the Web could include integration with the telephone service for voice mail and video-telephone calls. As cable companies and high-speed transmission connections enter the scene, it's possible that Web browsers could also access radio and television channels.

Web Automation

A second major area of development at this time is the issue of how to allow Web documents to become active rather than passive elements on the Internet. The basic idea is quite simple: allow a page that you access over the Web to use your computer to interact with you. To do this, it is necessary that both the Web page and the browser that you are using allow this.

The most notable exponent of this new technology is Sun Soft, a division of Sun Microsystem, who have released a new Web browser, called HotJava, and a new interpreted language, called Java, that do just that. When reading a page in HotJava that contains the new HTML tag APP, the browser downloads the required code, called an *applet*, and executes it. The code must be written in the Java language for execution. In this way, the entire transaction takes only a short time (for the download) but may execute for some time on its own system. There are obvious issues in this, including resource problems on its computer, security issues and so on, but basically,

this is a start on a new type of interactive document. Currently Sun's HotJava site includes examples of embedded spreadsheets, animations and three-dimensional models that can be rotated with the mouse. The HotJava browser is currently only available for Sun workstations, but editions for both Macintosh and Windows are in the works. The whole concept is so compelling that Netscape has announced that it has licensed the Java architecture from Sun and will support the Java language at some point in future releases of Netscape Navigator. You can get more information on HotJava and the Java language from http://java.sun.com/.

UserLand, the creators of the Frontier scripting language for the Macintosh, have also added extensions to allow similar capabilities. The latest edition of Frontier has several new and impressive features, including automating many tasks of Web page management. The most exciting capability of the latest release, however, is its ability to ask a browser to execute a script located on the browser's own machine. Of course, Frontier must be running on your computer for this to work or you'll get an error. In addition, this doesn't actually download the script—the script must already exist on your computer. In this regard, this is different than the Java scripts mentioned earlier, which will be automatically loaded and executed by the browser. Nevertheless, this does open up a whole new type of interactive application.

Frontier scripting is not for the faint-of-heart, but it does provide a rich and effective method for handling multiple Web documents. We have included the latest version of Frontier on the Companion CD, along with several cool scripts (so you don't need to learn how to program just yet!) that will help you work with your tools to manage Web data, both incoming and outgoing.

CD-ROM

In addition to Netscape Communication's announcement to include Adobe Acrobat's Portable Document format, HotJava, Netscape announced it will also include support for Macromedia Director files. Director is a powerful multimedia authoring and playback tool that can create multimedia presentations that can be played back on Macintosh, Windows and OS/2 platforms. Director support will be included in Netscape as a run-time engine called ShockWave. For more information on Macromedia Director, check out the URL http://www.macromedia.com/.

Another area that is getting a lot of attention by Web publishers is VRML (Virtual Reality Markup Language). VRML supports 3D and dynamic objects on the Web. The VRML is not an extension to HTML. In fact, it isn't even compatible with HTML. VRML defines objects that can contain different data types, such as JPEG images, sound files, video clips, etc. VRML is based on the Open Inventor file format developed by Silicon Graphics. The VRML specification is available at http://vrml.wired.com/. A white paper by David Raggett titled "Extending WWW Support to Platform-Independent Virtual Reality" is available at http://vrml.wired/.com/concepts/raggett.html.

Silicon Graphics already has a VRML Web server and Web browser, named WebSpace, available for SGI workstations. The browser and server are going to later be available for the Macintosh and other platforms. For information on the availability of WebSpace check out the URL http://www.sgi.com/Products/WebFORCE/WebSpace/WebSpaceAvailability.html.

Moving On

With a possible audience of millions, the Web is becoming the new frontier of publishing. After browsing Web sites, you're bound to wonder what you need to publish your own Web documents. This book will guide you through the process providing hands-on examples you can easily modify to match your own publishing needs.

In order to publish on the Internet, you'll first want to take a look at the types of tools you have to work with. Although HTML is a fairly easy language to master, entering HTML commands can quickly become a tedious process. The next chapter gives you an overview of the editors and converters that can save you time when creating HTML documents.

2

HTML Editors & Converters

While it's possible to create even the most complex HTML documents with nothing more than a plain text editor, there are a number of programs that can save you time and effort in the process. If you are creating the content for your Web pages from scratch—and if the Web is the only place your work will be published—start with an HTML editor. HTML editors focus on the creation of new HTML documents.

If you're going to be working with an existing document, such as a brochure or press release, your best bet may be an HTML converter. An HTML converter is a program that translates your existing document from its current format (or a format your word processor or page layout program can export) into a set of HTML pages. This means you can save yourself the trouble of starting over when you want to publish your work on the Web. There are some drawbacks to this method, however. HTML is still in its infancy and is far more limiting than existing page layout programs and word processors. A document that looks splendid when produced with a desktop publishing package will lose many of its endearing charms when shoehorned into the HTML format. For example, you could lose control of margins, indents and fonts.

In this chapter we'll look at HTML editors and HTML converters. Before you rush into creating HTML pages, take a look at the benefits and limitations of these editors and converters and try both approaches to see which works best for you.

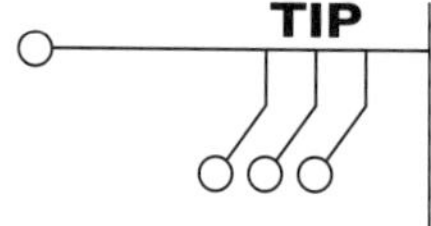

Don't worry if you don't understand what all the markup does right now. What you need to understand is the range of editor and converter programs available and how to choose the ones that best meet your needs.

HTML Editors

There are two basic types of HTML editing packages available: stand-alone editors and word processor templates. Choosing between the two types is a matter of personal preference and practice. Since you can get versions of all these programs for free, there is almost no reason not to try both types, and see which you prefer. To help those of you who don't want to know about all the editors and templates, we have included coverage of our favorite editor and template at the beginning of each section.

One thing you'll notice right away about many HTML editors is that when you create the HTML document, you will see the actual HTML markup. A few editors, such as Webtor and Arachnid, hide the actual HTML code; most others, including HoTMetaL PRO, show the markup in some form—often in a different color, or using special tokens. (You can, however, "hide tags" in HoTMetal PRO.)

There is a good reason for this. There is no such thing as true WYSIWYG (What You See Is What You Get) with publishing on the Web. Every Web browser, such as Netscape or Mosaic, has its own way of rendering the page, and the user has complete control over page size and font styles. So, by forcing you to look at the HTML markup, you are reminded that you are merely creating a text document with hints to the viewer programs about what different parts of your document mean.

There are a large number of editors for the Macintosh, and more appear, it seems, almost daily. As a result, no attempt has been made to make this list exhaustive. Instead, we have tried to find several good ones, each with some special feature that makes it notable. Your ideas may differ from ours, or you may have needs that we didn't consider in selecting these editors for review. Also, in addition to new editors, the old ones are updated frequently, with new features and new extensions to handle the new variants of HTML. As a result, you should be prepared to do a little looking around to find out both exactly what versions of what tools are current and which tools suit you the best.

One of the best places to look for information like this is on the set of pages entitled *Macintosh WWW Development Guide* at http://www.uwtc.washington.edu/Computing/WWW/Mac/Directory.html. This is a great site for all kinds of information about developing and viewing WWW pages from your Macintosh. The page was created and is maintained by Jon Wiederspan, who has done the Macintosh community a great service by creating, collating and maintaining all this information.

In this chapter, there are a few criticisms that can be leveled at each of the packages. Keep in mind that most of these editors are *free*, and the authors of these packages spent a lot of time on programs that may never bring them a dime. Some of the program creators are working on advanced versions of their programs that they can make money on, but for now they are offering their work to the public in the hope that someone will find them useful. This is indicative of the spirit of the Internet—sharing work and offering to help without expectation of compensation. Without authors like these, there would not be an Internet, or the World Wide Web, as we know it today.

Rules-based & Unchecked HTML Editors

HTML editors and templates fall within one of two categories: rules-based HTML editors and unchecked HTML editors. Rules-based editors require you to follow carefully HTML formatting conventions. You must insert the right tags in the right locations. The major benefit of using a rules-based editor is that it helps you create HTML documents correctly. If you try to open a document that includes nonstandard tags, the editor will typically display an error message when it tries to load the document. Unchecked HTML editors don't check the validity of the document—you can insert tags incorrectly and the editor will not let you know. The benefit of an unchecked editor is that you can use nonstandard tags.

Stand-alone Editors

Typically stand-alone editors don't require support from other software in order to work. This section explains the benefits and limitations of five popular stand-alone editors, including HoTMetaL and HoTMetaL PRO, Webtor, Arachnid and HTML Web Weaver.

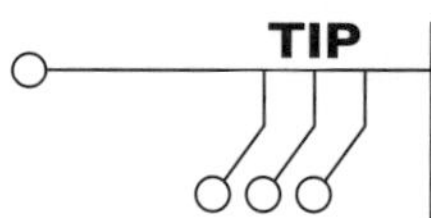

Although most stand-alone editors allow you to create and edit HTML documents, they also mostly require that you have a document viewer, like Netscape or Mosaic, to actually see what your documents will look like. All of these editors make some effort to display your work as it may look; but, as we said before, every browser is different. So, most of these editors allow you to automatically transfer pages to your browser of choice for a final view.

HoTMetaL PRO & HoTMetaL

Our favorite stand-alone HTML editors are HoTMetaL PRO and its freeware counterpart, HoTMetaL, from SoftQuad. Note that the Companion CD-ROM contains HoTMetaL LITE, a fully working lighter version of HoTMetaL PRO 2.0. HoTMetaL PRO is a rule-based HTML editor that includes several features not available in the freeware version that you'll find useful for heavy-duty HTML editing, including

- *Importing files through a filter*—This feature allows you to import files that are not correct HTML, but are close. The HoTMetaL freeware version simply refuses to open these files.
- *Spell-checking and thesaurus*—The addition of spell-checking and the thesaurus is an invaluable aid.
- *Additional editing flexibility*—The PRO version gives you fine control over editing and makes the creation process easier. It also provides additional HTML tag types not supported in the free version.
- *Macro language*—You can create, save, load and run keystroke sequences you define to speed your editing process—a handy feature.
- *Tables*—Although tables are not supported in HTML 2.0, some browsers have recently added table support based on future HTML version standards. HoTMetaL PRO allows you to insert tables into your HTML document.
- *Online documentation*—HoTMetaL PRO provides an extensive online help system that saves you from having to refer to the documentation for help.
- *Online tutorial*—An HTML document that guides you through the creation of an HTML document.

HoTMetaL PRO is based on SoftQuad's SGML editor, which makes moving from the HTML product to SoftQuad's SGML editor an easy transition.

SoftQuad is one of the founding members of *SGML Open*, "a non-profit, international consortium of providers of products and services, dedicated to accelerating the further adoption, application, and implementation of the Standard Generalized Markup Language, the international standard for open interchange of documents and structured information objects." If you're interested in learning more about this organization, check out the Web page at http://www.sgmlopen.org/sgml/docs/index.html.

Other features of HoTMetaL PRO include the ability to look at the structure of the HTML markup, enforce HTML structure, open existing HTML files, edit large files, preview images and have the program guide you through changing all the URL references from local references to network-name references.

Although you can open HTML pages created by other editors (or right off the Web), be aware that HoTMetaL PRO is a rules-based editor that checks for correct HTML syntax, so it will reject a good number of pages that seem to work okay on the Web. This is because most Web browsers are very accepting of bad HTML coding. You will be able to view HTML pages that bear little resemblance to properly structured HTML. HoTMetaL PRO is fussy and therefore may not be the best choice for making a few small edits to an existing HTML page that isn't well coded.

On the other hand, speaking as long-time developers, we often find that it is penny-wise and pound-foolish to avoid the hassle of correcting an existing page that isn't done according to the rules. Too often you will find yourself later having to make more corrections, each time getting deeper and deeper into the morass. Eventually, you may have to correct the page anyway, which will take longer and be more difficult because of the changes on the way; under those conditions, you may well be advised to simply make the corrections initially and then work from that point on with a correctly formatted page. Of course, you have to assess the tradeoffs and make the choice for yourself.

Installing HoTMetaL

HoTMetaL PRO is not shareware or freeware. You can't copy it and give it away. SoftQuad's HoTMetaL program, however, is freeware and can be found at several locations on the Internet. SoftQuad isn't giving away the store. They believe that by giving away their basic product, they can convince you to upgrade to their professional edition. Also, by giving you a way to get started on HTML authoring for free, they are luring yet another writer into the larger field of SGML and electronic document publishing, a field in which SoftQuad is one of the leaders. To get the latest version of HoTMetaL check out the URL: ftp://ftp.ncsa.uiuc.edu/Web/html/hotmetal/.

SoftQuad plans to make a free version of HoTMetaL available for the Macintosh by September 1995. You can find a list of sites that carry the free versions of HoTMetaL on the SoftQuad Web server at http://www.sq.com/products/hotmetal/hm-ftp.html. You can also e-mail SoftQuad for more information at hotmetal@sq.com.

All in all, the free version of HoTMetaL is an excellent HTML editing tool. It still suffers from an intolerance of incorrect HTML markup and insists on presenting the nitty gritty of the HTML markup, even when you'd rather be focusing on content and structure. If you run into problems using this version, you're on your own—SoftQuad offers no technical support for the free version.

Webtor

Webtor is a good, stand-alone WYSIWYG (What You See Is What You Get) HTML editor. Webtor has two floating palettes that you can use to see the current structure of your document in outline form and to inspect and alter the attributes of your HTML code. Although Webtor provides a good approximation of how your document will look, it also allows you to preview the document using your choice of a Web browser. Unlike HoTMetaL PRO, Webtor does not show you any of the HTML codes that are in your document, which make creation and organization of the document easier, in our opinion. The document structure and inspector palettes show you how your document is put together at all times, and you can see the HTML code in a separate, edit window as well. However, to see the HTML code directly, Webtor launches your choice of an ASCII text editor. (You can use TeachText, if you don't have anything else; however, we recommend BBEdit Lite, which comes on the Companion CD.) You can find out more about Webtor, and get a copy of the current version, at http://www.igd.fhg.de/~neuss/webtor/webtor.html. Webtor was written by Jochen Schales, of the Fraunhofer Institute for Computer Graphics, Darmstadt, Germany, who can be reached at schales@igd.fhg.de.

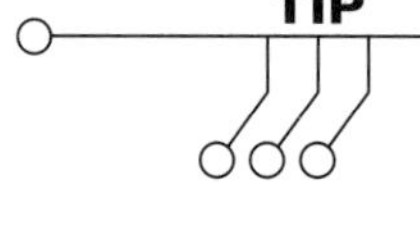

At the time of writing this Webtor is still in a pre-release version and is "under construction," as they say. The basic structure and features currently available make it clear that Webtor is going to be one of the more successful HTML editors available. At the present time, however, it is subject to unexplained errors and problems, as you would expect from pre-release software, and not all features are fully implemented as yet. For that reason, we have not included it on the CD-ROM, but we encourage you to check it out for yourself. As Jochen Schales, the author of Webtor, says, "Remember: to err is human—to forgive is Macintosh."

Installation

To install Webtor, uncompress the Webtor self-extracting archive file. The compressed file creates a new folder that contains the executable program and two subsidiary folders, which contain documentation and examples for your use. Webtor was written in C++.

Figure 2-1 shows a typical Webtor screen, including the two floating palettes that show document structure and allow you to inspect and edit HTML tags. The top palette shows the overall document structure. The lower palette shows the HTML tags at the current cursor location; in Figure 2-1, the cursor is located at the first store location.

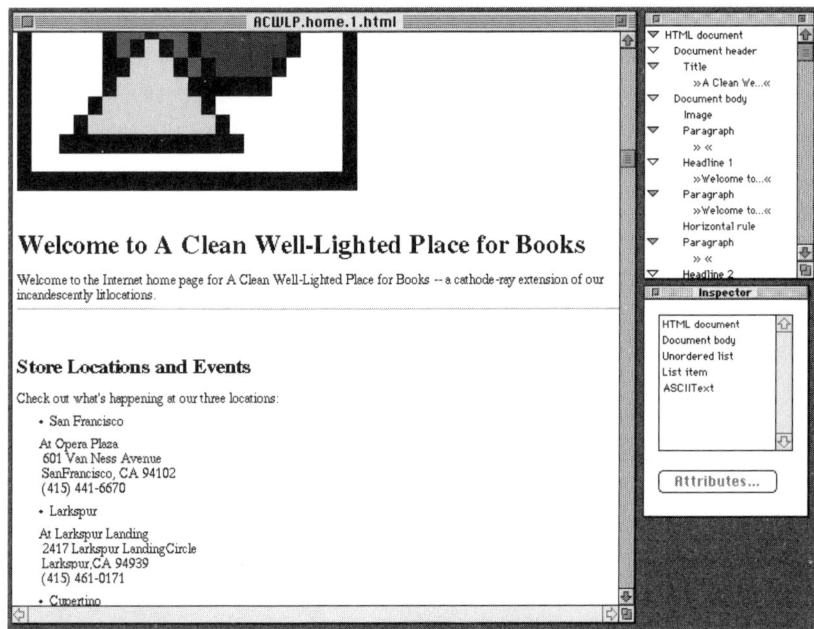

Figure 2-1: *A typical Webtor editing screen with the floating structure and inspector palettes shown.*

Getting Started

Using Webtor is very simple: you select the markup element you want from the HTML Elements menu, and the program enters the markup for you. All inline markup, such as text styles and anchors, are entered by selecting the text you want to treat in a special way (such as bold, italic, etc.) and then choosing the markup you want from the pop-up menu HTML Elements>>Inline. You can display the document structure and Inspector palettes by selecting Windows>>Document Structure or Windows>>Inspector respectively; you hide them by clicking on the close box in the upper left-hand corner of the individual palette. A particularly nice feature of the document structure palette window is that you can collapse the structural elements by turning the arrow icons next to each element, just as you hide or display folders in the Finder. This makes a very useful outline presentation of the document.

The Extras menu allows you to view your HTML document in two alternative ways. First, Extras>>Test Document allows you to preview your document in your choice of a Web browser. Second, Extras>>View Source allows you to see the document in ASCII text format, with all the codes and attributes in your choice of a text editor. In both cases, you must first use the Edit>>Preferences dialog box to set a Web Browser and a Source Viewer for use with these menu selections.

HTML Web Weaver

HTML Web Weaver is similar to Webtor in that it uses several floating palettes to display information. In the case of HTML Web Weaver, however, the palettes contain HTML tag information. By default, HTML Web Weaver defines three different floating palettes, each displaying a different set of tags: font and header tags in one, major structural tags in another, and the remaining tags in a third. The program also has a toolbar that you can use to insert HTML tags and markup existing text. The program has several nice features, most notably the ability to be customized extensively. For example, you can create custom entries for new or special tags. It also allows you to customize the floating palettes to include any set of tags that you want. The biggest drawback is that all this customization comes at a price: the program is slow to load and run. HTML Web Weaver also has extensive balloon help to enable you to get to work quickly. You can get an overview of Web Weaver and download it from http://www.potsdam.edu/Web.Weaver/About.html. HTML Web Weaver is shareware; you may use it for up to 30 days for evaluation, but after that you must send a $25.00 registration fee. HTML Web Weaver was written by Robert C. Best III, who can be reached via e-mail at Robert.Best@potsdam.edu.

Installing HTML Web Weaver

To install HTML Web Weaver, decompress the program archive in a new folder. The compressed file is not self-extracting, so you should have Stuffit (or an expander that will accept Stuffit files) available. The program comes with extensive documentation (in HTML format, naturally) and tutorial files. The entire set of files

requires about 1.5MB on disk. Figure 2-2 shows HTML Web Weaver with a sample HTML page and all the standard floating palettes and toolbar active.

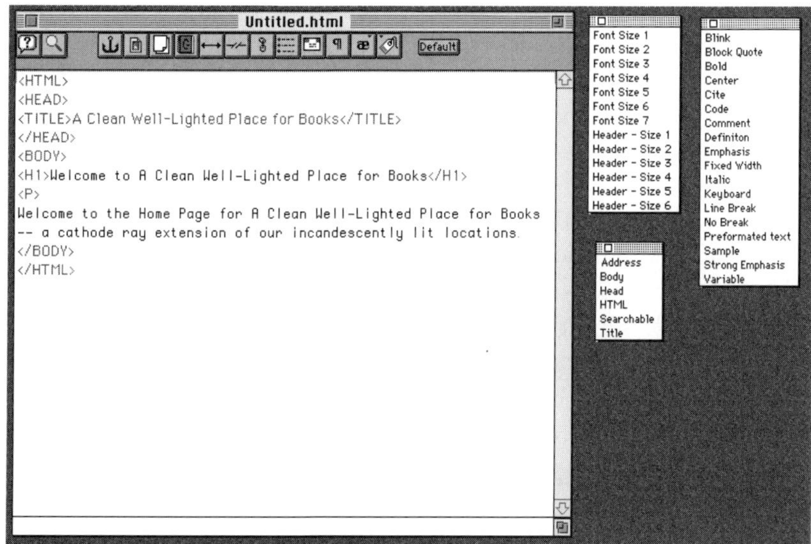

Figure 2-2: *A typical HTML Web Weaver editing screen with floating palettes and toolbar active.*

Getting Started

One of the nice features of this program is the floating palettes and the easy access to the "extended" character set used by most European languages by using a custom floating palette. Once you've set up the floating palettes to your satisfaction, simply select the text that you want to tag and then select the tag for that text. This works even for large blocks of text used for lists, for example, and HTML Web Weaver will correctly break the section of text down into list items and so on, as required. The program is definitely set up to aid in marking up existing text and is by far the easiest entry method of all the HTML editors covered in this chapter for that task.

HTML Web Weaver does not provide any type of WYSIWYG display. It displays text with tags in an alternative font. To get a preview, you must first choose a browser by pressing the Select Preview Helper in the Preferences dialog box (Edit>>Preferences). Then choose File>>Preview (-E) to view your document.

This version of HTML Editor, like some other editors, suffers from a limit on the file size: files cannot be larger than 32K bytes (and processing becomes noticeably slower when files get larger than about 28K).

Arachnid

Arachnid is a different kind of HTML editor; in fact, its author calls it "an HTML file builder" rather than an HTML editor. Arachnid is based on an object-oriented, drag-and-drop approach to HTML document construction. The drawback to this approach is that Arachnid maintains documents in its own format, and documents must be exported to HTML format before using them on the Web. Arachnid also comes with a free player application, which allows others to play back your documents in Arachnid format. Arachnid uses a floating tool palette, with automatic help and a variety of tools to help you insert and work with links and forms in your document. The tool palette also contains a Tool Description row that allows you to get immediate information on what each tool does. You can get a copy of Arachnid by linking to the home page located at http://sec-look.uiowa.edu/. This has a link to a page containing the latest information on Arachnid and links for downloading it. The program was written by Robert McBurney, who can be reached via e-mail at robert-mcburney@uiowa.edu.

Installing Arachnid

To install Arachnid, decompress the self-extracting archive file. The compressed file creates a new folder that contains the executable program and a simple ReadMe file. You can download the complete Arachnid documentation separately in Acrobat PDF format. (The Acrobat Reader is available on the Companion CD-ROM.) The documentation is quite good. It describes the Arachnid project setup and structure and covers most functions

CD-ROM

that you may want to use when creating an HTML document. Arachnid was written using SuperCard, which makes it somewhat slow in launching and operation. Figure 2-3 shows you a typical Arachnid editing display with the full floating tool palette open.

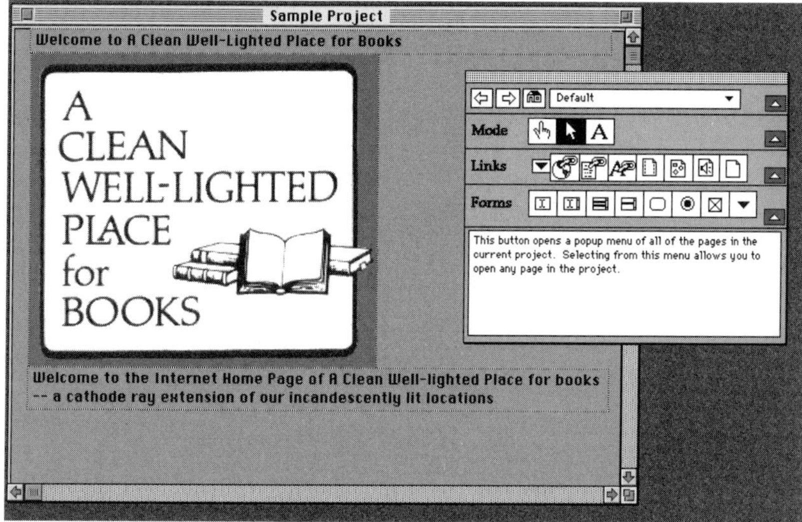

Figure 2-3: *Arachnid main screen with floating tool palette.*

Getting Started

Arachnid takes a distinctly original approach to creating Web documents. One of the strengths of this program is its drag-and-drop approach to adding interactive elements, such as links to video, audio and URLs, to a document. To add a new link to an Arachnid project, simply select the type of link that you want from the tool palette and drag the tool image to the position in your document where you want to place the link. For URLs, Arachnid also allows you to create a list of URLs that you can then add directly into the project. All of these features make adding links quite easy.

The form tools allow you to create a form just as easily. In addition, Arachnid has an Active mode that allows you to play back links in your document. This is a great help in building a new, interactive page.

Arachnid does have some significant drawbacks, however. The fact that it does not work in HTML makes it more difficult to use. It does have the capability to both load existing HTML documents and export an Arachnid project as an HTML document. Unfortunately, these functions are extremely slow in the current beta version of Arachnid, making their use very problematical for repetitive work. Overall, Arachnid shows some real innovation in user interface for creating and testing new Web documents, but is probably not a good choice for editing existing documents.

Templates

As mentioned at the beginning of this chapter, the second way to create an HTML document is to use an existing editor or word processing program and add special templates that allow you to add HTML tags directly into your document. While there is a great benefit in using an editor you are already familiar with, there are some real limitations when using templates to create an HTML document. Depending on what you want to do you may find that you will want to use both a template and an HTML editor to create your Web documents.

BBEdit Extensions

BBEdit is one of the most popular text editors in use in the Macintosh world, and for many good reasons. It is simple to learn but will grow with you: it has many abilities for automation and extensions. For these reasons, it is natural that several extension packages for BBEdit are available that help you create HTML documents in your favorite editor.

BBEdit Lite

BBEdit Lite is a freeware version of the full BBEdit application. It is quite useful in its own right and is fully capable of being used alone for many editing tasks. In addition, the HTML editing

extensions that are available for BBEdit also work with BBEdit Lite. BBEdit Lite is included on the Companion CD-ROM. Like SoftQuad's policy on HoTMetaL, Bare Bones Software, the developers of BBEdit, have found it a good commercial venture to distribute this free version of their editor to allow users to become familiar with the great set of tools and excellent features that are part of BBEdit.

You can install BBEdit Lite from the compressed, self-extracting archive by copying it to your hard disk and double-clicking on it; then select the location you want the BBEdit Lite folder placed.

Installing BBEdit HTML Tools

BBEdit HTML Tools are extensions to BBEdit or BBEdit Lite that allow you to insert HTML tags into your text documents. The BBEdit HTML Tools are free and are available on the Companion CD-ROM. You can also get a copy of them from ftp://ftp.york.ac.uk/pub/users/ld11/ with a file name of BBEdit_HTML_Tools.sea.hqx. As the author notes, these extensions are updated regularly, so you may wish to check that you have the latest version. These extensions were written by Lindsay Davis, who can be reached via e-mail at LD11@unix.york.ac.uk.

To install the tools, simply copy the self-extracting archive to your hard disk and uncompress the tools into the same folder where you have BBEdit or BBEdit Lite installed. Note that the tools must end up in the same folder as the BBEdit application itself. Then, follow the directions in the file ReadMe.html to install the extensions and configure BBEdit for their use.

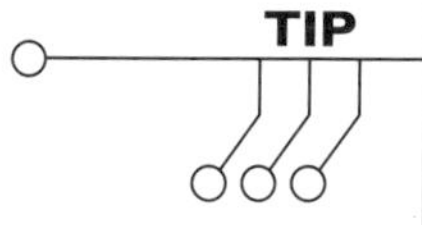

As you can tell by the file name, the ReadMe.html file is designed to be read as an HTML document. That means you can open it in your favorite browser and read it, using the embedded links to jump to the information you need. However, the author has cleverly included the entire text as a comment at the beginning of the document, so that you can also open and read it with any simple text editor—such as BBEdit itself.

Setting Up BBEdit HTML Tools

Once you have installed the tools extensions, according to the directions in the ReadMe.html file, you need to set some preferences for your editor. When you launch BBEdit, you should see a new series of extensions under the Extensions menu. Select Extensions>>Utilities and press the Preferences button to bring up the Preferences dialog box. Here you should at least set a Web client, such as Netscape, and select a Document Template. The HTML Tools comes with a simple document template that gives you the basic attributes for an HTML document; you can also create others as you want or need them. Once you've set up your browser and template, you're ready to go. You can begin a new HTML document by selecting Extensions>>Document and filling in the dialog box. Note that you don't use the standard, File>>New command; if you do, you'll only open a new text document, not an HTML one. If you use the template provided, the resulting dialog box will look like Figure 2-4. Fill in the Title and other attributes for your document, set the New Document checkbox and click OK. The resulting document will appear in BBEdit as shown in Figure 2-5.

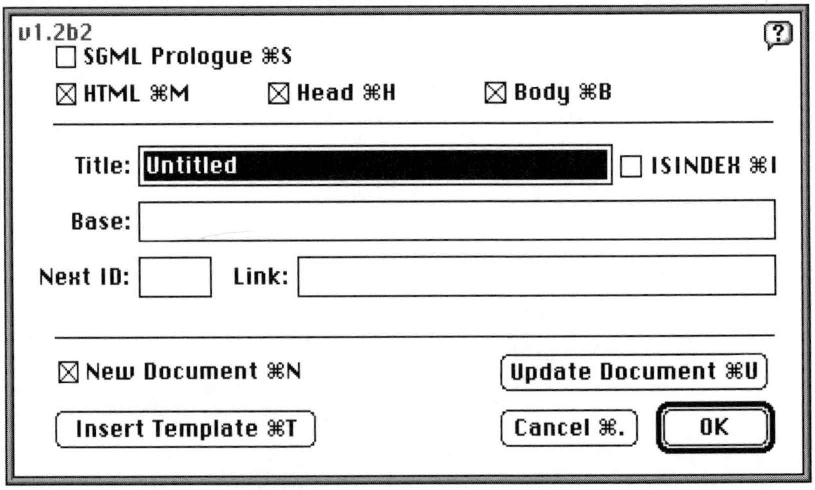

Figure 2-4: *The HTML Tool Extensions to BBEdit present a special dialog box for a new HTML document.*

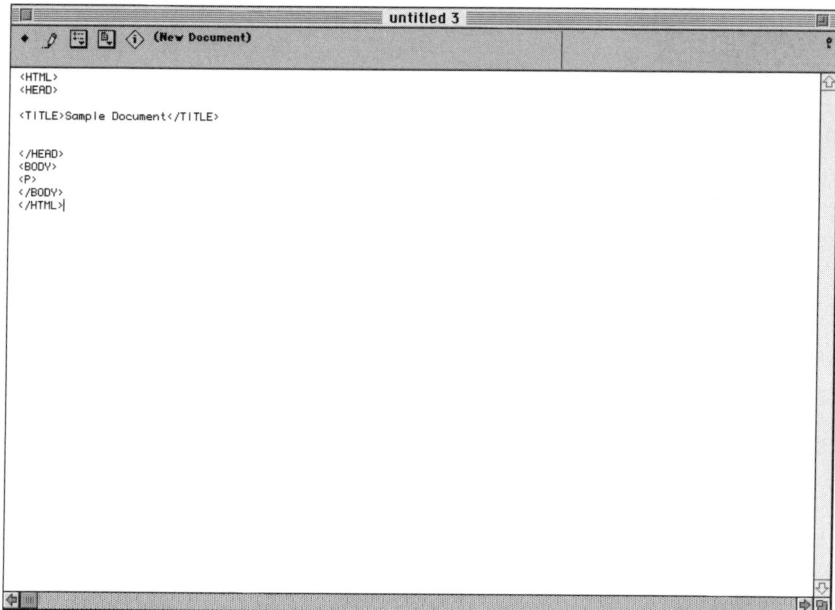

Figure 2-5: *This is a start on a new document in BBEdit when you use the HTML Tools Extensions to create it.*

Microsoft Word Templates

There are a large number of templates available for Microsoft Word for Windows. Unfortunately, none of these have as yet been made available for Word for Macintosh—and, when they are, they are likely to require using the notoriously slow and poorly received, Word 6.0. While there is a great benefit of using a word processor you are already familiar with, there are some real limitations when using a Word template to create an HTML document. Depending on what you want to do, you may find that you'll be better off using Word to create a document, exporting it in RTF (Rich Text Format) and converting it to HTML using the RTFtoHTML converter discussed in the next section. Then you can use an HTML editor to fine-tune your Web documents.

HTML Converters

In the first part of this chapter you were introduced to a number of tools that made it easier for you to create new HTML documents, or to use text editor templates to create documents with HTML markup. If you have a large set of existing documents you want to put on the Web, however, original authoring or extensive modifications to existing documents may not be a viable option. The following section explores an HTML converter that lets you create HTML documents from files in other formats. There are many converters and filters available, but most of them are created for the UNIX operating system, where sophisticated filter tools are already available for other purposes. If you don't find what you want in this chapter, be sure to check the Web archives for new conversion tools.

For converting existing documents, the best conversion utilities are those that work with existing document processing packages. Currently, there are flavors for almost any word processing or page layout application, including Quark Xpress, PageMaker and FrameMaker. Information about all types of conversion programs is available at Jon Weiderspan's Macintosh WWW Development tools site at http://www.uwtc. washington.edu/Computing/WWW/Mac/HTMLEdit.html.

The Quark XPress converters come in two types: some are standalone converters that require you to export your Quark pages as files and then convert them, and some are Quark Xtensions, that link directly into XPress itself. Of the QuarkXTensions, the most full-featured—and the most expensive by far—is BeyondPress, an extension from Astrobyte LLC. Information on BeyondPress is available from Astrobyte and http://www.astrobyte.com/astrobyte/BeyondPressInfo.hhtml. There are, however, a number of other XTensions that may provide enough functionality for your requirements at a lower cost.

RTF to HTML

This converter is the best we found. Almost all word processors can export documents in Rich Text Format (RTF). This program is a top-notch converter program with plenty of options to handle even the most complex formatted documents. As mentioned previously, this converter, along with all other HTML converters, is limited by what can be represented in HTML. If you're a programmer, one of the best features about the RTF to HTML converter is that the source code is available. You can get a copy of the converter at ftp://ftp.cray.com/src/WWWstuff/RTF/latest/binaries. The file name is rtftohtml-mac.sit.hqx. The program is copyrighted by the Free Software Foundation, which gives liberal redistribution rights but insists that the programs stay free and may not be incorporated into commercial software.

The main features of the RTF to HTML converter are:

- Bold, italic and underlined text are converted to HTML properly.
- Courier font text appears in HTML as the Teletype font.
- Tables will be converted to the "Pre-formatted Fixed Pitch Text" style, with the borders removed. (The current version of HTML does not directly support tables, although HTML 2.1 will.)
- Footnotes are placed into separate documents, and hypertext links are added.
- Table of contents entries and heading styles one to six are generated (as created with Microsoft Word). These will be included in a generated hypertext table of contents in a separate file. Each table of contents entry will link to the correct location in the main document.
- Document styles are directly supported through the use of the html-trans file, which comes predefined with many standard document styles as used in Word for Windows. If you use a style that is not in the html-trans file, you'll see a warning message. You can define your own styles in the "html-trans" file to support whatever document styles you use in your own work.

- Graphics that have been inserted into the RTF will be written to individual files in Macintosh PICT format. These files must then be converted to the GIF format supported by most Web browsers. (See Chapter 8, "Getting Graphic With Images," for more information about graphics and graphics file formats.)
- Text that has been inserted into a document with a Copy/Paste/Link command will be connected via hypertext links.
- Headers, footers, tables of contents and indexes are ignored.
- You may manually embed HTML in a source RTF document and have the converter simply copy the HTML to the output HTML document.
- You may specify hypertext links in the RTF source that will be converted to HTML hypertext links.
- You may customize the converter to manage almost any special case of text conversion you encounter.
- The converter supports nested lists.
- Output files are created using the same name as your input file, with the suffix HTML.

As you can see from this list, the RTF to HTML converter is a very powerful tool for you to add to your HTML creation toolbox. Until the stand-alone HTML and SGML editors or Word add-on programs have fully matured, editing in your favorite word processor and then converting the RTF to HTML may be the best way to go for large documents.

There are a number of other converters available for UNIX-based systems, as well as for other operating systems. If you are interested, you can get additional information at http://www.w3.org/hypertext/WWW/Tools/Filters.html and http://oneworld.wa.com/htmldev/devpage/dev-page.html.

Moving On

Now that you've got a handle on the tools you can use to create HTML documents, it's time to explore the possibilities the Web brings to structuring information for publishing on the Web. If you're anxious to begin using HTML skip to Chapter 5, "Creating Your First Web Document," but be sure to come back to Chapter 3, "Structuring Information in Web Documents," for information about designing and creating nonlinear documents.

3

Structuring Information in Web Documents

At first glance publishing on the Internet may appear to be fairly easy. So easy, in fact, that the temptation exists to slap some words on a page, toss in some favorite hyperlinks, throw in a few images and put your creation on the Net for the world to see. Unfortunately, many Web authors have taken this approach by constructing documents that show little consideration for the reader. This chapter will help bring structure, efficiency and elegance to your documents by addressing the special needs and circumstances presented by the structure of the Web. It also offers some tried-and-true design principles from the world of "paper publishing" that apply to Web documents as well.

Linear vs. Hypermedia Documents

Typically when you pick up a book, you flip it open to the first page and start reading. Perhaps, you'll look at the Table of Contents to see what's there, and you skip around, awkwardly, by going to a particular chapter and skimming it until you find the reference or thought that aroused your interest in the first place.

In a book, the author has structured the information in a way that best presents the point he or she is trying to make, and you have little say in the way the author feels you should absorb information. This kind of a publication is called linear. You start at point A, and go to point B and so on in a predetermined straight line. If the writer feels you should learn about birds before bees are discussed, that's the way it is going to be. If the process of gathering honey has captured your interest and you want to learn a bit about it before continuing on with the book, you have to wait until the author is ready to present this information before you can learn about it. You could shuffle through the book looking for references to the process. It is also possible, but not probable, that you could go to the library and get another book that discussed the honey-gathering process in detail to find the information you want. If you want to learn about something, you want it now. You don't want to have to wade through a lot of text that has little or no bearing on what you want to learn about.

That brings us to hypermedia. On the Web, *nonlinear* publications are the rule. Nonlinear publishing taps the power of the computer and the client/server model to let a reader follow almost any tangent he or she wants. (If the author provides the pathways, that is.) In the above example, if you wanted to learn about acquiring honey, and the path to that information had been presented in a Web document, you could simply position your cursor on the hyperlink, click and be transported to the beekeeping home page of the Entomology Department at a local university, or wherever the relevant information happened to be. When you got your fill of information on honey, and wanted to go back and learn something about birds, another click could zip you back from whence you came.

Structuring Your Web Document

The first decision you must make when creating a Web document is how to structure the information you want to present. Web documents most often contain a series of linked elements presented one idea or action at a time. If, for example, one part of

your document included a customer survey or a large collection of links to software, this would be a stand-alone element accessed by a link from other pages in your document.

These pages may also be visited directly from links that other authors have added to their documents at sites anywhere in the world. Keeping this one-at-a-time approach in mind, it becomes necessary to impose a structure on your document.

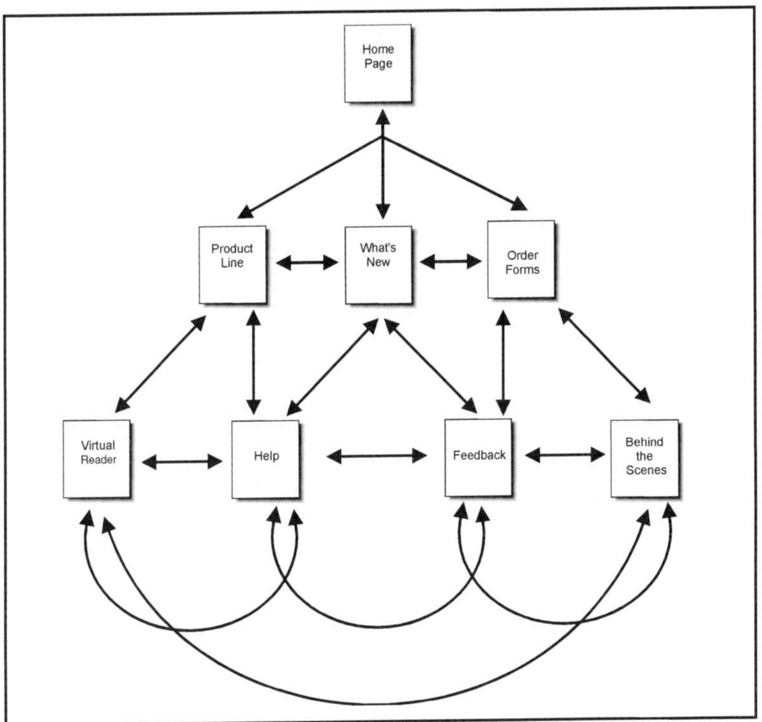

Figure 3-1: *It's a good idea to sketch out Web documents and links before creating your Web document.*

Establishing Hierarchies

The best way to initiate a structure is to create an outline. This helps you create a structured document and determines the links you need to create to documents or sites elsewhere on the Web, or within your own document. The following outline of Web pages and links is based on a real world example from A Clean Well-Lighted Place for Books, one of the premier retail booksellers in the San Francisco Bay area.

Home Page: A Clean Well-Lighted Place for Books

a. About ACWLPFB
b. What's New (link to page 2)
c. Store Locations and Events (link to page 3)
d. Mystery Quote! (link to page 4)
e. Best of the Books (link to page 5)
f. Guides for the Virtual Reader (link to page 6)
g. Ordering (link to page 7)
h. Feedback (link to page 8)
i. Behind the Scenes (link to page 9)

Page 2: What's New

a. New Fiction
b. New Non-Fiction

Page 3: Store Locations and Events

a. San Francisco
b. Larkspur Landing
c. Cupertino

Page 4: Mystery Quote!

a. The Mystery Quotation
b. How to Play the Game

Page 5: Best of the Books

a. Newsletter
b. Buyer's Choice
c. Staff Favorites
d. From Other Countries

Page 6: Guides for the Virtual Reader

a. Calendars of Interest
b. Reader's Resources
c. Zines
d. Antiquarian or Out-of-print Books
e. Newpapers Online
f. Miscellaneous References
g. Other Bay Area Resources
h. San Francisco Museums
i. Bay Area Restaurant Guides

Page 7: Order Forms
- a. Ordering Books
- b. Special Orders
- c. Return Policies

Page 8: Feedback
- a. Comments
- b. Mailing List
- c. Customer Survey

It's often beneficial to give each topic its own page. This makes updating easier and allows you to refer to the same page, like the Ordering Forms or Feedback page, over and over from various places within the document. The next item we need to consider is how to tie these documents together in a coherent way.

Determining Your Links

Once the Web documents have been outlined, you're ready to consider how you will link the various parts together. The actual process of linking will be covered in Chapter 6, "The Art of Linking," but you need to decide what you want to link early in the design process. Therefore it's a good idea to sketch out the structure of your Web pages. Make the home page the front door to your document so that visitors can move to other pages from the home page. Figure 3-1 shows the structure of A Clean Well-Lighted Place for Book's pages.

Be aware that the very nature of the Web allows visitors to enter in places other than the uppermost level. Readers can jump to a specific Web page by following a link that someone else established and find themselves on a page that is far removed from any introductory material. For this reason, one of your initial design considerations is to provide the visitor with an easy way to your home page, if they wish. This can be accomplished by providing a hyperlink to your home page on all your Web pages. By creating a hyperlink to the home page, people can easily find the points of interest by the links established in the directing document (the home page). As well as providing links to your home page, you may also want to include links for readers to visit or return to other pages within the document. Figure 3-2 shows the bottom of Interactive Age magazine's Web page. Interactive Age can be found at http://techweb.cmp.com:80/ia/current. Notice that there are several navigational icons and hyperlinks to aid the reader visiting the Web site.

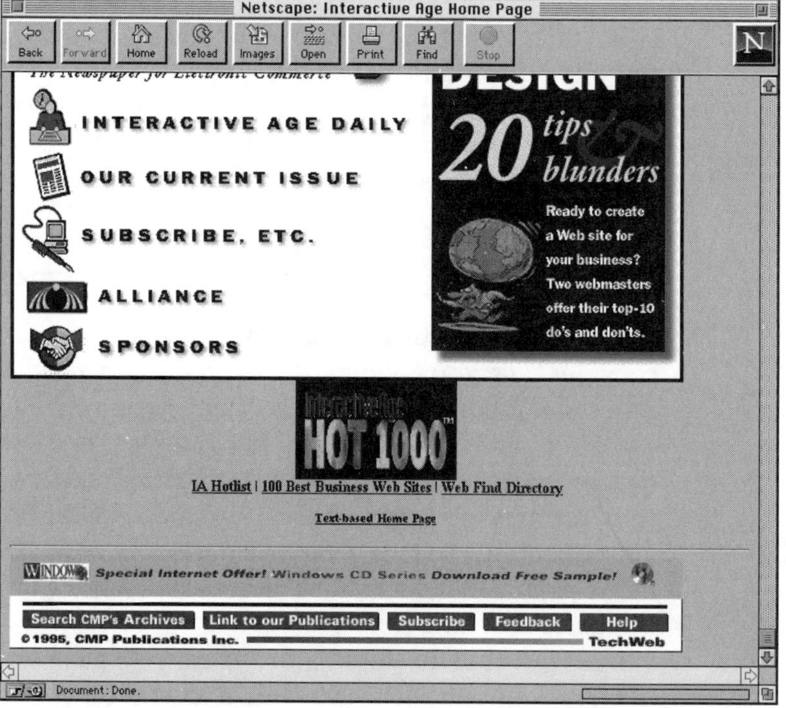

Figure 3-2: Interactive Age's *Web page is a good example of how to include navigational icons and hyperlinks, so people can easily move back to the home page or to another page.*

Designing Web Pages

Structuring and designing Web documents is not a simple job. Be prepared to make changes. It's a good strategy to plan it as if the home page will be the first page read. If you include a link on

every page of your document that takes the reader to the first page, it really doesn't matter where the reader starts reading. The following sections examine determining your Web document's structure by defining your document's goals and designing your Web pages to capture the audience you want to address.

Defining Your Documents Goals

At the same time that you are creating an outline, you also need to articulate the document's goals, or purpose. A document that simply provides information can be successful by just including pointers to Web sites that have the information your reader wants to see. A corporate page, on the other hand, needs to provide a message of what the company is offering or trying to accomplish.

It may sound simplistic, but the most important thing you have to do is decide *what* you want to do. And, the best way to define this is often to ask yourself, "When a reader has finished reading my work, what do I want him or her to know?" Everything else you do will be judged by this standard. Keep focused and don't lose sight of your goal.

The bottom-line goal for A Clean Well-Lighted Place for Books is to generate sales by interesting readers in specific titles and by increasing traffic in the stores. People come into a bookstore for two reasons. First, to find a book that they already know that they want and, second, to browse the book selections to see if there is something that interests them. Therefore, the pages need to inform the reader of specific titles that are currently available at the stores, and let them acquire enough information to make them want to either place an order for the book or come into the store for it. Also, the pages need to provide information on store events and types of books available to encourage readers to come by the store to browse. Sometimes people mistakenly think that, because the Web is itself computer-related and computer-generated, Web pages have to focus on computer products. This is simply not true, as you can see in the case of ACWLP's Web site.

Document Aesthetics

Even after the material you want to present has been selected, there are many other design elements yet to consider. Your publication needs both a "look" and a well-defined audience. It is also important, and prudent, to consider the limitations your readers may have due to the browser and equipment they may be using, such as a 14,400 bps modem or a high-speed ISDN connection.

Developing Your Look

Because readers will be jumping into, out of, or within your Web pages, the importance of maintaining a consistent look throughout your work is not quite as important as if the work were to be published in print. However, it is still highly desirable to develop a look that will carry throughout your pages.

A consistent look accomplishes several purposes: First, you may decide to publish the document on paper sometime, and it will be ready to go; second, especially for commercial pages, readers should constantly be aware of who you are, and one good way to achieve this is through consistent visual cues—a logo on each page, for example; third, and equally important, lack of consistency presents a scattered, unprofessional image you may not want to broadcast. Even if you're publishing an anarchistic newsletter, readers are more likely to keep reading when they are presented a consistent structure and design.

Capturing Your Audience

A considerable amount of thought should be devoted to defining the characteristics of your target audience. If you make your message too simple, or too complex, you will either insult or bore many of the people who visit your site. You are safe in assuming that anyone accessing your work through the Web is literate, and a possessor of sufficient resources to get into the Web in the first place. You are certainly sure that any reader has a curious bent of mind. This definition, however, includes the fourteen-year-old hacker, as well as the forty-year-old rocket scientist.

The trick then becomes how to structure your presentation and language to appeal to your ideal audience. Most of this selection process is accomplished by the style of writing you choose. For example, including puns, word games and hyperbole, or adding too lighthearted a style could affect your credibility, causing others to view your site as a frivolous pastime, rather than presenting a serious professional image. This isn't to say you can't create a fun Web page, just be sure your writing style doesn't distract from the goal of your Web page.

It is also important to keep in mind the equipment that will be used to view your message—there are many differing hardware/software configurations and capabilities out there. Some machines just won't display graphics at all, and Chapter 5, "Creating Your First Web Document" discusses how to write for both graphic- and text-based Web browsers. However, even limiting our discussion to graphics-capable machines, there is still a wide diversity of possibilities. For example, there are many different Web browsers: NCSA Mosaic, Netscape Navigator, MacWeb, etc., and each of these browsers displays your presentation differently.

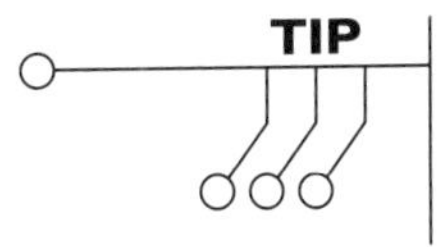

There has been a trend in some Web documents to include information about the browser that was used when testing the document, such as a message that goes something like: "Use Netscape to view this document at its highest quality." You might want to create a link to a formatted version designed specifically for the Netscape Navigator browser.

You should also consider the constraints placed on a reader by his or her hardware. There is probably someone out there who has figured out how to connect to the Net at 2400 bps. You could also find someone who is trying to be "graphical" using a 7- x 5-inch monochrome screen at a 72 dpi resolution. You can be pretty safe in ignoring their needs. After all, making your presentation simple enough to be adequately viewed on equipment of this nature would detract from your message. (You would not be able to include any but the simplest graphics, since the download time would be unacceptable at 2400 bps.)

What you do need to consider is the browser displaying on a screen using eight-bit color or better. Also, the lowest modem connection you may want to test with is 9600 bps.

Constructing Web Pages

Up to this point, we've talked about the collection of pages that, when assembled, make up your Web presence. Our consideration has also been directed toward the "big picture" design. Now, it's time to examine the process of constructing and designing individual pages. Each individual page in your document should contain certain elements: identity, look, links and information.

How to Let Them Know Who You Are

Remember that a reader does not, necessarily, use the front door (or your home page) to get into your document. Therefore, it's important for you to include some information that identifies yourself on each page. This can be a simple logo or some text that is linked to your home page or another page, where information about you can be found. Your purpose is to get your name and message out. You don't want the reader scratching his or her head wondering who you are.

How to Develop the Look You Want

The look of your presentation is very important. Consider how you look at your "snail" or postal mail. There are some publications you get that you know by sight. It could be a logo, a color, an envelope or almost any unique identifier. You immediately know that this is a publication you want to read (or toss). You want your Web document to be read. Many of the same things that attract you to a mailed document can be used to make your Web publication stand out, too. The visual appeal of a page, the amount of white space, the depth of content and the ease of access all must be thought through.

Ask yourself, how you can make your pages artistically pleasing, given the limitations of your authoring tools? Can you stand back from the page, when it is displayed in a browser, and feel welcome? Everyone senses the artistic page on one level or another, however, and often this element above all others has an almost subconscious effect on how a reader perceives you and your organization. If you're not an artistic type, seek out someone who is and have them review your work. Several individuals and companies exist that provide Web design services. If you're interested in contacting a Web design service, check out the resources section at the back of this book for a list of some Web design service companies.

Another consideration is the size of your graphics. The amount of text on the screen at any given time should not be out of proportion to the size and placement of graphic elements. Don't clutter your page with too much text. Pages that contain a lot of text are often called *gray pages*. Not only does looking at gray pages make you feel intimidated by the amount of information they appear to contain, they look cluttered and unappealing.

One way to break up your pages without using too many graphics is to use white space. White space includes the space between lines of text, called *leading*, the space between words and characters, called *kerning*, and the size of the margins and breaks between paragraphs. All of these elements help to give the reader an overall impression of your page.

Because browsers are trying to display the same page on a wide variety of hardware and software, you don't have any control over the leading or kerning, and you only have limited control over the margins and what font is used. What you do have is absolute control over the number of words used in any paragraph. Most HTML editors insert extra space after a paragraph; use this as a design tool.

The depth of content is another major issue. The beauty of publishing on the Web is the ability to link elements within (and outside of) your document. Keep your pages short, concise and dedicated to one issue or topic. Include branches that lead to pages containing other ideas or issues. The reason for this is one of maintenance, as well as aesthetics and ease of use. If all information about a topic is included in a known place, you only have to update it once.

Ease of access is another issue. While unfortunately ignored by many Web authors, a page's ease of use probably leads to many instances of readers bailing out of publications without reading them. Even though most browsers give the reader the option of not loading graphics, not all readers are aware of this. If your pages contain large graphics, the process of downloading the graphic to the reader's browser can take so much time that the reader becomes impatient, and unreceptive to your message. If you want to include graphics (and you should), keep them small. You can offer the option of viewing a more complex version of the graphic by linking the smaller (thumbnail) version of it to the larger one.

Make sure all the links you add jump to other Web pages and all these sites work. All too often authors use links to sites that have changed. Surfing the Internet and encountering a dead link or a link to a site in which the URL has changed is frustrating. You should check your links and plan to recheck them regularly. Otherwise you're sending a subliminal message to the reader that not only is the link dead, but the information you are presenting is also out-of-date.

How to Design Your Home Page

A good design idea is to use the home page as a table of contents for the rest of your document. Figure 3-3 shows the Internet Business Center's home page (http://www.tig.com/IBC/index.html).

Notice that the page starts off with a graphic, the Center's logo. Following that is the identifying information, a very brief statement about what the center does. Three feature articles are then listed with links to their pages. (These pages are most likely more table of contents style pages that allow the reader to further refine what he or she wants to read.) Finally, a list of other sites is included in bullet-style. Even though the Netscape Navigator is set up to use a gray background, the page is still pleasing to view. The varying design elements (graphics, text and lists) make the page interesting and the appearance crisp and clean.

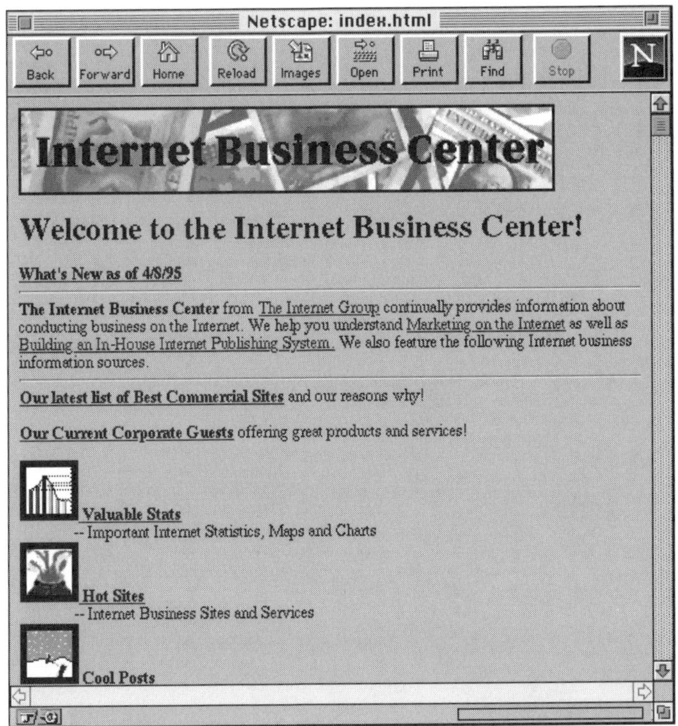

Figure 3-3: *The Internet Business Center's home page is an example of a simple uncluttered Web page.*

Another aspect of good design is to show sensitivity to all viewers. For example, you may want to present your pages in different formats: one for users that can handle large graphics and another for text browsers. If you are going to include browser specific features, it's also a good idea to give users a link to take them to a version of the document that has been optimized for the browser. Figure 3-4 shows the Ventana Media's home page (http://www.vmedia.com), which lets users choose between a rich-presentation format or a simple-presentation method.

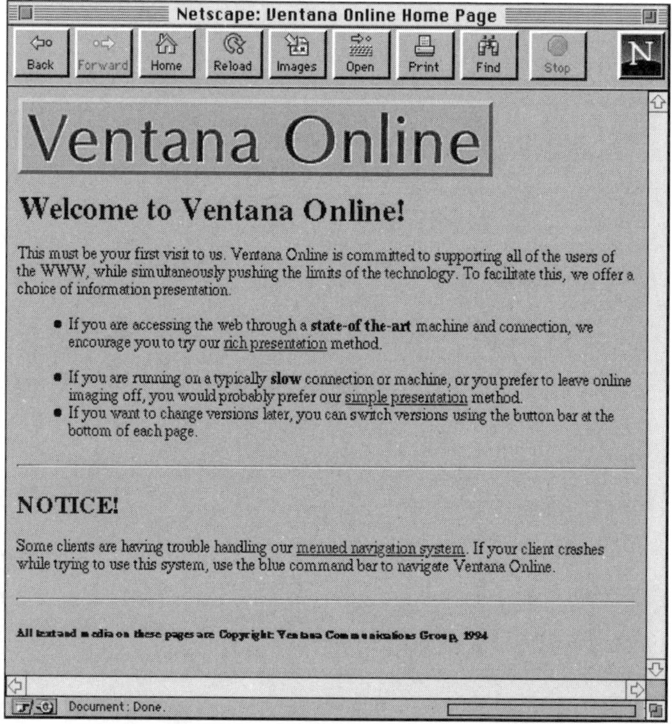

Figure 3-4: *Ventana Media lets users choose between a rich-presentation format or a simple-presentation method.*

How to Design Subsequent Pages

Many of the structure and design issues are the same for pages that are linked to your home page. The following are some general guidelines for creating subsequent Web pages.

An important design consideration is to include only one or two topics per page. Your readers came to this page expecting to see what they had selected on your home page, and little else. If you're going to include large Web documents, such as documentation or an online book, it is helpful to create a table of contents. A good example of a Web page that presents a table of contents can be found in The Magellan Venus Explorer's Guide at http://newproducts.jpl.nasa.gov/magellan/guide.html.

Figure 3-5 shows how a Web page can use links to create a table of contents that let the reader quickly move to information they want.

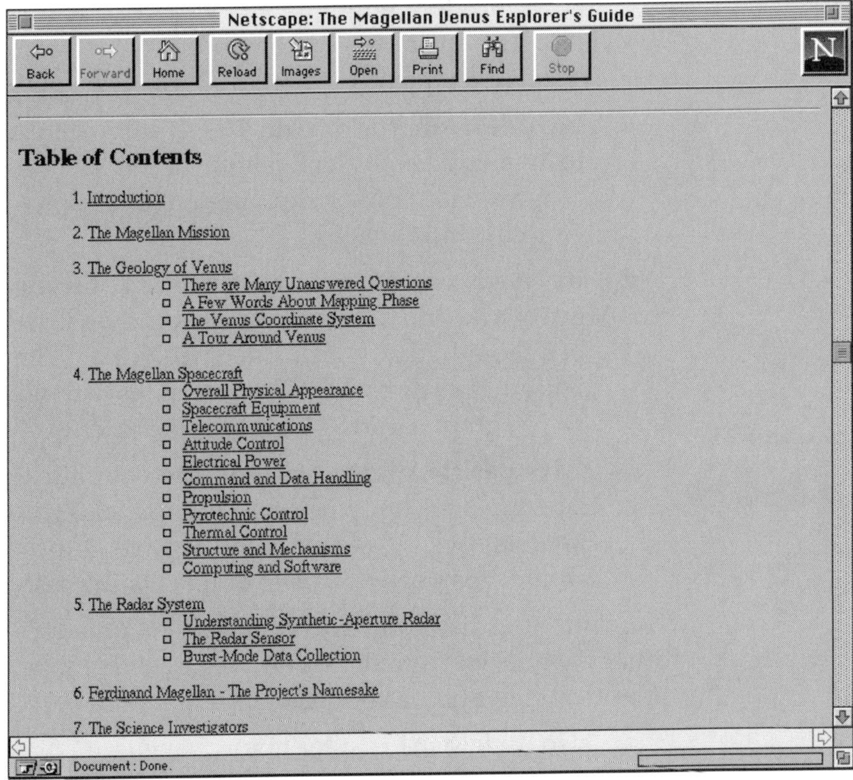

Figure 3-5: *The Magellan Venus Explorer's Guide is a good example of a linked table of contents.*

Some other items to keep in mind are:

- **Keep it simple.** Pages that contain massive amounts of text are typically not read. A good rule of thumb is never to have more than 50 percent of the screen covered with anything. When you are viewing your page, step back from the monitor so you can't read any of the text, and look to see if the appearance of the gray (text-filled) areas and the rest of the screen is pleasing to the eye.

- **Vary the text styles.** Break your information down in such a way that you can use different levels of headings, when appropriate. Each level displays differently and gives your document eye-appeal. Include, when called for, text attributes that emphasize key points. Headings, body text and text attributes are discussed in Chapter 7, "Creating Your Text Appeal."
- **Include a graphic or two.** Use graphics as design elements to break up text or lend a little variety to your presentation. You will learn how to link images in Chapter 8, "Getting Graphic With Images."
- **Be consistent.** It is easy to view each document as a separate work, and in a sense you should do just that. Remember, though, that your readers will jump from page to page within your document. Be consistent with your usage of styles, graphics and other design elements.
- **Give people a reason to return to your site.** Many Web sites are one-shot wonders. Add value to your site to entice readers back by adding a hotlist page, tutorial, weekly comic, tips page or a page of links to interesting software.

The third, fourth and fifth level pages of a Web document do not differ a whole lot from the second page. Remember, however, to provide pathways for your readers to

1. Go back to the first, or home, page.
2. Go forward in your presentation to the next logical place.
3. Go directly to the Order Form, if you have one.
4. Go back and see what came before the current page.

Do's & Don'ts

We've covered a lot in this chapter. Much of it will be reinforced as you continue reading and using Web authoring tools. Below is a list of ten design issues you'll want to keep in mind when creating Web documents.

1. *Decide what you want to do.* If you don't know where you're going with your document, you will never get there. It is really difficult to keep yourself focused when you are writing any document, and the more structure you can bring to the process, the better the results.
2. *Identify yourself.* It's your turn on stage, take advantage of it. Each page should contain some kind of identifier, like a logo and a brief statement of purpose.
3. *Know your audience.* Design a publication that will be pleasing to view on a "normal" computer system. Structure your language, vocabulary and syntax to the audience you want to address. This can serve as a gatekeeper, welcoming in those you want and excluding those you don't. If you have high-quality graphics you want to include (pictures of your product, for example) consider creating a thumbnail of those images or linking those pictures to a page that individuals with slower modems can skip if they wish.
4. *Keep your design simple.* Allow linked documents to provide more in-depth information and keep all of your pages as simple and uncluttered as you can.
5. *Vary your styles.* Use the different levels of text (headings, etc.) as design elements to break up your page.
6. *Include a graphic or two.* Graphics are a great way to provide interest and style to your page. Keep inline graphics small, in bytes, and simple, in colors. They'll load faster.

7. *Keep your design tight.* There is no limit on the number of pages you can create. Keep the information presented highly focused on your goals. If you think a reader may want to go off on a tangent, provide a link instead of placing the extra verbiage on the current page.
8. *There's no place like home.* Be sure to provide links that will take readers back to where he or she may want to go—home or the previous page.
9. *Be consistent.* Try to develop your own style and carry it through the entire publication. People remember the feel and look of your publications, a consistent approach will gain you recognition much quicker than an inconsistent one.
10. *Know your writing and artistic skills and get feedback.* Publishing documents is a blend of art and craft. A publishing house employs designers, artists and page layout professionals in addition to the editors, marketers and accountants. If you're publishing Web pages on your own, ask other people their opinions about your finished document.

Moving On

Take the time to determine the goal of your site and design your Web pages to meet that goal—it will save you time in the long run. A site that has an efficient structure and a consistent, visually appealing design improves the chances that people will return to it. Designing a well-structured site is only the first step, it's time to begin learning how to use HTML and start creating your individual Web pages. The next chapter introduces you to the HoTMetaL PRO editor and shows you how to install it and use it to create Web pages.

4

Getting Started With HoTMetaL PRO

HoTMetaL PRO is an easy-to-use graphical editor for creating files in the HTML format. Because HoTMetaL PRO is a rules-checking HTML editor, it ensures that you create correctly marked-up documents. This chapter tells you how to set up and start HoTMetaL PRO and gives you an overview of the HoTMetaL PRO environment. It also explains how to work with HoTMetaL's menus and toolbars to create, edit and save HTML documents. Additionally, it explains how to customize the program and how to get additional help, so you get the most out of HoTMetaL PRO.

CD-ROM

Note: We are privileged to offer a special version of HoTMetaL PRO on the Companion CD-ROM for your use. This version, called HoTMetaL LITE, does not have all of the features available for the full, commercial release of HoTMetaL PRO. In particular, it lacks the Thesaurus and conversion features that can be very valuable for transforming existing documents into HTML pages. However, for the work in this book, and for any work where you are creating pages from scratch, the LITE version that you now own is a perfect tool. Once you have mastered these techniques using the LITE version, you may wish to upgrade your current version of HoTMetaL LITE to the full, professional version. Contact SoftQuad for details on how to do this.

For the most part, the instructions presented in this book cover both versions of HoTMetaL: our special HoTMetaL LITE version, and the full professional version, HoTMetaL PRO. We use the name HoTMetaL PRO when we are working with or discussing the general application. All instructions in this book that reference HoTMetaL PRO work for both versions of the application. For installation and other tasks, where you are working specifically with the version on the Companion CD-ROM, we have used the name HoTMetaL LITE to distinguish this version from the professional version.

Installing HoTMetaL LITE

HoTMetaL PRO and HoTMetaL LITE both require using a Macintosh with an 68030 or better processor with 8MB or more memory. (However, you can substitute disk space for memory, if you have available disk space, by turning on Virtual Memory in the Memory Control Panel.) Remember that, in addition to running HoTMetaL PRO, you will need to be able to run a browser at the same time to preview your documents and to view HoTMetaL PRO's help files and documentation. The optimal amount of memory is 12MB or more. The installation requires approximately 6MB of disk space.

To install HoTMetaL LITE, start your Macintosh and be sure no other applications are running, then perform the following steps:

CD-ROM

1. Insert the Companion CD-ROM into your CD drive and display it on the desktop. Double-click on the icon representing your CD to open it and then double-click on the HoTMetaL LITE Installer file in the hmpro2 folder.
2. A dialog box appears asking you to select the drive where you want to store HoTMetaL PRO. The default is your current drive. If you want to store HoTMetaL in another drive, use the Drive button to cycle through the drives available on your system.
3. Click Install. If you wish to cancel the installation for some reason, click on the Quit button.

The Installer program displays the amount of room required to install HoTMetaL PRO in the installation dialog box, along with the available space on the currently selected drive. If you don't have enough space on the current drive, use the Drive button to select another drive or else cancel the installation and free up some disk space. The dialog box changes to indicate the status of the files being copied to your hard disk. You may click the Stop button at any time during installation to terminate the process—however, this leaves some files partially installed, which you may have to delete manually.

If you already have a previous version of HoTMetaL PRO installed in the same folder in which the new version is being installed, you may wish to keep certain files intact. For certain files in the distribution, a dialog box appears allowing you to install the new version of a file and create backup copies of the old file, or else leave the old file as it is without installing the new file.

5. When the installation is completed, you will see a dialog box telling you whether all files were successfully installed. Click OK to return to the Finder.

That's all there is to it. You have now installed HoTMetaL LITE and its associated files.

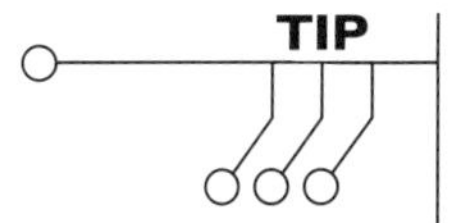

The entire HoTMetaL PRO documentation is available as part of the installed files. The files are in HTML format and stored in the Help folder inside your HoTMetaL PRO folder. You can view them with your favorite browser.

Starting HoTMetaL PRO

After installing HoTMetaL PRO or HoTMetaL LITE, the new HoTMetaL PRO folder will be on the top level of the selected drive. You may want to move this folder to a more convenient location inside some other folder at this time. To start HoTMetaL PRO, double-click on the program icon, or select the program icon and choose Open from the File menu.

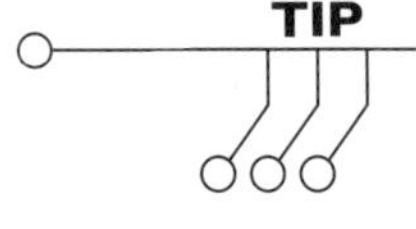

If you want to move HoTMetaL PRO, you may also want to make an alias to the application and store that in the Apple Menu Items folder inside the System folder. This allows you to easily open HoTMetaL PRO by simply selecting it from the Apple menu at any time.

After an introductory copyright screen, you'll see the three tool palettes displayed beneath the HoTMetaL PRO menu bar and an empty screen. By default, HoTMetaL PRO does not open a new document. Figure 4-1 shows the initial HoTMetaL PRO screen.

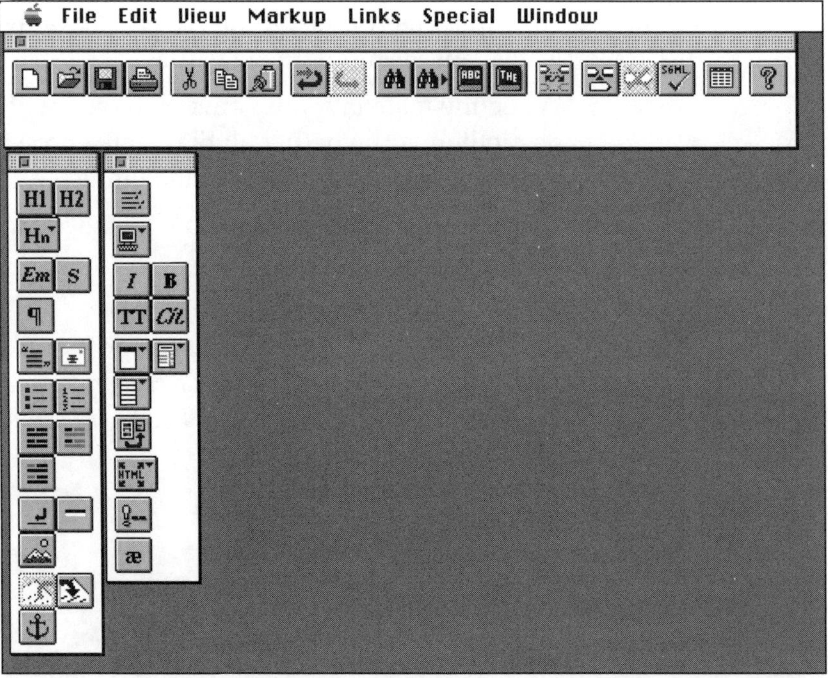

Figure 4-1: *The initial HoTMetaL PRO editing screen showing the floating tool palettes.*

Creating a New HTML Document

To create a new HTML document, choose File>>New. This displays a document named document1 with the beginning and ending tags essential to all HTML documents. Figure 4-2 shows the results of choosing the File>>New command. The next chapter explains the purpose of each of these tags.

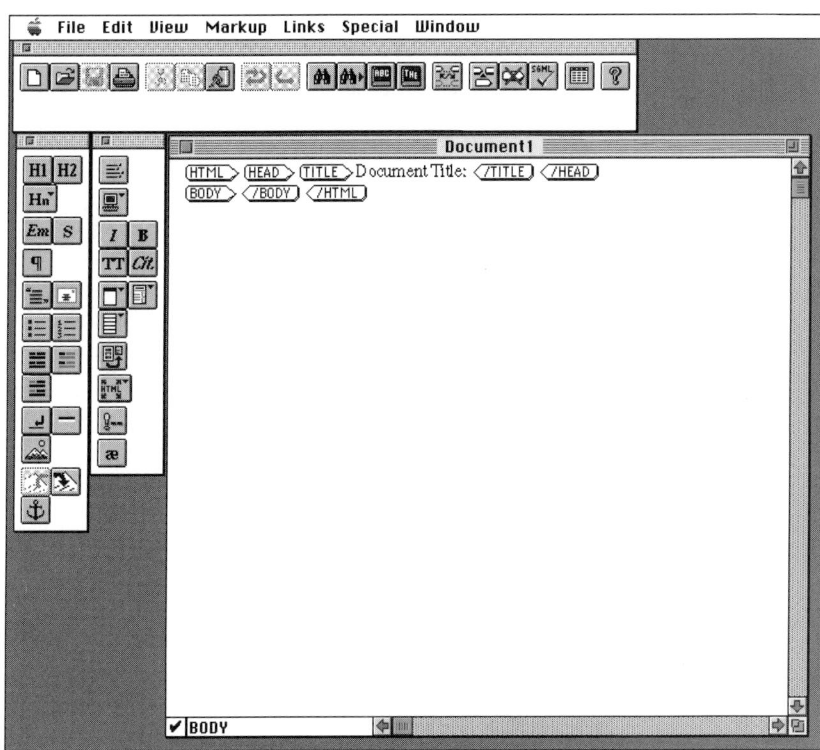

Figure 4-2: *The HoTMetaL PRO screen after choosing the File>>New command.*

Working With Templates

The default template is the file that is opened whenever you create a new document with the File>>New command. The hmpro2.stl file, in the Styles folder, is used as the default template. You can use any HTML document as your default template; you can change the default template using the Preferences command in the Special menu.

Editing an HTML File

Once you've started the program, the simplest thing to do is to open one of the many template files SoftQuad has included. Samples range from a few simple paragraphs to a Web home page, to a customer service forms–based page. If you find something similar to what you want, you're set. Even if you need to make modifications, using the template saves you the effort of figuring out how to create an HTML page from scratch. A number of additional document templates come with HoTMetaL PRO, in the Template folder. These templates are HTML documents you can edit to meet your needs. You can open an HTML document with the File>>Open command, or with the File>>Open Template command. Figure 4-3 shows the homepage.html file opened in the HoTMetaL PRO window. The file aareadme.html in the Templates folder gives you an index of available templates.

If you already have an HTML file that you want to edit, choose the File>>Open command. A dialog box appears. Change to the drive and folder of your HTML document and double-click on the icon for the file. HoTMetaL PRO opens the file for editing. The text is displayed with varying font sizes to suggest how the page may look when viewed with a Web browser.

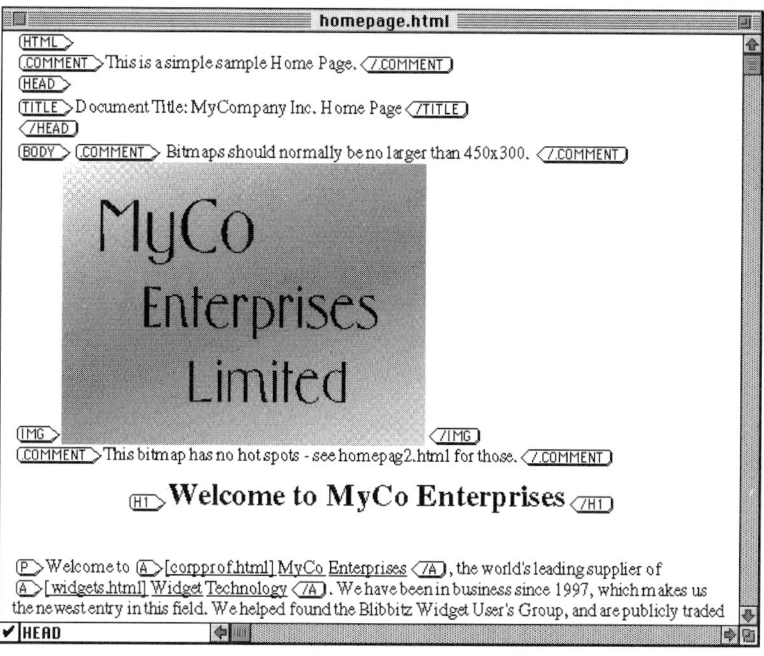

Figure 4-3: *The homepage.html file opened in HoTMetaL PRO.*

Now that you have an open file, you can start entering text and markup. The markup consists of elements that begin with start tags and end with end tags. You can enter elements by using the toolbars or the Markup menu. The name of the current element is displayed in the lower left corner of the document window, just to the left of the horizontal scrollbar.

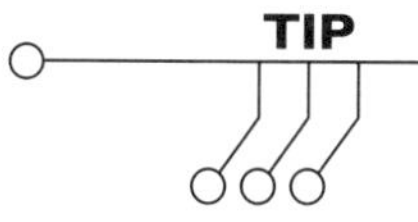

Although you can open HTML pages created by other editors (or right off the Web), be aware that HoTMetaL PRO is a rules-based editor that checks for correct HTML syntax, so it will reject some documents that seem to work okay on the Web. This is because most Web browsers are very accepting of bad HTML coding, allowing readers to view HTML pages that are improperly structured. HoTMetaL PRO 2 will try to open an HTML file even if it contains errors, but occasionally it will not be able to open documents that are incorrectly structured or use unsupported extensions.

Getting Familiar With HoTMetaL PRO's Tool Palettes & Menus

HoTMetaL PRO has three tool palettes (also called toolbars in the menus), which are used to provide fast access to a number of frequently used menu commands and common operations. The top tool palette is called the Standard palette, and is located horizontally below the menu bar by default. By default, two additional tool palettes are displayed vertically beneath the Standard palette. The left tool palette is the Common HTML palette. This tool palette contains buttons for inserting common HTML elements; the right tool palette is called the Other HTML palette. It is for creating less common HTML elements.

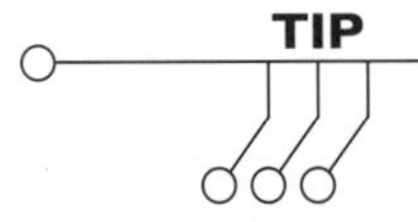

When you position the mouse pointer over a button on any of the tool palettes, a tooltip appears in the lower part of the Standard palette that displays a short description of what that button does.

Moving a Toolbar

You can move any of the three tool palettes. With the pointer on the bar at the top of the palette, press and hold the mouse button down and drag the tool palette wherever you want. When a tool palette is not in its default position, HoTMetaL PRO remembers where you have placed the palette and will display it there the next time you start the application. To return the tool palettes to their default positions, use the View>>Toolbars command to display the Toolbars dialog box. If you've moved the palettes, the Custom radio button will be selected. Choose the Default button to return the tool palettes to their default locations. Choosing the Custom button returns the palettes to the last non-default postion where you had placed them. This dialog box also lets you choose which tool palettes are visible. Figure 4-4 shows HoTMetaL PRO with floating tool palettes repositioned to allow maximum editing area for a document on a large display.

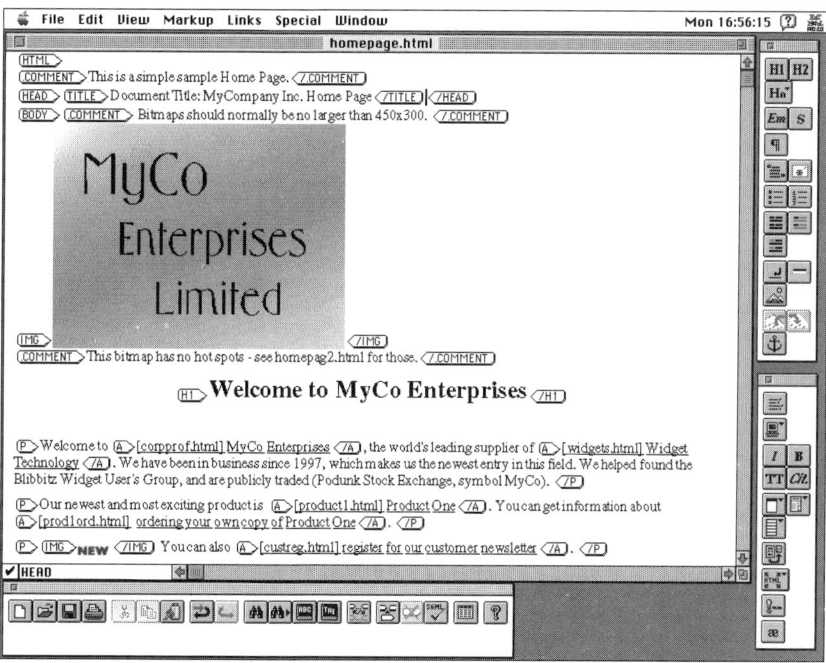

Figure 4-4: *HoTMetaL PRO toolbars can be moved anywhere on the screen.*

Hiding & Showing Toolbars

The View>>Toolbars dialog box lets you choose which toolbars are visible. You can hide a tool palette by clicking on the control button in its upper left corner. When you click on a button in any of the tool palettes, HoTMetaL PRO performs the appropriate action. Table 4-1 shows each tool palette's buttons and lists the button's menu command and the keyboard shortcut equivalent.

Standard Tool Palette

Button	Name	Menu	Shortcut
	New	File>>New	⌘-N
	Open	File>>Open	⌘-O
	Save	File>>Save	⌘-S
	Print	File>>Print	—
	Cut	Edit>>Cut	⌘-X
	Copy	Edit>>Copy	⌘-C
	Paste	Edit>>Paste	⌘-V
	Undo	Edit>>Undo	⌘-Z
	Redo	Edit>>Redo	—
	Find	Edit>>Find and Replace	⌘-F
	Find Next	Edit>>Find Next	⌘-G
	Check Spelling	Edit>>Check Spelling	—
	Thesaurus	Edit>>Thesaurus	—
	Show/Hide Tags	View>>Show Tags/ Hide Tags	⌘-??
	Insert Element	Markup>>Insert Element	⌘-I
	Remove Tags	Markup>>Remove Tags	⌘-D
	Validate SGML	Special>>Validate Document	⌘-/
	Insert Table	Markup>>Insert Table	—
	About	Apple Menu>>About HoTMetaL PRO	—

Table 4-1: *Tool palette buttons and their associated commands.*

The Common Tool Palette

Button	Name	Menu
	Heading 1	Markup>>Insert Element, H1
	Heading 2	Markup>>Insert Element, H2
	Headings 3-6	Markup>>Insert Element, H3/H4/H5/H6
	Emphasis	Markup>>Insert Element, EM
	Strong	Markup>>Insert Element, STRONG
	Paragraph	Markup>>Insert Element, P
	Block Quote	Markup>>Insert Element, BLOCKQUOTE
	Address	Markup>>Insert Element, ADDRESS
	Unordered list	Markup>>Insert Element, UL
	Ordered list	Markup>>Insert Element, OL
	Definition list	Markup>>Insert Element, DL
	Definition term	Markup>>Insert Element, DL, DT
	Definition description	Markup>>Insert Element, DL, DD
	Break	Markup>>Insert Element, BR
	Horizontal Rule	Markup>>Insert Element, HR
	Image	Markup>>Insert Element, IMG
	Connect Link	Links>>Connect Link
	Name Target	Links>>Name Link
	Anchor	Links>>Insert Anchor or Markup>>Insert Element, A

Table 4-1: *Tool palette buttons and their associated commands (cont.).*

Other HTML Palette

Button	Name	Menu	Shortcut
	Preformatted	Markup>>Insert Element, PRE	—
	Code	Markup>>Insert Element, CODE, SAMP, KBD, VAR	—
(Drop-down list includes CODE, SAMP, KBD, and VAR)			
	Italic	Markup>>Insert Element, ITALIC	—
	BOLD	Markup>>Insert Element, B	—
	TeleType	Markup>>Insert Element, TT	—
	Citation	Markup>>Insert Element, CITE	—
	Head elements	Markup>>Insert Element, BASE, ISINDEX, LINK, META and TITLE	—
(Drop-down list includes BASE, ISINDEX, LINK, META and TITLE)			
	Form elements	Markup>>Insert Element, FORM, INPUT/OPTION/SELECT/TEXTAREA	—
(Drop-down list includes FORM, INPUT OPTION, SELECT and TEXTAREA)			
	Other lists		—
(Drop-down list includes UL Compact, OL Compact, DL Compact, DIR, DIR Compact, MENU, and MENU Compact)			
	ISINDEX	Markup>>Insert Element, ISINDEX	—
	Extensions to HTML	Markup>>Insert Element, BIG, BLINK, CENTER, DFN, FONT, S, SMALL, SUB, SUP, U, WBR, and NOBRK	—
(Drop-down list includes BIG, BLINK, CENTER, DFN, FONT, S, SMALL, SUB, SUP, U, WBR, and NOBRK)			
	Insert comment	Markup>>Insert Comment	⌘-'
	Special characters	Markup>>Special Characters	⌘-E

Table 4-1: *Tool palette buttons and their associated commands (cont.).*

Editing HTML Documents

As we mentioned at the beginning of this chapter, HoTMetaL PRO is a rules-based editor that, unlike most HTML editors, protects you from making mistakes when inserting and editing markup tags. The process of inserting tags may take a little more time with HoTMetaL PRO than some HTML editors, but it saves validation time. HoTMetaL PRO automatically ensures that your document doesn't contain incorrect and unmatched tags. The Markup menu contains commands that let you add, split, join, change and remove markup tags and element attributes. The Links menu lets you create and edit hypertext links. Table 4-2 lists the commands for the most common operations found in the Markup and Links menu.

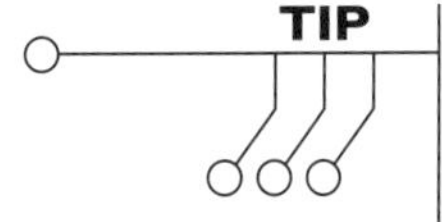

Because you don't know which browser will be used to view your documents, you should follow all the rules in the HTML language as closely as possible. Currently, using some HTML editors and editing templates you can get away with ignoring some elements and still produce a readable document. Keep in mind, however, that anyone can easily download your source code. If you don't follow HTML formatting rules, others may make judgments about you and your company from the quality of your documents.

Pinning Dialog Boxes

Most HoTMetaL PRO dialog boxes automatically close after you perform an action. A special feature of HoTMetaL PRO is that you can pin frequently used dialog boxes. Pinning a dialog box allows it to remain open and saves you from having to continually choose menu commands to display the dialog box. For example, to pin the Insert Element dialog box, press ⌘-I and click the pin icon in the upper right hand corner of the Insert Element dialog box. Simply clicking on the pin changes the icon from a side view of a pin to an end-on view, showing you that the dialog is pinned. You can also click on the pin icon and select Pin Dialog from the pop-up menu.

Command	Description	Shortcut
Markup>>Insert Element...	Displays the Insert Element dialog box, so you can insert a new, empty element in which you can type text or insert other elements.	⌘-I
Markup>>Change...	Changes the markup. Select this command to get a list of valid elements to replace the current element.	⌘-L
Markup>>Split	Splits the current element into two elements at the current insertion point or selection.	⌘-P
Markup>>Join to Preceding	Joins the current element with the element preceding it, provided both are of the same type.	⌘-J
Markup>>Remove Tags	Removes the tag icons that delimit the current element, leaving the content unaltered.	⌘-D
Markup>>Edit SGML Attributes...	Displays the Attributes dialog box for changing the attributes of a selected element.	⌘-]
Markup>>Special Characters...	Displays a dialog box that lists special characters, such as symbols and foreign characters.	⌘-E
Links>>Insert Anchor...	Inserts anchor tags and displays the Edit URL dialog box, which lets you create or edit the attributes of a selected URL.	—
Links>>Edit URL...	Displays the Edit URL dialog box, which lets you add or edit the attributes of a selected URL.	—

Table 4-2: *Common Markup and Link menu commands.*

HoTMetaL PRO is context sensitive, so only valid choices appear in the dialog box even when it is pinned. You can drag the dialog box anywhere on the screen by moving the pointer on the title bar and pressing and holding down the mouse button and dragging the window so that it doesn't cover part of the document window.

Making Selections in HoTMetaL PRO

Like most word processors and editors, HoTMetaL PRO works on the *select then operate* principal. For example, you need to first select text for which you want to perform a cut or copy operation. It may take a little time to become familiar with how HoTMetaL PRO lets you select tags and text. HoTMetaL PRO only lets you select tags and text as groups. In other words, you can't edit a selection of text and an end tag. Instead, you must select the text only, or you must select the beginning tag, the text and the closing tag.

Showing & Hiding Tags

When you first open a document, the HTML tags appear on the screen as small tag icons. The tags that point to the right are start tags, indicating the beginning of an element. The tags that point to the left are end tags, indicating the end of an element. If you choose View>>Hide Tags, the tag icons will not display. The View>>Hide command toggles to View>>Show Tags. Choosing View>>Show Tags displays the tag icons.

HoTMetaL PRO Editing Commands

HoTMetaL PRO's Edit menu includes standard editing commands, including Cut (⌘-X), Copy (⌘-C), Paste (⌘-V) and Delete (Del). At this point, the one command you're bound to find most helpful is the Edit>>Undo command. The shortcut key for the Undo command is ⌘-Z.

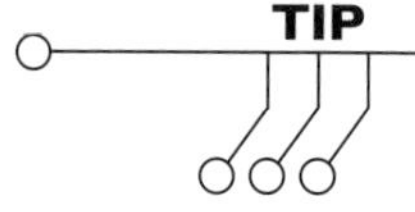

TIP

HoTMetaL PRO lets you paste raw HTML tags and text into an HTML document displayed in HoTMetaL PRO. The raw tags are replaced with HoTMetaL PRO tag icons. This lets you cut or copy tags consisting of text in a word processor, such as Microsoft Word, or a text editor, such as BBEdit, and paste the text directly in as tags in HoTMetaL PRO. Conversely, you can select and copy or cut HoTMetaL PRO tags and text and paste raw tags into your text processing application.

Using a Document Outline

HoTMetaL PRO lets you expand and collapse elements to show a rudimentary outline view of your document. The outline view is helpful for rearranging your documents or creating an outline for your document. To display a document in an outline view window, choose the View>>Show Outline command. You can display an outline view window for each open document.

Expanding & Collapsing Outline Levels

When you first choose the View>>Show Outline View command, a small window appears with a single line. A black arrow appears next to the tag. Click on the tag to expand the outline to show the next level of elements. Each line in the outline view shows a start tag, an end tag and some text between them. The amount the line is indented indicates the level of the element. When you expand an element, the next level of elements it contains is shown as indented lines. To see the next level of an indented element, click on the element's start tag. Figure 4-5 shows a document's elements expanded in outline view.

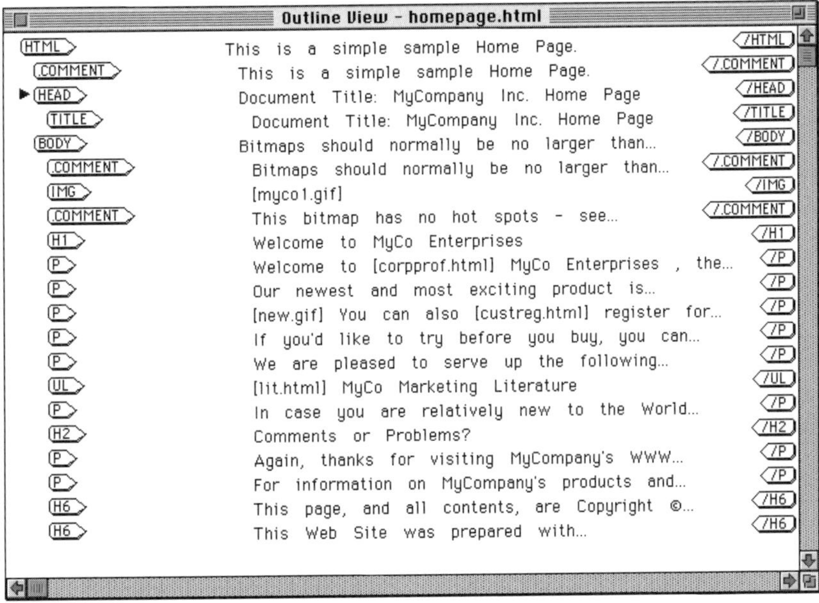

Figure 4-5: *Clicking on a tag expands the elements in outline view.*

Editing Elements in the Outline View Window

The text in outline view cannot be edited directly; however, you can use the toolbar and Edit and Markup menus. While in outline view you can insert, remove, split and join elements. To select an element in the outline view, you can either click to the left of the start tag and drag the cursor across the tag, or double-click to the left of the start tag. More than one element can be selected by clicking with the pointer to the left of a start tag and then dragging down to select additional elements. The View>>Show Outline View command is a toggle, so by choosing this command the menu command changes to View>>Hide Outline View. Choosing View>>Hide Outline View closes the Outline View window.

Setting Preferences

Some of HoTMetaL PRO's preferences can be set using the Special>>Preferences command. Figure 4-6 shows the Preferences dialog box. Any changes you make apply to all open documents and will be saved for the next editing session. The following sections explain each of the options in the Preferences dialog box. To save your preference settings, click on the Apply button.

Preferences

☒ Display images after open.

Default Template: [ ] Choose...

☐ Make backup file when saving changes.

Automatically save after

64000 changes. 1000 minutes.

☒ Inform when automatically saving.

Tag Icons

Size: 10 Font: System

Supplementary Dictionaries

Dictionaries: hmpro2.dct

Path: Macao:HTML Pub ƒ:HoTMetaL PRO

Browser for Help: [ ] Choose...

Apply Reset Cancel

Figure 4-6: *The Preferences dialog box.*

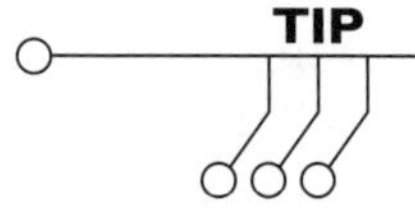

Netscape Communications has added many extensions to overcome some of the layout limitations of HTML. Unlike previous versions of HoTMetaL PRO, you no longer need to make configuration changes in order to work with Netscape and Netscape's extensions to HTML by changing the browser and the rules setting. By default, HoTMetaL PRO is set up to use the Netscape extensions.

Specifying How to Display Images

To display inline images that you have specified in your document, click in the check box labeled Display images after open, so a check mark appears in the check box. If you want to override this setting for an individual document, choose the View>>Show/Hide Inline Images command. For more information on working with graphic images, see Chapter 8 "Getting Graphic With Images."

Changing the Default Template

The Default Template text box lets you specify the HTML document file that is opened whenever you choose the File>>New command. You can use any HTML document as your default template. Clicking on the Choose button displays the Choose Template dialog box, as shown in Figure 4-7. This dialog box is similar to the dialog box that displays when choosing the File>>Open command. Using this dialog box you can choose any HTML document in any drive or folder as your default template.

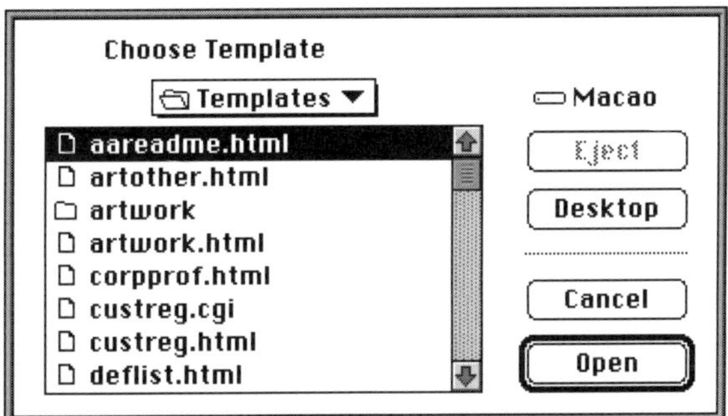

Figure 4-7: *The Choose Template dialog box lets you specify the default template.*

Automatically Backing Up Your Work

By default HoTMetaL PRO doesn't automatically save your changes in a backup file. If you want HoTMetaL PRO to automatically save your changes to a backup file when it saves changes, click in the check box labeled "Make backup file when saving changes." A check mark appears in the check box. HoTMetaL PRO names the backup file with the current filename but adds a .bak extension to the existing filename.

To have HoTMetaL PRO automatically save the current document file, you need to specify the number of minutes and/or the number of changes to trigger the automatic save operation. The default values are 64000 changes and 1000 minutes, which essentially is the same as disabling the Autosave feature. A reasonable setting is to save your files every ten minutes. We don't recommend using the number of changes as a save measure, as it can be hard to predict exactly what constitutes a "change" in your document and therefore difficult to know exactly what state the document was in when it was last saved. A timed backup is usually easier to use if you need to recover a lost document. If you want HoTMetaL PRO to warn you each time it automatically saves a file, check the "Inform when automatically saving" check box.

Changing the Size & Font of Tag Icons

You can specify the font and font size that HoTMetaL PRO uses to display the start- and end-tag icons of elements. The default font is the System font, and the default size is 10 points. Figure 4-8 shows tags displayed using a different font and font size.

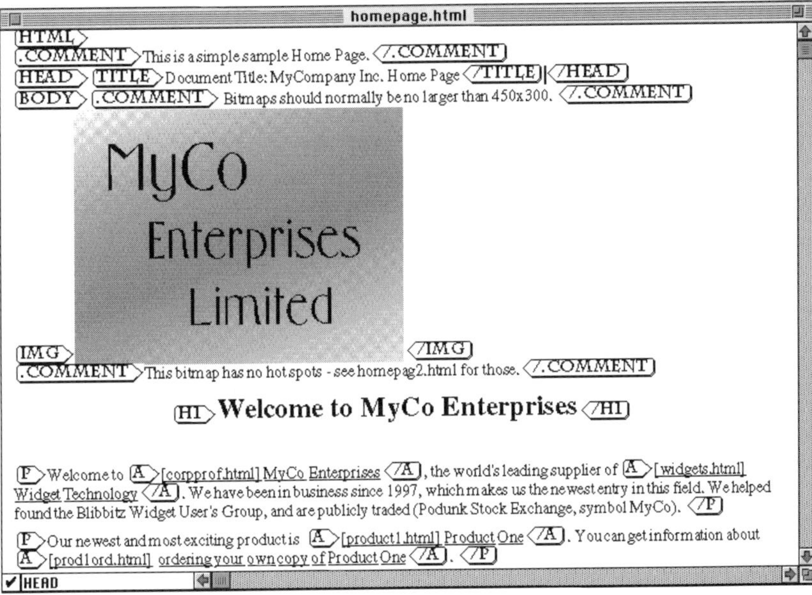

Figure 4-8: *Tags can appear in any font or size you specify.*

Adding Supplementary Dictionaries

HoTMetaL PRO lets you create and use supplementary dictionaries for checking your spelling. You can specify up to 24 special dictionaries. To add a dictionary, enter the name of the dictionary in the Dictionaries text box. Each dictionary name needs to be separated by a colon, for example:

```
legal.dct:tech.dct:medical.dct
```

Enter the path of the folder containing your dictionaries in the Path text box. HoTMetaL PRO is shipped with a default supplementary dictionary, hmpro2.dct., which is stored in the Spell folder inside the Lib folder in your HoTMetaL PRO folder.

When you launch HoTMetaL PRO, it automatically loads the dictionary file user.dct, also located in the Spell folder. You can add words to the user dictionary during a spell checking session. Changes that you make to the user.dct file will be loaded the next time you start up HoTMetaL PRO. Alternatively, you can create and load a different dictionary during a HoTMetaL PRO session.

User dictionaries are binary files and cannot be modified with a text editor. To create a new personal dictionary,

1. Choose Edit>>Edit Dictionary. The Edit Dictionary dialog box appears, as shown in Figure 4-9. The name of the currently loaded dictionary is shown at the bottom of the dialog box.

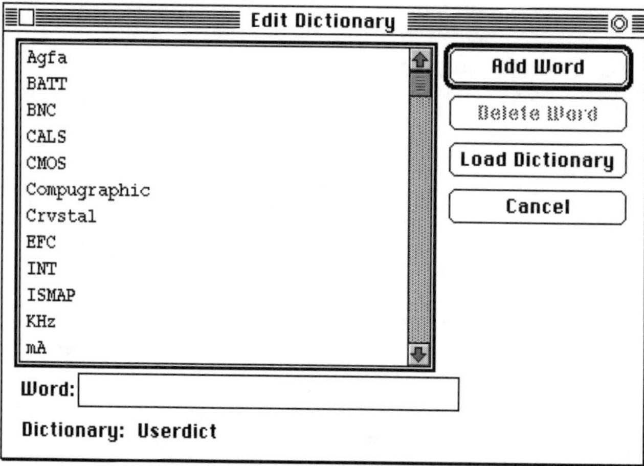

Figure 4-9: The Edit Dictionary dialog box.

2. Click on the Load Dictionary button. The Load Dictionary dialog box appears.
3. Click on the New button to display the New User Dictionary dialog box. Enter the name of the dictionary you want to create.
4. Click on the New button.
5. You are automatically returned to the Edit Dictionary dialog box, shown in Figure 4-9, with your new dictionary loaded.
6. Enter the word you want to add in the text box labeled Word and click on the Add Word button to add the word to the dictionary. To delete a word from the dictionary, click on the word in the list and click on the Delete Word button.

7. When you are through entering items, click on the Close box in the upper left corner to close the dialog box and save your changes to the dictionary.

Getting Help

The Help menu includes options for searching for help when working with HoTMetaL PRO. To display the Help menu, click on the Balloon help icon at the top right of the menu bar. The bottom element of this menu will be Help for HoTMetaL PRO 2.0. Choose this to display HoTMetaL's help information. You'll need to choose a Help browser (normally, the same browser you use for previewing your documents) the first time you select the Help function.

If you encounter a problem that is not documented in this book or the help file, check Ventana's Web page that is associated with this book at the URL http://vmedia.com/pim.html. You can get free technical support about HoTMetaL PRO installation-related questions by sending e-mail to help@vmedia.com or by calling Ventana technical support at (919) 544-9404.

If you need technical assistance for noninstallation related issues, contact SoftQuad directly by sending e-mail to hotmetal-support@sq.com or call SoftQuad technical support at (416) 239-4801. You can also fax your question using the fax number (416) 239-7105. Be aware that SoftQuad is based in Canada.

Additional Help options are available from the Apple menu: SoftQuad Home Page, HoTMetaL PRO Registration and Submit Problem Report. All of these also require a browser. The SoftQuad Home Page option is the same as using a browser to connect to the URL http://www.sq.com. To register your version of HoTMetaL PRO with SoftQuad, choose HoTMetaL PRO Registration from the Apple menu. This prompts you for a browser to display a registration form, which you should fill in and submit. You can also print the registration form and fax it to SoftQuad. If you choose Submit Problem Report, you also need to specify a browser which in turn displays a report form that you can fill in and submit over the Web or by fax.

Moving On

In this chapter you've learned a lot about installing, starting and using HoTMetaL PRO. This chapter barely scratches the surface of HoTMetaL PRO's numerous features. Many other exciting HoTMetaL PRO options, such as previewing, validating and publishing HTML documents, are covered later in this book as you need them. The next chapter explains how you can use HoTMetaL PRO to insert the most common elements to create your own HTML documents.

5

…ment

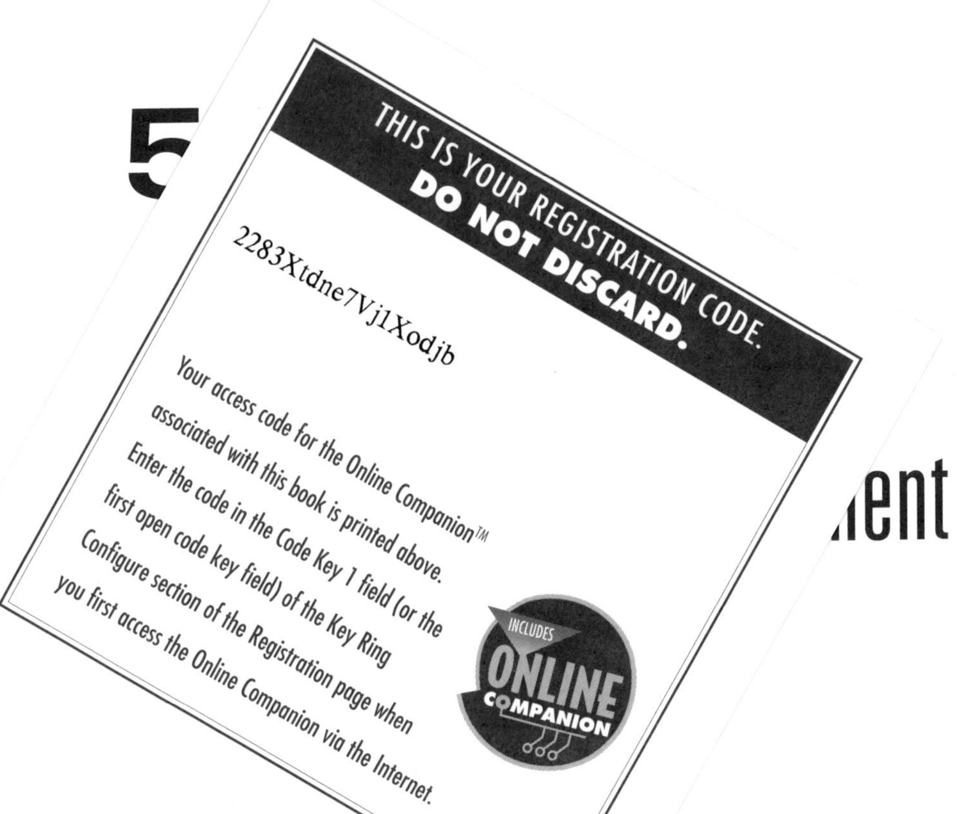

…ou can start creating a Web document. Yo… …mplate and modify it to meet your needs or dow… …ify the source code of an existing Web document … …ernet. Web browsers, such as Netscape Navigator and Mosai… let you display a window containing the HTML codes and text used to create documents on the Web or save the HTML codes and text to a file. The problem with this method is that it is amazing how many Web documents break the basic rules of HTML. Just because you're viewing a home page for a large company is no guarantee that the page is created correctly.

This chapter takes a different approach. It discusses the basic elements used to create a simple home page and presents valid elements and procedures you can follow to construct your own HTML documents. References are made throughout this chapter to other areas in this book where you can obtain more detailed information about each subject. To help you create correct Web pages we'll focus in this chapter on inserting elements and verifying your document using HoTMetaL LITE, which is included on the Companion CD-ROM.

Adding Markup to HTML Documents

As mentioned in Chapter 1, "The World Wide Web & Hypermedia Publishing," the elements that specify how to display text are collectively called *markup*. Markup is the use of codes that tell the Web browser how to display your words. The document is composed of text that takes its cues from the markup.

Using markup is a lot like using parentheses in algebra or entering a formula into a spreadsheet. Instead of parentheses, HTML markup uses codes within angle brackets. Markup typically consists of a beginning code, commonly referred to as a *tag*, that specifies the effect, and an ending tag that includes a forward slash to identify the end of the markup. For example *<TITLE>* signifies the beginning and *</TITLE>* marks the end. The beginning and ending tags are sometimes referred to as *elements*. Each element has a name that corresponds with the tags, for example, <TITLE> </TITLE> specifies the title element. When text or data appears within a beginning and ending tag, the entire element is sometimes called a *container*.

Not all elements demand a closing markup, and not all tags must contain text. Elements that don't contain text and don't require an end tag are sometimes referred to as *empty elements*. A few tags let you define *attributes* to the element specific to the element type. HoTMetaL PRO includes the Edit SGML Attributes command in the Markup menu to let you specify an attribute. For example, using an attribute you can define where text is placed next to an image or define alternative text to accommodate viewers that are unable to handle images.

If you choose to use a text editor or an HTML editor other than HoTMetaL PRO that doesn't automatically insert tags, it's helpful to know that markup tags are not case sensitive; for example <title>, <TITLE> and <Title> all can be used for the title tag.

There is one other point to note if you are using a standard text editor to insert markup tags. It sometimes isn't clear from HTML documentation whether you need to include an ending tag for specific markup elements. If you are in doubt, generally it's better to include one. Many browsers will allow you to get away without ending tags where the language says they should be, but you may easily end up with a page that won't display correctly on some systems. Of course, using HoTMetaL PRO will avoid this, since it handles inserting both tags where required.

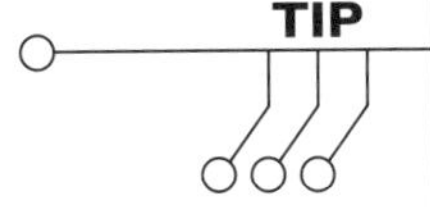

Because you don't know which browser will be used to view your documents, you should attempt to follow all the rules in the HTML language as closely as possible. Currently, some HTML editors and templates allow you to get away with ignoring some elements and still produce a readable document. Keep in mind, however, that anyone can easily download your source code. If you don't follow HTML formatting rules, others may make judgments about you and your company from the quality of your documents.

Beginning Your HTML Document

A Web document is composed of two parts: the *head* and the *body*. Each document contains some common elements: a beginning HTML tag, a title, a body, some headings and an ending tag. To begin creating a home page, start HoTMetaL PRO. Select File>>New to open a new document. A window appears named Document1. This is the default window for creating a document. You will be asked to change the name to something other than Document1 later when you save your document.

If you are using the standard document template, your page starts out with the essential HTML tags already included in the document: <HTML>, <HEAD>, <TITLE> and <BODY>. This shows how useful templates are: They save you having to enter these standard, required elements separately. In fact, you can't enter them directly from HoTMetaL PRO at all—the Insert Elements entry in the Markup menu is dimmed when you position the insertion point outside of the existing tags.

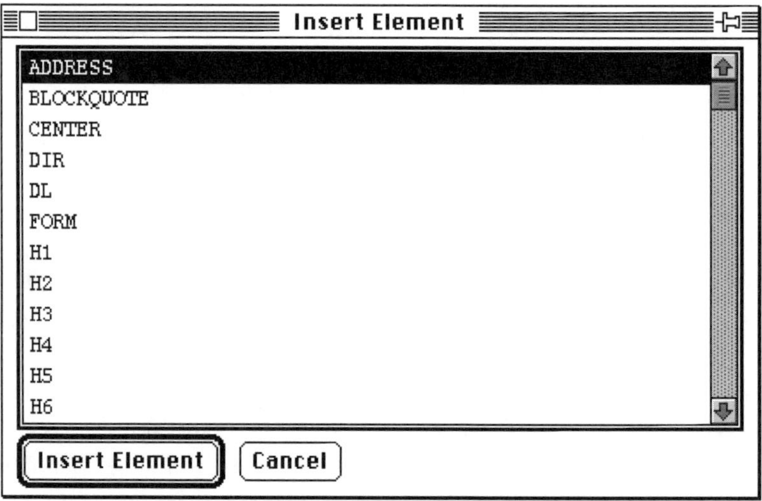

Figure 5-1: *The Insert Element dialog box.*

An HTML Comment

One element that can be included in the head or the body is the comment tag. Comments don't appear in the Web browser. HoTMetaL PRO supports the comment tags with the special Markup>>Insert Comment command, or you can use the Insert Comment button on the Other HTML tool palette. The opening tag for a comment is <!— and the closing tag is —>. Because some Web browsers balk at multiple line comments, it is best to keep comments short or use the comment element for each line you want to add.

The Head Tags

Every HTML document starts with the markup tag <HTML>. The initial <HTML> tag informs the browser what kind of document it's looking at, so it can be displayed properly. This becomes more

important as other documents, such as SGML documents for Panorama and other non-HTML browsers, start being used. The end tag </HTML> instructs the browser that the document is complete. It's included as the last tag in your document.

Immediately following the <HTML> tag is a tag called <HEAD>. The <HEAD> tag allows the HTTP server software to discover information about the document.

The next item that should be included is a document title. The title of a document, contrary to what you would expect, doesn't appear at the top of your document. Typically the title appears in the title bar of the window. The title is used for index information by Web searching programs, such as Web spiders and robots.

When you create a document using HoTMetaL PRO, the words "Document Title" appear in the HoTMetaL PRO document window. This text appears only in the editing window display, it is not part of the text of the document.

The insertion point is initially positioned between the <BODY> tags in your document. To create a title, move the insertion cursor to the point after the words 'Document Title:' between the <TITLE> tags. Type a title for your sample document. Keep the title short yet descriptive. A descriptive title is important because many browsers will use this title if the reader saves your page as a bookmark or hotlist item. When you display this document in a browser, the contents of the title element will be displayed in the window's title bar. It is possible that the title will display in some browsers on a Document Title line. The following is a sample of the head tags.

```
<HTML> <HEAD> <TITLE> A Clean Well-Lighted Place for
Books
</TITLE> </HEAD> </HTML>
```

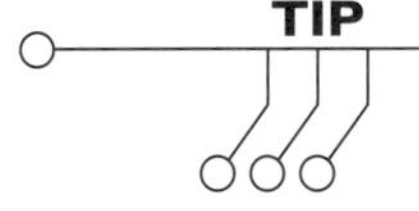

Other tags can appear in the head of a document, including the ISINDEX, BASE, LINK, NEXTID and META tags. For more information on these heading tags, see Appendix C, "An Illustrated HTML Reference."

The Body Tags

The main part of your document is the body, contained within the BODY element. Except for the ending </HTML> tag, everything from here on is a body element, including headings, paragraphs, special characters, lists, images, hyperlinks and so on. The following sections explain how to identify the beginning and the contents of the body of your Web page.

Identifying the Body of Your Document

The body of your document is the material between the BODY tags. The BODY tags are added directly before the closing </HTML> tag, as shown below:

```
<HTML> <HEAD> <TITLE> A Clean Well-Lighted Place for
Books
</TITLE> </HEAD> <BODY> </BODY> </HTML>
```

To begin the body of the document, move the insertion point back between the BODY tags. If you simply wish to insert text, you can now start typing. HoTMetaL PRO will automatically insert the required PAR tags to enclose your new text. However, if you want to insert other elements, you need to open the Insert Elements dialog box. To do this, choose Markup>>Insert Element or press ⌘-I. The Insert Element dialog box appears, as shown in Figure 5-1. (Alternatively, you can use the tool palettes to choose an element to insert.)

Once the insertion point is placed between the <BODY> tags, the Insert Element dialog box will present many element choices. Because you will frequently be inserting elements between the beginning and ending BODY tags, you may find it helpful to pin the Insert Element dialog box at this time. To pin the Insert Element dialog box, press ⌘-I, and click once on the pin icon in the upper right-hand corner.

Organizing Your Document With Headers

Like any well organized document, it's a good idea to start with a heading. There are six possible heading tags, <H1> through <H6>. Each tag works just like a heading style in a word processing document, or levels in an outline, providing structure and division in your document. The type style and size of the heading changes depending on how the individual browser that is displaying your document is configured.

To create headers, select the <H1> element from the Insert Element dialog box. The insertion point appears between the starting and ending H1 tags. The following is a sample heading.

```
<H1>Welcome to A Clean Well-Lighted Place for Books </H1>
```

Even though you can use up to six different levels of headings, it is best to stick to only four. Many browsers are not set up to display higher-level heads with font and character attributes that differ enough from each other to make them noticeable. Keep your headings structured like any outline. For example, you wouldn't put a lower-level heading before a higher-level heading in an outline. The same holds true for HTML headings.

If you're using an editor other than HoTMetaL PRO, don't try to combine the heading and title tags for the first level of a document. For example: <H1><TITLE> A Clean Well-Lighted Place for Books </TITLE></H1> is incorrect. The TITLE tag can only appear inside the HEAD at the start of the document while the heading tags are only valid within the body of the document.

Inserting Paragraphs & Line Breaks

Unlike typical word processor documents, how lines wrap in your document has no effect on how the HTML document displays in a browser. Pressing Enter may add line spaces to your HTML document, but the lines will not appear when displayed in a browser. Multiple spaces are also ignored. All spaces and multiple returns are collapsed to a single space. In order to specify a paragraph, you use the standard paragraph tag. The paragraph tag ends the current line and inserts additional spacing prior to the start of the next line.

Although the paragraph tag in version 2 of HTML doesn't require an ending counterpart, HTML version 3 does. This is partially to make HTML more compatible with SGML, but more importantly, it opens the way to include attribute information for the paragraph, such as centering or justification. HoTMetaL PRO automatically adds a starting and ending paragraph tag.

To start adding text, choose P from the Insert Elements dialog box. You can then enter the text you want between the beginning and ending paragraph tags. The following is the HTML source code for the first paragraph of A Clean Well-Lighted Place's home page:

```
<P>Welcome to the Internet home page for A Clean Well-
Lighted Place for Books—a cathode-ray extension of our
incandescently lit locations.</P>
```

The line-break tag <BR> lets you break a line without adding a space between the lines. The line-break tag is an empty element. It appears in HoTMetaL Pro with a starting and ending tag, although when displayed as raw HTML code the <BR> tag does not have an end tag. Line-break tags commonly are used with the address tags, which are explained later in this chapter.

Adding Horizontal Rules

The horizontal rule element is another way to divide your document into sections. The default rule is a shaded line that when viewed with a gray background looks like an inset 3D bar drawn across the width of the page. You may see some impressive horizontal rules in Web pages. Many people use inline graphic images in place of horizontal rules. To include a horizontal rule, use Markup>> Insert Elements and/choose HR from the Insert Elements dialog box.

```
<HR> </HR>
```

Netscape adds four proprietary extensions to the horizontal rule to let you specify the thickness, width, alignment and shading of horizontal rules. For example, you could specify a rule that is a line ¼-inch thick that appears centered and is 50 percent of the width of the document. Figure 5-2 shows the Edit Attributes dialog box for horizontal rules. Table 5-1 describes Netscape tag extensions that allow the document's author to describe how the horizontal rule should look.

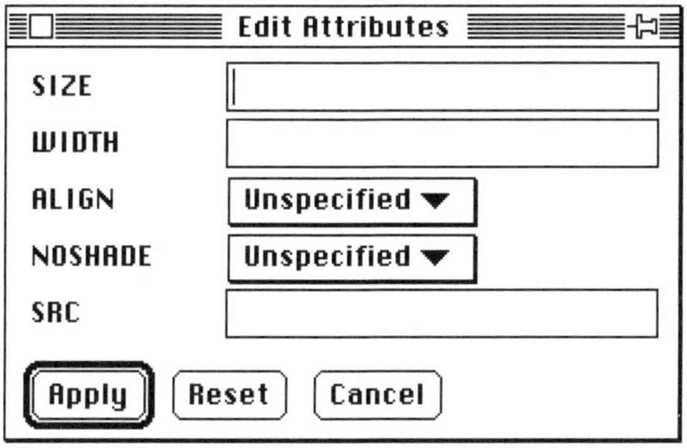

Figure 5-2: *The Edit Attributes dialog box for horizontal rules.*

Attribute	Description
<HR SIZE=*n*>	Specifies the thickness of the horizontal rule in pixels. The *n* stands for the number of pixels.
<HR WIDTH=*n*>	Specifies an exact width in pixels, or a relative width measured in percent of document width. The *n* stands for a number of pixels.
<HR ALIGN=*alignment*>	Specifies the alignment of the rule. The three choices are LEFT (left aligned), RIGHT (right aligned) or CENTER (centered).
<HR NOSHADE>	Specifies that you do not want any shading of your horizontal rule.

Table 5-1: *Attributes for horizontal rules.*

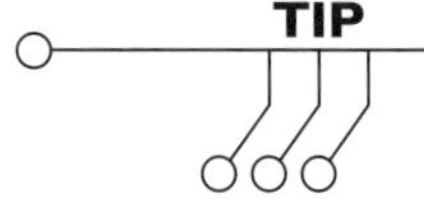

Just because something looks great in your browser doesn't mean it will look great when viewed in other browsers. Because we are creating a simple home page in this chapter, we recommend that you use the Netscape extensions. (See Chapter 3 for how to set these.) Once you have a handle on building pages, you can edit your pages to create a version that takes advantage of these extensions or not, as you choose. Many of the features that the Netscape extensions bring to HTML will be available in HTML version 3.

Including Lists

There are four types of lists you can use in an HTML document: unordered lists, ordered lists, discursive lists and directory lists. An *unordered* list is another way of saying a bulleted list. An *ordered* list is a numbered list. A *discursive* or *definition* list is also called a *glossary* list. Discursive lists let you create two columns, one for terms and one for the description of the term. A *directory* list is a list of short items (less than 24 characters). Directory lists display a list of items with no bullets and without a hanging indent. Because lists are so common to HTML documents, we'll briefly cover these lists in this chapter. Many home pages, however, typically only include the unordered (bulleted) list.

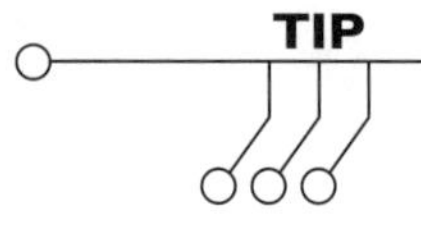

It's possible to nest lists in a Web document for an outline effect. Chapter 7, "Creating Your Text Appeal," explains creating nested lists.

Unordered (Bulleted) Lists

The unordered list tag, <UL>, is used to mark the beginning of a bulleted list. The unordered list uses the list item tag <LI> to indicate each separate list entry. This tag appears before the text used to denote the list item. The browser determines what character to use for a bullet. Some browsers, for example, may use an asterisk or a dash. You can combine the paragraph tag to help add space around list items, as shown in the following example:

```
<P>Check out what's happening at our three locations:</P>
<UL>
<LI><P>San Francisco (Opera Plaza)</P></LI>
<LI><P>Larkspur</P></LI>
<LI><P>Cupertino</P></LI>
</UL>
```

This would appear similar to Figure 5-3 in your document.

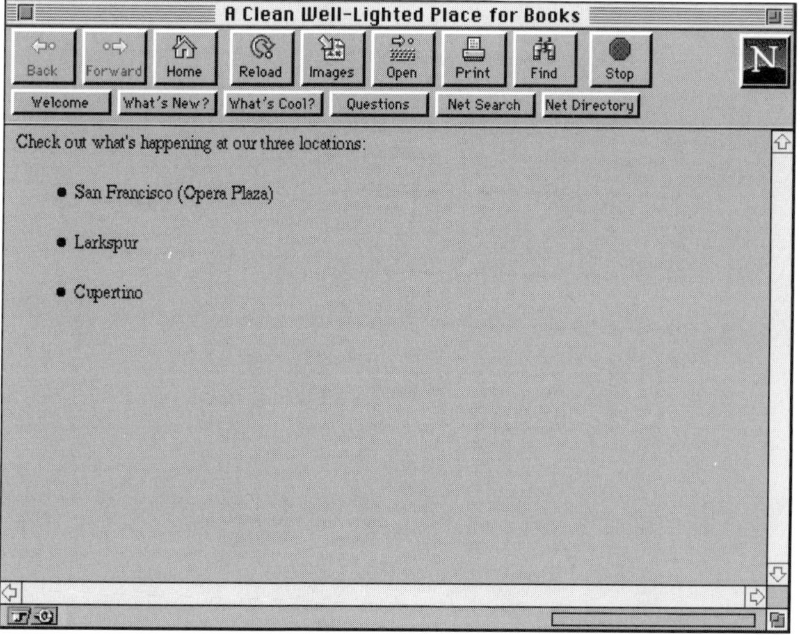

Figure 5-3: *An unordered list.*

A common mistake is to embed a heading within a list to make the list font larger. Doing this will lead to unpredictable results. It may look fine on your screen, but it will most likely cause problems when viewed with other browsers.

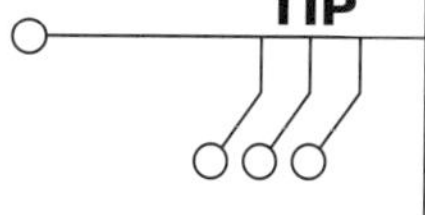

HTML version 3 adds a new TYPE attribute to the unordered list. The TYPE attribute lets you define one of three types of bullets: circle, disc or square.

Ordered (Numbered) Lists

The ordered list tag <OL> is used to mark the beginning of a numbered list. Like the unordered list, this tag must be followed by list item tags <LI> to denote the actual text used in the list. The end tag, </OL>, must be included at the end of the ordered list.

When the page is displayed the browser automatically inserts the numbers for each list item. This is convenient because it eliminates numbering errors. The following is an example of an ordered list:

```
<H2> Order Forms </H2>
<OL>
<LI><P> Ordering Books </P></LI>
<LI><P> Special Orders </P></LI>
<LI><P> Return Policies </P></LI>
</OL>
```

This code would appear onscreen like Figure 5-4.

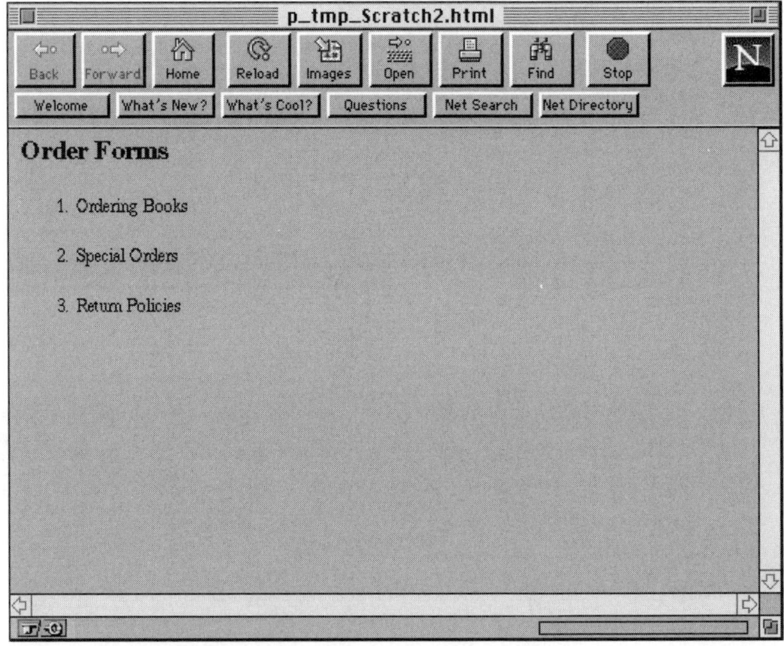

Figure 5-4: *An ordered list.*

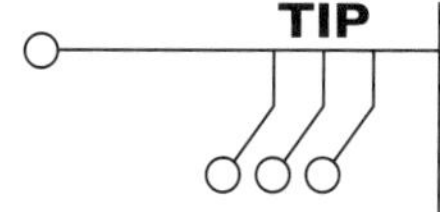

HTML version 3 adds a new TYPE attribute to ordered lists. The TYPE attribute lets you define the character used at each level of nesting. The number or the count can now be changed in the middle of a list. You also can specify uppercase roman numerals, lowercase roman numerals, uppercase letters or lowercase letters. For more information on the ordered list, see Appendix C, "An Illustrated HTML Reference."

Descriptive (Glossary) Lists

The descriptive list tag is used to construct a glossary-like entry. A descriptive list contains two elements: a descriptive title, <DT>, and its related list entry. Each description list entry is preceded by the markup descriptive definition <DD>. Descriptive lists can also include the <P> markup to include spaces between entries.

```
<DL>
<DT>The Crossing by Cormac McCarthy (Vintage Paper-
back, $13.00)
<DD><P>Young Billy Parham traps a she-wolf and decides
to return her to the mountains across the Mexican border.
</P>
<DT>Shipping News by E. Anne Proulx (Simon & Schuster
Paperback, $12.00)
<DD><P>The unblessed, hapless Quoyle retreats to his
ancestral home in Newfoundland with his two young
daughters and take-charge Aunt. Won the Pulitzer Prize for
fiction.</P>
<DT>In The Lake of the Woods by Tim O'Brien (Houghton
Mifflin Paperback, $21.95)
<DD><P>The hero's traumatic Vietnam past intrudes upon
his present political ambitions in the totally absorbing
novel.</P>
</DL>
```

Inserting Inline Graphic Images

Most Web documents contain an inline graphic or two. This chapter contains an example of a logo added as an inline graphic. For this example the logo is kept on your local drive. In its simplest terms, a local inline graphic can be included in a document using raw HTML by including its source after the <IMG markup, in the form <IMG SRC= "*path/filename.gif*">. When you use HoTMetaL PRO, choose Markup>> Insert Element and choose the IMG element from the Insert Elements dialog box. This displays the Edit URL dialog box. In the Name text box, specify the path to the image file using a forward slash between folder names and the filenames. To view the URL in HoTMetaL PRO, choose View>>Hide Inline Images and choose View>>Show URLs; the URL for the inline image appears as <IMG SRC: path/filename.gif>. If you are storing the HTML document in the same directory as the graphic file, you can omit the path. For example, the raw HTML entry for an inline image without a path may appear as

```
<IMG SRC="logo.gif">
```

Not all browsers can display graphic images. To make sure that others viewing your page are not left in the dark, choose Markup>>Edit SGML Attribute. This displays the Edit Attribute dialog box shown in Figure 5-5.

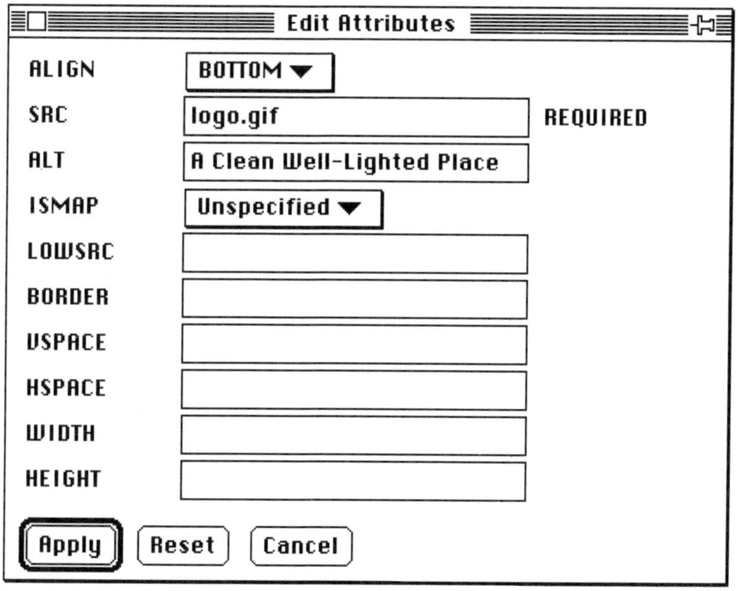

Edit Attributes
ALIGN BOTTOM
SRC logo.gif REQUIRED
ALT A Clean Well-Lighted Place
ISMAP Unspecified
LOWSRC
BORDER
VSPACE
HSPACE
WIDTH
HEIGHT
Apply Reset Cancel

Figure 5-5: *The Edit Attribute dialog box lets you specify text for text-based Web browsers and other image attributes.*

Edit the ALT attribute field to specify text to display in place of the image. This lets a person viewing the page from a text-based browser, such as Lynx on a VT100 terminal, see the words "A Clean Well-Lighted Place for Books Logo" at the location of the logo.

```
<IMG SRC="logo.gif" ALT="A Clean Well-Lighted Place for
Books Logo">
```

By default HoTMetaL PRO doesn't display the ALT attribute and text. There are two ways you can see the text that ALT attribute is set to display: choose the Markup>>Edit SGML Attribute or choose the View>>Show Link and Context View. In order to see the ALT attribute and text using the Show Link and Context, the insertion point must be in the line containing the URL for the image.

This adds the logo to the document, so it now looks like Figure 5-6. By default text is aligned with the bottom of the image. You can choose Markup>>Edit SGML Attribute to specify that the text is aligned at the top or the middle of an inline graphic using the ALIGN attribute.

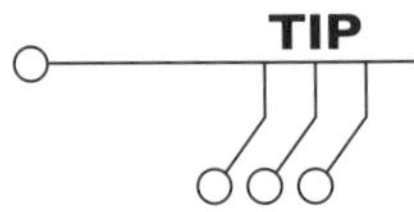

TIP

A complete discussion of inline and external graphics is the subject of Chapter 8, "Getting Graphic With Images."

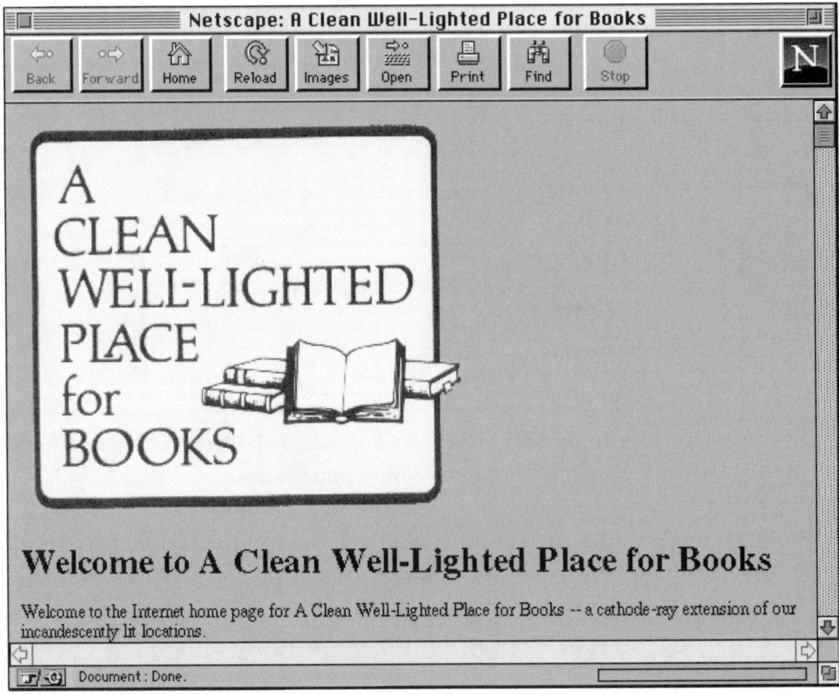

Figure 5-6: *A Clean Well-Lighted Place for Books's logo is added to the top of the Web document.*

Adding Links

A *hyperlink* is a term used to describe hypertext or an image in your document that acts as a pointer to another location or a file. The location could be another Web document on a remote system, another local Web document or another part of the current document. The following section explains how to create a link to another location within the same Web document. Creating links to remote documents is discussed in-depth in Chapter 6, "The Art of Linking." In order to create a link, you must identify the destina-

tion and create an anchor name that identifies the anchor's destination. The starting point and the destination points are referred to as *anchors* and appear between the <A> and </A> tags. Anchors can include one or more attributes, but each must have NAME and/or HREF attributes.

The HREF attribute specifies that the anchor is the start of a hypertext link and is followed by an equals sign (=) and the destination anchor or URL. The browser presents the text between the <A> and </A> tags as a hyperlink. The text after the <A> tag and immediately before the </A> shouldn't include any spaces, otherwise space characters will be highlighted. If the hyperlink text appears at the end of a sentence, it's good design to put the period directly outside the closing </A> tag. The path to the destination is established in the document by including the markup:

```
<P>Check out our special
<A HREF="#staff">staff recommendations</A>.
</P>
```

The NAME attribute specifies that the anchor is the destination of the link.

```
<P><A NAME="staff"></A>Staff Recommendations
</P>
```

In this example, #staff label is used to specify the destination of the link. The words "staff recommendations" appear in the document as the hyperlink text. If you click the "staff recommendations" hypertext, you will be sent to the Anchor with the NAME="staff" in the document.

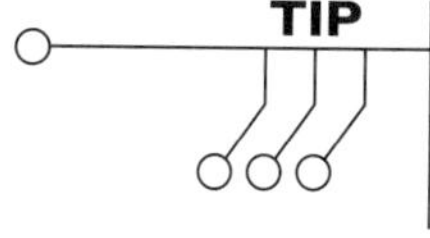

The above is a very simplistic execution of a link. To learn how to link to documents outside your system, or to get a deeper understanding of the linking process, refer to Chapter 6, "The Art of Linking."

Adding an Address

The <ADDRESS> tag is usually an e-mail address and is generally used to identify the author of a document or the Webmaster, thereby letting users contact the document's author. The output appears as italic text. In most cases you'll want to use the <BR> tag to provide line breaks for each part of the address.

```
<P>For additional information, please send e-mail to
<B>information@bookstore.com</B>, phone us at +1 415-
555-7999, or FAX your request to +1 415-555-6195. If you
have problems or comments concerning our Web service,
please send e-mail to the following address:
</P>
<ADDRESS>webmaster@bookstore.com</ADDRESS>
<P>You can also contact us via ground mail at</P>
<ADDRESS>
A Clean Well-Lighted Place for Books<BR>
601 Van Ness Ave<BR>
San Francisco, California 94402 USA<BR>
</ADDRESS>
```

A Sample Home Page

CD-ROM

The following is the raw source for a page that includes most of the tags that have been introduced in this chapter. The graphic image file used as the logo in this sample is supplied on the Companion CD-ROM. The CD-ROM also includes the code for this example. At this point, of course, the page is still quite simple, but this gives you a good idea of how all these elements work together to make an HTML page.

```
<HTML>
<HEAD>
<TITLE> A Clean Well-Lighted Place for Books </TITLE>
</HEAD>
<BODY>
<IMG SRC="images/logo.gif" ALT="A Clean Well-Lighted
Place for Books Logo">
```

```
<H1>Welcome to A Clean Well-Lighted Place for Books'
Home Page</H1>
<P> Welcome to the Internet home page for A Clean Well-
Lighted Place for Books—a cathode-ray extension of our
incandescently lit locations.</P>
<HR>
<H2>Store Locations and Events</H2>
<P>Check out what's happening at our three locations:</P>

<UL>
<LI><P>San Francisco</P>
<P>At Opera Plaza<BR>
601 Van Ness Avenue<BR>
San Francisco, CA 94102<BR>
(415) 441-6670</P></LI>
<LI><P>Larkspur</P>
<P>At Larkspur Landing<BR>
2417 Larkspur Landing Circle<BR>
Larkspur, CA 94939<BR>
(415) 461-0171</P></LI>
<LI><P>Cupertino</P>
<P>At the Oaks<BR>
21269 Stevens Creek Boulevard<BR>
Cupertino, CA 95014<BR>
(408) 255-7600</P></LI>
</UL>

<P><B>OPEN 7 DAYS, 10:00 AM to 11:00 PM</B><BR>'til
Midnight on Fridays and Saturdays</P>

<HR>

<H2>Best of the Books</H2>

<P>Our staff members (naturally!) read a lot of books. The
<A HREF="#staff">staff recommendations</A>.
is a list of what they feel are the best books they have read
in the last year. This briefly annotated list represents only a
portion of the diverse books that they championed.
```

```
<HR>
<H2> Order Forms </H2>
<OL>
<LI><P> Ordering Books </P></LI>
<LI><P> Special Orders </P></LI>
<LI><P> Return Policies </P></LI>
</OL>
<HR>
<H2><A NAME="staff"></A>Staff Recommendations</H2>
<DL>
<DT>The Crossing by Cormac McCarthy (Vintage Paper-
back, $13.00)
<DD><P>Young Billy Parham traps a she-wolf and decides
to return her to the mountains across the Mexican border.
</P>
<DT>Shipping News by E. Anne Proulx (Simon & Schuster
Paperback, $12.00)
<DD><P>The unblessed, hapless Quoyle retreats to his
ancestral home in Newfoundland with his two young
daughters and take-charge Aunt. Won the Pulitzer Prize for
fiction.</P>
<DT>In The Lake of the Woods by Tim O'Brien (Houghton
Mifflin Paperback, $21.95)
<DD><P>The hero's traumatic Vietnam past intrudes upon
his present political ambitions in this totally absorbing
novel.</P>
</DL>
<HR>
<H2>How to Contact A Clean Well-Lighted Place for Books
</H2>
<P>For additional information, please send e-mail to
<B>information@bookstore.com</B>, phone us at +1 415-
441-6670, or FAX your request to +1 415-567-6885. If you
have problems or comments concerning our Web service,
please send e-mail to the following address:
</P>
<ADDRESS>webmaster@bookstore.com</ADDRESS>
<P>You can also contact us via ground mail at</P>
```

```
<ADDRESS>
A Clean Well-Lighted Place for Books <BR>
601 Van Ness Avenue<BR>
San Francisco, California 94102 USA<BR>
</ADDRESS>
</BODY>
</HTML>
```

Validating Your Web Document

One simple but important final step you should take is to validate your document before publishing it. To validate your document with HoTMetaL PRO, choose the Special>>Validate Document command or use the shortcut key, ⌘-/. In addition to checking your entire document, HoTMetaL PRO lets you check an individual section of your document. If text in your Web document is selected, only the selection is checked, otherwise the entire document is checked. HoTMetaL PRO checks for all required beginning and ending elements and checks to make sure the attributes are in the correct form. If HoTMetaL PRO finds an error, a message box appears notifying you of the error and the insertion point moves to its location, as best as HoTMetaL PRO can determine, so you can fix the error.

Publishing Your Web Document

When you get ready to publish your work on the Internet, you'll need to replace all the local references with URLs that point to your system as the network sees it. For example, during development, a local reference might be:

```
file://documents/page1.html
```

but the network reference might be:

```
http://www.mycompany.com/info/documents/page1.html
```

HoTMetaL eases this transition by prompting you for the URL changes. To replace the local references, choose the File>>Publish command. HoTMetaL PRO displays the Publish dialog box, which lets you choose whether to find and replace the URLs on a one-by-one basis or replace all the local file references to network HTTP references.

Moving On

Now you have an idea of how easy it is to write a simple HTML document. You've only scratched the surface, however. Until you delve into the power of links, you really can't take advantage of the global publishing capabilities of the World Wide Web. The next chapter builds on the HTML tags you learned in this chapter to show you how to exploit the power of links to publish complex Web documents and connect to files and other Web documents around the world.

SECTION II

Working With the Pieces

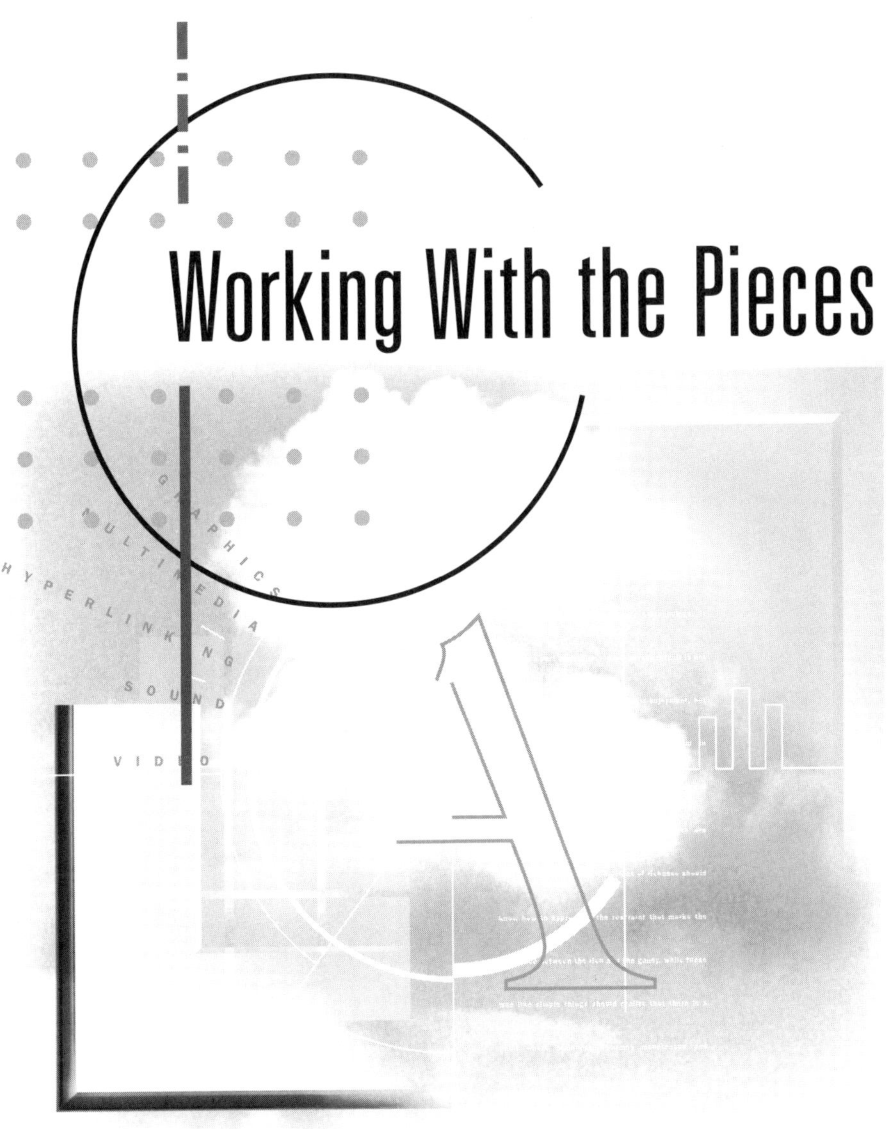

6 The Art of Linking

The last chapter took you through HTML basic training, showing you how to create a Web page and include a link to another part of the same page. A Web page with links only to the same page, however, is a little boring. This chapter lets you create more exciting interactive HTML pages by explaining how to create links that connect to additional pages on your own system and how to create links to connect to Web pages at other sites anywhere in the world.

An Introduction to Links

There are three types of links you can create: intra-page links, intra-system links and inter-system links. Intra-page links link to another place in the current page; intra-system links link to other pages on the current server; and inter-system links link to a page on another server.

The Anchor tag lets you create a link. Well-designed HTML pages have multiple links to produce easy-to-use, easy-to-read Web documents. The text examples in this chapter show the raw HTML source code, rather than the HTML tag icons, which HoTMetaL PRO displays. A typical Anchor tag for an inter-system link in a raw HTML document looks similar to the following:

```
<A HREF="http://www.vmedia.com/">Ventana Online</A>
```

The opening <A> tag specifies the place you are linking to, that is, the destination URL or the name of a file. In this case, the destination is the URL http://www.vmedia.com/. Between the opening and closing tags is the text that will be highlighted on the page as the "hyperlink text," in this case, Ventana Online. The closing tag </A> indicates the end of the link text and hypertext reference.

How to Create a Link

There are two ways to create a link with HoTMetaL PRO. The most intuitive method is to first type the text you want, without inserting the hyperlinks. This keeps you focused on the information you want to convey and helps you avoid the undistinguished, worn-out "click here" phrase that infests so many otherwise well-written pages. When you have completed your text, go back and select the text that will become the linked text, then use the Links>>Insert Anchor command to add an Anchor tag. As a shortcut, use the anchor button in the Common HTML tool palette. This displays the Edit URL dialog box for adding a link, as shown in Figure 6-1. Enter the file name or URL for the jump destination in the HREF field and choose the OK button.

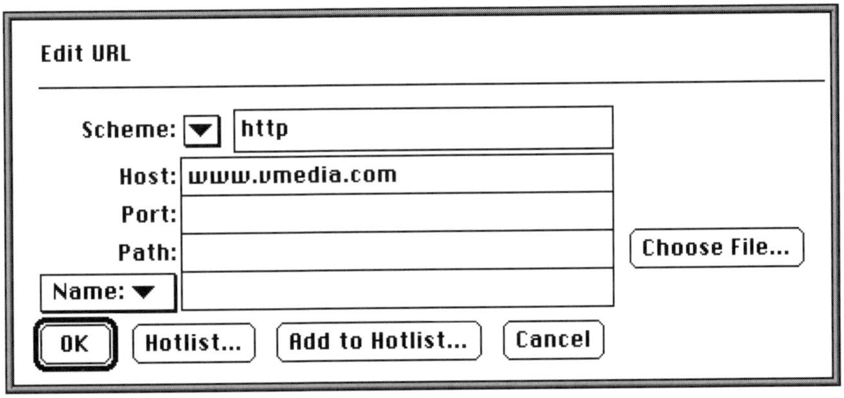

Figure 6-1: *The Edit URL dialog box lets you add a hypertext link.*

Alternatively, when you have not already entered the linked text that you want to use, you can choose the Markup>>Insert Element command. This displays the Insert Element dialog box. Select Anchor, which automatically displays the Edit URL dialog box shown in Figure 6-1. Enter the URL information in the same way you did before.

If you have already entered an anchor, you can change the anchor reference by using the Markup>>Edit SGML Attributes command. This displays the Edit Attributes dialog box shown in Figure 6-2. Enter the revised filename or jump destination in the HREF field and choose the Apply button.

Edit Attributes

METHODS

REL

REV

URN

TITLE

HREF http://www.vmedia.com/

NAME

Apply Reset Cancel

Figure 6-2: *The Edit Attributes dialog box is another way to add a hypertext link.*

When you have entered the link information, enter the text to display in your document to identify the link. This goes after the link data but before the ending Anchor tag. All the text within the tag will be displayed as linked text.

By default HoTMetaL PRO displays the hypertext reference next to the HREF anchor. If HoTMetaL PRO doesn't show the content of a link, choose View>>Show URLs.

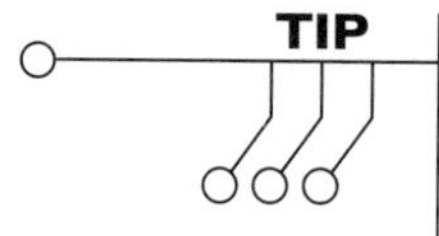

TIP

If you're not using HoTMetaL PRO, you can enter the text with an HTML editor or a text editor, such as SimpleText. Remember that the Macintosh system allows you to name files with longer file names and extensions, provided the file name and any extensions don't exceed 31 characters.

Creating a Link to a Local Page or File

When you're authoring for the Web, keep individual pages as short as is practical. This means you'll wind up with a lot of inter-page links to individual pages. The following is a hands-on example that steps you through the process of creating two pages that point to each other with links using HoTMetaL PRO. Figure 6-3 shows the results of these two pages.

1. Start HoTMetaL PRO.
2. Display at least the Common HTML tool palette and choose File>>New to begin a new document. By default, the standard document template supplies the required HTML tags (HTML, HEAD, TITLE and BODY) for a basic document.
3. Place the insertion point after the phrase "Document Title:" between the TITLE and /TITLE tags. The phrase Document Title: is not a part of the document's title and will not display in a Web browser.
4. At the insertion point, type the title of the document **Link Sample Page 1**.
5. Move the insertion point between the BODY and /BODY tags in the document.
6. Add a heading by pressing the H1 button on the Common HTML tool palette. This adds an H1 element between the BODY tags. The insertion point appears between the H1 and /H1 tags.
7. Type the heading **Link Sample Page 1** at the insertion point.
8. Move the insertion point between the /H1 and /BODY tag. Switch back to the dialog box, select the P (paragraph) element, and choose the Insert Element button. The insertion point appears between the P and /P tags.
9. At the insertion point, type **This is a reference to page two**.
10. Select the text "page two," and then choose Links>>Insert Anchor menu item or press the Anchor button.
11. This displays the Edit URL dialog box. In the PATH field, type **page2.html** as the link destination and choose the OK button.
12. Choose File>>Save or press ⌘-S and save the file as "page1.html."
13. To create the second page, choose File>>Save As and enter **page2.html** as the file name.

14. Change the "Page1" references to "Page2" and change the anchor references from "page one" to "page two."
15. Choose Markup>>Edit SGML Attributes or press ⌘-]. This displays the Edit Attributes dialog box. Replace the **page2.html** with **page1.html** for the link destination in the HREF field and choose the Apply button.
16. Choose File>>Save or press ⌘-S to save your changes.
17. Close the Insert Element dialog box.
18. To test your sample link pages, choose File>>Preview. Alternatively you can open either page with the File>>Open File or the File>>Open Local File command on your Web browser.

The Link Sample Page 1 includes a link (page2.html) that points to Link Sample Page 2. The Link Sample Page 2 includes a link (page1.html) that points back to Link Sample Page 1. The source for the first page appears similar to the following:

```
<HTML><HEAD><TITLE>Link Sample Page 1. </TITLE>
</HEAD>
<BODY><H1>Link Sample Page 1</H1>
<P>This is a reference to
<A HREF="page2.html">page two</A>.
</P>
</BODY></HTML>
```

Page two appears similar to the following:

```
<HTML><HEAD><TITLE>Link Sample Page 2.</TITLE>
</HEAD>
<BODY><H1>Link Sample Page 2</H1>
<P>This is a reference to
<A HREF="page1.html">page one</A>.
</P>
</BODY></HTML>
```

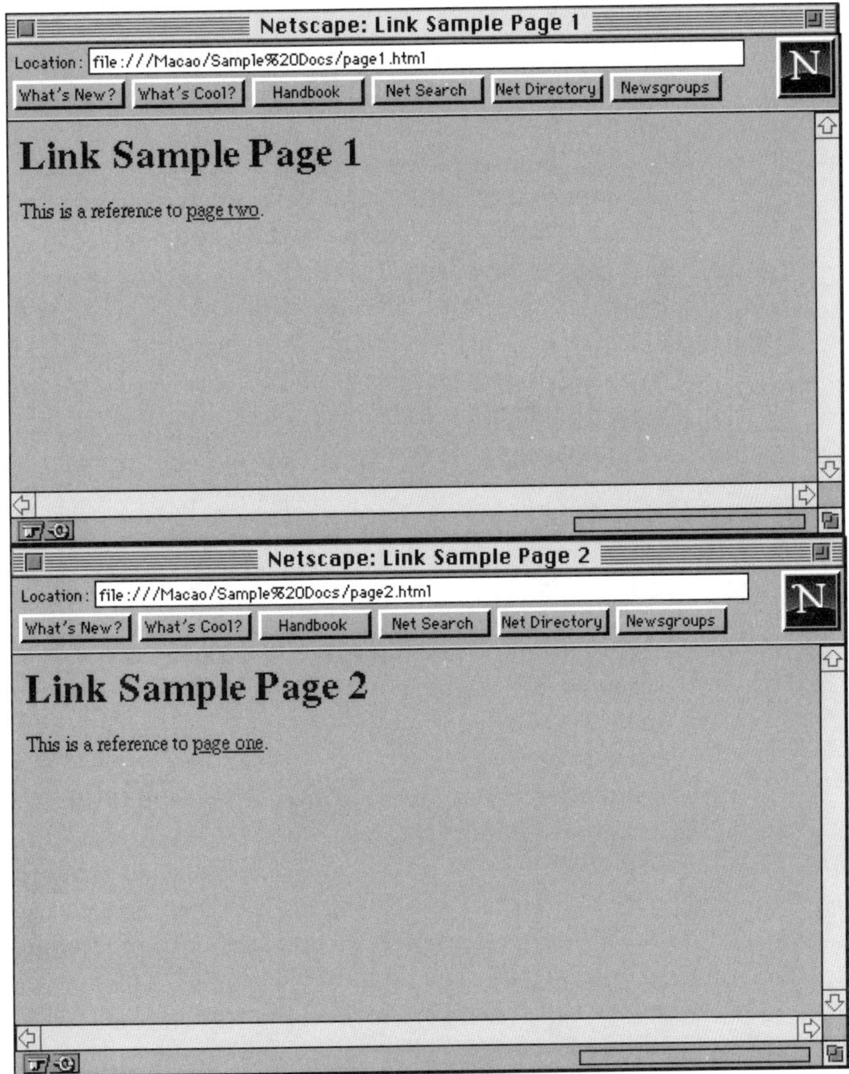

Figure 6-3: *How "page1.html" and "page2.html" appear in the Netscape Navigator browser.*

Relative Paths

In the previous example, the HREF attribute specifies only a file name. Notice there isn't a full URL prefix. This is allowed because your browser uses the HREF as a *relative* path. That is, if you opened the first file with the File>>Open command, the browser assumes that all HREFs that do not have a prefix specified, such as HTTP: or FILE:, are located in the same relative directory as the first file you opened. This is a handy feature, since you can move both files to another directory, and the links will still work. If you look at the "jump destination" in the status line of your browser (typically found at the bottom of the screen), you'll see the complete path to the file; for example,

```
file:///MyMac/HTMLDocuments/page2.html
```

The Importance of Local Links

It's important to use links that assist users when navigating through your pages in both directions. A common problem with many HTML pages on the Web today is the lack of good backward links.

Imagine for a moment you've navigated through the Web to a particularly interesting page. You add it to your bookmark list for future reference. Now, several days later, you call up the bookmark to look at that page again. At this point, you may wish to look at other pages on the same site, but unfortunately there are no links on the page you are viewing. At this point, you are effectively "lost in hyperspace," with little or no idea how to move around to other pages on the same server.

As a rule, you should *always* include a link from every HTML page back to your home page. From your home page you can create links to other pages or to other interesting places on the Web.

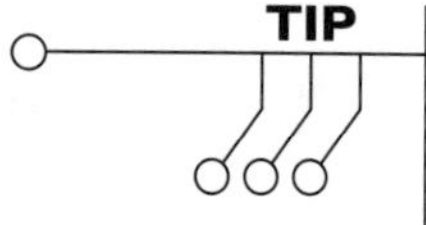

In addition to the text-based links discussed in this chapter, there are links that you can add to graphical images. For example, a common practice is to use a logo as a link to your home page. Making an inline graphic image a link is covered in detail in Chapter 8, "Getting Graphic With Images."

Creating a Link Within a Page

In most cases, it's a good idea to keep your Web pages short. This ensures that the text will fit in a screen or two on the reader's computer. There are cases, however, where this isn't practical or desired. For example, you may have a long price list or a FAQ (Frequently Asked Questions) you may want to keep together so people can easily print it out. When you have long pages, it's convenient to provide links between sections of the same page. This is done with *intra-page links*.

Now HoTMetaL PRO makes creating intra-page links very simple. The easiest way to create these links is to enter all the text for your page before creating any links within the page. For clarity, the *source* anchor is the text that points to the jump-to point, or *destination* anchor, on the same page.

There are a couple of unique steps for creating intra-page links, specifically, establishing names or labels for the jump-to destinations in the page. Labels in pages are also created with the Anchor tag, using the NAME attribute of the Anchor tag to create the label. The following example steps you through the process of creating a link within a page.

1. Enter all the text you want to use for your page.
2. Move to the destination you want to let users jump to in your document. Select the text that you wish to be the anchor for the destination and choose Links>>Name Target or press the Anchor button on the Common HTML tool palette. This displays the Insert Named Location dialog box shown in Figure 6-4.
3. The dialog box automatically displays the first word of the selected text as the default name of the anchor. Click OK to accept the default, or type in a new name and click OK. You can enter any name that you want for the link. For example, Figure 6-4 shows the destination label "questions" added as the Name field.
4. Move to the text in your document that you want to make the source link. This is the text that points to the destination you just selected.

5. Select the word or phrase you want to use to point to your destination and choose Links>>Connect Link or press the Connect Link button on the Common HTML tool palette. This automatically creates a new anchor link that points to the previous destination. Note that this item is only available immediately after you have created a destination anchor.
6. Choose File>>Save or press ⌘-S to save your changes.
7. Choose the File>>Preview command or press ⌘-M to test the intra-page links.

Although this is the simplest way to create intra-page links, you may not always want or be able to make the links immediately. You can always use this technique to create a destination link. Sometimes, however, you may need to make a source link before you make the destination, or when the destination is already created. In that case, you can make any selected text into a source anchor by replacing the single step 5 in the previous example with these steps.

1. Select the word or phrase that you want to use to point to your destination and choose Links>>Insert Anchor. This will display the Edit URL dialog box shown in Figure 6-5.
2. Type the text to match the label for the destination in the Name field and choose the OK button. For example, Figure 6-5 shows "questions" added to the name field to match the destination label named "questions" in the same document. HoTMetaL PRO automatically adds the required '#' character in front of the label to indicate that this is a link to another part of the same page.

In the previous chapter, we explained how to create a link to a specific part of the page using HoTMetaL PRO. This chapter shows a different example that includes the label within a heading. In order for this to be a practical example, we included enough text so the link points to a section that isn't on the screen at the same time. Remember all the examples are included on the Companion CD-ROM, so you don't have to type in all the text.

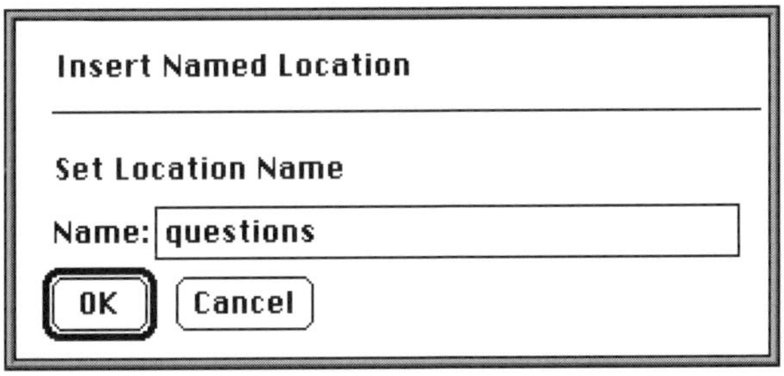

Figure 6-4: *The Insert Named Location dialog box.*

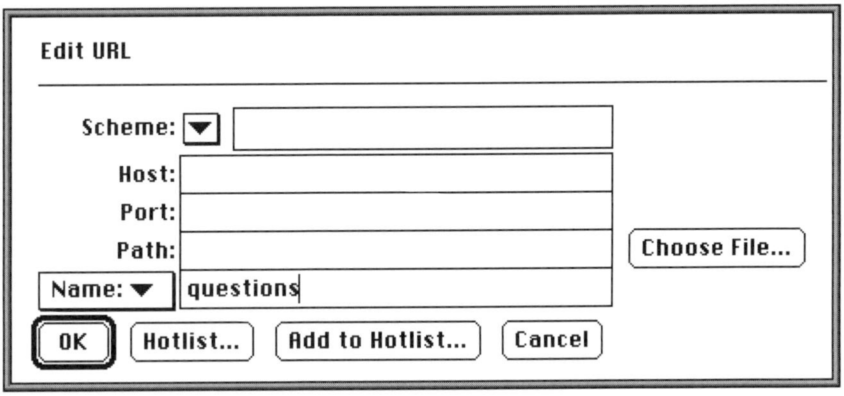

Figure 6-5: *The Name field lets you label the jump-to destination.*

```
<HTML><HEAD><TITLE> Frequent Buyer Club</TITLE>
</HEAD>
<BODY><H1>ACWLP's Frequent Buyer Club </H1>
<P>This page includes details about A Clean Well-Lighted
Place for Books' Frequent Buyer Club and answers to fre-
quently asked questions about our Frequent Buyer Club.
</P>
<P>If you have some specific questions, you can move
directly to our <A HREF="#questions">question and an-
swer</A> section. If you already know that you'd like to
join, simply fill out our Club <A> HREF="#join.html"
>enrollment form</A></P>
<HR>
```

```
<H1>Frequent Buyer Club</H1>
<P>Buy 20 books or other items and get a free award
coupon. </P>
<P></P>
<H2>Frequent Buyer Club Rules and Limitations</H2>
<OL>
<LI>No membership fee to join.</LI>
<LI>Sign up by filling out the <A> HREF="#join.html">
enrollment form</A>. </LI>
<LI>When we ring up your purchase at the cash register,
please tell us your enrollment number and we'll credit your
account. </LI>
<LI>Our computer will track and record each purchase and
issue your frequent buyer award coupon automatically.
</LI>
<LI>The amount of your award coupon will be equal to the
average cost of the last twenty books or other items you
have purchased.</LI>
<LI>You may use your award coupon at any of our three
locations for any purchase after the last qualifying pur-
chase.</LI>
<LI>Every purchase of books, cards, gifts, or CD-ROMs
counts toward your award coupon. Purchases of news-
papers, magazines, postage fees, event tickets, and Golden
Gate Bridge tickets are not counted.</LI>
<LI>Purchases made under other discount programs, such
as the Teacher's classroom discount or the City Arts
Patron's discount, do not count toward the award coupon.
However, books that are sold at a discounted price, such as
our NY Times Bestsellers, do count.</LI></UL>
<HR>
<H2>How can I join the Frequent Buyer Club?</H2>
<P>Simply go to the information desk at any one of our
three locations to join the Frequent Buyer Club for that
store. Or, you may join for any one of our store locations,
as well as for on-line purchases, by filling out an on-line
<A>HREF="#join.html">enrollment form</A>. </P>
<P>Follow these steps to enroll:</P>
<UL>
<LI>Pick up an enrollment form.</LI>
```

```
<LI>Fill out the required information.</LI>
<LI>Select an account code number from four to seven
digits or letters. (We suggest using all, some portion, or a
variation of a familiar telephone number.)</LI>
</UL>
<P>That's all there is to it! Tell the cashier your account
number when you make your purchase and our computer
system does the rest. It keeps track of all your eligible
purchases and issues your award certificate automatically!
<P>Thanks for joining A Clean Well-Lighted Place for Books'
Frequent Buyer Club</P>
<P></P>
<HR>
<H2><A NAME="questions"></A>Frequently Asked Ques-
tions</H2>
<H4>Q: How much does it cost to join ACWLP Frequent
Buyer Club?</H4>
<P>A: Nothing.</P>
<H4>Q: How do I keep track of my purchases?</H4>
<P>A: You don't have to because our computer does it for
you. When you enroll, you select an account number (4 to 7
digits) which we will enter into our computer/register sys-
tem. When you purchase something, tell us your account
number. Through this number we will track your purchases
and issue an award coupon automatically after the twentieth
item.</P>
<H4>Q: What purchases are credited toward my ACWLP
Frequent Buyer account?</H4>
<P>A: Almost everything at A Clean Well-Lighted Place for
Books will be credited to your account total except news-
papers, magazines, postage fees, event tickets, and Golden
Gate Bridge tickets. This means books, greeting cards, gifts,
audio cassettes, CD-ROMs, t-shirts, calendars, stationery,
and lots more are included when you purchase from us.
</P>
<H4>Q: What about gift certificates?</H4>
<P>A: Since gift certificates are gifts for the person receiv-
ing them, the recipients rather than the donors will have
purchases credited toward their accounts when they use
them.</P>
```

```
<H4>Q: What if I shop at more than one location?</H4>
<P>A: You can redeem your award coupon at any of our
three locations, but since our computer systems are not
interconnected you must register at each store separately. If
you register on-line, you may choose any one location for
your enrollment. In that case, all on-line purchases, as well
as any in-store purchases at the selected location, will be
credited toward your award. You may have accounts at each
store accumulating credit toward award coupons. If you
wish, you may use the same number for each account.</P>
<H4>Q: What about privacy? Who else will see information
about me and my purchases?</H4>
<P>A: Privacy is a great concern to us, too. That's why A
Clean Well-Lighted Place for Books has never and will never
sell, rent, or loan our mailing list. Our Frequent Buyer Club
is operated solely by A Clean Well-Lighted Place for Books,
and information about your purchases will not be shared
with <EM>anyone</EM>.</P>
<H4>Q: Does my membership ever expire?</H4>
<P>A: No program is forever, but currently we only plan to
allow membership to expire if the member makes no pur-
chases for 12 months.</P>
<PRE>
</PRE>
</BODY>
</HTML>
```

In the above example, you can see the destination for the jump specified as a label in the same page, "questions". The pound sign prefix in the parameter: HREF="# questions" tells your viewer that the jump is internal to this page, to a place with the label "questions". At the Frequently Asked Questions section of the page, you see another Anchor tag, this time using the NAME= questions attribute instead of the HREF= attribute. The NAME specifies the label to be used as a jump destination. If you create a file with this content, open the file in a browser and click the "questions and answers" hyperlink, the page jumps to the Frequently Asked Questions section.

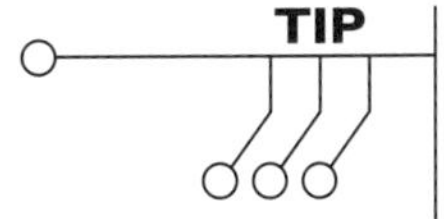

Anchor tags can be used for creating hypertext jumps and creating labels at the same time, if you use both HREF and NAME parameters. Also, you can combine inter-page jumps with jumps to specific labels so that you can jump from a particular point in one page to a particular point in another page. See the end of this chapter for a more complex example.

Creating a Link to a Page at Another Site

This is the most powerful type of Web link. It allows you to create a link from your page to any page anywhere on the Web. You need to be careful, however, to check the correctness of the link on a regular basis. Because you generally don't control the location of the destination page you are linking to, it's possible that the link may change. It is also possible that the network or host system you're linking to will be down at various times, making your link inoperative. Remember that since this is an actual inter-system link, you'll need to be connected to the Internet for it to work.

To create an inter-system link, you need to specify a full URL as the jump destination.

1. Enter and select the text you want to make a hyperlink to identify the place you want to let users jump to.
2. Choose the Markup>>Surround command or press ⌘-U. The Surround dialog box appears. Choose the Surround button to surround the selected text with Anchor tags.
3. Choose the Markup>>Edit URL. This displays the Edit URL dialog box.
4. Click the arrow located to the right of the Protocol field. Choose the http option to indicate a Web server. If you want to connect to a host using a different protocol, such as an FTP or Gopher site, choose the appropriate protocol from the list.

5. Enter the host address in the Host field. Because you specified the http protocol in the previous step, you don't need to enter the http:// prefix. For example to specify the URL for Ventana Online, enter **www.vmedia.com**. Choose the Apply button. If the link doesn't appear, you can choose the View>>Show Link and Context View to display the link.

Links in a Sample HTML Document

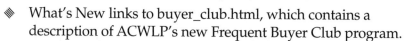

To help you better understand links, take a look at the following example. The following HTML sample document follows the structure set up in Chapter 3 and builds on the sample HTML page presented in the previous chapter. It includes local intra-page links and intra-system links, as well as an inter-system link to a page on another server.

Don't worry, the linked documents don't have to be created at this point. In fact, you don't even have to create the linked documents. Simply use the sample destination documents that we've included on the Companion CD-ROM. Later you can replace the text and images in these sample files with your own. Here are some of the links and pages that you will ultimately create for this document:

- What's New links to buyer_club.html, which contains a description of ACWLP's new Frequent Buyer Club program.
- Store Locations and Events shows each of the three store locations, with address and telephone number, and links to an individual page for each location, which contains a month's calendar of events for each store location, along with a description of any new services and store promotions.
- Mystery Quote! is ACWLP's monthly contest to identify a "mystery" quotation and links to quote.html.
- Best of the Books links to best.html, which itself is broken down into several different sections relating to book recommendations, including the staff recommendations that you saw earlier.

- Guides for the Virtual Reader links to vreader.html, a page containing links to a variety of resources for the readers from the Bay area, including lists of events at other bookstores, information on locating antiquarian and out-of-print books, links to electronic magazines and other materials of general interest to readers.
- How to Order links to an order form orders.html, which provides a form for ordering any books from ACWLP along with a description of how to place special orders and a discussion of return polices.
- Feedback links to feedback.html, which lists links to a mailing list and offers a customer satisfaction form for requests and comments to A Clean Well-Lighted Place for Books.
- Behind the Scenes links to behind.html, which displays a look at A Clean Well-Lighted Place for Books, Inc., its philosophy and key employees.

Because the content of a link is not obvious when viewing a HoTMetaL PRO document, the examples below show the source of the final HTML text, rather than HoTMetaL PRO. If you want to view the content of the links, open the sample document using HoTMetaL PRO and choose View>>Show URLs. View>>Show URLs should show all the URLs inline in HOTMetaL PRO.

```
<HTML>
<HEAD>
<TITLE> A Clean Well-Lighted Place for Books </TITLE>
</HEAD>
<BODY>
<IMG SRC="images/acwlp3.gif" ALT="A Clean Well-Lighted
Place for Books Logo">
<H1>Welcome to A Clean Well-Lighted Place for Books'
Home Page</H1>
<P> Welcome to the Internet home page for A Clean Well-
Lighted Place for Books—a cathode-ray extension of our
incandescently lit locations.</P>
```

```
<HR>
<H2>Store Locations and Events</H2>
<P>Check out what's happening at our three locations:</P>
<UL>
<LI><P><A HREF="opera.html"> San Francisco </A> </P>
<P>At Opera Plaza<BR>
601 Van Ness Avenue<BR>
San Francisco, CA 94102<BR>
(415) 441-6670</P></LI>
<LI><P><A HREF="larkspur.html"> Larkspur </A> </P>
<P>At Larkspur Landing<BR>
2417 Larkspur Landing Circle<BR>
Larkspur, CA 94939<BR>
(415) 461-0171</P></LI>
<LI><P><A HREF="oaks.html"> Cupertino </A> </P>
<P>At the Oaks<BR>
21269 Stevens Creek Boulevard<BR>
Cupertino, CA 95014<BR>
(408) 255-7600</P></LI>
</UL>
<P><B>OPEN 7 DAYS, 10:00 AM to 11:00PM</B><BR>'til
Midnight on Fridays and Saturdays</P>
<HR>
<H2>Best of the Books</H2>
<P><IMG SRC="images/bestbook.gif" ALT="Best Books
Logo"> Here are some interesting and, we hope, unex-
pected recommendations for books that you may not have
heard about or read yet.</P>
<P>Our staff members (naturally!) read a lot of books. Our
<A HREF="news.html">newsletter</A> for May presents a
list of what they feel are the best books they have read in
the last year. This briefly annotated list represents only a
portion of the diverse books that they championed.</P>
<P>Also check out our new <A HREF="fbclub.html">
Frequent Buyer Club</A> for a special award program that
will keep you coming back for more! And we have answers
to any <A HREF=fbclub.html#questions>questions</A>
about the Frequent Buyer Club as well.</P>
```

```
<P>There is a whole world of books out there, and many of
the best are written by authors in other countries. Check out
our special list of authors <A HREF="forauth.html"> from
other countries </A>. This list presents many authors, both
well-known and less so, arranged by region and country.
</P>
<HR>
<P> When you find a book that you like, you can place an
order by filling in the <A HREF="orders.html"> order form
available on-line. You can also look here for a description of
how to place special orders and for an explanation of our
return policies. </H2>
<HR>
<H2>The Virtual Reader</H2>
<P><IMG SRC="images/vreader.gif" ALT="Virtual Reader">
Of course, if none of this is of interest to you, there are
many other <A HREF="otherres.html">reader's resources
</A> on the net. Check out Eric De Mund's <A HREF=ftp://
www.culturewave.com/pub/culturewave/ba-bookstore-
events/>calendars</A> for events at bookstores in the Bay.
Or check out local newspapers and electronic magazines
(familiarly referred to as 'zines, or e-zines), or even <A
HREF=http://w3.com:80/bayfood>pick a place for dinner</A>
tonight.</P>

<HR>

<H2>Feedback </H2>

<P>Before you leave, drop us a line or two or get on our <A
HREF=maillst.html>mailing list</A>. We'd love to hear from
you!</P>
<HR>
<H2>How to Contact A Clean Well-Lighted Place for Books
</H2>
<P>For additional information, please send e-mail to
<B>info@bookstore.com</B>, phone us at +1 415-441-6670,
or FAX your request to +1 415-567-6885. If you have prob-
lems or comments concerning our Web service, please
send e-mail to the following address:
</P>
```

```
<ADDRESS>webmaster@bookstore.com</ADDRESS>
<P>You can also contact us via ground mail at</P>
<ADDRESS>
A Clean Well-Lighted Place for Books<BR>
601 Van Ness Avenue<BR>
San Francisco, California 94102 USA<BR>
</ADDRESS>
<P>This page, and all contents, are Copyright (C) 1995 by
Canyon Software Inc., San Rafael, California, USA.
</P>
<HR>
<B>[
<A HREF="news.html">Newsletter</A>
|
<A HREF="fbclub.html">Frequent Buyer Club</A>
|
<A HREF="orders.html">Order</A>
|
<A HREF="vreader.html">Virtual Reader</A>
|
<A HREF="maillst.html">Mailing List</A>
</B>
</BODY>
</HTML>
```

All the anchors that include a hypertext reference following the form HREF=document.html point to other HTML pages; for example, HREF=fbclub.html and HREF=news.html reference HTML documents.

The sixth anchor's hypertext reference combines a document name and a label within the document. In the paragraph on the Frequent Buyer Club, the second anchor's hypertext reference points to the document named fbclub.html and the label questions within that document. Choosing this link lets the reader jump directly to the location labeled questions in the fbclub.html document.

The tenth anchor's hypertext reference is HREF=ftp://www.culturewave.com/pub/culturewave/ba-bookstore-events/. This example of an inter-system link points to the FTP site www.culturewave.com. The additional information moves the reader directly to the directory where the list of bookstore events is kept. Clicking on this link displays the directory and allows readers to download the event list to their own computer.

In a similar way, the eleventh anchor is another example of an inter-system link. This hypertext reference, HREF=http://www.childsoft.com/ims/rest/ba_rest_guide.html, points to an HTML page on another computer system that maintains a list of restaurants. Clicking on this link transfers readers directly to that page, which will then display in their browser.

Figure 6-6 shows how this document appears when viewed in Netscape.

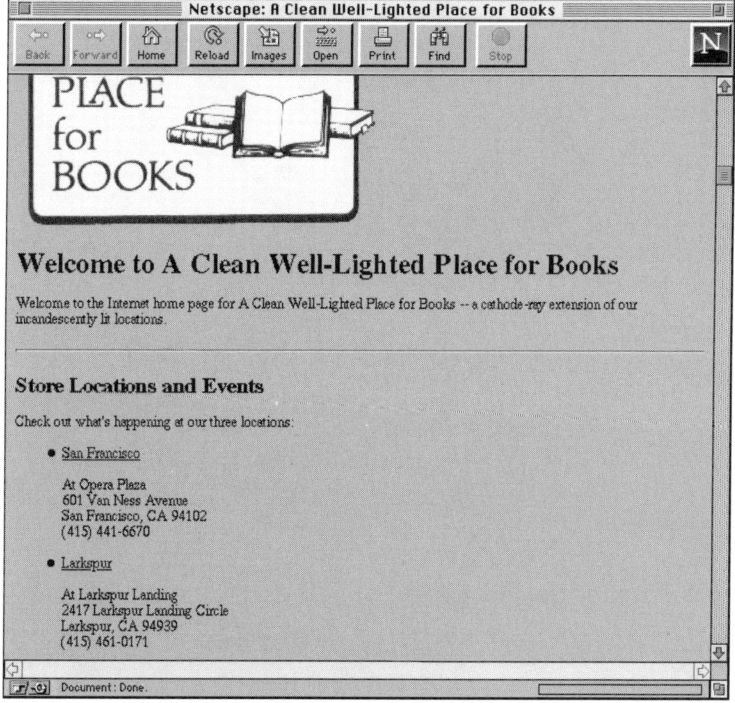

Figure 6-6: *The sample HTML document.*

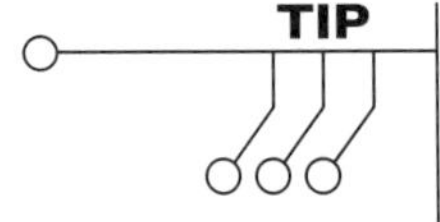

Normally, you will only use the HREF and/or the NAME Anchor tag attributes. As the Web evolves, however, use of other tags may become more prevalent. For more information on the different attributes that are available for links, see Appendix C, "An Illustrated HTML Reference."

Moving On

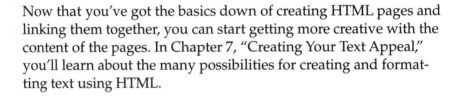

Now that you've got the basics down of creating HTML pages and linking them together, you can start getting more creative with the content of the pages. In Chapter 7, "Creating Your Text Appeal," you'll learn about the many possibilities for creating and formatting text using HTML.

7

Creating Your Text Appeal

By now you can see the striking difference between how HTML documents are written and how documents are created with a word processor. Instead of focusing on a physical description of a page's margins, fonts and formatting, the tag structure of HTML focuses on the content of a document and what the various parts of a document mean. The focus of HTML markup is on the classification and content of a paragraph or group of words, instead of the look of the displayed or printed page. There are still a few tags that give explicit directions about rendering text, such as bold or italic, but most are focused on the *logical* meaning instead of the *physical* rendering. In this chapter, you'll learn about the options you have as an author to describe the various parts of your page, and see how the different Web browsers will render that page.

Netscape's Extensions to HTML

Most of the tags described in this chapter are part of the HTML standard. A few, however, have been added by Netscape Communications. Use these extensions with care because a page created to look great on the Netscape browser using their extensions may look positively dreadful on another browser. Theoretically, a browser should ignore any markup elements or attributes that it doesn't understand; unfortunately, not all of them do so. You should always check your work with an assortment of browsers to make sure the rendering is acceptable on all of them.

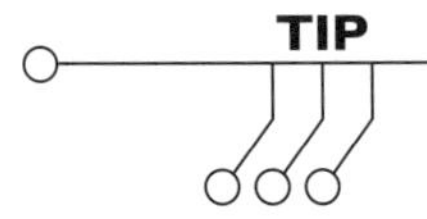

One of the reasons to use HoTMetaL PRO as your editor is that it automatically enforces basic rules about inserting HTML tags in your document. This carries over into the area of tag attributes as well, so if you are using HoTMetaL PRO as your editor, then the default is to not allow you to enter the Netscape extensions into your HTML tags—HoTMetaL PRO won't understand them. However, HoTMetaL PRO can be configured to enable the Netscape extensions if you want to use them. To do that, you have to specify a special rules file in the HoTMetaL PRO configuration file, sqhmpro Preferences. *This changes the rules that HoTMetaL PRO uses for validation of your HTML tags, and allows you to use the Netscape extensions for tags and attributes. See Chapter 2 for information on changing your configuration file.*

If you find you want to edit the initialization file frequently to switch between the standard HTML rules and Netscape rules, you can use the following trick. Make two copies of the preferences file and name them something different, like Preference-Netscape and Preferences-Standard. Then edit each one with the changes you want. To use one or the other, simply return to the Finder, select the file you want, and choose File>>Make Alias. Retitle the alias file as sqhmpro Preferences. *Now, when you launch HoTMetaL PRO, it will use the file pointed to by the alias as its configuration file. If you forget which file the alias points to, simply use File>>Get Info (-I) to display the file information, which includes the name of the original file.*

Inserting Paragraph Elements & Attributes

Chapters 4 and 5 explained the two basic procedures to insert elements using HoTMetaL PRO. You can first type and select your text, then select the style in HoTMetaL PRO by choosing the Markup>>Surround menu items. This surrounds the selected text with the chosen tag. Alternatively, you can choose the Markup>> Insert Element and select the tag from the Insert Elements dialog box. If the tag acts as a container, you can then enter your text between the opening and closing tags. The most basic element is the paragraph. The paragraph element has changed from HTML 1.0 to HTML 3; HTML 1.0 specified only one tag at the end of the paragraph. HTML 3 requires a beginning tag <P>, the text to be displayed, and an ending tag, </P>. The browser displays a single line space after an ending paragraph tag. It is a common mistake to include multiple paragraph marks for spacing, but if you add multiple paragraph elements, only one space will appear. The following sections describe additional methods of working with paragraphs.

Displaying Preformatted Paragraphs

If you want to create a block of text on a page and be sure that the style of text will not change when rendered by a Web browser, use the preformatted text element. This shows up as the PRE tag in HTML text. When rendering this tag, Web browsers use a fixed width font, like Courier, and break lines exactly where they are broken in your source document. Preformatted text is useful when you want to create a computer listing or a simple table (we'll cover more complex tables, using HTML tags, later in this chapter). You can also use the PRE tag to insert a text file like a USENET News article, or if you want to add white space to a document. Any white space you add between the opening <PRE> and the closing </PRE> tags displays when viewed in a browser. When you use the <PRE> tag you can add character styles and links, but not paragraph elements, such as headings. Keep your text between 60 to 80 characters when using the <PRE> tag. If you exceed 80 characters it's likely that the text will not display correctly since most screens are only 80 characters wide and the browser will not break lines of text within the PRE tags.

Centering Paragraphs

One of the more exciting extensions to the HTML specification by Netscape is the <CENTER> paragraph tag. Note that this is an actual tag not just an attribute. The <CENTER> tag causes the paragraph or other element, such as a header or image, to be centered on the browser's screen. While this is a common feature in word processors, not all Web browsers support this nonstandard extension. Since a <CENTER> tag will generate a line break—as do all paragraph tags—if a browser ignores the <CENTER> tag, it will also leave out a line break you may have been expecting. For this reason, try to avoid using the <CENTER> tag for headings. Instead, use one of the standard heading tags. If you're creating a page especially for Netscape browsers, go ahead and use the <CENTER> tag to center elements. Figure 7-1 shows the logo and first heading centered on A Clean Well-Lighted Place for Books's home page.

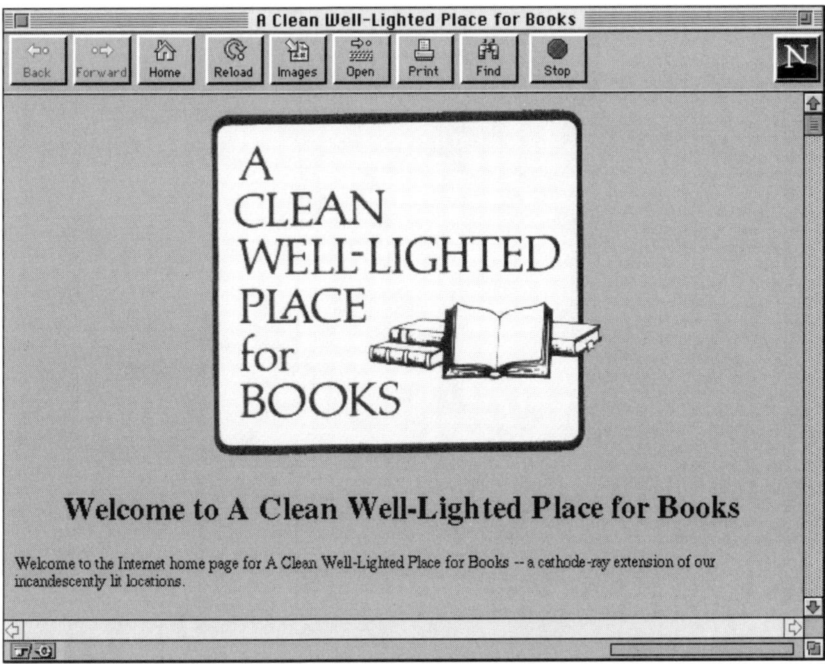

Figure 7-1: *The <CENTER> tag lets you center elements, such as images and headers.*

Adding a Quotation

The final paragraph style available is the BLOCKQUOTE style. This paragraph style should be used when you create text that is quoted from another source. Typically, Web browsers render this text as indented. Some Web browsers display block quotes in italics. Figure 7-2 shows examples of block quotes. In this example, the <BR> tag is used to place the name of the person quoted on a separate line, and the person's name, title and other information appears emphasized using the <EM> tag, discussed later in this chapter.

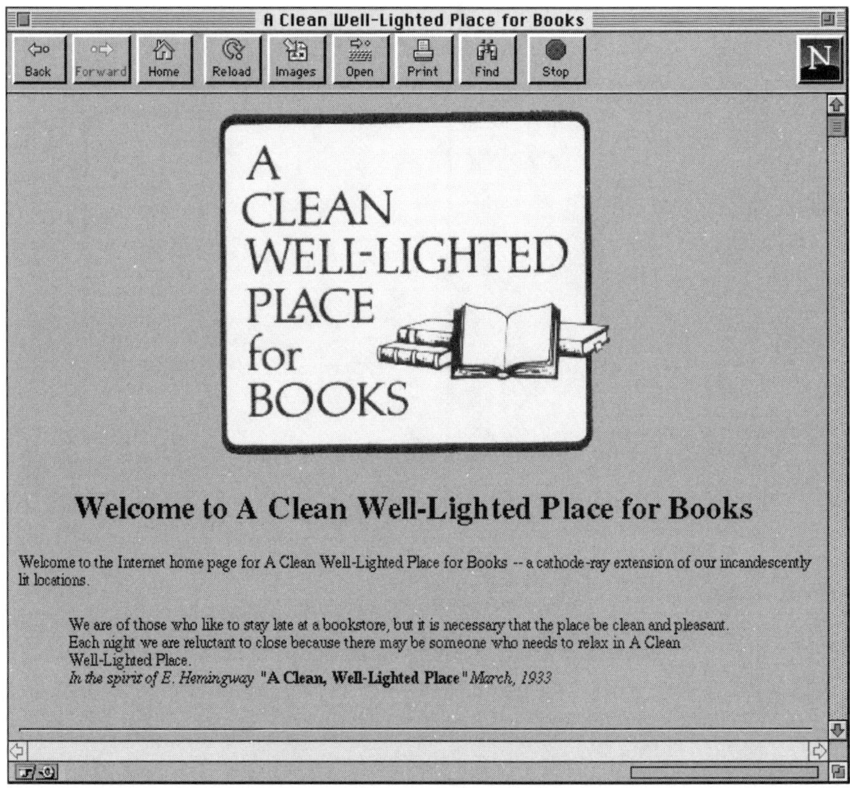

Figure 7-2: *The <BLOCKQUOTE> tag automatically indents quoted material.*

Using Lists

In Chapter 5 we introduced including lists in a Web page. The following sections include additional information on the four types of lists: unordered lists, ordered lists, directory lists and discursive lists (also called glossary lists). When you want to insert list items, move the insertion point before the end list item tag and use the Markup>>Split command or press -P. This automatically places the insertion point between empty beginning and ending list item tags.

Creating Unordered Lists

The unordered list (UL) is also commonly called a bulleted list. Figure 7-3 shows how an unordered list appears in HoTMetaL PRO and Figure 7-4 shows how it appears rendered in Netscape. The standard handling for this list is to use bullets for various indent levels. The first indent level displays a disc, which appears as a round bullet. The second level displays a circle, which we found indiscernible from the disk. The third and last level displays a square bullet. An unordered list is started with the <UL> tag. Each entry in the list is created with an <LI> (List Item) tag. The list item may consist of more than one line. The menu list is another type of unordered list. Using the <MENU> tag instead of <UL> creates a more compact list than an unordered list. Each list item in a menu list should be no longer than one line.

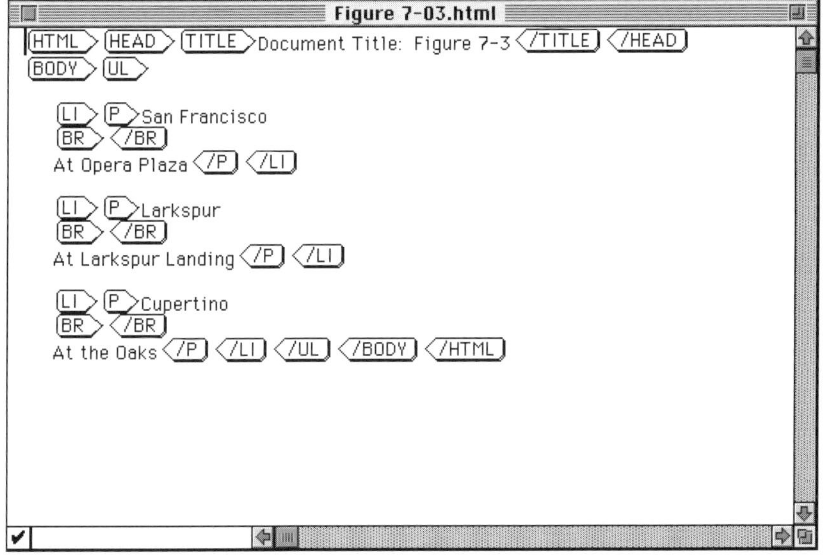

Figure 7-3: *An unordered (bulleted) list in HoTMetaL PRO.*

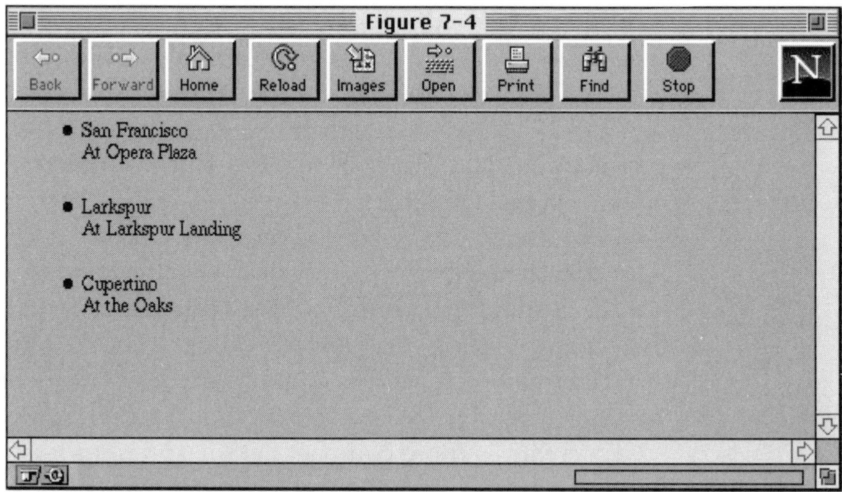

Figure 7-4: *An unordered (bulleted) list in Netscape Navigator.*

Netscape has added the TYPE extension to control the bullet type. To use this Netscape extension, move the cursor between the beginning and ending line-item tags for the item you want to change and choose Markup>>Edit SGML Attributes. This displays the Edit Attributes dialog box. In the TYPE attribute field, enter disc, circle or square. While there are three possible types, the only noticeable difference in Netscape occurs when you change from the disc to the square attribute.

This extension breaks from the preferred "logical style" concept into the "physical style" concept, since you control the actual bullet style, and browsers other than Netscape will not recognize the extension. For example, Mosaic will only display disc bullets.

Creating Ordered (Numbered) Lists

Ordered lists, or numbered lists, are lists that have numerals as the list-item bullet. By default, lists are ordered in ascending numerical order, 1, 2, 3, 4, etc. The numbering implies that the order of the elements in a list has special significance.

Netscape has added an extension so lists can be ordered in ways other than just 1, 2, 3, 4, etc. Netscape extensions also allow you to use capital letters, small letters, capital roman numerals and small roman numerals. Since non-Netscape browsers just default to numbers, be sure your text does not explicitly refer to "Item C" or "Item II."

To use a Netscape extension numbering scheme, move the cursor between the beginning and ending list item tags for the item you want to change and choose Markup>>Edit SGML Attributes. This displays the Edit Attributes dialog box. In the TYPE attribute field, enter one of the choices listed in Table 7-1.

Tag	Description
A	Specifies that the current list item and subsequent list items begin with capital letters.
a	Specifies that the current list item and subsequent list items begin with lowercase letters.
I	Specifies that the current list item and subsequent list items begin with uppercase roman numerals.
i	Specifies that the current list item and subsequent list items begin with lowercase roman numerals.
1	Specifies that the current list item and subsequent list items begin with numbers (the default setting).

Table 7-1: *TYPE attributes for lists.*

Another Netscape extension lets you start a list at a value other than 1. To enter a different value, you need to edit the START attribute field of the OL element, listed in the Edit Attributes dialog box. This Netscape extension changes the current list item value and acts as a starting value for subsequent list items. The START attribute has no effect on the TYPE setting; for example, entering 3 displays the current list item as "C" (TYPE=A), "c" (TYPE=a), "III" (TYPE=I), "iii" (TYPE=i) or "3" (TYPE=1). Figure 7-5 illustrates how an ordered list is entered in HoTMetaL PRO. Figure 7-6 shows how this looks when rendered with Netscape Navigator.

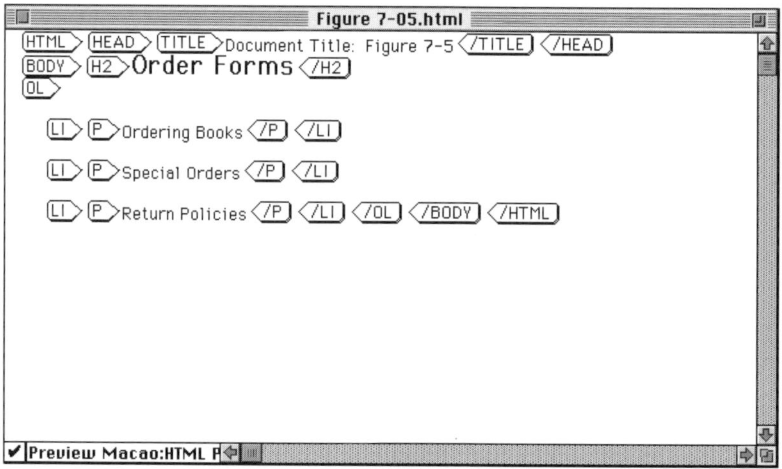

Figure 7-5: *An ordered (numbered) list in HoTMetaL PRO.*

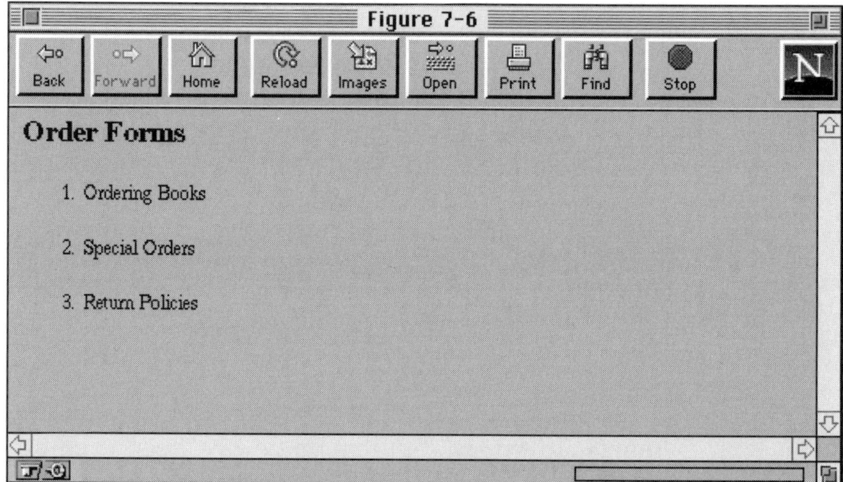

Figure 7-6: *An ordered (numbered) list in Netscape Navigator.*

Creating Directory Lists

A directory list is specified in the standard as a list of items that are less than 24 characters in length. Web browsers render this as a list of items with no bullets and no hanging indent, so while you can include items that are longer than 24 characters, if the line wraps around, there is no indication that it is part of a single list item.

Creating Discursive Lists

Discursive lists, also known as *definition lists* and *glossary lists*, are used to create lists in which each item also has a descriptive paragraph. Typical uses for discursive lists are for glossaries, and lists of definitions and their meanings. A discursive list is started with the <DL> tag. Each entry in the list is created with a single line *term* indicated by a <DT> tag, and a *definition* indicated by a <DD> tag. The definition may consist of more than one line. Figure 7-7 shows the HTML example of a directory and a discursive list in HoTMetaL PRO. Figure 7-8 shows how the directory and discursive lists appear in Netscape Navigator.

There is a "COMPACT" option for discursive lists that is specified in the standard, but at the time this was written, none of the Web browsers tested did anything about it. Theoretically the compact option displays the list in a more condensed format.

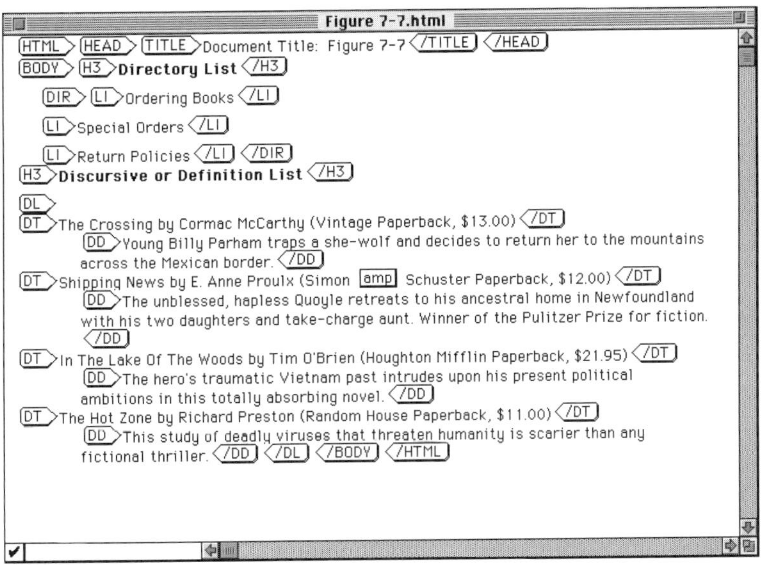

Figure 7-7: *HoTMetaL window for directory and discursive lists.*

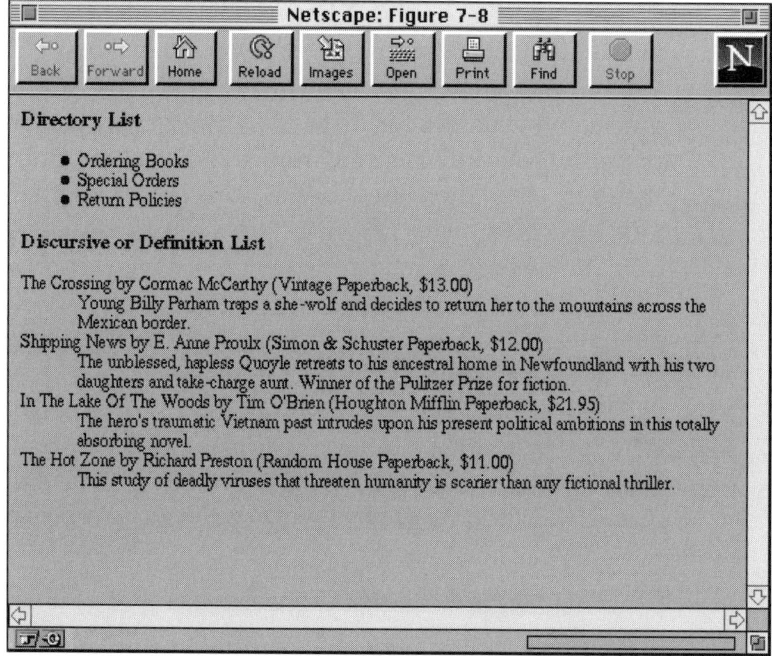

Figure 7-8: *Directory and discursive lists in Netscape Navigator.*

Creating Nested Lists

You can insert, or nest, a list within a list by inserting a list element, such as UL or OL, inside a list item (LI). We recommend you don't nest lists deeper than three levels. Be aware that different browsers handle nested lists differently—just because the nested list appears with a round bullet in Netscape doesn't mean all browsers will use the same style bullet.

Adding an Address

The <ADDRESS> tag, as the name implies, is used to identify a block of text that contains an address. As with most HTML tags the address is rendered in a distinctive fashion by Web browsers. Although different browsers choose different styles, typically the address will appear in italics. As mentioned in Chapter 5, the <ADDRESS> tag is frequently used with the <BR> tag to separate each line of the address.

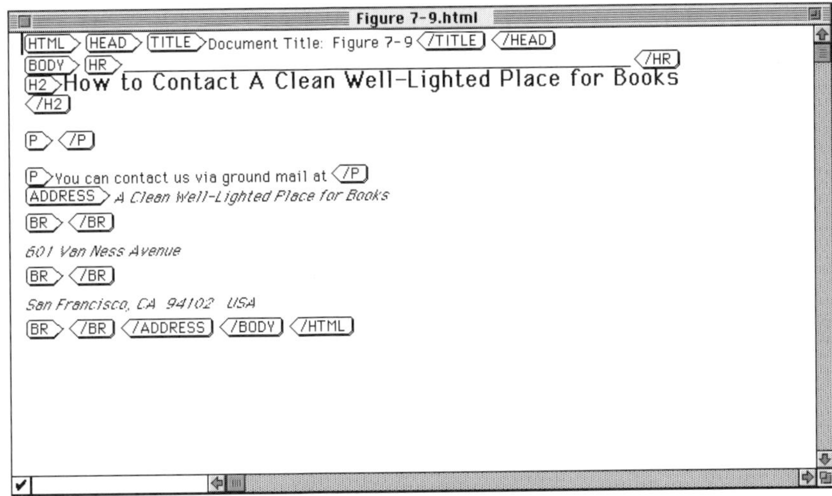

Figure 7-9: *An address style in HoTMetaL PRO.*

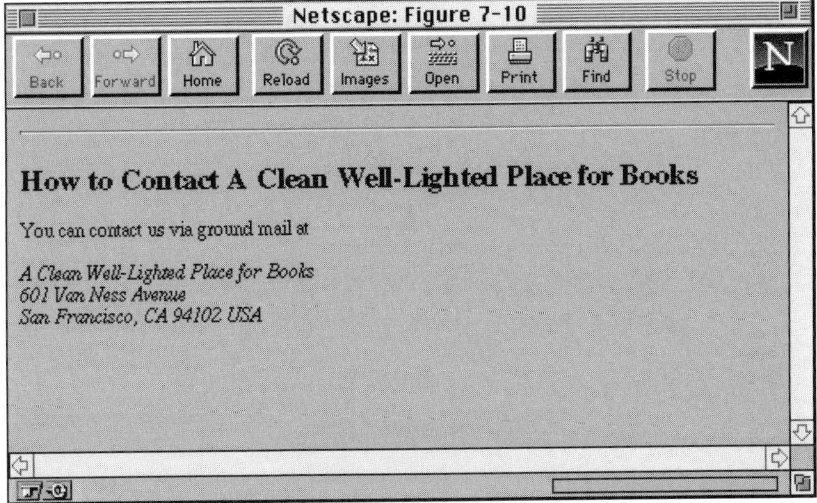

Figure 7-10: *An address style rendered by Netscape Navigator.*

Using Logical Styles to Format Characters

Logical styles tell the browser the kind of text to be presented and leave the rendering decisions to the browser. In general, you should use a logical representation instead of the physical representation whenever possible. Logical style tags are preferred over physical tags, because logical styles allow for more intelligent handling of text. Logical styles also give users more flexibility, allowing anyone to set up their browser however they see fit. The biggest limitation to logical styles is that you often find instances that have no corresponding logical style. For example, if you have text that is the "legalese" in a document, you may want it rendered in as small a font size as possible. This calls for a style to define small text, but such a style is not defined in HTML. This is handled in the electronic, multiplatform publishing world by using SGML with author-definable logical tags, but at the expense of great complexity, which has so far been spared in HTML. Suffice it to say that the use of logical styles versus physical styles is a subject of great contention within the Web community.

Emphasizing Text

There are two forms of emphasis used on an HTML page, EM for emphasis and STRONG for strong emphasis. Typically, EM is rendered as *italic*, and STRONG is rendered as **bold**.

Computer Code & Examples

For sections of your text that are computer code (or similar), use the <CODE> tag. This is usually rendered by a browser in Courier fixed-pitch font, and in most browsers, the size of the font is controlled separately from the size of other logical styles. If you have an entire paragraph of text that needs to be rendered in this fashion, use the <PRE> tag, which is a paragraph style. Do not use CODE—it is a character style, not a paragraph style, and, therefore, will not generate a line break.

Other logical styles include SAMP, which is defined in the standard as a sequence of literal characters; KBD, which would be text that a user would type on a keyboard; and VAR, which is used for variable names. It seems clear that the original designers of the HTML styles were computer users and programmers. The final logical style currently in the standard is the CITE style, which should be used when text on your page is a citation for a title or a reference. The citation text is typically displayed in italics.

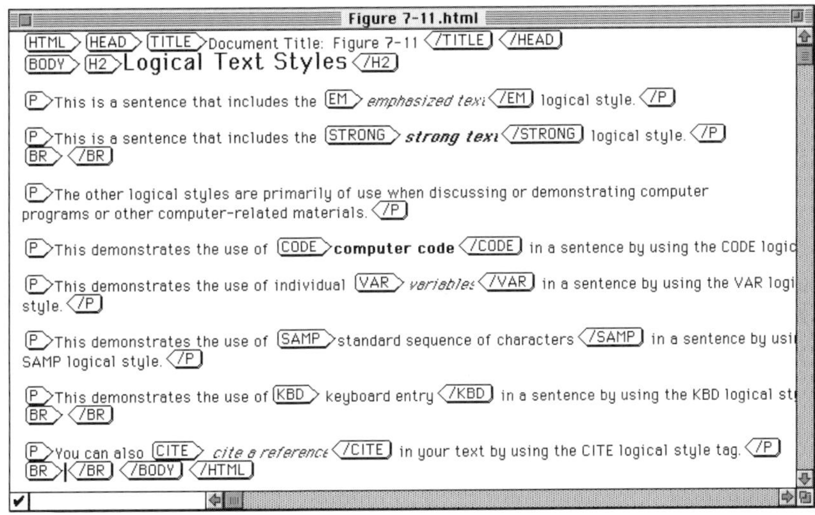

Figure 7-11: *Logical character styles in HoTMetaL PRO.*

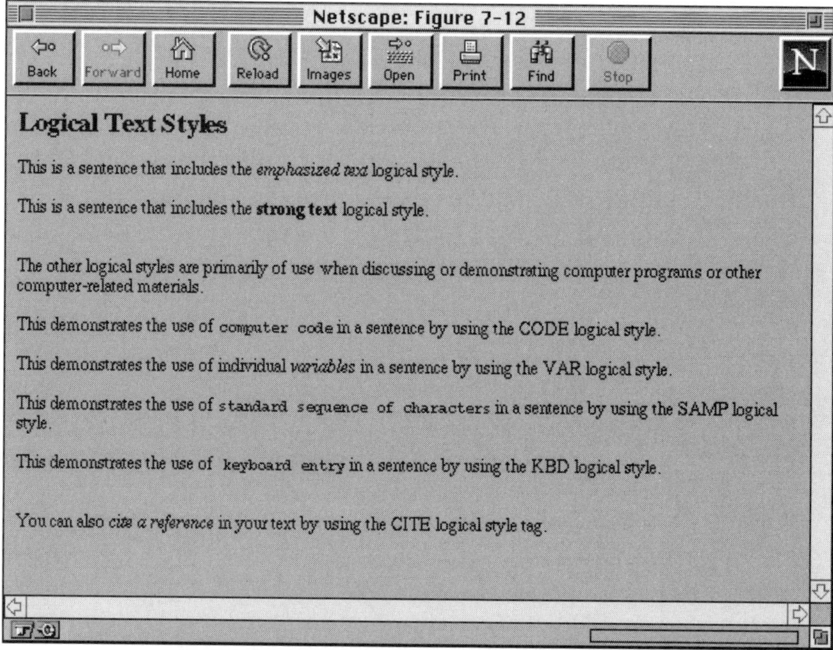

Figure 7-12: *Logical character styles rendered by Netscape.*

Using Physical Styles to Format Characters

The second category of styles for formatting characters is *physical styles*. Physical styles give an explicit direction to a Web browser about how to render a character. There are several physical styles, including bold, italic, underline, blink and fixed-width font. Examples of these styles (except the underline font) are shown in Figure 7-13 as HTML code and in Figure 7-14 rendered with Netscape Navigator.

Unlike the paragraph formatting tags, the character formatting tags do *not* cause a line break, and you can use multiple styles in the same sentence. Character formatting tags always *surround* the text that is to appear formatted; for example, emphasis text would start with EM and end with /EM.

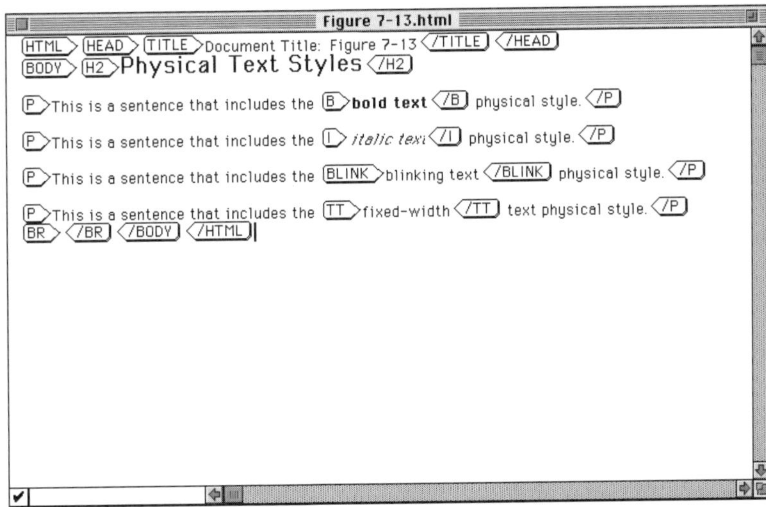

Figure 7-13: *Physical character styles in HoTMetaL PRO.*

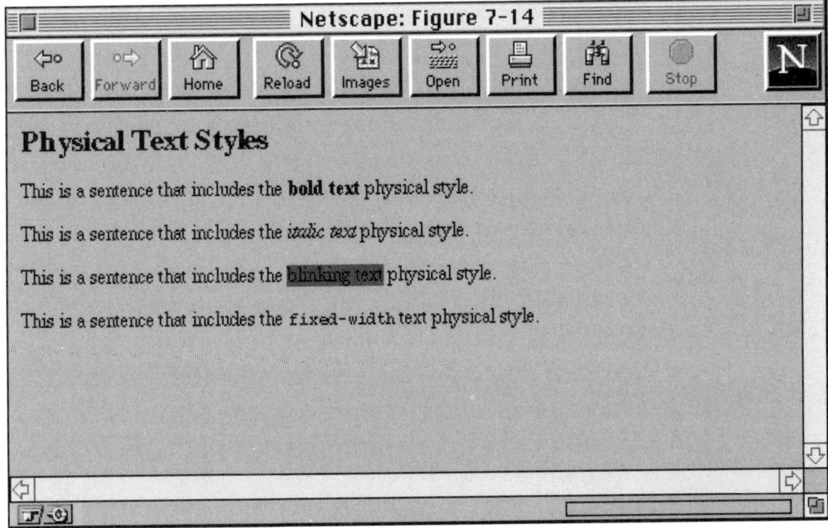

Figure 7-14: *Physical character styles rendered by Netscape Navigator.*

Adding Bold & Italics

Bold (B) and Italic (I) styles are the same as you would expect: bold text and italic text. As always, place the text you want treated with these styles between the opening and closing tags. With HoTMetaL PRO, you have the option to type away at your page, then go back later to add character formatting with the Markup>>Surround menu option. A particular advantage to formatting text after it's typed is that you avoid the overuse of formatting changes on a single page.

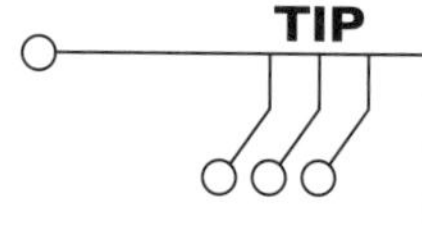

Use the <STRONG> tag instead of <B> wherever possible, unless you want to ensure that only a bold font is used. Use the <EM> emphasis tag instead of <I> wherever possible, unless you want to ensure that only an italic font is used. These two suggestions will keep your document as portable as possible.

You would need to specify physical rendering if you need to refer to the formatting explicitly in the text, such as: "The **bold** text is from the original document, and the *italic* text is from the first revision." Of course, some browsers cannot render bold or italic text, so include alternate ways of identifying specific areas of text, or provide an alternate page for browsers that don't support character-formatting properties.

The Underline style is a proposed standard and cannot be entered with HoTMetaL PRO at this time. Underlines are typically converted to italics for most professionally published documents. Instead of using the underline use italics. Underline has no corresponding logical style, so if you must underline text, you need to manually use the beginning <U> and ending </U> tags.

Including Blinking Text

An extension added by Netscape is the <BLINK> tag. The Blink style causes text to blink on and off on the viewer's screen. At first this may look like a nifty feature, but like using multiple exclamation points, it calls undue attention to itself. Just because it's new doesn't mean you have to use it. Looking at blinking letters can easily become a distraction and detract from your overall message. Use this extension sparingly, if at all. Since it is an extension to the HTML specification added by Netscape, you should not expect this to work on all browsers, but in general if the browser can't display the blinking text, the browser will ignore the <BLINK> tag and display the text.

Changing Fonts & Font Sizes

The control of the font point sizes in HTML is left to the discretion of the Web browser. Netscape, however, has decided that some control over the *relative* size of a font in a document is needed. Netscape has defined two tags for controlling font sizes, <BASEFONT> and <FONT>. The <BASEFONT> tag defines the relative size of the standard font for a portion of your text. You can use any number from 1 to 7 with 3 as the "middle" size to define the size. Size 3 is also the default. Netscape also lets you use the plus (+) and minus sign (-) followed by an integer to specify the font size relative to the basefont size. For example, <BASEFONT SIZE=+4 > specifies the font should be incremented 4 units larger than the standard base font, and <FONT SIZE=+4>*a section of text* </FONT> applies a relative font size 4 units larger than the base font to the words "a section of text." Note that you can indicate increased or decreased sizes for any part of your text, even an individual letter or word. Figure 7-15 shows an example of the font size tags as they appear in HoTMetaL PRO, used to increase the size of the first letters in a heading. Figure 7-16 shows the resulting page in Netscape Navigator.

For specifying parts of paragraphs that use a fixed-width font, such as typewriter text, use the <TT> tag. Typically, the Web browser will use a Courier font. If you have an entire paragraph to be rendered in a fixed-width font, use the PRE paragraph style.

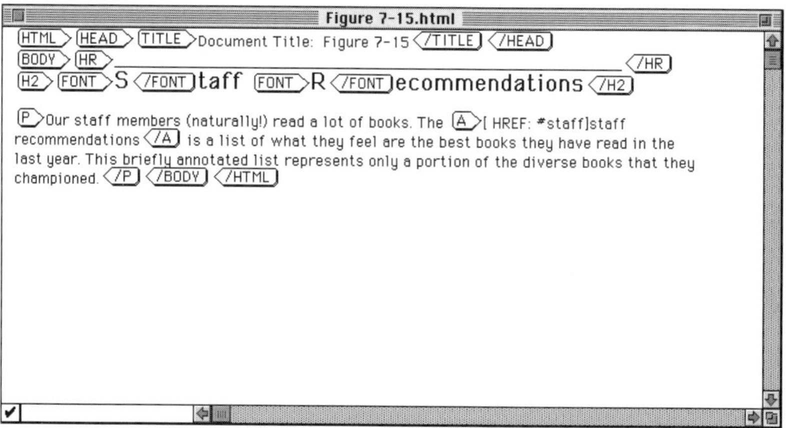

Figure 7-15: *An example of different font sizes in HoTMetaL PRO.*

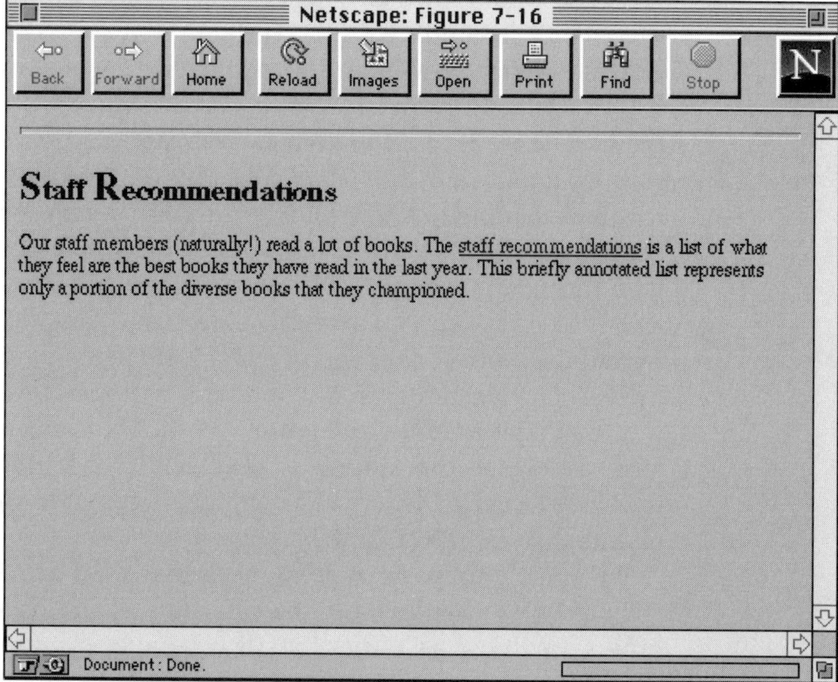

Figure 7-16: *An example of different font sizes in Netscape Navigator.*

Controlling Line Breaks

When the page you create is rendered on a computer screen with a Web browser, the size of the screen is entirely beyond your control. The browser itself flows your paragraphs to fit the width of the view screen (except for preformatted text, of course), so you can never tell where a line break is going to occur. There are instances, however, where you'll want to force a line break, or ensure that no line break occurs. To do this, use the break (BR) tag and the nobreak (NOBR) tag.

The <BR> tag inserts a line break at the point in the text that it occurs. The <NOBR> tag is used to surround text you don't want broken. This tag is a Netscape extension, so it may not work with all browsers. All text that appears between the starting and ending <NOBR> tag will not be broken on the screen. This is useful for long text strings with spaces that should not be broken across a line, such as a code example, or a line a user should enter in a computer program. Another place the <NOBR> tag is useful is in phone numbers, or the multiword links such as "Frequent Buyer Club" and "from other countries" found on the ACWLP home page. In addition to the <NOBR> tag, Netscape has added another tag called WBR, which stands for Word BReak. The <WBR> tag is inserted in strings of text where the text *could* be broken, if needed, for formatting.

Using Special Characters

HTML lets you include a large number of "special" characters that can be entered but are not normally found on a U.S. keyboard. The word "special" is in quotes, because for many writers of HTML pages these characters are simply part of the alphabet, but because of the limitations of the original definition of the 7-bit character set, we are now forced to take special measures to create these characters. In HTML parlance, these special characters are called *character entities*. Most of these characters are accented characters, currency marks and characters that have special meaning to the HTML language: such as the double quotation mark (") the greater than (>) and less than signs (<) and the ampersand (&).

What's Special & What's Not

Most characters that appear on a U.S.-style keyboard are regular characters that can be typed directly in an HTML document. This includes all alphabetic and numeric characters, and most commonly used punctuation. With HoTMetaL PRO, all you need to do is type these characters, and the corresponding HTML code will be inserted. If you're entering raw text, you need to identify that you're referring to a special character. HTML uses a special escape code to identify characters that have special meaning to HTML. The escape code begins with an ampersand (&) and ends with a semicolon, as shown in the following list of characters.

Character	Code
>	>
<	<
&	&
"	"

The special characters of HTML include all accented characters, plus special punctuation and currency marks. A complete list of these characters can be found in the "Illustrated HTML Reference" section at the end of this book. With HoTMetaL PRO, you can enter special characters in one of two ways: First, you can type the character on the keyboard using the standard Macintosh keyboard commands, or you can select the desired character from the Character Entity list provided by HoTMetaL Pro.

You can enter most specical characters directly from the Macintosh keyboard using standard keyboard sequences. For example, to enter a copyright symbol, you can use the key combination Option-g. To enter characters that aren't directly available from the keyboard, such as accented characters, you first set the accent then enter the letter to be accented. For example, to enter an "e" with a grave accent, press Option-' and then press the "e" key. If the character you've entered has a special representation in HTML, HoTMetaL PRO will enter that code. If there is no dedicated code, HoTMetaL PRO creates a general entity tag that inserts a standard three-digit code for the character.

The Macintosh provides direct keyboard entry of almost every possible character that is normally used in any European language. If you are not sure of how to get the character that you need, first look at the KeyCaps display (normally shown under your Apple menu). This shows you the keys of your keyboard and displays the various characters available as you press keys on your keyboard. If the character that you want isn't there, check your Macintosh System Guide documentation for a description of how to enter special accented characters.

The other way to enter special characters with HoTMetaL PRO is to use the Markup>>Special Characters command. This brings up the Special Characters dialog box, shown in Figure 7-17, from which you can choose the special character you want to insert.

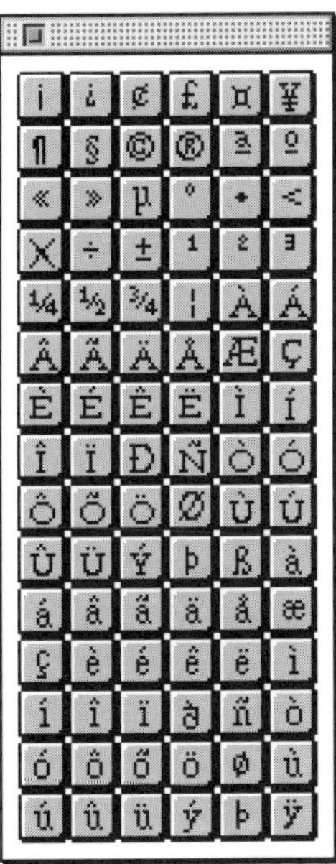

Figure 7-17: *The Special Characters dialog box lets you insert special characters.*

Netscape includes two new entities: the registered trademark symbol (®) and the copyright symbol (©). Both appear in the Special Characters dialog box. The escape code for the registered trademark is ®. The code for the copyright symbol is ©.

As you create your Web document, keep in mind that the World Wide Web is a global network and for many of the people who can access your pages English is a second language. If you have the ability to author pages in more than one language, by all means do so. You'll help foster the globalization of the Web and attract an audience that might otherwise not have access to your site. Figure 7-18 helps show how special characters are used in an HTML document. Figure 7-19 shows a page that includes special characters. Take a look at http://www.csr.ists.ca/w3can/Welcome.html for the complete references.

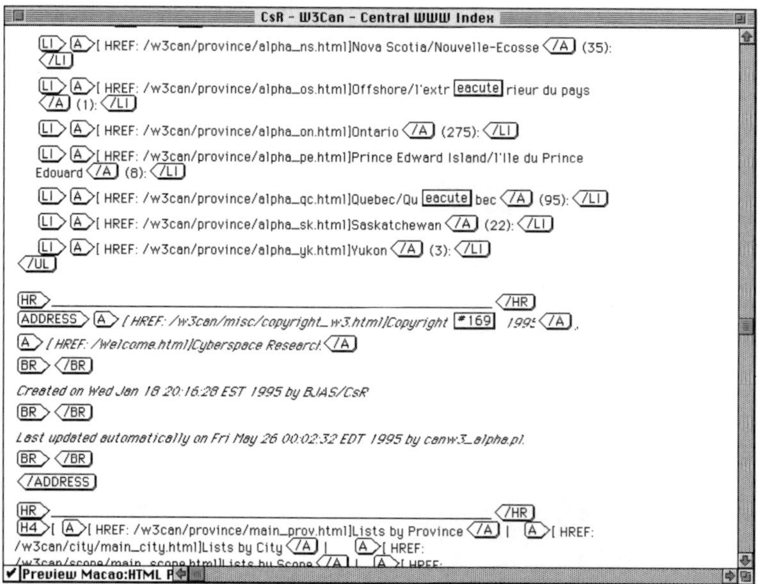

Figure 7-18: *Fragment of a multilingual Web page in HoTMetaL PRO.*

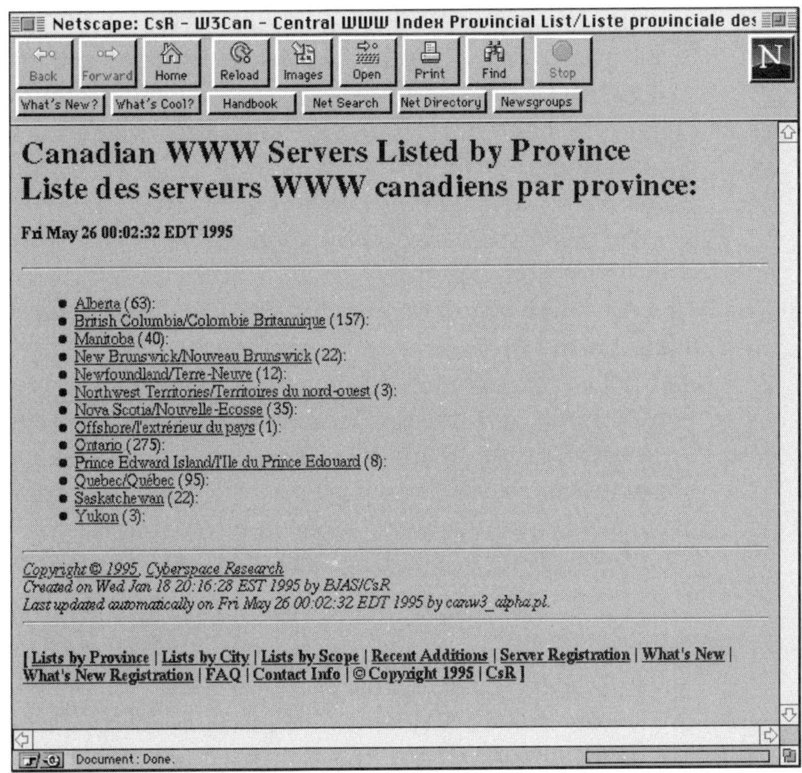

Figure 7-19: *A multilingual Web page as displayed by Netscape Navigator.*

Using Horizontal Rules

The use of special elements, such as horizontal rules and repeating graphics, can add a special look to your pages, as well as provide the reader with visual cues as to the location of information on the page.

The horizontal rule, specified in HTML by HR, is used frequently to break up the page and separate elements on a page. This can be very useful to keep topics marked clearly, since you have very little other control over the formatting of a page. When converted to raw HTML, the horizontal rule is specified with the

<HR> tag and *no* closing tag. (Note: HoTMetal PRO displays start and end tag icons for the <HR> tag, although only the start tag is saved as text.) In addition to the standard use of the horizontal rule, Netscape has defined the ability to specify the width of a rule as a percentage of the displayed page width. This can produce some very striking effects when using the Netscape browser, and some really ugly effects when viewed with any other viewer. Use the extensions carefully!

Although graphics are not specifically part of a chapter on text, it's worth noting here that some graphics can be used to provide a stronger presence to your pages. For example, the common horizontal rule could be replaced with a graphic element. This also gives the person reading your pages a hint as to how wide you really wanted the page to be. Use of common graphics is handy when you want to create a navigation bar at the top and/or the bottom of your pages. Check out Chapter 8 to find out about using graphics on your pages.

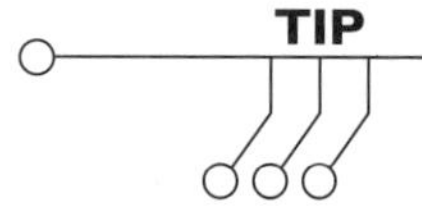

When a graphic is used as a control bar, you also need to tie your page in to the Common Gateway Interface (CGI), discussed in Chapters 8 and 10.

Netscape adds four Netscape HTML extensions to the horizontal rule to let you specify the size, width, alignment and shading of horizontal rules. For example a ¼-inch rule that takes up 50 percent of the width of the document can appear centered. Just because something looks great in your browser doesn't mean it will appear the same in other browsers. Figure 7-20 shows the Edit Attributes dialog box for horizontal rules. Table 7-2 describes Netscape tag extensions that allow the document's author to describe how the horizontal rule should look. Although Netscape lets you use percentages to define the width, HoTMetaL PRO doesn't. Instead you must enter the number of pixels.

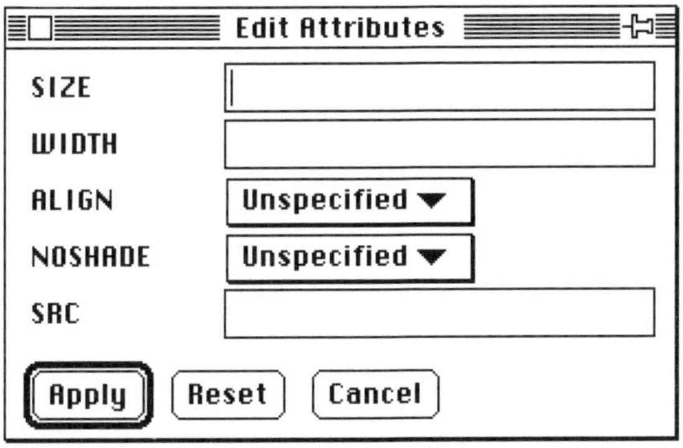

Figure 7-20: *The Edit Attributes dialog box for horizontal rules.*

Attribute	Description
<HR SIZE=*n*>	Specifies the thickness of the horizontal rule in pixels. The *n* stands for the number of pixels.
<HR WIDTH=*n*>	Specifies an exact width in pixels, or a relative width measured in percent of document width. The *n* stands for a number of pixels.
<HR ALIGN=*alignment*>	Specifies the alignment of the rule. The three choices for *alignment* are LEFT (left-aligned), RIGHT (right-aligned) or CENTER (centered).
	Specifies that you do not want any shading of your horizontal rule.

Table 7-2: *Attributes for horizontal rules.*

Figure 7-21 shows an example of horizontal rules using Netscape extensions. In this case, a series of progressively thicker and longer rules have been used to create a dramatic entry to the Staff Recommendations section of the document. Here are the settings for each of these rules, from the top down, as you would see them in HTML.

1. <HR SIZE="2" WIDTH="10" ALIGN="CENTER">
2. <HR SIZE="4" WIDTH="60" ALIGN="CENTER">
3. <HR SIZE="6" WIDTH="120" ALIGN="CENTER">
4. <HR SIZE="8" WIDTH="300" ALIGN="CENTER">
5. <HR SIZE="10" ALIGN="CENTER">

You'll notice that the last rule has no width setting, so it will default to the width of the browser window. The other rules are fixed sizes, so that, if the browser window is smaller than the width specified (unlikely, for these widths, but possible) then the rules would extend out of the window.

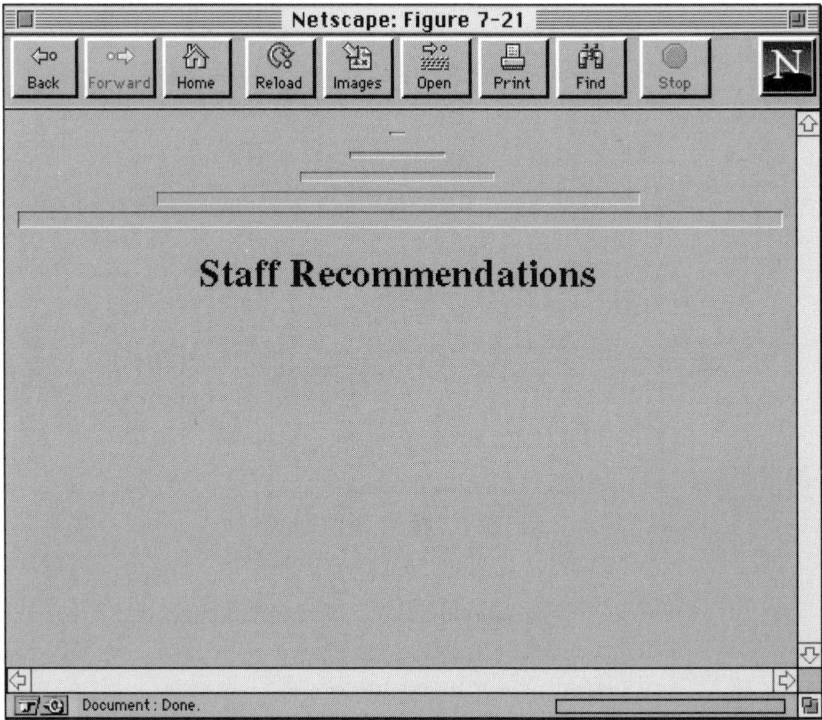

Figure 7-21: *Horizontal rules using Netscape extensions.*

Using Tables

Tables are a new addition to the HTML language and are not officially supported in the current version (HTML 2). They are in such demand, however, that you can already edit tables with HoTMetaL PRO and view them with Netscape Navigator and the NCSA Mosaic browser. Keep in mind that the table features are still experimental, and the table tag markups are still subject to modification. Naturally, the implementation of the tables can vary widely, so what you write in HoTMetaL PRO is not exactly what appears in a browser. This is not a flaw in HoTMetaL PRO or the browser—merely an illustration of the problems you'll face when working with not-quite-yet-standard features.

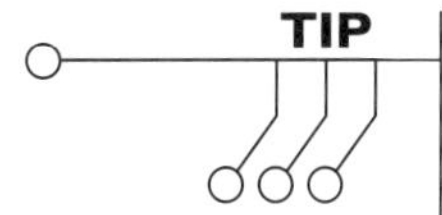

Netscape has added a few attributes for working with tables. HotMetal PRO automatically supports these options, but remember that all browsers may not recognize them.

Adding a Table

Tables are an important element in many technical documents, and as such, the availability of tables in HTML is a boon to those people trying to create HTML versions of existing technical documents. For the purposes of illustration, this chapter explains how to add table elements using HoTMetaL PRO and presents three sample tables. The following steps explain how to add a table with a border and a caption using HoTMetaL PRO.

1. In the body of your Web page, choose Markup>>Insert Table. The Insert Table dialog box is displayed, as shown in Figure 7-22.

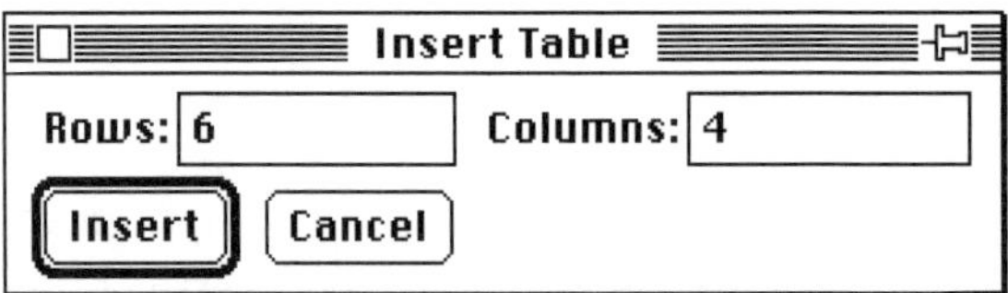

Figure 7-22: *The Insert Table dialog box.*

2. Specify the number of columns in the Number of Columns field and the number of rows in the Number of Rows field. Choose the Insert button. A grid appears, as shown in Figure 7-23.

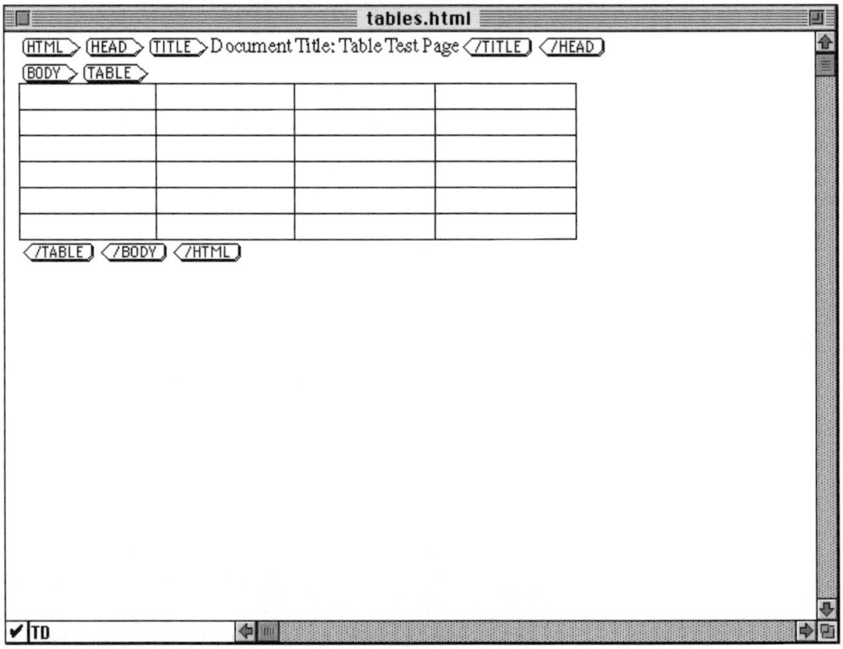

Figure 7-23: *When you insert a table a grid appears.*

3. Click to the right of the starting Table tag and choose the Markup>>Edit SGML Attributes or press -]. The Edit Attributes dialog box appears.
4. Select a number in the Border drop-down list to specify the border size (number of pixels) you want for your table and choose the Apply button.
5. Choose Markup>>Insert Element or press -I. The Insert Element dialog box appears.
6. Select the Caption element from the Insert Element dialog box and choose the Insert Element button. The insertion point appears between the starting and ending caption tags.
7. Enter the caption you want to appear above your table.

Editing a Table

Once you've added a table and moved the insertion point in the table, the four table commands become active in the Markup menu, provided the insertion point is inside a table. Table 7-3 lists and describes the Markup menu options you can use to edit a table.

Option	Description
Cell Properties	Displays the Cell Properties dialog box as shown in Figure 7-24. This allows you to change the properties of an individual cell. The changes apply only to the cell where the cursor is currently located. You can specify the Vertical Alignment (Unspecified, TOP, MIDDLE or BOTTOM), the Horizontal Alignment (Unspecified, LEFT CENTER JUSTIFY or RIGHT) and the Width of the cell in pixels. You can also specify that the cell not wrap text by checking the NoWrap check box.
Row Properties	Displays the Row Properties dialog box as shown in Figure 7-25. This allows you to change the properties of an entire row at one time. The changes apply only to the row where the cursor is currently located. You can specify the Vertical Alignment (Unspecified, TOP, MIDDLE or BOTTOM) or the Horizontal Alignment (Unspecified, LEFT CENTER JUSTIFY or RIGHT). You can also specify that the cells in the row not wrap text by checking the NoWrap check box.
Edit Table	Displays the Edit Table dialog box as shown in Figure 7-26. This dialog box contains two sections. The top section lets you choose buttons that extend or contract the boundary of the current cell by one grid cell in the direction of the arrow on the button. The merged cell (the one in the direction of the arrow) must be empty. The lower section allows you to choose buttons that let you insert rows above or below the current row or insert columns to the left or right of the current column. You can also choose to delete a row or column.

Table 7-3: *Table editing options.*

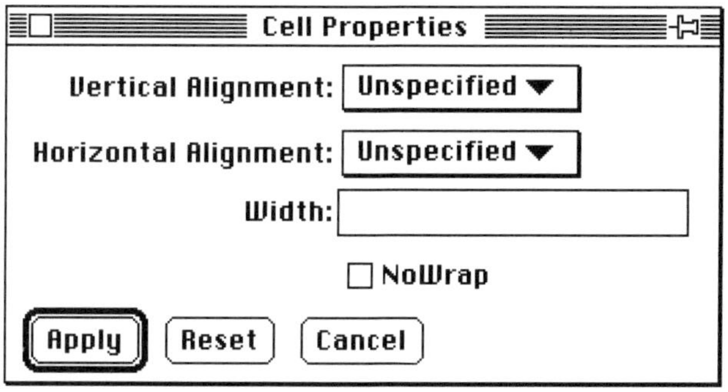

Cell Properties

Vertical Alignment: Unspecified

Horizontal Alignment: Unspecified

Width:

NoWrap

Apply Reset Cancel

Figure 7-24: *The Cell Properties dialog box.*

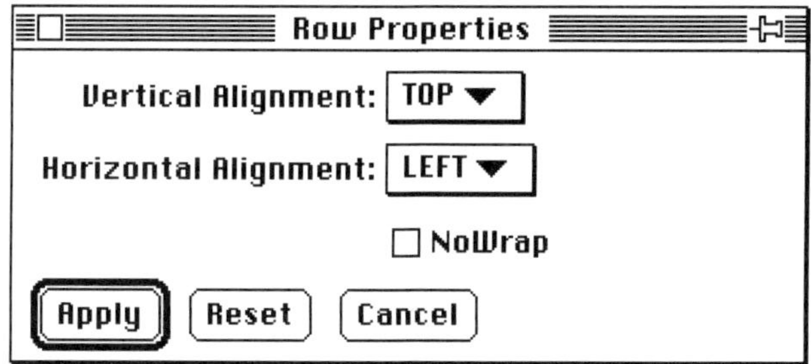

Figure 7-25: *The Row Properties dialog box.*

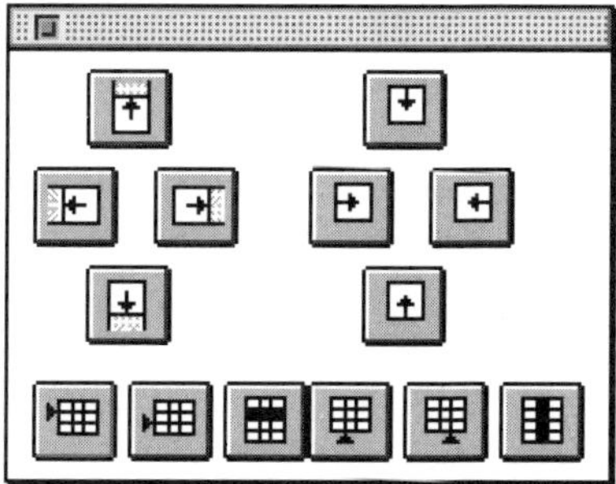

Figure 7-26: *The Edit Table dialog box.*

Sample Tables

Netscape and Mosaic browsers both support tables and can render tables with 3D borders. The following table takes advantage of HoTMetaL PRO's table tags. This code matches the results displayed in Figure 7-27. Table 7-4 on pages 172–173 lists and describes the tags used to create tables. Remember you can find the code for the tables presented in this chapter on the Companion CD-ROM.

CD-ROM

```
<!DOCTYPE HTML PUBLIC "-//SQ//DTD HTML 2.0 HoTMetaL
+ extensions//EN">
<HTML><HEAD><TITLE>Table Test Page</TITLE></HEAD>
<BODY><H1>Sample Table 1</H1>
<TABLE BORDER="2"><CAPTION>Sales Figures for 1995</
CAPTION>
<TR ALIGN="LEFT" VALIGN="TOP"><TD COLSTART="1"></
TD>
<TD COLSTART="2">Eastern Region</TD>
<TD COLSTART="3">Central Region</TD>
<TD COLSTART="4">Western Region</TD></TR>
<TR><TD COLSTART="1">January</TD>
<TD COLSTART="2">2345.44</TD>
<TD COLSTART="3">1120.33</TD>
<TD COLSTART="4">1436.35</TD></TR>
<TR><TD COLSTART="1">February</TD>
<TD COLSTART="2">5300.00</TD>
<TD COLSTART="3">1923.33</TD>
<TD COLSTART="4">1212.33</TD></TR>
<TR><TD COLSTART="1">March</TD>
<TD COLSTART="2">2343.22</TD>
<TD COLSTART="3">1232.10</TD>
<TD COLSTART="4">1123.53</TD></TR>
<TR><TD COLSTART="1">April</TD>
<TD COLSTART="2">2345.10</TD>
<TD COLSTART="3">1750.50</TD>
<TD COLSTART="4">1565.35</TD></TR>
<TR><TD COLSTART="1">May</TD>
<TD COLSTART="2">5434.22</TD>
<TD COLSTART="3">1654.30</TD>
```

```
<TD COLSTART="4">1110.40</TD></TR>
</TABLE>
</BODY></HTML>
```

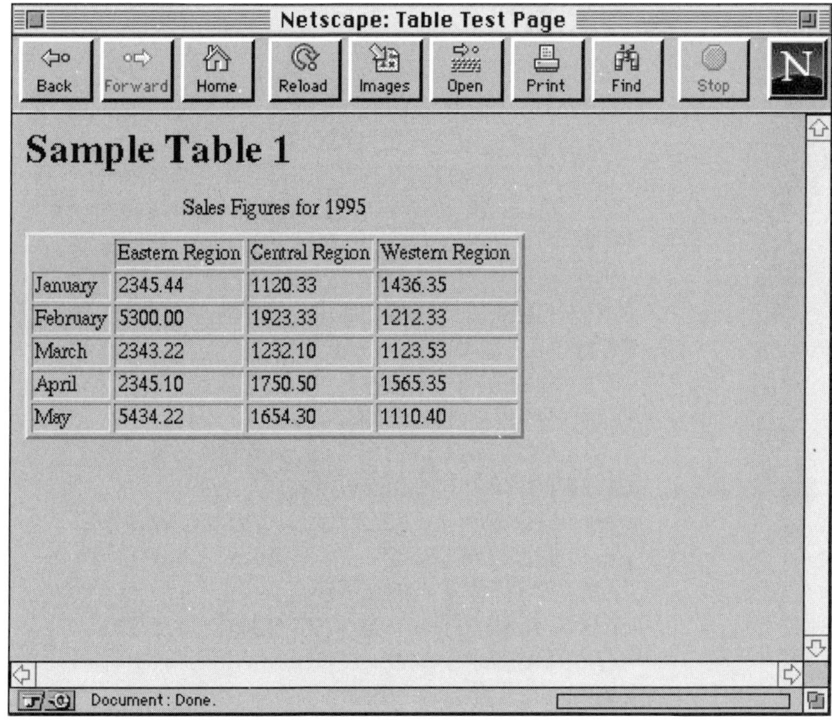

	Eastern Region	Central Region	Western Region
January	2345.44	1120.33	1436.35
February	5300.00	1923.33	1212.33
March	2343.22	1232.10	1123.53
April	2345.10	1750.50	1565.35
May	5434.22	1654.30	1110.40

Figure 7-27: *A simple table created using Netscape.*

The following is a more complex example. This table builds on the previous example by including row and column spanning. To create this table, first add an additional row for the new subheads, just beneath the regional titles. To do that, use the Edit Table dialog box to add a new row. Then use the Edit Table dialog box to add new columns to the right of each sales column. Finally, use the Edit Table dialog box to change the regional titles in the top row to each span two adjacent columns by merging them with the empty column to the right. Now fill in the Verified data elements in your new rows. Figure 7-28 shows the results of the following HTML code.

```
<!DOCTYPE HTML PUBLIC "-//SQ//DTD HTML 2.0 HoTMetaL
+ extensions//EN">
<HTML><HEAD><TITLE>Table Test Page</TITLE></HEAD>
<BODY><H1>Sample Table 2</H1>
<TABLE BORDER="2"><CAPTION>Sales Figures for 1995</
CAPTION>
<TR ALIGN="LEFT" VALIGN="TOP"><TD COLSTART="1"></
TD>
<TD COLSTART="2" COLSPAN="2">Eastern Region</TD>
<TD COLSTART="4" COLSPAN="2">Central Region</TD>
<TD COLSTART="6" COLSPAN="2">Western Region</TD></
TR>
<TR><TD COLSTART="1"></TD>
<TD COLSTART="2">Sales</TD><TD
COLSTART="3">Verified</TD>
<TD COLSTART="4">Sales</TD><TD
COLSTART="5">Verified</TD>
<TD COLSTART="6">Sales</TD><TD
COLSTART="7">Verified</TD></TR>
<TR><TD COLSTART="1">January</TD>
<TD COLSTART="2">2345.44</TD><TD
COLSTART="3">No</TD>
<TD COLSTART="4">1120.33</TD><TD
COLSTART="5">No</TD>
<TD COLSTART="6">1436.35</TD><TD
COLSTART="7">No</TD></TR>
<TR><TD COLSTART="1">February</TD>
<TD COLSTART="2">5300.00</TD><TD
COLSTART="3">No</TD>
<TD COLSTART="4">1923.33</TD><TD
COLSTART="5">No</TD>
<TD COLSTART="6">1212.33</TD><TD
COLSTART="7">No</TD></TR>
<TR><TD COLSTART="1">March</TD>
<TD COLSTART="2">2343.22</TD><TD
COLSTART="3">Yes</TD>
<TD COLSTART="4">1232.10</TD><TD
COLSTART="5">Yes</TD>
<TD COLSTART="6">1123.53</TD><TD
```

```
COLSTART="7">Yes</TD></TR>
<TR><TD COLSTART="1">April</TD>
<TD COLSTART="2">2345.10</TD><TD
COLSTART="3">No</TD>
<TD COLSTART="4">1750.50</TD><TD
COLSTART="5">Yes</TD>
<TD COLSTART="6">1565.35</TD><TD
COLSTART="7">Yes</TD></TR>
<TR><TD COLSTART="1">May</TD>
<TD COLSTART="2">5434.22</TD><TD
COLSTART="3">Yes</TD>
<TD COLSTART="4">1654.30</TD><TD
COLSTART="5">Yes</TD>
<TD COLSTART="6">1110.40</TD><TD
COLSTART="7">Yes</TD></TR>
</TABLE>
</BODY></HTML>
```

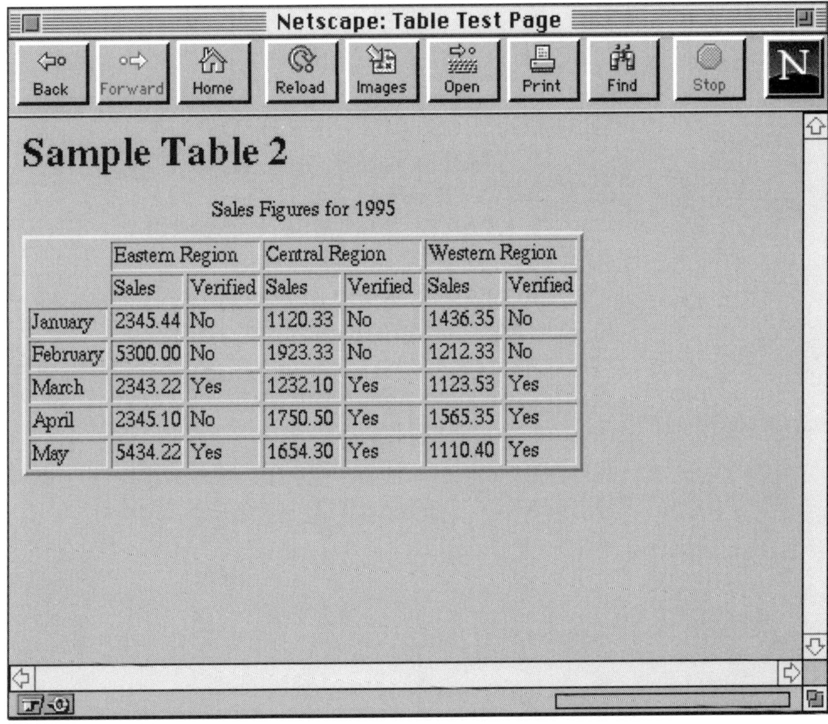

Figure 7-28: *A sample table showing row and column spanning.*

The third and last example builds on the previous example, adding some finishing touches by centering the table, aligning the caption at the bottom of the table and including a larger border with cell padding and cell spacing. It also centers the regional titles in their row, using the Markup>>Now Properties dialog box. Figure 7-29 shows the results of the following HTML code.

```
<!DOCTYPE HTML PUBLIC "-//SQ//DTD HTML 2.0 HoTMetaL
+ extensions//EN">
<HTML><HEAD><TITLE>Table Test Page</TITLE></HEAD>
<BODY><H1>Sample Table 3</H1>
<CENTER>
<TABLE BORDER="8" CELLPADDING="4" CELLSPACING="4"
ALIGN="CENTER">
<CAPTION ALIGN="BOTTOM">Sales Figures for 1995</
CAPTION>
<TR ALIGN="CENTER" VALIGN="MIDDLE"><TD
COLSTART="1"></TD>
<TD COLSTART="2" COLSPAN="2">Eastern Region</TD>
<TD COLSTART="4" COLSPAN="2">Central Region</TD>
<TD COLSTART="6" COLSPAN="2">Western Region</TD></
TR>
<TR><TD COLSTART="1"></TD>
<TD COLSTART="2">Sales</TD><TD
COLSTART="3">Verified</TD>
<TD COLSTART="4">Sales</TD><TD
COLSTART="5">Verified</TD>
<TD COLSTART="6">Sales</TD><TD
COLSTART="7">Verified</TD></TR>
<TR><TD COLSTART="1">January</TD>
<TD COLSTART="2">2345.44</TD><TD
COLSTART="3">No</TD>
<TD COLSTART="4">1120.33</TD><TD
COLSTART="5">No</TD>
```

```
<TD COLSTART="6">1436.35</TD><TD
COLSTART="7">No</TD></TR>
<TR><TD COLSTART="1">February</TD>
<TD COLSTART="2">5300.00</TD><TD
COLSTART="3">No</TD>
<TD COLSTART="4">1923.33</TD><TD
COLSTART="5">No</TD>
<TD COLSTART="6">1212.33</TD><TD
COLSTART="7">No</TD></TR>
<TR><TD COLSTART="1">March</TD>
<TD COLSTART="2">2343.22</TD><TD
COLSTART="3">Yes</TD>
<TD COLSTART="4">1232.10</TD><TD
COLSTART="5">Yes</TD>
<TD COLSTART="6">1123.53</TD><TD
COLSTART="7">Yes</TD></TR>
<TR><TD COLSTART="1">April</TD>
<TD COLSTART="2">2345.10</TD><TD
COLSTART="3">No</TD>
<TD COLSTART="4">1750.50</TD><TD
COLSTART="5">Yes</TD>
<TD COLSTART="6">1565.35</TD><TD
COLSTART="7">Yes</TD></TR>
<TR><TD COLSTART="1">May</TD>
<TD COLSTART="2">5434.22</TD><TD
COLSTART="3">Yes</TD>
<TD COLSTART="4">1654.30</TD><TD
COLSTART="5">Yes</TD>
<TD COLSTART="6">1110.40</TD><TD
COLSTART="7">Yes</TD></TR>
</TABLE>
</CENTER>
</BODY></HTML>
```

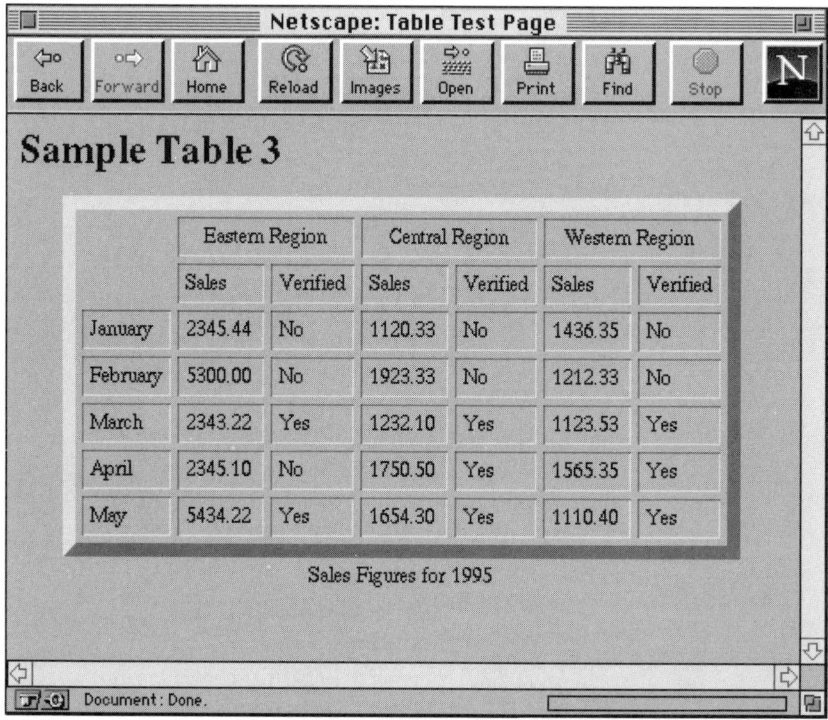

	Eastern Region		Central Region		Western Region	
	Sales	Verified	Sales	Verified	Sales	Verified
January	2345.44	No	1120.33	No	1436.35	No
February	5300.00	No	1923.33	No	1212.33	No
March	2343.22	Yes	1232.10	Yes	1123.53	Yes
April	2345.10	No	1750.50	Yes	1565.35	Yes
May	5434.22	Yes	1654.30	Yes	1110.40	Yes

Sales Figures for 1995

Figure 7-29: *A table centered with a large border and cell spacing and cell padding.*

Tag	Description
</TABLE>	Specifies the beginning (<TABLE>) and ending (</TABLE>) of the table. If the BORDER attribute is added, as it is in the previous examples, then Mosaic displays the table with a border. Netscape adds three attributes to the Table tag: CELLSPACING, CELLPADDING and WIDTH. The CELLSPACING attribute lets you specify the amount of space inserted between the cells in a table. The CELLPADDING attribute lets you specify the amount of space between the border of a cell and the contents of the cell. The WIDTH attribute lets you specify the width of the table in pixels. The WIDTH attribute can also be used with the TH and TD tags to specify the width of a cell.

</CAPTION>	Adds a caption or heading for the table. The caption for the sample Table 1 is "Sales Figures for 1995." The ALIGN=BOTTOM attribute lets you position the caption directly underneath the table.
</TR>	Begins and ends a Table Row. Two attributes let you position the row. HALIGN determines the horizontal alignment and VALIGN determines the vertical alignment. The rows in the sample table are all set to HALIGN=RIGHT. The other HALIGN options are LEFT and CENTER. The VALIGN options are TOP, MIDDLE and BOTTOM.
</TH>	Specifies the Table Header cell. You can specify the horizontal alignment (HALIGN) and the vertical alignment (VALIGN). The available alignment attribute settings are the same as the TR tag. In addition to the alignment attributes you can also specify the number of columns (COLSPAN=*n*) or rows (ROWSPAN=*n*) a cell spans. In order to specify the number of columns or rows to span, you need to use the Markup>>Cell Spans menu item. You can view the COLSPAN or ROWSPAN setting by choosing the View>>Show Link and Context View. You can manually edit the COLSPAN or ROWSPAN attribute settings by using the Markup>>Edit SGML Attributes. Another option that is not yet available from HoTMetaL PRO menus is to turn off word wrapping in a cell using the NOWRAP attribute. By default the table header cell's text is bold and centered. Attributes specified by the TH tag take precedence over the default alignment set in the TR (Table Row) tag. (Note: Be careful when editing tables. Changing COLSPAN or ROWSPAN could cause HoTMetal PRO to be unable to display the table in graphical form.)
</TD>	Begins and ends each cell's table data. Table data can use all the alignment attributes available to the TH tag. By default text is left aligned and vertically centered. Attributes specified by the TD tag take precedence over the default alignment set in the TR (Table Row) tag.

Table 7-4: *Table tags.*

Entering Equations

Equations are not yet directly supported by the current version of HTML or by other widely used browsers. To put an equation in your text, you need to convert the equation to a bitmap and include it with your text as an inline image.

Entering equations is simplified when you use Word as your authoring tool. Whenever you want to use an equation, enter it with the Microsoft Equation Editor. Save the file as an RTF file, then use the RTF to HTML converter. The converter saves all the equations (as well as other images) as PICT images and inserts references to GIF files in the text. Use a graphics program, such as Photoshop, to convert the PICT graphics files into GIF files. The Web browser will pick up the GIF graphics files for all the equations. Check out Chapter 8 for more information about graphic programs files and conversions.

Moving On

You can create professional looking pages with the text elements you've learned about in this chapter. And with HoTMetaL PRO you have a jump start on getting the work done quickly. But to really capture your audience you'll want to mix text with images. The next chapter reveals how to effectively add images to the text components to create even more effective and more powerful Web pages.

8 Getting Graphic With Images

No matter how impressive your message, people respond best to images. The reader's eye is naturally drawn to a picture before text, and the choice and quality of the images you use will largely determine whether someone will take the time to read your Web page or pass it by. Much of the Web's success is due to its ability to include graphic images. Cliché though it may be, a picture *is* worth a thousand words. Because images are so important to publishing on the Internet, you need to to take the time to master the tags and graphics editing options necessary to include graphics.

Graphics is one of the richest fields of computing. Tools abound to help you create and present eye-catching images. This chapter covers creating and working with images in the GIF and JPEG graphics formats and points out the benefits and problems that those file formats present to a Web publisher. This chapter also covers one of the most important aspects of graphics on the Web: the ability to create interactive graphic images with image maps.

HoTMetaL PRO & Images

HoTMetaL PRO includes commands for previewing and working with images. Many of the commands that control viewing inline images can be found in HoTMetaL PRO's View menu. By default, the View menu displays the Show Inline Images option. This option toggles to Hide Inline images, which shows only the IMG tag used to include inline images in your Web pages.

You can open a graphic file in an editor when previewing a page by pointing HoTMetaL PRO to a graphic editor program. This way you can easily display and edit the images in your HTML document. To view the picture from HoTMetaL PRO, choose View>>Show Image. This command works if HoTMetaL PRO can display the image in your document.

When you select View>>Show Image, HoTMetaL PRO will display an image viewer selection dialog box, similar to the Browser selection dialog box you saw earlier, if you have not already chosen an image viewer. If you don't have an image viewer already, you may want to use JPEGView, a shareware

viewer that is on the Companion Disk. To do that, use the dialog box to navigate to the folder where you've stored JPEGView and select it. HoTMetaL PRO will ask you to confirm that you wish to use this as your viewer for the selected image.

This will point HoTMetaL PRO to your JPEGView application. If you have a more powerful commercial editor, such as Adobe Photoshop, you can easily select it instead, using the same navigational technique.

Once you have selected and confirmed the choice of a viewer, HoTMetaL PRO will launch the viewer application and pass the image file location to it. You can then view and edit the file.

Graphics Formats

There's a world of graphics file formats, but to publish on the Internet you have to concentrate on just two main types, Graphics Interchange Format (GIF) and Joint Photographic Experts Group (JPEG). It's easy for browsers to be set up to include other formats, such as Tagged Image File Format (TIFF) and Encapsulated PostScript (EPS), but most Web documents contain only GIF files and point to larger, high-resolution files in the JPEG format.

The Lowdown on the GIF Format

The GIF format was created by CompuServe to provide a way to quickly exchange graphics image files over phone lines. GIF files are stored in a compressed format so that the time to download graphics files is minimal. GIF files support indexed color image types, as well as line art and grayscale images. A major benefit of GIF files is that they can be displayed on UNIX, Macintosh and Windows platforms.

There are two types of GIF file formats: GIF89a and GIF87a. GIF89a includes a transparency index that causes the background color of the display to remain unchanged for the color indexed as transparent. Interlaced images means the image can be progressively displayed. When an interlaced file is downloaded, it appears with a "venetian-blind" effect. Interlaced files let the user begin viewing the rest of the document while the GIF image is downloading. Interlaced GIF files are supported by both NCSA Mosaic (version 2.0) and Netscape Navigator. Unfortunately, some graphics editors don't support both GIF formats. Even Adobe Photoshop, powerhouse that it is, only produces GIF87a format. However, the Transparency application, which is included on the Companion CD-ROM, allows you to set a tranparency index for an existing GIF image and save the image in GIF89a format. (You'll read about creating transparent images with Transparency later in this chapter.)

CD-ROM

The GIF LZW Controversy

In December 1994, a controversy arose over the GIF file format. The controversy started because CompuServe and Unisys, the two companies that own the rights to the GIF file format, decided to start charging developers for products that include GIF support. Until that announcement, the GIF format was treated as a public-domain standard—although it really wasn't. The GIF file format uses LZW compression. LZW comes from the names Lempel, Ziv and Welch. Lempel and Ziv were mathematicians who were originators of several compression schemes. Welch later added his input to Lempel and Ziv's compression algorithm. Unisys, a large networking and information management company, owns the patent for LZW and is requiring licensing for all software developers (*not* end users) using LZW compression. CompuServe Information Services has provided an optional licensing agreement that CompuServe-related software developers can enter into, instead of dealing with Unisys directly. Software developers whose software is not "primarily for use with the CompuServe Information Service" will have to obtain a license from Unisys. CompuServe is licensing the use of LZW in GIF products for 1.5 percent of the product's selling cost. Of the 1.5 percent, 1 percent goes to Unisys. Unfortunately this has caused a lot of confusion and has been a stumbling block to many software vendors. If you want to follow up on this controversy, check out Unisys at http://www.unisys.com/ and CompuServe's Web site at www.compuserve.com/ or Yahoo's collection of GIF links at http://www.yahoo.com/Computers/Software/Data_Formats/GIF/.

CompuServe has proposed a new standard called GIF24 as a successor to the GIF89a specification. GIF24 ups the ante on GIF by supporting 24-bit images. A file format named PNG is being used as the basis for GIF24. PNG uses a compression technology called "deflation" that is used in many freeware programs. It was developed to be a free and open standard. You can check out the draft of the PNG specification at Thomas Boutell's Web server at http://sunsite.unc.edu/boutell/png.html.

The Lowdown on the JPEG Format

JPEG is the standard of choice because of its high resolution and high compression. Many graphics editors, such as Adobe Photoshop, let you choose a quality setting for the compression. High quality is less compressed, with a ratio of about 5:1 to 15:1. JPEG images are decompressed automatically when they are loaded into the browser. JPEG reduces image files to about 10 percent or less of their original size.

The JPEG algorithm is referred to as *lossy*, meaning that some data is lost. JPEG identifies and ignores pixels that are not essential to the overall quality of the image, such as a large area of a single color. Typically, the absence of subtracted information is not noticeable. Once an image is compressed using JPEG, it loses some information, so the image file will be much smaller and yet will, hopefully, appear indistinguishable from the original image. Another advantage of JPEG is that it's directly supported in PostScript Level 2 printing and display devices. PostScript has long been a standard on the Internet. When a JPEG-compressed image is sent to a PostScript Level 2 printer with the proper commands, the file is sent to the printer where it is decompressed and rendered. Unlike GIF, JPEG supports 24-bit color. JPEG, unfortunately, doesn't support interlacing.

Including Inline Images

An inline image is an image that is displayed without the help of an external helper application. Netscape and Mosaic both support inline images in GIF and JPEG formats. The IMG tag <IMG> is used to insert graphic image files. Inserting an image in your document using HoTMetaL PRO is as easy as choosing Markup>> Insert Element and choosing the IMG element from the Insert Elements dialog box. There is no limit to the number of inline images you can use in a document.

Providing Alternative Text for an Image

Not everyone can view or chooses to view inline images. Many people who have modem connections turn off inline images to receive information faster. To address people accessing your page using a text-based browser, such as Lynx, be sure to include alternative text to clue them in to what they can't see. To add alternative text, move the insertion point in the IMG tag and choose the Markup>>Edit SGML Attributes. This displays the Edit Attributes dialog box, shown in Figure 8-1, which includes the Alternative (ALT) attribute. In the ALT attribute field, enter the text you want displayed where the image occurs.

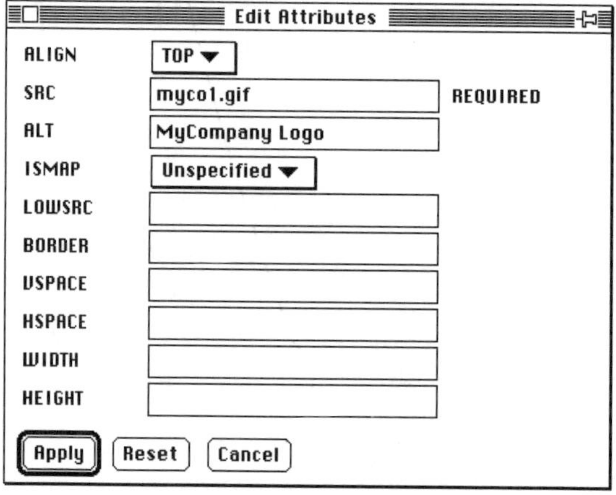

Figure 8-1: *The Edit Attributes dialog box includes the ALT field for specifying alternative text for text-based Web browsers.*

Making an Inline Image a Hyperlink

Any inline image can also be used as a hyperlink to another HTML document or file. When you insert an image tag in the hypertext part of the anchor, a border is displayed around the outside of the image. The following example displays an image named acwlp.gif as a hyperlink:

```
<A HREF = "store_info.html"><IMG SRC = "acwlp.gif"></A>
```

Clicking the image lets the user jump to an HTML document named store_info.html. Figure 8-2 shows an inline image that's also a hyperlink.

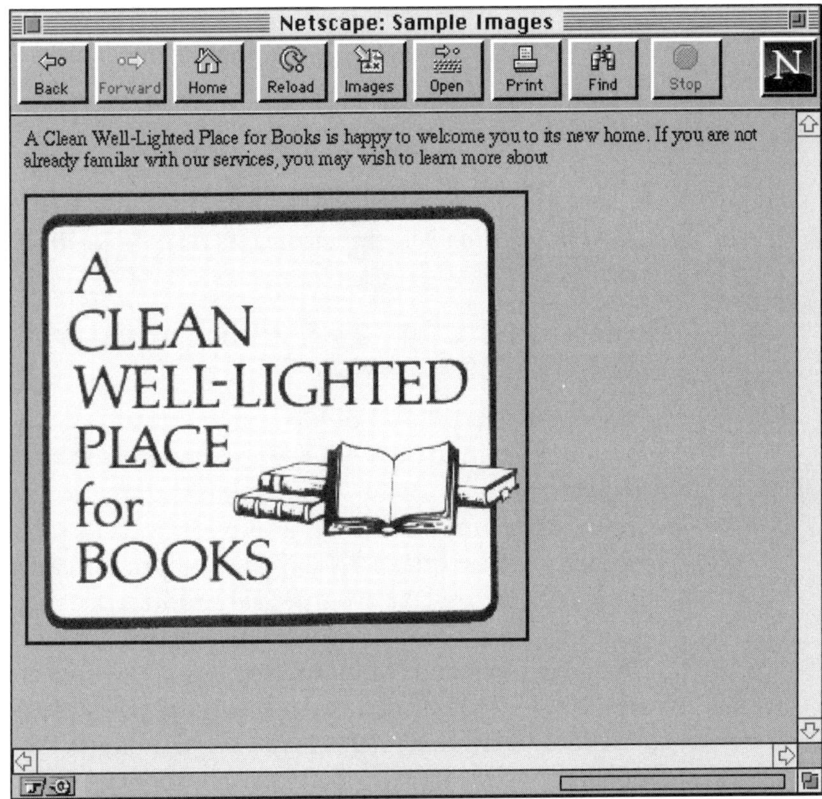

Figure 8-2: *An inline image can also be a hyperlink. The outline around the image indicates it's a hyperlink.*

Acquiring Graphic Image Files

Adding images to your Web pages can give them a polished, professional look, thereby making a strong statement about you and your company. The biggest hurdle in creating a Web page, however, is acquiring and editing images to add to your page. If you're creating a Web site for your business, you may want to hire a desktop publisher to scan or create pictures for your page. Even if you have the graphics tools, there's a long learning curve to becoming a graphic artist.

To add an inline image, you'll need to create a GIF image, which requires a bitmap editing program like Adobe Photoshop; have access to an existing GIF image; or acquire an image with a scanner.

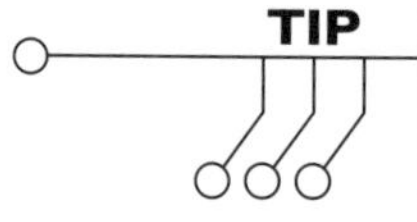

If you want to present a Web page for your business, consider using digitized photos rather than illustrations. Readers tend to show more trust in photographic images than in illustrations.

Professional Clip Art & Photo Images

Commercial clip art and photo images are everywhere. Clip art and photos seem to be the most popular add-on for most graphics and multimedia programs. Many application packages include samples from various clip-art and photo vendors. Be aware, however, that the quality of clip art and photos can vary dramatically. Just because it's a commercial product doesn't mean that it belongs in the professional-quality category.

Image Club is one company that has always stood out as a leader in the professional-quality clip-art category. Image Club also offers affordable professional photo images. Another company that offers impressive digital photos is CMCD, an offshoot of Clemont Mok's design firm. A trend in photo images is to use single, everyday objects as metaphors. You can check out CMCD's latest releases of everyday objects at http://www.cmdesigns.com.

Keep in mind that there's no standard format for clip-art and photo files. For example, Image Club's graphics are in EPS format, while CMCD ships photos in Kodak's PhotoCD format. The

Companion CD-ROM contains image samples from Image Club and CMCD. Check the back of the book for other sources of clip art and photos.

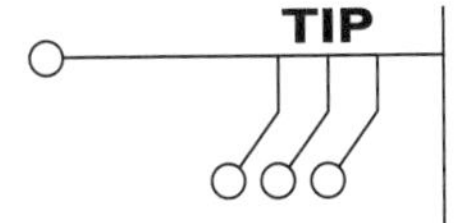

Don't mix different types of graphic images. Black-and-white illustrations, color photos and clip art all have definite looks and moods. Choose images carefully, so that the images complement your document's message. Using black-and-white illustrations and color photos on the same page may leave readers with a mixed message and will most likely leave readers cold.

Scanning Images

One way to acquire an image is to scan an existing picture or photo. Scanning images is dangerous. If you scan a photo from a magazine or other publication, most likely you're infringing on someone's copyright. It's much safer to create your own images or purchase royalty-free images. Many copy centers and service bureaus will scan your logos or pictures for a small fee. If you plan to have your own Web site, you might want to consider purchasing a color flatbed scanner, such as a Hewlett Packard LaserJet IIIc.

If you would like more information on copyrights, Thomson & Thomson, a trademark and copyright research firm that provides some helpful resources on copyrights, is located at http://www.thomson.com/thomthom/resmain.html. A copyright FAQ is also available at http://www.cis.ohio-state.edu/hypertext/faq/usenet/Copyright-FAQ/top.html. You can also check the U. S. Copyright Office, a department of the Library of Congress at gopher://marvel.loc.gov/11/copyright.

Free Images at Web Sites

There are thousands of GIF files on the Internet. Several sites on the Web include free images you can use to create your Web documents. You can get collections of decorative elements, such as bullets, icons and line drawings that enhance the appearance of your Web document. You simply download the files to your system. Because GIF images are internally compressed, you don't need a decompression program. The viewer or paint program you use to display the image will automatically decompress the GIF file. Collections of clip art may be stored in BinHex or MacBinary

format and may be compressed. To help you expand compressed files, check out the version of Stuffit Expander included on the Companion CD-ROM. Stuffit Expander works both stand-alone and with browsers to decompress a wide variety of files on the fly. Table 8-1 lists some sites that include graphic images, including bullets, icons and lines.

URL	Contents
http://www.yahoo.com/yahoo/computers/multimedia/pictures	A great inventory of picture files.
http://www.yahoo.com/Computers/World_Wide_Web/Programming/Icons/	A huge listing of icons and clip-art links.
http://www.idb.hist.no/~geirme/gizmos/gizmo.html	GIF images, icons, buttons, bullets and lines, plus links to other resource archives.
http://inls.ucsd.edu/y/OhBoy/icons.html	GIF images, icons, bullets and lines.
http://ns2.rutgers.edu/doc-images/small_buttons/	Standard GIF icons.
http://white.nosc.mil/images.html	Space, travel, medical and other images, plus links to other resource sites.
http://www-ns.rutgers.edu/doc-images/icons/	Standard GIF bullets.
http://www.cit.gu.edu.au/~anthony/icons/	Standard GIF icons.
http://www.cs.yale.edu/homes/sjl/clipart.html	Pointers to archives filled with clip art.
http://www.di.unipi.it/iconbrowser/icons.html	A large collection of icons.

Table 8-1: *URLs for image collections.*

Images & Copyrights

Publishing on the Web carries with it the same restrictions as traditional publishing. You're still subject to copyright and trademark laws. Be careful of what you use in your document. Many files are available that break copyright restrictions; just because they're available at a site doesn't mean you have the legal right to publish them in your document.

Image Editing Fundamentals

While graphics editors let you convert, trim, apply filters, adjust the number of colors, etc., be warned—mastering bitmap editing programs can be a time-consuming task. If you find a usable image but it needs editing or is in the wrong format, you can use a graphics editor program to edit and save the file in the GIF format. If you want, you can also include other image files, such as JPEG images, that users can view using an external viewer. See the Resources section for information on GIF and JPEG bitmap editing programs.

Graphics Editors & Tools

Editing image files can be a tricky proposition. Several shareware and commercial graphics editors let you create and, to some extent, edit GIF and JPEG images. One of the most popular shareware image converters, which also allows you to do some basic editing, is GraphicConverter. As its name implies, this application is primarily for conversion of images between graphics formats, but it does allow you to manipulate images in basic but useful ways. Version 2.1.2 is included on the Companion CD-ROM. Figure 8-3 shows the GraphicConverter image editor.

CD-ROM

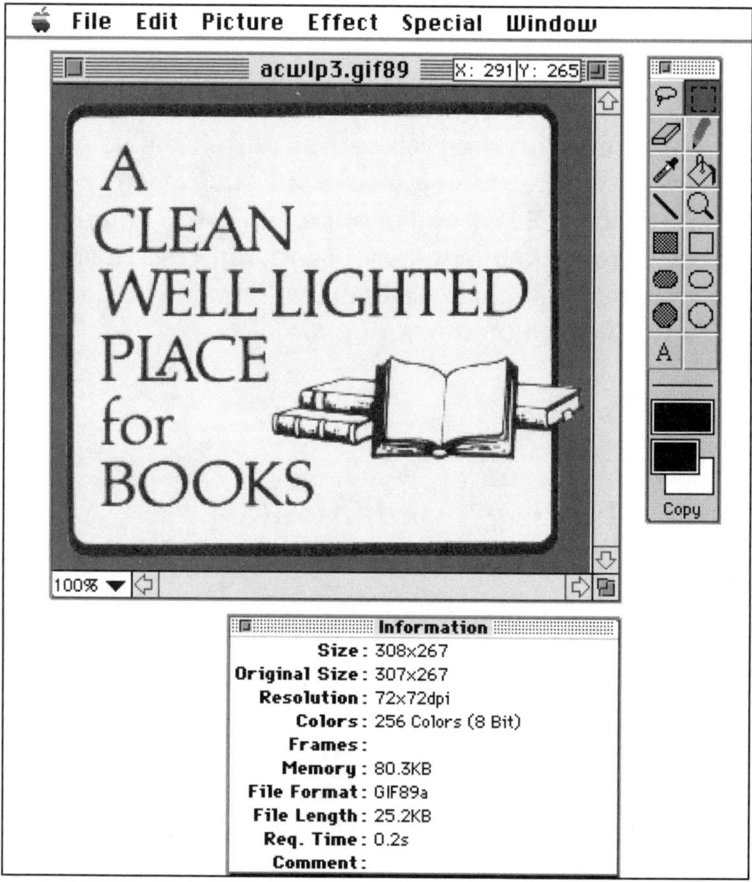

Figure 8-3: *The GraphicConverter image editor.*

A wide range of full-featured commercial graphics editors exist, from low- to high-end. However, anyone planning to work with graphics should also consider purchasing Adobe Photoshop. This is the best image editor we've ever used. While it is expensive, it includes just about every feature you could want in an image editor. Version 3.0 lets you work with layers and add lighting effects. Once you've tried Photoshop, it's hard to go back.

One primary concern when publishing on the Web is to create memorable graphics. Numerous graphics applications and utilities exist that go beyond simple graphics editing. One impressive graphics application is Fractal Design Painter. Painter lets you create images using tools that emulate traditional artist's tools, such as water colors, oil-based paints, charcoal, pastels and so on. We used Painter with the Kurta XGT graphics tablet to produce some marvelous images. Painter includes several other features for creating and editing animations and videos. 3D-rendering applications, such as Adobe Dimensions, are more complex than graphics editors, but they let you work with three-dimensional images to create eye-catching graphics that simulate materials and textures, as well as allowing you to change the lighting to create objects that reflect light and cast shadows. Most 3D-rendering applications can also create and edit animations, which are discussed in the next chapter. Both graphics programs and 3D-rendering applications let you use filter programs, also called *plug-ins*. Kai's Power Tools is probably the best known plug-in that works in conjunction with graphics editors like Adobe Photoshop to create unique special effects. Before you can effectively use a graphics editor and other graphic-related applications and tools, it's important that you understand the basic components of an image and the factors that affect the image's output when published on the Web.

Understanding Pixels & Color Palettes

A *pixel* is the smallest unit of an image. The *pixel-depth* or *bit resolution* refers to a measurement of the number of bits of stored information per pixel. In other words, each pixel is assigned a numeric value to represent a color. The greater the pixel depth, the more colors you have available. GIF files have a color-depth of 8 bits per pixel, for a possible 256 values. GIF files are indexed color images that use a *color palette*. A color palette, sometimes called a color look-up table (CLUT), is a mathematical table that defines the colors of pixels. Like a paint-by-numbers kit, each displayed pixel has a value that matches one of the indexed locations in a palette. For this reason, a palette is sometimes referred to as an *indexed color system*.

Most graphics editors provide a palette tool for displaying available colors. Some image editors let you use a color picker to display or specify a particular color. As we mentioned, the GIF format uses a color palette with up to 256 colors. The colors can be 256 colors out of millions of possibilities. Only one combination of 256 colors can be used at a time. As a Macintosh user, you've probably never had to worry about this—the Macintosh Palette Manager (a portion of the Color QuickDraw software that is part of every recent Macintosh) automatically handles all color transformations as you switch from window to window and maintains individual palettes for each window. However, if you have multiple images in a single window that use conflicting palettes, you may have a problem displaying the images at the same time.

Basically, the Macintosh uses two modes of color display: indexed color, described above, and direct color. The mode you use is determined by the type of color display and video device driver installed on your system. The indexed color mode was created for the original color displays on systems like the Mac II. On those systems, the Macintosh Toolbox uses the indexing system described above. On such systems, you may have color display problems if you use GIFs with multiple, conflicting palettes. The second mode, called *direct color*, removes the need for color indexes, palettes and color lookup tables. When you specify a color to a direct color device, the Macintosh operating system simply passes the color value request directly to the video driver, bypassing any palette or color-indexing scheme. As a result, there is no color conflict, no matter how many colors you use, and no matter whether you have several GIFs with conflicting color requirements on a page. At this time, most Mac systems have video cards that support direct color, so most Mac users don't worry much about color handling.

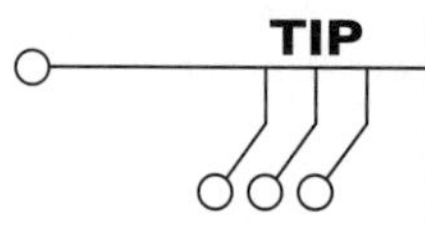

You can quickly check to see if your system uses direct color with this simple test. Open the Monitors Control Panel on your system. If the Monitors Control Panel shows any entries greater than 256 colors, your system uses direct color. If the last entry in the Control Panel is 256, then your system uses indexed colors.

Because color handling is a function of the device driver and not the application or sytem software, even using the Monitors Control Panel to set the number of colors for your display to 256 will not cause the system to use indexed colors. Instead, the system simply limits each image to 256 possible colors, which isn't really the same result at all. As a result, for direct display devices, even this setting will not cause the types of display problems that arise with indexed-color devices. Therefore, you should always be aware of possible problems in display for readers of your pages who are using more limited, indexed systems, such as many UNIX systems and Microsoft Windows.

However, since your Web pages will be seen by people using lots of different platforms, you should understand the limitations of using color images on platforms using indexed color. In particular, Microsoft Windows reserves 20 colors for displaying standard window information, like titles, frames and so on. If you use a palette of 256 colors for one image and use another color palette that includes additional colors not in the other palette, strange colors may flash on the screen while the system creates a new palette and the old colors change to the new palette.

Using more than 256 colors can also distort images. Colors are allocated as they are requested, until 256 colors are used. Any additional graphics displayed onscreen can only use colors that have already been allocated, unless a new color table is used. That's why images may display correctly at the beginning of a Web page but subsequent images will appear distorted. For example, if your page has two images that use more than 256 colors, when the browser displaying your page runs out of colors, the remaining colors will not be created. Instead, the colors closest to those already allocated will be used, which can distort your image.

The best way to keep images distortion-free when displayed is to use the same palette for all images appearing on the same page. Graphics editors let you remap, optimize and customize palettes. JPEG files, on the other hand, support 24-bit color, which gives you up to 16.7 million colors. Using 16-bit and 24-bit images, you don't have to worry about palettes.

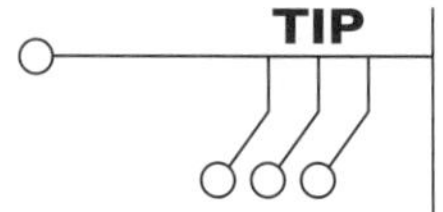

TIP

If you want to edit a color palette, convert the image to RGB (red, green, blue) mode. This gives you more editing options. After editing the graphic image, convert the file to an indexed image type.

Changing Resolutions, Cropping & Resizing Images

It's helpful to understand how resolution affects your image. First, it's important that you don't confuse the two types of resolution: image resolution and monitor resolution. *Image resolution* refers to the spacing of pixels in the image and is measured in pixels per inch (ppi). If the image has a resolution of 96 ppi, it contains 9,216 pixels per square inch (96 x 96 = 9,216). *Monitor resolution* is the number of dots per inch that your monitor uses to display an image. It determines how large or small images appear onscreen. Typically, monitors have a resolution of 72 dpi for displaying graphics.

It's important to keep icons and buttons the same size to give your page a uniform and consistent feel. To maintain one size, you may want to crop your graphics to include only the part of the image you want to show.

Images can be distorted when you change their resolution or size. As we mentioned earlier, most clip art comes in high-resolution format. It's best to edit, resize and crop an image in its original high-resolution format before you convert it to GIF format. You should also make sure that the number of pixels per inch doesn't change when saving a high-resolution image to a different format, otherwise the image will be saved with different dimensions. Be careful when enlarging images in GIF or JPEG format. This usually ends up giving your image the "jaggies." If you do enlarge an image, you'll probably need to edit the image in the enlarged form to get a reasonably good display.

Dithering Images

After you've resized your image and reduced the color depth to 8 bits (256 colors), the next step is to select a dither type. *Dithering* is a process that adjusts the color value of a pixel, based on the color values of adjoining pixels, to the closest matching color value in the target palette. Dithering helps reduce the number of colors needed to display an image by simulating colors. The process of dithering is somewhat complex in calculation, but simple in theory. Suppose, for example, that you have a section of color in your image that is purple, and your current palette contains only two elements: red and blue. Without dithering, each pixel in the purple area would be analyzed and then rendered in (say) blue, which would be the closest match available in the existing palette to the desired color. With dithering, however, the process is more complex, but provides a better match. After the first pixel in the area is analyzed and mapped to a color, the difference between the actual color used and the desired color is taken. The color-mapping process notices that the desired color had some element of red in it that is not represented in the actual color value used, so red is added to the desired values of the surrounding pixels. Now, when the next pixel is analyzed, the desired value falls more on the red side, so that it is rendered in red. Again, the difference is used to adjust the surrounding pixels that have not yet been adjusted, moving them toward blue. This process continues over the entire area, with the result that the area becomes a mix of red and blue pixels. When you look at the image from a distance, your eye integrates mixture into a single area that will look more or less purple. In this way, dithering effectively simulates a color that is not actually present in the palette, giving the appearance of more colors in an image than there really are. This creates a smooth transition between two different colors. Dithering options are built into most image-editing programs. Using various dithers can also extend the range of perceived colors. For example, diffusion dithering, a popular option available in most image editors, randomly positions pixels instead of using a set pattern.

Anti-aliasing Type

When you add text to images, the pixels can create text with jagged edges. These jagged edges are sometimes called *stairsteps* or *the jaggies*. If you want to add text when using a graphics editor, make sure you choose the anti-aliasing option. The anti-aliasing option in image editors helps eliminate the jaggies by making the edges of text appear smooth and blend into the background.

Displaying Type as Graphic Images

HTML doesn't let you specify fonts in Web documents. If you want to present text in a decorative font, you need to use images to display the type. Some graphics editors, such as Adobe Photoshop, include the capability to add text and save the files as a GIF or JPEG graphic image.

Many drawing and paint graphics programs let you add special effects to text. For example, Adobe Photoshop lets you create layered, shadowed, recessed, embossed, glowing and translucent text. Other products, such as Adobe Dimensions, allow you to extrude text elements into three dimensions, change lighting and display features, and wrap text around three-dimensional objects. Figure 8-4 shows a sample of text in the GIF format created using Adobe Photoshop.

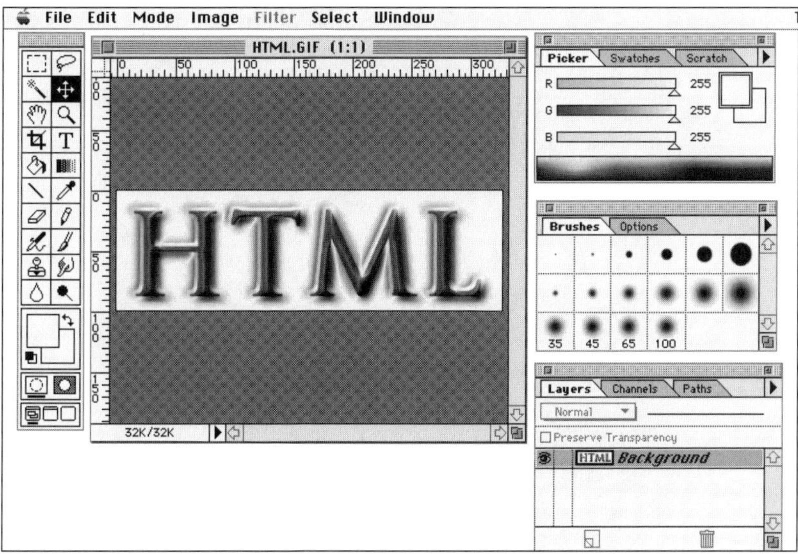

Figure 8-4: *Text created using Adobe Photoshop.*

Converting GIFs to Transparent, Interlaced Images

You can use several methods to create transparent images. A transparent image is sometimes called a floating image because it appears to float on the Web page. Figure 8-5 shows a transparent image with a gray background.

Most clip art and photos don't come in a format ready for Internet publishing. Luckily, converting an image into the GIF or JPEG format is as easy as saving a file. Most graphics editors let you use a Save As option to save files in GIF and JPEG formats. In creating these images, you should consider a couple of important conversion options: *interlacing* and *transparent backgrounds*.

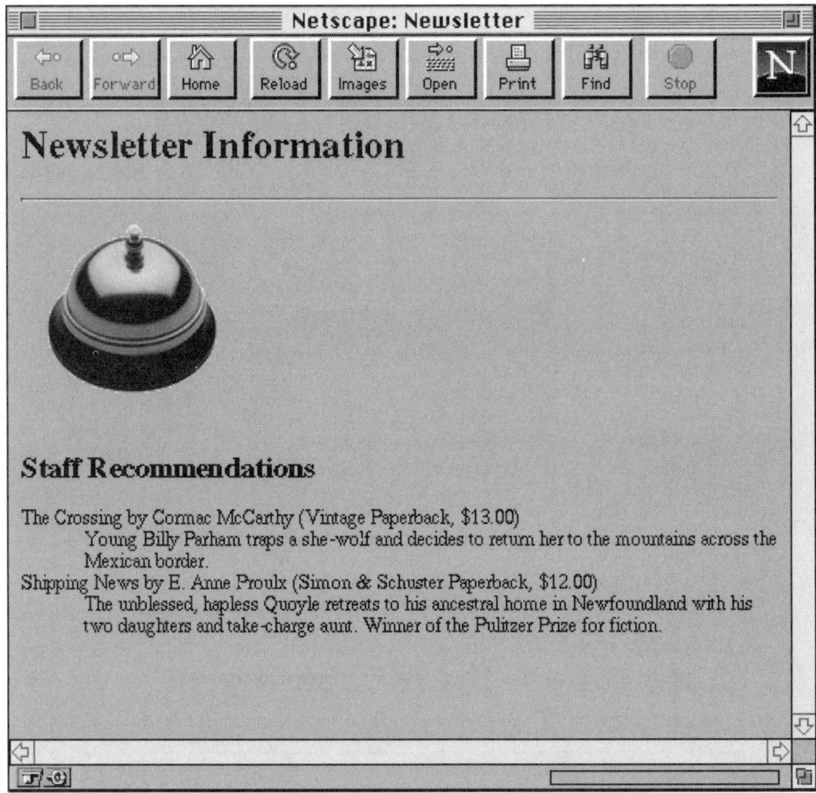

Figure 8-5: *A transparent image shown with a gray background.*

You can interlace GIF images in several ways. It's surprising that many graphics editors don't let you save GIF graphic files in the interlaced format. On the Companion CD-ROM, the program called GraphicConverter automatically saves GIF files as interlaced image files. You can then use Transparency, which is also on the CD-ROM, to make a selected color transparent in the image and save it in GIF89a format. The following sections explain how to determine the background color and describe different ways to create a transparent background and save files in a GIF89a format.

Determining the Background Color

If you don't know what the background is set to, you'll need to display the image and check the background color. You can use any graphics editor to find out the background color. Generally, you don't need to know the exact color to change the background to a transparent value—your eyes will tell you quickly enough what color is in the background. If you want to be more precise, however, you can determine the exact color value for the background. In order to display the background color using Adobe Photoshop, click the color picker (the eye dropper in the floating toolbox) on the background color. The picker's floating palette will display the chosen color. The actual RGB (red, green, blue) values appear next to the color bars displayed in the picker's palette.

Make sure you use a unique color for the background of your image before changing the background to be transparent, or any portion of the picture that shares the background color will also be transparent. For example, if you have an image of a person and convert the picture of a face with a white background, the whites of the eyes and the teeth may also become transparent, which will cause a problem when viewed on a non-white background.

The way to correct for this is to change the background color to a specific, unique color that does not otherwise exist in the image. You can use Photoshop's bucket fill to do this. Simply change the image to RGB mode, select a unique color in the color picker palette, and then fill the background with that color. If any of the color shows where you don't want it, you can use Photoshop's editing tools to remove the color. When you're done, only the parts of the picture that you want to be transparent should be in your special background color. You can also use GraphicConverter's bucket fill tool to do this, but the process takes longer, since the fill process is slower and less accurate.

Creating an Interlaced Image With GraphicConverter

To create a transparent, interlaced image for use in your Web pages, you'll need to transform the image you want to display using two tools included on the Companion CD-ROM. You can do this in two steps. First, use the GraphicConverter application to add interlacing to the image, resize the image, and perform any basic editing that you need. Then make the background color in your image transparent and save the image in GIF89a format, using Transparency.

CD-ROM

The GraphicConverter program, written by Thorsten Lemke, is an image conversion and editing program that lets you change an image from one format to another. If you change your image to a GIF format, you have the option of interlacing it, as well as selecting the GIF format. The following steps explain how to use the GraphicConverter program included on the Companion CD-ROM.

CD-ROM

1. Launch the GraphicConverter application and open the image that you want to edit or convert. The image editing window of GraphicConverter was shown in Figure 8-3.
2. Make any editing changes that you want. It's often helpful to magnify the image to see the exact area that you're working with if you're changing colors.
3. Choose Save As from the File menu.
4. In the Save As dialog box, choose the GIF format from the Format list.
5. Click the Options button to display the GIF options dialog box. The GIF Options dialog box is shown in Figure 8-6.
6. Select 89a for the Version and Interlaced for the Row Order.
7. Click OK to set the options, and then save the file under a new name.

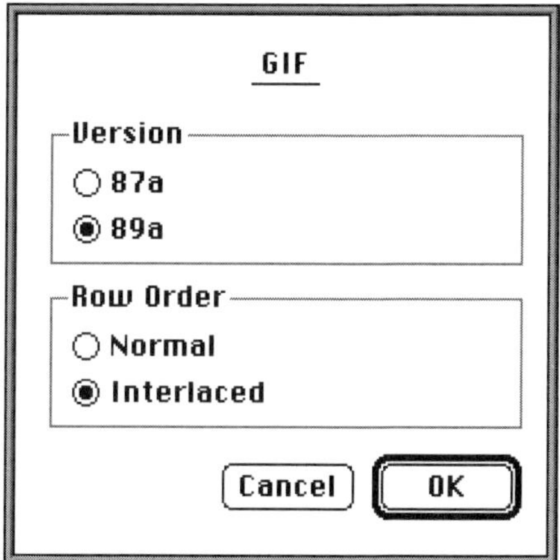

Figure 8-6: *The GraphicConverter GIF Options dialog box lets you set how you want to save your GIF file after editing.*

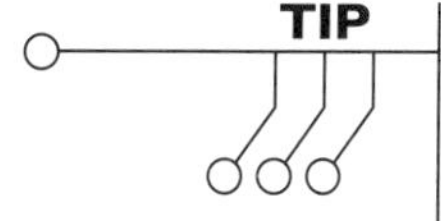

The GraphicConverter program also allows a transparency value for any color in the image. This is done by navigating to the Transparent GIF Settings dialog box (Picture>>Colors>>Transparent GIF Color) and selecting the transparent color in the dialog box. However, this is more difficult and less precise than simply using the Transparency application.

Creating a Transparent Image Using Transparency

The Transparency program lets you create a transparent image from any GIF file and save the file in GIF89a format. The Transparency program is included on the Companion CD-ROM.

Using the Transparency program is simplicity itself.

1. Launch the Transparency application and open the image that you want to edit. The image you have chosen is displayed.
2. Click on the background color in the image. That converts the color to a transparent value.

3. The image will change so that the new transparent value is shown in gray. Verify that the parts of the image to be transparent are now set correctly.
4. If the file is not in GIF89a format, choose Save as GIF89 and save the image under a new name. If the image is already in GIF89 format, simply Close the image and choose Save when asked if you want to save the changes.

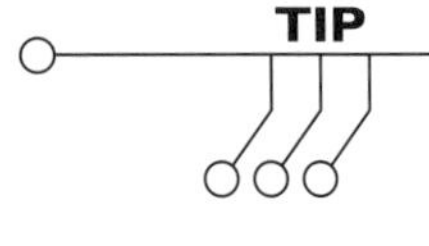

If you hold down the mouse button when you click on the background color in the image, Transparency will display the color palette for your image, with the selected background color selected and displayed under the cursor arrow. This can be helpful if you're not sure that you have chosen the correct color.

Saving Bandwidth by Using Thumbnails

An inline image can only be displayed in a 800 x 600 resolution, whereas an external JPEG image can be in 24-bit format. Say you have a killer 24-bit graphic you want to show off. Don't include the JPEG as an inline image. Instead, present a thumbnail in the GIF format that links to the JPEG image. Clicking the inline image hyperlink automatically opens the JPEG image file in a larger, higher resolution. Figure 8-7 shows a thumbnail image, and Figure 8-8 shows the larger file it points to. To create a thumbnail image that's linked to a larger image, use the Anchor tag. The following is a raw HTML example of a GIF thumbnail file named small.gif linked to display a file named large.jpeg:

```
<A>HREF=large.jpeg><IMG SRC=small.gif></A>
```

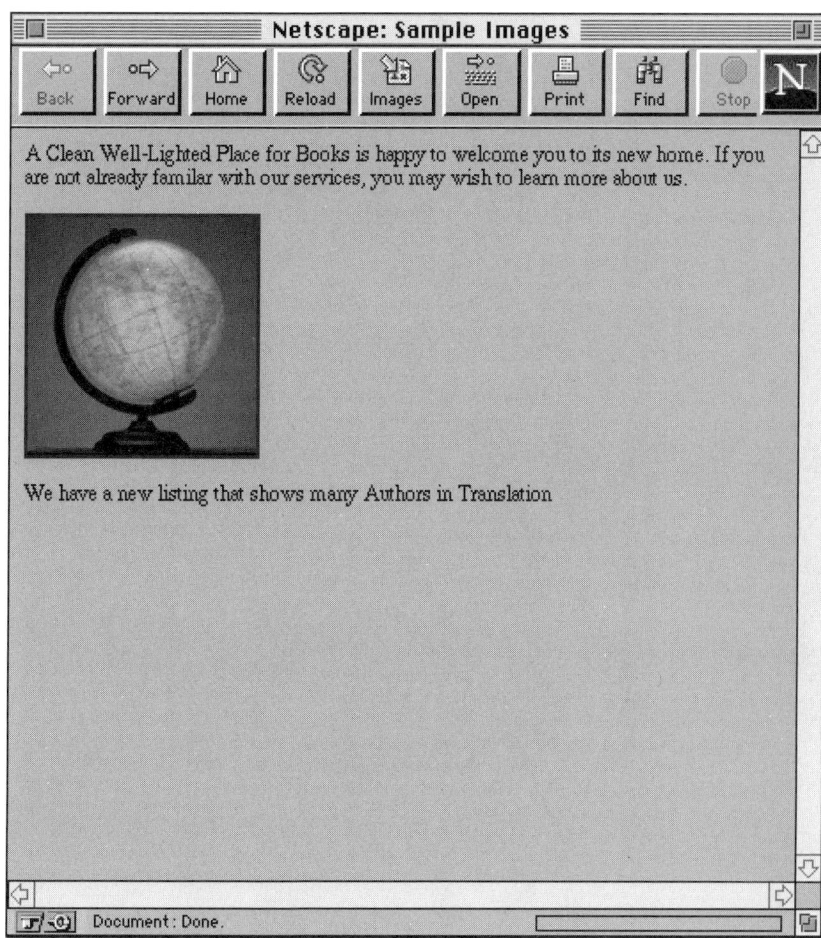

Figure 8-7: *A thumbnail of a globe in a Web page.*

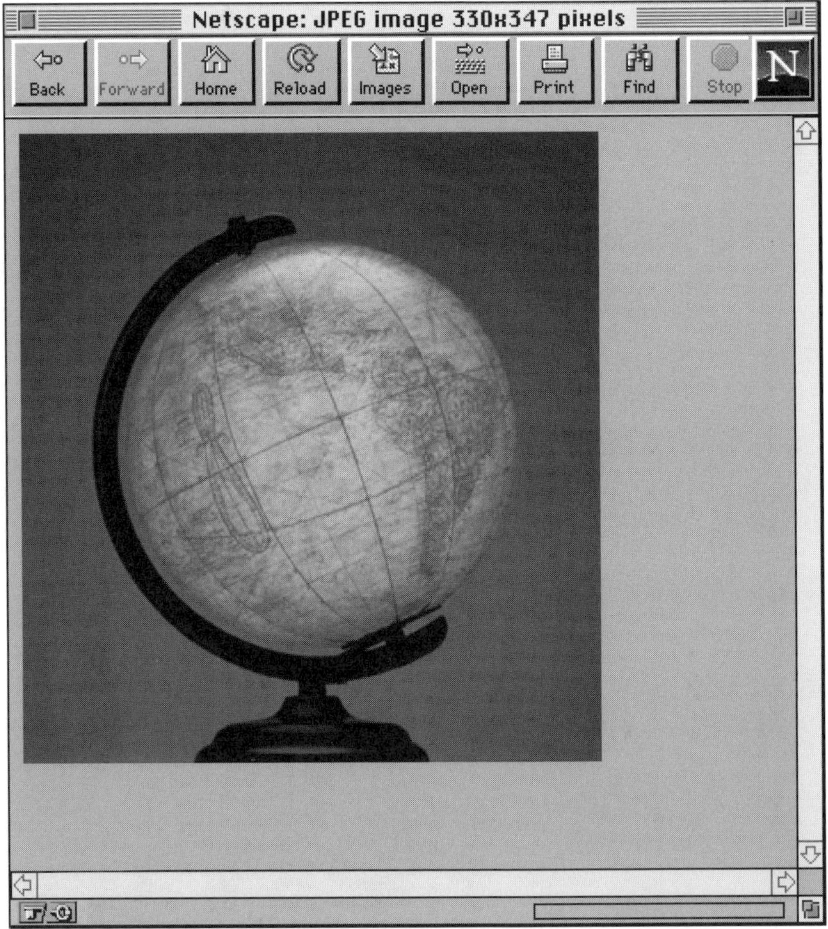

Figure 8-8: *The larger, linked image of the globe.*

Positioning Images

Considering the importance of graphics, it's little wonder that of all the added Netscape tags, the image tag has the most extensions. Several extensions have been added to help you align text and images. Two powerful attribute additions are the "left" and "right" settings. These attribute settings let you align images that

can float in margins. The rest of the align options correct what Marc Andreeson thought were "horrible errors" he made when first implementing the IMG tag.

To align an image using HoTMetaL PRO, move the insertion point between the starting and ending IMG tags and choose the Markup>>Edit SGML Attributes. The Edit Attributes dialog box appears, as shown in Figure 8-9. The raw HTML syntax for the alignment attribute is <IMG ALIGN=*postion*>. Table 8-2 explains the alignment options.

In order to use Netscape extensions with HoTMetaL PRO, you need to make sure the rules setting in the sqhmpro Preferences file is set to the Netscape extensions rules file (html-net.mtl).

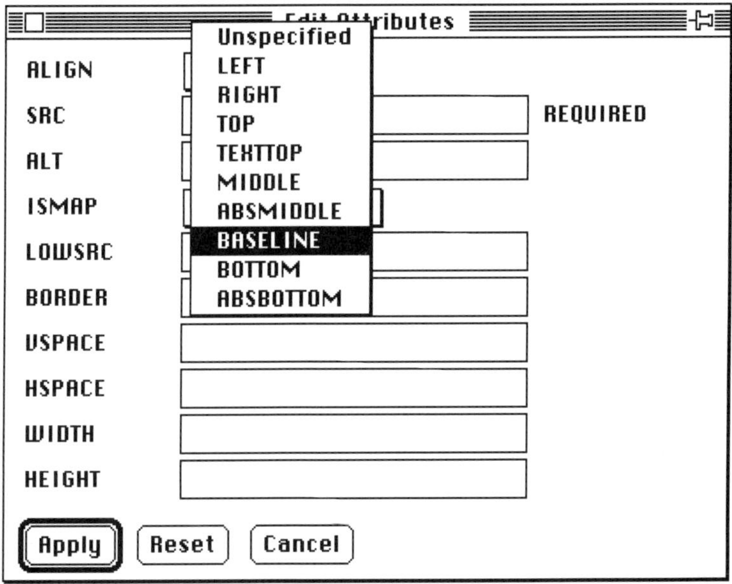

Figure 8-9: *The Edit Attributes dialog box for images.*

Position	Description
left	Aligns the image in the left margin. Subsequent text will wrap around the right-hand side of that image.
right	Aligns the image in the right margin. Subsequent text wraps around the left-hand side of that image.
top	Aligns the image with the top of the tallest item in the line.
texttop	Aligns the image with the top of the tallest text in the line. The texttop attribute is usually the same as the top attribute.
middle	Aligns the image so the baseline of the current line appears aligned with the middle of the image.
absmiddle	Aligns the middle of the current line with the middle of the image.
baseline	Aligns the bottom of the image with the baseline of the current line.
bottom	Aligns the bottom of the image with the baseline of the current line. This is the same as baseline.
absbottom	Aligns the bottom of the image with the bottom of the current line.

Table 8-2: *Position attributes for images.*

Adding Space Around an Image

Netscape includes two attributes for adding space around a floating image: <IMG VSPACE=*n* HSPACE=*n*>. Without those commands, floating images could press up against the text wrapped around the image. The VSPACE attribute sets the vertical space above and below the image. The HSPACE attribute sets the horizontal space to the left and right of the image.

To help you place images more easily, Netscape added a CLEAR attribute to the BR tag. The CLEAR tag has three settings: left, right and all. CLEAR=left breaks the line and moves down vertically until you have a clear left margin. CLEAR=right breaks the line and moves down vertically until you have a clear right margin. CLEAR=all moves down until both margins are clear of images.

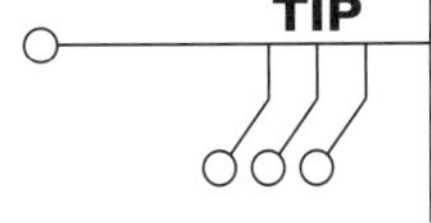

Transparent GIFs can be used as spacers to position images evenly or wherever you want them on the page. The best way to use a transparent GIF is to create a transparent GIF that is only one pixel high and as many pixels wide as you need. The smaller the space, the faster the image will download.

Adding Borders & Drop Shadows to an Image

A border can help accent an image, drawing the reader's eye to a graphic. Netscape has added the BORDER attribute to let you control the thickness of a border framing an image. In most cases, you don't really want to set a border for images that are also part of anchors. This can confuse people, because they're used to having a colored border indicate that an image is an anchor.

To add the BORDER attribute to an image, choose Markup>> Edit SGML Attributes. This displays the Edit Attributes dialog box. In the Border field, enter the number of pixels you want to define as a border to your image. The raw HTML tag for adding a border appears as <IMG BORDER=*n*>, where *n* is the width of the border in pixels. Figure 8-10 shows an image with a two-pixel border.

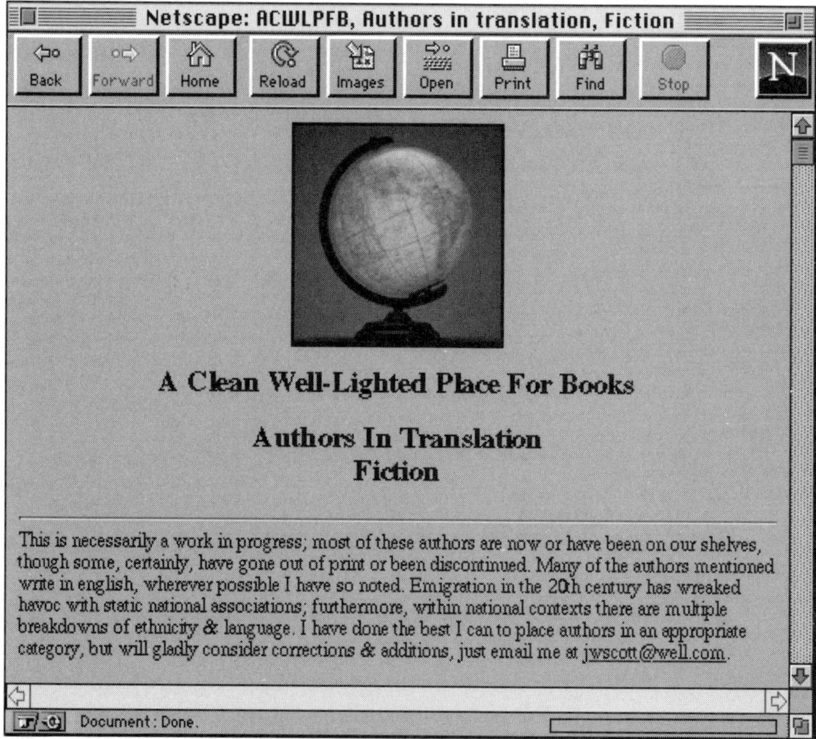

Figure 8-10: *An image with a two-pixel border.*

Another technique for calling attention to a graphic image is adding clip art as a border or including a drop shadow to the graphic. Adding a drop shadow is accomplished by editing the image and adding a dark border around a portion of the image. Drop shadows can be quite effective when you save the graphic with a transparent background. Figure 8-11 shows an image with a drop shadow and a transparent background.

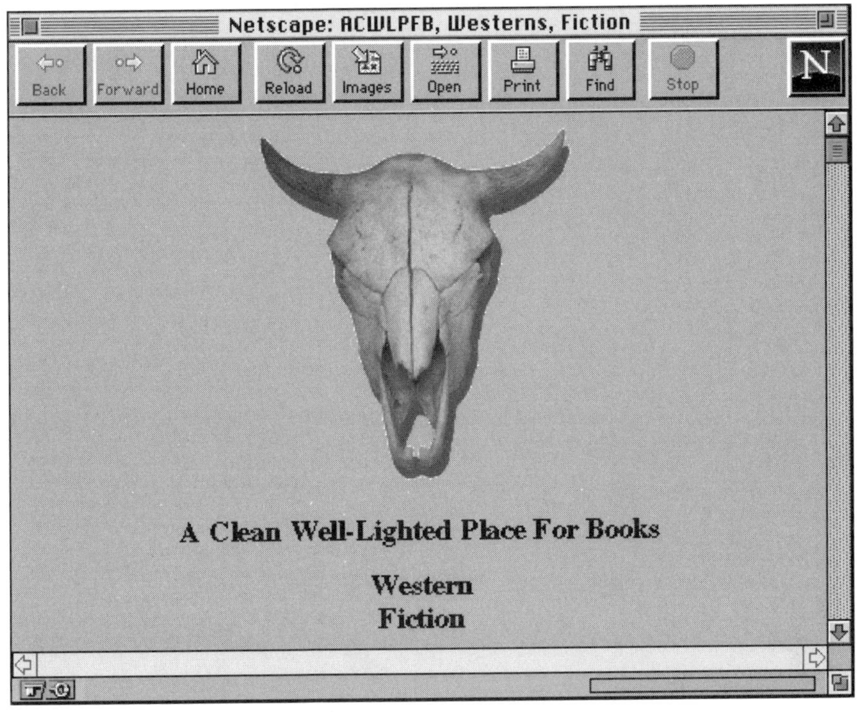

Figure 8-11: *An image with a drop shadow and a transparent background.*

Using an Inline Image as a Horizontal Rule

Horizontal rules are an effective way of visually breaking up your Web page. To enhance the separators in your Web documents, you can use colored lines or colored bars as horizontal rules. The bars aren't created by using the <HR> tag, but instead are graphic inline images. Using inline images as horizontal rules is a great way to add color and pizzazz to your document. Many pages include rules that are made up of color gradients. Colored horizontal rules are a great way to accent the image colors in your document. Figure 8-12 shows inline images used as horizontal rules. You can pick up graphics files of horizontal rules by checking out some of the sites we listed earlier in this chapter.

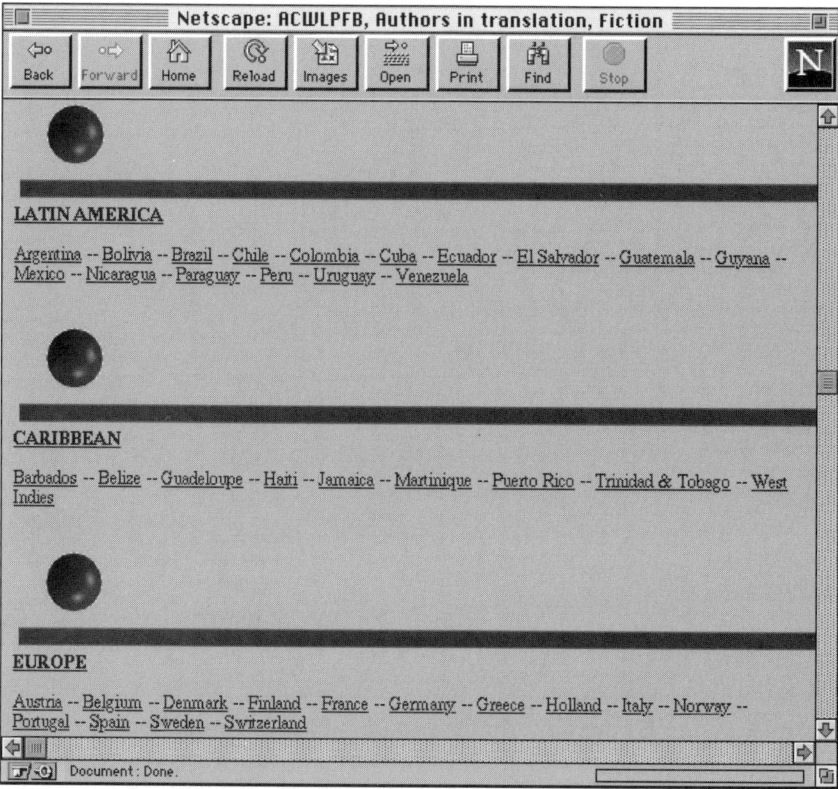

Figure 8-12: *Inline images used as horizontal rules.*

Using Inline Images as Bullets in a List

Besides using graphics for horizontal rules, you can substitute graphics for bullets to create unnumbered lists. Many of the sites containing images that were listed earlier in this chapter used icons and images to replace bullets in lists. The following lines show how to create a list of hyperlinks using an image as a bullet instead of the standard unordered list (<UL>) tag's bullets. Figure 8-13 shows a transparent image used as a bullet to present an unordered (bulleted) list.

```
<P>
<IMG SRC="book.gif" ALT="Book"><A HREF="#
latin_america"><B>Latin America</B></A>
</P>
<P>
<IMG SRC="book.gif" ALT="Book"><A
HREF="#caribbean"><B>Caribbean</B> </A>
</P>
```

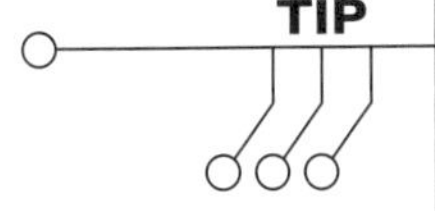

Note that this construction entirely replaces the <UL> tag and the associated <LI> tags. You don't want to leave those tags in the document, because the browser will add the standard bullets every time it sees the old tags.

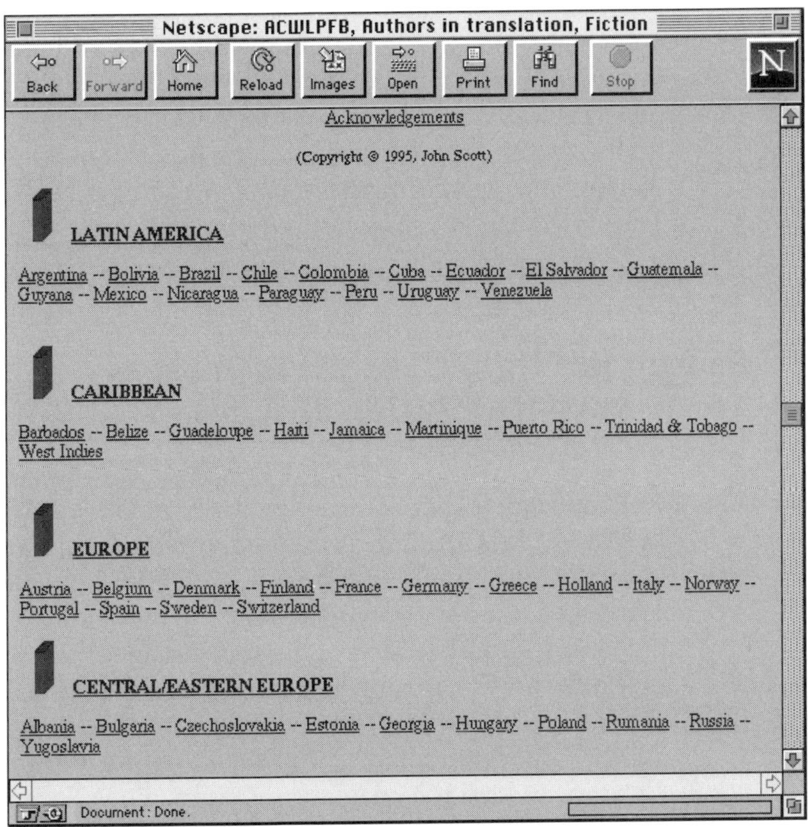

Figure 8-13: *Customized bullets in an unordered list.*

Specifying the Width & Height of an Image

Netscape also added the WIDTH and HEIGHT attributes to the IMG tag, primarily to help speed display of the document. When Netscape encounters a new Web page, it has to create an area for the image called a *bounding box*. Including the WIDTH and HEIGHT attributes saves the browser the time needed to calculate the size of the image. If a Web browser doesn't support the WIDTH and HEIGHT attributes, it ignores them. However, if you specify the wrong size for an image, it will be scaled to fit in the dimensions you specified, which may take more time than simply loading the image would have.

You can find the width and height of your images using a graphics editor. GraphicConverter, for example, lists the width and height, along with the number of colors and other useful information about the image in the Information Palette. Like the other IMG attributes, you use the Markup>>Edit SGML Attributes to display the Edit Attributes dialog box. Fill in the Width and Height fields to specify the image's width and height in pixels. The HTML tag appears similar to the following:

```
<IMG WIDTH=125 HEIGHT=125>
```

Fading in High-Resolution Images From Low-Resolution Images

Netscape has added yet another attribute to the IMG tag, called LOWSRC. This attribute is not supported by HoTMetaL PRO. The LOWSRC attribute is added to the IMG SRC tag to let you specify a low-resolution version of an image to load first, and then load a higher-resolution version of the same image. You can include the LOWSRC attribute using any text editor, such as BBEdit, or unchecked HTML editor. The high-resolution image fades in replacing the low-resolution graphic. The LOWSRC attribute instructs Netscape to load the image specified by the LOWSRC attribute on its first pass through the document. When all of the images are displayed in full, Netscape performs another pass and loads the image specified by the IMG SRC. Browsers that don't recognize the LOWSRC attribute load the image specified by IMG SRC. You can include both GIF and JPEG images using this method. If you also specify the width and height values, both the high-resolution and the low-resolution versions of the image will be scaled to fit. The following is an example of an IMG tag including the LOWSRC attribute:

```
<IMG SRC="high-res.jpeg" LOWSRC="low-res.gif">
```

Changing the Window's Background & Foreground

With the introduction of Netscape Navigator 1.1, Netscape has included extensions that allow you to control the display of the background and foreground colors of the browser's Netscape window. You can specify the color of the background or you can tile an image in the background, similar to using a pattern or color for the Desktop Pattern feature that you can set through the General Controls Control Panel. Keep in mind that right now this is a specific feature of Netscape, so users using a different browser will not see the background color or the background tiled image and the foreground colors. The following sections explain how to include these background and foreground extensions in your Web pages.

Specifying Colors

To specify a color, you need to choose a color and convert the RGB (red, green, blue) decimal settings to hexadecimal. As we mentioned earlier, the Microsoft Windows platform reserves 20 basic colors for displaying windows, and each image uses a palette of 256 colors. If you use more than 256 colors, images will not display correctly. Since all MS Windows devices reserve these standard 20 colors, it is a good idea to stick with these standard Windows colors for your work. This minimizes the possibility that you will use a color that will affect the display of your inline graphics on systems such as Windows. To help save you the time of converting the RGB decimal settings to hexadecimal, Table 8-3 lists the hexadecimal settings for the standard Windows palette. Note that the table separates each red, green and blue setting with a comma, but you do not include commas when specifying a color.

Color	Decimal RGB Values	Hexadecimal RGB Values
Black	0,0,0	00,00,00
Dark Red	128,0,0	80,00,00
Dark Green	0,128,0	00,80,00
Dark Yellow	128,128,0	80,80,00
Dark Blue	0,0,128	00,00,80
Dark Magenta	128,0,128	80,00,80
Dark Cyan	0,128,128	00,80,80
Light Gray	192,192,192	C0,C0,C0
Grass Green	192,220,192	C0,DC,C0
Light Blue	166,202,240	A6,CA,F0
Cream	255,251,240	FF,FB,F0
Medium Gray	160,160,164	A0,A0,A4
Dark Gray	128,128,128	80,80,80
Red	255,0,0	FF,00,00
Green	0,255,0	00,FF,00
Blue	0,0,255	00,00,FF
Yellow	255,255,0	FF,FF,00
Magenta	255,0,255	FF,00,FF
Cyan	0,255,255	00,FF,FF
White	255,255,255	FF,FF,FF

Table 8-3: *Decimal and hexadecimal codes for the standard Windows palette colors.*

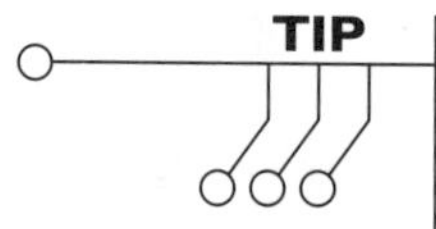

You don't have to use these colors, of course. You can use your graphics program to display any color that you want and determine what the RGB values for that color are. Then use any scientific calculator to calculate the correct hexadecimal equivalents. However, remember that this may cause any images on your page to display poorly on some systems.

Specifying the Netscape Window's Background Color

The Netscape extension BGCOLOR is not available in the current version of HoTMetaL PRO. BGCOLOR is added as a BODY attribute. The syntax for specifying the background color is

```
<BODY BGCOLOR="#rrggbb"> Body text </BODY>
```

You must enter the red, green, blue color settings (rrggbb) in hexadecimal format. To enter a color, use Table 8-3 in the previous section to find the color you want, or calculate the value manually.

Using an Image for the Netscape Window's Background

One of the many additions to the specifications for HTML 3.0 is the addition of the BACKGROUND attribute to the BODY tag. The BACKGROUND attribute lets you specify a URL pointing to a tiled image forming a background of the Netscape window. The syntax for using the BACKGROUND tag is

```
<BODY BACKGROUND="path/image.gif"> Body text</BODY>
```

The URL can point to any location. Netscape has supplied numerous background files, including fabrics, weaves, rocks, dots and water. You can check out these backgrounds at http://home.netscape.com/home/. The following is an example of using a background stored at Netscape.

```
<BODY BACKGROUND="http://home.netscape.com/home/
bg/water/raindrops_light.gif "> </BODY>
```

Figure 8-14 shows a page of text displayed using the Netscape raindrops_light.gif as a background.

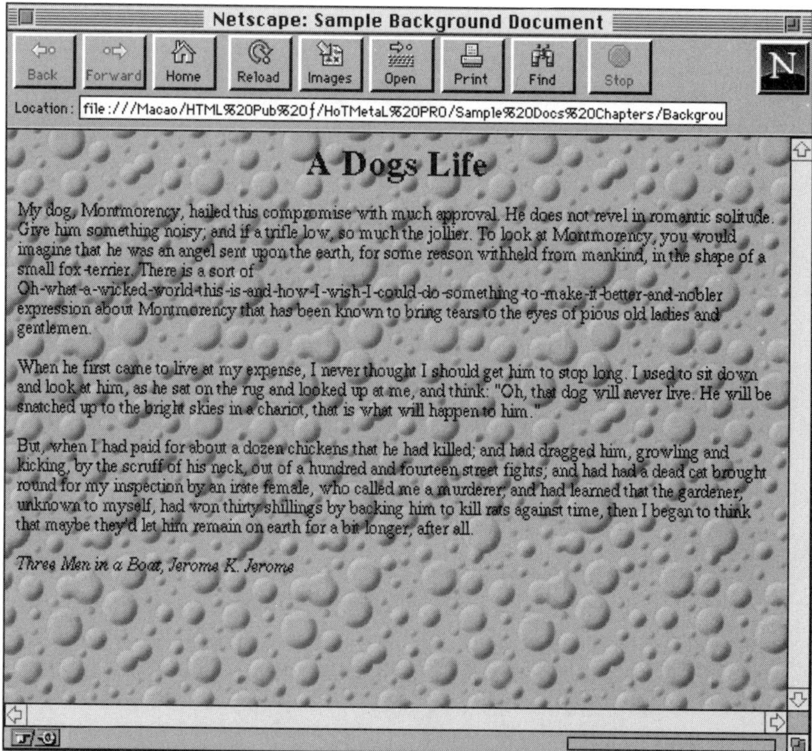

Figure 8-14: *A page of text displayed using a Netscape background.*

Changing the Foreground Text & Links

In addition to changing the background colors, Netscape also lets you specify the color of text and links in a Web page. The TEXT attribute lets you specify the color of text other than links in your Web page. The syntax for the TEXT attribute is

<BODY TEXT="*rrggbb*">Body Text</BODY>

Like the background color, text color is specified in hexadecimal format (rrggbb). To enter a color, use Table 8-3 in the previous section, "Specifying the Netscape Window's Background Color," to find the color you want, or use manual calculations to determine the hexadecimal setting for the color you want.

Three attributes let you specify the color of links: LINK, VLINK and ALINK. LINK refers to the links as they first appear on the page. The default color for links is blue. The V in VLINK stands for *visited.* VLINK changes the color of links that the user has chosen. The default color for visited links is purple. The A in ALINK stands for *active.* ALINK changes the color when the hyperlink is choosing. The default for active links is red. The following is an example that includes a dark cyan color for the background, white for text, yellow for links, medium gray for visited links and magenta for active links.

```
<BODY BGCOLOR="#000080" TEXT="#FFFFFF" LINK="#FFFF00"
VLINK="#A0A0A0" ALINK="#FF00FF"> Body Text goes here
</BODY>
```

Creating an Image Map

The IMG element also lets you set up image maps. *Image maps* are graphic images that have defined "hot spots." Each hot spot is a link. Clicking on the graphic is the same as clicking on a hyperlink. The image lets the user jump to the URL that is defined for that region of the graphic. Image maps bring new ways to publish interactive Web pages. For example, a graphic can be a series of labeled buttons with each button image set to a different location.

Remember, if you use an image map, anyone using a text-based browser will not be able to see the image. If you use image maps, be sure you create a text-only version of the links for text-based browsers.

In order to create an image map, you first need to create an image that you want to include hot spots in. You might want to use a motif or a metaphor for your images. For example, you might want to use an image of different buildings or an image of several planets, with each identifying a different link. Novell's home page presents a series of graphic images, including several sculptured buttons, to direct users to appropriate locations, as shown in Figure 8-15.

Figure 8-15: *Novell's Web page displays buttons and various graphics to specify each hyperlink.*

Specifying Hot Spots

There are different ways of identifying the parts of the image to specify a hot spot. You can manually enter the coordinates in a file and specify the URL you want to jump to, or you can use an image-mapping program to create the file.

It's possible to identify the areas by noting the coordinates for the region you want to include, but there's an easier way. One of the biggest time savers for specifying hot spots is to use a program like Rowland Smith's WebMap. WebMap is a utility that lets you

draw rectangles, circles and arbitrary polygons; it automatically adds the coordinates to an image map file. The WebMap program is included on the Companion CD-ROM. As of this writing, a new version of WebMap is in the works. You can check for the latest version at http://www.city.net/cnx/software/webmap.html. The current WebMap file is named webmap.1.0.1.sea.hqx (of course, the version number will change for newer versions).

Hot spots can be a variety of shapes, including a circle, rectangle or polygon. The most upper-left pixel is used as the beginning coordinate of an x axis, and the y axis begins at the upper-left corner to the end of the right side of the image. This x and y grid lets you identify pixels you want to include as a hot spot. Most graphics editors use the same type of grid, allowing you to easily display specific coordinates. The next section explains how to use the WebMap program to create a map file.

Using WebMap to Create an Image Map

If the WebMap program is not installed, create a folder and copy the WebMap1.0.1.sea file to the folder, then double-click on the file to install the entire WebMap application. The following steps explain how to use WebMap to create a map file.

1. Launch the WebMap program.
2. Choose File>>Open. The standard File Open dialog box appears.
3. Select the GIF file you want to use. For the examples in this chapter, enter shapes.gif. The shapes.gif image file is included on the Companion CD-ROM.
4. Choose OK. WebMap loads your image for you to begin editing. Be patient, this may take several seconds if the image is large. Figure 8-16 shows the sample image, shapes.gif, loaded in the WebMap window. This image consists of a polygon, a circle and a rectangle. The shapes.gif image was created using the trueSpace 3D graphics and animation program.

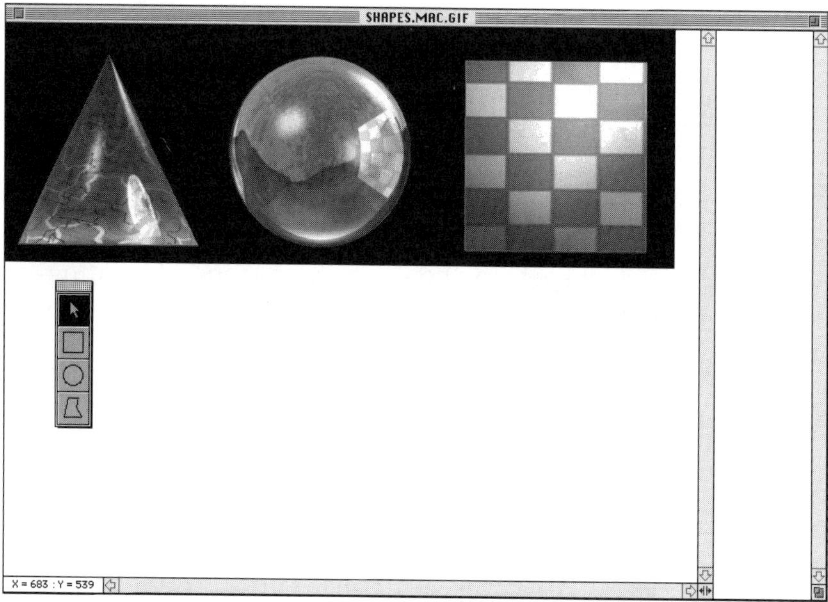

Figure 8-16: *The shapes.gif file loaded in the WebMap window.*

5. Use the floating Tools palette and choose the tool that specifies the shape you want to use to define a hot spot. The Tools palette includes three choices: Polygon, Rectangle and Oval. The following sections explain how to define these regions. If two defined areas overlap, the first matching shape in the map file determines the URL that will be returned. If you don't like the region you created, use the selection tool (the arrow) to select the problem area or use Clear from the Edit menu to cancel the defined area and start over. This example includes each of the three hot spots.

Polygon

Click the mouse button at some point on the edge of an area of interest in the image. Move the mouse pointer to another point on the edge of the area of interest. Note that a line follows you from the point of the initial click. Click again at this second point. Continue clicking points until you have outlined all but the final connection back to the first point. For the last point, click the starting point of your path to close the selection area.

Rectangle

Click the mouse button in one corner of a rectangular region of interest in the image. Now move the mouse pointer to the opposite corner, tracing out a rectangle.

Oval

Position the mouse pointer in the edge of the oval. Click the mouse button and then move the mouse pointer down and to the right to define the desired oval. Hold down the Shift key while dragging to constrain the defined area to an exact circle.

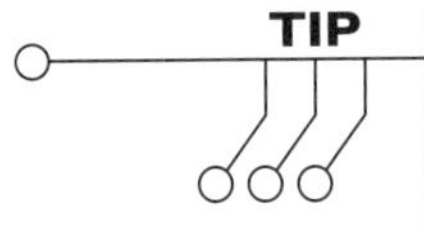

You can use the Preferences dialog box to allow you to define ovals or circles from the center instead of from the edge. This is often a better and more intuitive way to define your curved hot spots.

6. When you draw your hot spot, it appears as a gray or light-colored area over your original image. As the hot spot is defined, its associated URL is listed in the area on the right of the image. At first, of course, no URL is defined for the hot spot, so the list entry is [Undefined]. Figure 8-17 shows you how the shapes look after a hot spot has been defined over each one.

Figure 8-17: *The hot spots with the URL definition list on the side.*

7. Choose Edit>>Set Default URL or press -U. The Default URL dialog box appears, as shown in Figure 8-18.

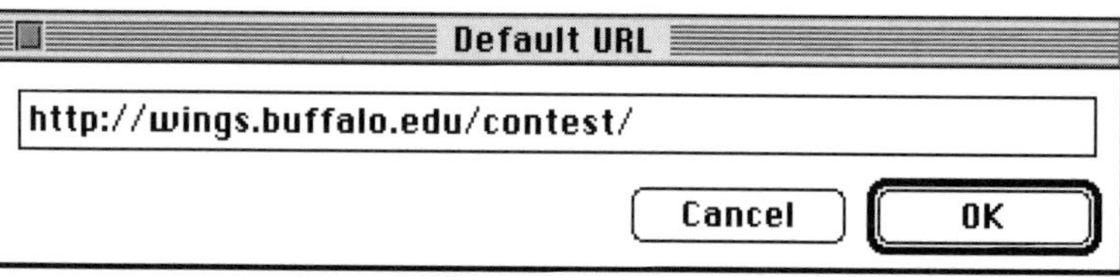

Figure 8-18: *The Default URL dialog box.*

8. Enter the URL you want to default to for clicks outside the regions you are about to specify. If you want to point to a local file, start with a forward slash. If you want to refer to a document on another server, enter the full URL. For this example, enter **http://wings.buffalo.edu/contest/** and choose OK.
9. Click the mouse button on the first item in your map. This will select the corresponding URL from the list to the right of the image. This is the URL that matches your selected item; at the same time, the selected hot spot is made lighter to indicate that it matches the highlighted URL entry. Double-click on the selected URL. The Object URL dialog box appears, as shown in Figure 8-19.

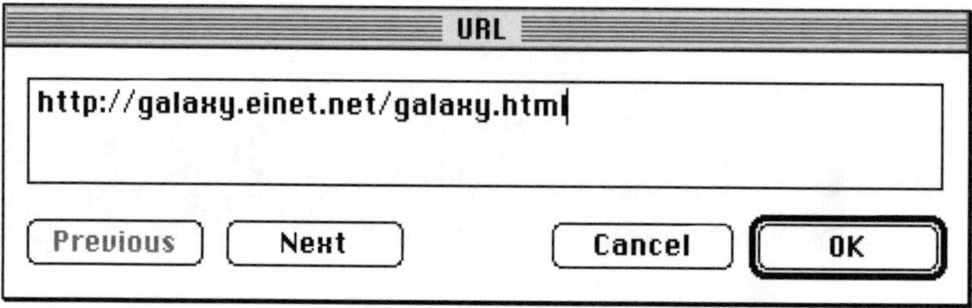

Figure 8-19: *The Object URL dialog box lets you specify the URL the object is to link to.*

10. Enter the URL to link to. You can also add any comments in the Comments window. Choose OK when you're fin-

ished. For this chapter's examples, enter **http:// www.yahoo.com/yahoo/** for the rectangle, **http:// www.vmedia.com/** for the circle and **http:// galaxy.einet.net/galaxy.html** for the triangle.

11. Choose the File>>Export As Text command.
12. Choose the NCSA radio button or the Cern radio button to determine the format of your map file output. The NCSA button is preferred for WebSTAR and MacHTTP servers.
13. Enter the name you want to use for your map. This file will store your hot-spot coordinates. The map files are stored in the same folder where your images are stored. It's important that you store your image map in the correct folder, because the image map script must be able to find the map files. To have your map match the examples in the rest of this chapter, enter **NcsaMap.map** if you chose the NCSA format, or enter **CernMap.map** for the Cern format.

If you open the image map file in a text editor, it will appear similar to Figure 7-20.

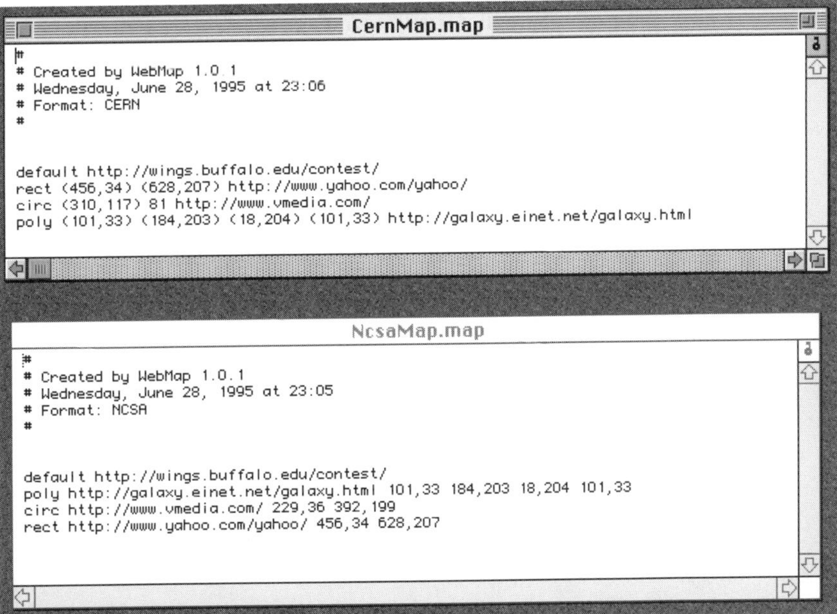

CernMap.map

```
#
# Created by WebMap 1.0.1
# Wednesday, June 28, 1995 at 23:06
# Format: CERN
#


default http://wings.buffalo.edu/contest/
rect (456,34) (628,207) http://www.yahoo.com/yahoo/
circ (310,117) 81 http://www.vmedia.com/
poly (101,33) (184,203) (18,204) (101,33) http://galaxy.einet.net/galaxy.html
```

NcsaMap.map

```
#
# Created by WebMap 1.0.1
# Wednesday, June 28, 1995 at 23:05
# Format: NCSA
#


default http://wings.buffalo.edu/contest/
poly http://galaxy.einet.net/galaxy.html 101,33 184,203 18,204 101,33
circ http://www.vmedia.com/ 229,36 392,199
rect http://www.yahoo.com/yahoo/ 456,34 628,207
```

Figure 8-20: *A sample Cern (CernMap.map) and a sample NCSA (NcsaMap.map) image map file.*

Understanding the Map File

The settings that appear in the resulting map file depend on whether you chose the NCSA server or the Cern server format. The map file is a text file consisting of definitions, comments and blank lines. You can edit the map file with any text editor. Map files end with the extension .map. The following section explains each type of entry in a map file.

The Default Setting

The Cern server lets you abbreviate default to def. The default setting defines the URL to jump to if the mouse click is outside a specified region. Both the Cern and NCSA servers use the same syntax for the default URL: default URL. The following example shows an example default setting that points to the site listing the winners of the "Best of the Web Awards."

```
default http://wings.buffalo.edu/contest/
```

Polygons

The Cern server lets you abbreviate the polygon setting to poly. The polygon is similar to a connect-the-dots puzzle. It defines a polygon with points at (x0,y0), (x1,y1), (x2,y2) and so on. The following is an example of a triangle defined for use on the Cern server that points to the EINet Galaxy home page.

```
poly (101,33) (184,203) (18,204) (101,33)
http://galaxy.einet.net/galaxy.html
```

The NCSA server also lets you abbreviate the polygon setting to poly. The NCSA server only lets you use a maximum of 100 points to define a polygon.

The following is an example of an NCSA setting for a triangle defined to point to the EINet Galaxy home page.

```
poly http://galaxy.einet.net/galaxy.html 101,33 184,203
18,204, 101,33
```

Circles

The circle setting for the Cern server defines a circle with center (*x,y*) and radius *r* and the URL to jump to if the user clicks inside the circle. The Cern server defines the circle using the center point and the radius; for this reason, WebMab will not let you create an oval hot spot if you have preset the Cern fomat for your map. The following is an example of a circle defined using a Cern server that points to Ventana Communications, the publisher of this book. You can abbreviate the circle setting as circ.

```
circ (310,117) 81 http://www.vmedia.com/
```

The NCSA server includes the URL between the circle setting and the coordinates defining the circle. The following is an example of a circle defined using the HTTPD server that points to Ventana Communications, the publisher of this book.

```
circ http://www.vmedia.com/ 229,36 392,199
```

Rectangles

The Cern sever lets you abbreviate the rectangle setting to rect. It defines a rectangle with top left at (x0,y0) and bottom right at (x1,y1) and the URL to jump to if the user clicks inside the rectangle. The following is an example of a rectangle defined using the HTTPS server that points to the Yahoo database of Web sites.

```
rect (456,34) (628,207) http://www.yahoo.com/yahoo/
```

The HTTPD server includes the URL before the definition of the rectangle. The following is an example of a rectangle that points to the Yahoo database of Web sites.

```
rect http://www.yahoo.com/yahoo/ 456,34 628,207
```

Using the ISMAP Tag

You identify an image map by including the ISMAP attribute in the IMG element. The ISMAP attribute tells the browser to append the mouse coordinates to the URL and send it to the server. The anchor URL <A> must refer to an image map file on the HTTP server. The image map file is the file that contains the mapping of the hot-spot coordinates, so the user can just click the mouse to move to another URL. Without the ISMAP attribute, the mouse coordinates will not be sent.

To add the ISMAP attribute using HoTMetaL PRO, move the insertion point between the starting and ending IMG tags. Choose Markup>>Edit SGML Attributes. The Edit Attributes dialog box appears. Choose the ISMAP attribute. The raw HTML code for a real-world example might appear as follows:

```
<IMG SRC="/images/shapes.gif" ISMAP>
```

The ISMAP attribute can also appear as

```
<IMG SRC="/images/shapes.gif" ISMAP="ISMAP">
```

The ISMAP attribute tells the browser that the image is an image map. The IMG element must be included in an anchor element to tell the browser where to send the request when the user clicks on the image. Clicking inside the image causes the coordinates of the point on the image where the user clicks to be sent to the server, along with the URL specified in the anchor. An external image map-processing program is usually started by the Web server to perform a mapping from the coordinates to another hypertext document.

Adding the Map to the HTTPD Configuration File

If you're using the NCSA server, you need to add a setting to the image map configuration file (imagemap.cnf). You'll find the file in the httpd/conf directory. The imagemap.cnf file is a text file. You can add your map file to the existing map entries with any text editor, such as BBEdit. The NCSA image map program requires that your image map be included in the imagemap.cnf configuration file, or the program won't work. The following example shows the addition of the map file, named NcsaMap.map, that we created using the WebMap program earlier in this chapter.

```
# Default imagemap.cnf
#
# -Casey Barton
#
imapdemo : HardDrive:httpd:conf:maps:imapdemo.map
wizflow : HardDrive:httpd:conf:maps:wizflow.map
NcsaMap: HardDrive:httpd:conf:maps:NcsaMap.map
```

Surrounding the Image With the Anchor

The WebSTAR server that comes on the Companion CD-ROM, also doesn't require you to use a program and configuration file to identify the map file. Instead, you specify both the script to process the request and the map file in the HREF attribute of the anchor surrounding the IMG tags. The following is an example of how to specify the location of the image map using the WebSTAR server.

```
<A HREF="scripts/MapServe.acgi$NCSAMap.map"><IMG
SRC="shapes.gif" ISMAP="ISMAP"></A>
```

You should store the .map file in the same directory as your map scripts. This example assumes that your scripts are stored in the 'scripts' folder within WebSTAR's own folder. See the WebSTAR documentation for more information.

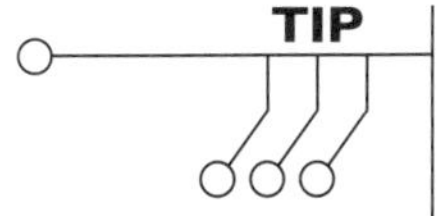

In order for your image map to work, you must test it over the Net with the server started. You must use the URL for your site to test the image map; you cannot test an image map locally.

Moving On

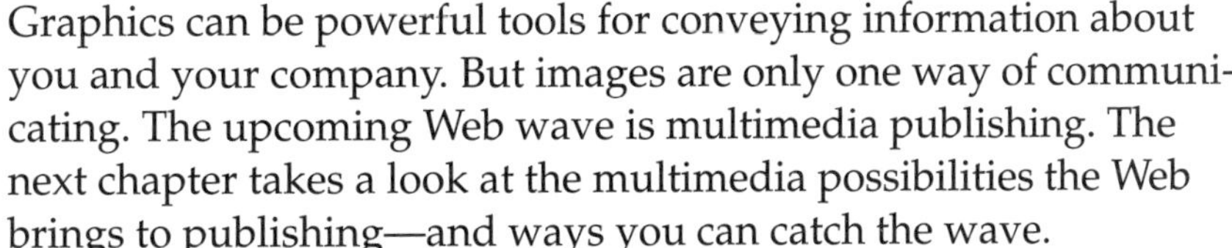

Graphics can be powerful tools for conveying information about you and your company. But images are only one way of communicating. The upcoming Web wave is multimedia publishing. The next chapter takes a look at the multimedia possibilities the Web brings to publishing—and ways you can catch the wave.

9

Adding Scintillating Sound & Vivid Video

One of the most exciting aspects of the World Wide Web is its inclusion of numerous forms of media. HTML and MIME typing has opened the doors to just about any kind of media files imaginable. Even though multimedia file formats abound, a somewhat informal standard has evolved for multimedia file types in use on the Web.

Luckily for Macintosh users, Apple has developed the Mac from the beginning with multimedia applications in mind. Many Macs come with the audio and video hardware necessary for creating and editing multimedia files, and there's enough shareware available on the Net to make it worth your while to explore your Mac's multimedia capabilities.

Even though current bandwidth limitations restrict many possible uses of audio and video applications over the Net, steady advances in compression and networking technologies are helping to remedy this situation. Some of those technologies have only been around for a couple of years, but they're already posing formidable challenges to traditional analog media distribution systems. To better prepare yourself for the coming dominance of digital media distribution, it's a good idea to become familiar with many of the multimedia technologies in use on the Net today.

If you plan to create original audio and video files, it's imperative that you understand the fundamental concepts of multimedia technologies. This chapter introduces you to the multimedia file formats currently in use on the Internet, as well as ways in which you can create high-quality files of your own with software included on this book's Companion CD-ROM.

Publishing Sound Files

The surge in multimedia-compatible computers has made the addition of sounds to Web documents commonplace. Thanks to MIME typing, you can easily include in your Web documents sound files that can be played by Web browsers with the appropriate helper applications specified. However, downloading and playing large sound files can be a time-consuming and processor-intensive operation, since sound files can easily exceed one megabyte for each minute of playing time. If you include hyperlinks to sound files on your pages, be sure the sound clips are relevant to your mission. You may be asking readers to devote a lot of time and hard disk space to get the sound, so don't disappoint them.

Digital Audio Basics: Sample Depth & Sampling Rates

You need to become familiar with a couple of fundamental digital audio concepts before you start digitizing your own audio clips. These concepts will give you the foundation for understanding how digital audio works and a working knowledge that will help you select the file formats most appropriate for your site.

The first concept, *sample depth*, refers to the number of discrete levels provided for each "sample" or output from an analog-to-digital (A/D) converter. Represented in bits, the sample depth determines the overall dynamic range, or span, between the quietest and loudest points of an audio sample. For instance, an 8-bit sample has 256 steps within the signal, while a 16-bit sample has 65,536. Obviously, the higher the sample depth, the greater the sound quality. Each bit contributes approximately 6 decibels (a measure of the ear's response to sound pressure levels, abbreviated dB) of dynamic range to the recording. Eight-bit audio files

are therefore able to reproduce a dynamic range of 48dB, roughly that of an analog cassette deck, while 16-bit audio files are capable of yielding the 96dB of dynamic range found on CDs.

The second concept you should understand is *sampling rate*, the frequency at which the A/D converter samples an incoming audio signal. The sampling rate is the highest frequency that can be recorded or played back, so the higher the sampling rate, the closer the audio file's fidelity is to the original sound. The *hertz* (Hz), or *cycles per second*, is the unit of measurement for a sampling rate. Therefore, an audio file with a sampling rate of 22kHz has been sampled 22,000 times every second. That means that the highest frequency stored in the file is 11kHz, since the highest possible sampled frequency is always one-half the sampling rate.

When preparing audio clips for use on the Web, keep in mind that you don't always have to use the highest possible sample depths and sampling rates. Higher sample depths and rates require more storage and throughput, so you need to decide whether or not you can sacrifice disk space and bandwidth for high-quality audio files. While one minute of an 8-bit mono file sampled at 8kHz is approximately 150k in size, a 16-bit stereo file sampled at 44.1kHz can take up 10MB. Since most people have a hearing range of 20Hz to 20kHz, it's rarely necessary to use sampling rates higher than the 44.1kHz CD standard, and that rate should be used only for the highest-quality samples. If an audio file consists solely of speech, an 8-bit, 8kHz file will usually suffice. If it's absolutely necessary for you to provide CD-quality audio samples, take advantage the various compression schemes discussed later in this chapter.

Sound File Formats

One of the issues surrounding any emerging technology is the flood of formats that appear. Seemingly, every hardware manufacturer has developed its own way to record and play sound files, and each of them needs its own software program to deliver the sound to the speaker. Fortunately, you don't need to become a master of formats to place sound files in your documents. As previously mentioned, MIME typing allows you to transmit any file format between a client and a server, but a handful of audio formats have come to prominence on the Net. The following sections explain the most standard sound file formats in use on the Web, including μ-law (AU), used by Sun and NeXt workstations; AIFF, used by Macintoshes; Microsoft's Wave (WAV) format, used by most PCs; and the increasingly popular MPEG compression format. This chapter also briefly discusses ways to convert more obscure audio formats, such as VOICE (.VOC) files created by SoundBlaster cards and Interchange File Format (.IFF) files created by Amigas.

While reviewing the following formats, keep in mind that some file format names are often used interchangeably with the compression/decompression algorithms, or *codecs*, on which they're based. For quick reference, we have included the appropriate MIME types for the formats before the descriptions.

If you're interested in learning more about sound file formats, compression schemes and sound-related technical information, check out ftp://ftp.cwi.nl/pub/audio/and get the FAQs titled Audio Formats.part1 and Audio Formats.part2. You can find the same at ftp://rtfm.mit.edu/pub/usenet news. answers/audio-fmts/.

Ventana Online also has a chapter from *The Web Server Book* dealing with the technical aspects of multimedia on the Internet at http://www.vmedia.com/vvc/onlcomp/wsb/ tmedia/.

μ-law: The Sun/NeXt Audio File Format

audio/basic au snd

The most widely used sound format on the Internet is the μ-law (pronounced *mu-law*) format. Often referred to as the Sun/NeXT audio format, the files are usually identified by the .AU extension, but occasionally end with the .SND extension. This can be rather confusing, since Macintosh System sounds are also frequently identified by the .SND extension.

The μ-law format allows for various sample depths and sampling rates, but most of the ones found on the Net are 8-bit, 8kHz monophonic files. These are ideal for use over relatively low-bandwidth computer networks, since they require a minimal amount of storage space and provide acceptable audio quality for users wanting to get an idea of what a sample sounds like, especially if the files are played back through a monophonic computer speaker. Even though most audio editing applications for the Mac don't directly support the μ-law format, there are ways to convert standard Mac file formats to and from μ-law. This conversion process is discussed in detail later in this chapter.

The Audio Interchange File Format (AIFF)

audio/x-aiff aif aiff aifc

Developed by Apple, the Audio Interchange File Format (AIFF) and AIFC (AIF-Compressed) formats are primarily used on Macintosh and Silicon Graphics workstations. Since AIFF files allow for the storage of monaural and multichannel audio data at a variety of sampling rates and sample depths, they are the default file type for most Macintosh audio editors. AIFC files are usually compatible with AIFF editing and playback software, yet they can be compressed at ratios as high as 6:1 (at the expense of the file's signal quality).

The Waveform (WAV) Sound Format

audio/x-wav wav

A proprietary format sponsored by Microsoft and IBM, the Resource Interchange File Format Waveform Audio Format (.WAV) was introduced in Microsoft Windows 3.1 and is most commonly used on Windows-based PCs. Like AIFF files, Waveform files can be saved as stereo or mono in 8-bit or 16-bit audio files. If you publish files in the Waveform format, Windows users will likely be the only people listening. In most cases, you'll want to save or convert the file to the μ-law format (see "Converting Sound Files" later in this chapter for more information).

The MPEG Audio Format

audio/x-mpeg mp2

MPEG is the acronym for Moving Picture Expert Group (http://www.crs4.it/~luigi/MPEG/), the organization responsible for the development for the MPEG codec. The name refers to the file formats that use the codec. MPEG is a constantly evolving standard, and it's sure to play an increasingly important role in multimedia file distribution over computer networks.

Four versions of the MPEG codec (MPEG-1 through MPEG-4) are available. MPEG-1 is the version most commonly used on the Internet, even though MPEG-2 (and higher) compressed files are sure to be introduced as communication technologies evolve. MPEG-1 audio compression specifies three layers, each specifying its own format. The more complex layers take longer to encode but produce higher compression ratios while keeping much of an audio file's original fidelity. Layer I takes the least amount of time to compress, but layer III yields higher compression ratios for comparable quality files. MPEG-1 layer II (.MP2 or .mp2) is the version used most frequently for audio files, but MPEG-1 layer III compression and playback packages are starting to be introduced. Both of these layers are based on psychoacoustic models that attempt to determine which frequencies within the signal can be discarded without sacrificing original audio fidelity. The quality of an MPEG-1 layer II-compressed audio file remains similar to the original uncompressed file at ratios from 5:1 to 12:1. You can create MPEG-compressed audio files with MPEG/CD, a software package discussed later in this chapter.

Including Sound Files in a Web Page

To include a reference to a sound, use the same format you would use with any hyperlink text or image. You might want to include the size of the file, since most audio files are quite large. For example, a link to a sound file uses the following syntax:
Want to check out <A HREF=" file://sunsite.unc.edu/pub/multimedia/sun-sounds/cartoons/speed_racer-complete-theme.au">Go Speed Racer</A> (498 Kb).

It's best to publish low-quality sound files in the μ-law format, since most browsers are already configured to play back this format. Some browsers even include embedded sound players that are launched when μ-law files are downloaded.

You may want to point to a sound file that is published at some other site because of space limitations on your host or other reasons. A little caution should be exercised if you do that, because external files may be changed without your knowledge. If you include the link, check occasionally to make sure the sound file is still available.

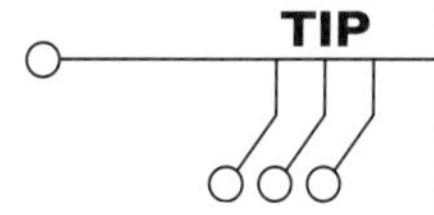

Make sure your intended audience has the necessary players. If there's a question as to whether or not your audience can listen to your sound files, refer them to the location of a player.

Acquiring Sound Files

Many sites on the Web include sound files. The problem is that many are poor quality clips, and it's sometimes hard to tell which ones break copyright laws—use audio files from the Internet at your own risk. Of course, you can always create a link to a sound in an archive. The following is a list of sites that include sound clips on the Web. Just because the sites are listed doesn't mean you can publish them at your Web site. However, you may want to experiment with the sound files, even if you don't add any of them to your Web pages.

URL	Description
http://www.acm.uiuc.edu/rml/Sounds/	A large collection of µ-law sounds, many from movies and cartoons such as *Roger Rabbit, Ren and Stimpy, Beavis and Butthead*. The site includes other clips, such as computer sounds, dinosaur noises, Monty Python routines, music, quotes, Christmas sounds and other sound effects.
http://sunsite.unc.edu/pub/multimedia/sun-sounds/	The University of North Carolina at Chapel Hill's SunSITE has numerous sound files in the µ-law format, including bird calls, cartoons, comedy, commercials, computer sounds, Monty Python routines, movies, clips from *Star Trek* and *Star Trek the Next Generation*, sayings, screams, sound tracks, TV, whales and other sound effects. Some sounds in the Waveform format are stored in a directory named PC Sounds.
http://www.cmf.nrl.navy.mil/radio/byte_RTFM.html	A short sound bite is added to this site just about every day. Most are single words or short phrases. Many are computer-related.
http://web.msu.edu/vincent/general.html	The MSU Vincent Voice Library collection of µ-law sound bites of famous people, such as Isaac Asimov, George Washington Carver, Amelia Earhart, Betty Ford, Will Rogers and Babe Ruth.
http://www.eecs.nwu.edu/µ-law~jmyers/sun_sounds/	Miscellaneous sound files in the format, such as a bark, bong, bubbles, birds chirp-ing, cowbell, crash, cuckoo, doorbell, drip, flush, gong, laugh, ring, rooster, space music, splat and several telephone sounds.
http://155.187.10.12:80/sounds/	Assorted bird calls from a cockatoo to a spinebill.

Table 9-1: *URLs for sound files.*

You can also find sound files in a few newsgroups such as *alt.binaries.sounds.music* and *alt.binaries.sound.misc*. The sound files are posted in ASCII format and must be decoded with a program like uuUndo before the clip can be played on a computer. The sound files posted in newsgroups change daily. Most of the postings are multipart files that have to be assembled before decoding. If you have a news reader that can put the parts together for you, such as NewsWatcher, this is a simple operation. If you're not using one of these programs, prepare yourself for some aggravation and read the newsgroup's FAQ (Frequently Asked Questions) file.

Audio on the Macintosh

Unlike many PCs, all new Macs come equipped with the hardware and software necessary to play digital audio files, and many have hardware for recording high-quality audio samples. If there's a particular audio file format that your Mac can't play, there are publicly available software packages that will enable you to listen to it. We've included some of these audio editing and playback packages with the Companion CD-ROM, including SoundEffects, MPEG/CD, SoundHack, and Brian's Sound Tool, all of which will be discussed shortly.

CD-ROM

The first step in making sure that your Mac is well-equipped to handle audio is to obtain the latest version of Apple's Sound Manager. First introduced in 1987, the Sound Manager allows any application to play and record sounds using built-in hardware. Support for 16-bit audio was added with the release of version 3.0 in 1993, and the newest version, 3.1, adds support for the IMA and µ-law audio codecs. It has also been streamlined for use with Power Macs, making audio handling much more efficient on the newest line of Power PC-based Macs. Sound Manager 3.1 (including a new version of the Sound control panel) can be downloaded for free from ftp://ftp.info.apple.com/Apple.Support.Area/Apple.Software.Updates/US/Macintosh/System/Other_System/Sound_Manager_3.1.sea.hqx.

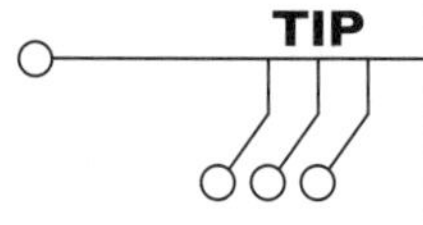

For the complete low-down on Macintosh audio/video hardware and everything relating to Macintosh-based multimedia, see http://www.csua.berkeley.edu/~jwang/AV/.

Sound Editors & Tools

Sound editors represent sound graphically, so you can cut and paste portions of the visual representation of the sound or insert silence in your sound file. Just as you can use filters in a graphics editing package to achieve different results, there are sound filters that let you control sound output. Editing software uses digital signal processing (DSP) algorithms to present tools and filters for controlling sounds, such as fades, delays, reverb, blending and equalizing sounds, adding distortion and other special effects.

A number of high-quality commercial audio editors are available for the Mac, including Digidesign's Sound Designer II (which comes with Audiomedia II), Digidesign's Pro Tools and Sound Tools (http://www.digidesign.com), Alaska Software's Digitrax, OSC's Deck II, and Opcode Systems's DigiTrax (http://www.opcode.com). All of these are multitrack editors, meaning that they allow you to overdub and mix down multiple audio tracks. They all provide onscreen mixers to control audio volume levels, as well as provide numerous filters and effects for modifying individual waveforms.

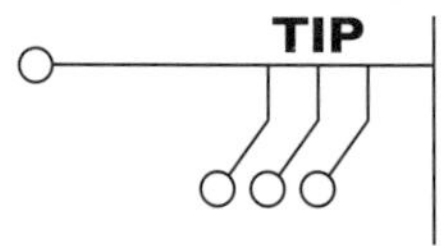

Looking for a high-end audio card with digital input/output? Check out Digidesign's Audiomedia II, a NuBus card providing digital I/O as well as hardware-based DSP processing. You can read more about it at http://www.digidesign.com.

CD-ROM

If you just want to edit samples graphically and don't need a multitrack sound editor, consider Macromedia's SoundEdit 16 ($379, 800-326-2128). Better yet, try out SoundEffects, a feature-rich shareware audio editor that we've included on the Companion CD-ROM. It provides many of the same capabilities as commercially available packages and is ideal for users new to the world of digital audio editing. SoundEffects imports and exports audio files in both AIFF and native Macintosh SND format, comes with a number of special effects and filters, and supports multichannel sounds. One of the nicest things about the package is that its developer, Alberto Ricci, included a Developer's Kit in the distribution to encourage people to write their own plug-in effects for the editor.

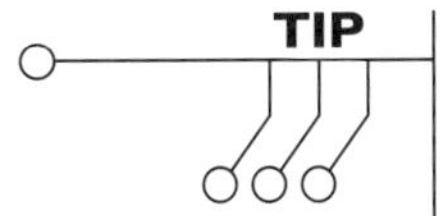

You can keep up with the latest versions of SoundEffects at ftp://ftp.alpcom.it/software/mac/Ricci.

Editing & Controlling Sound

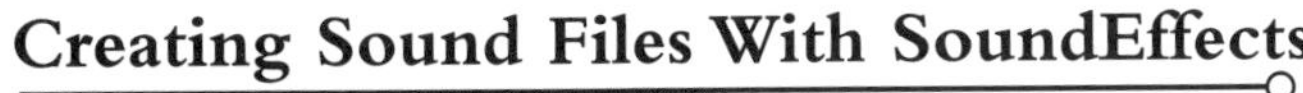

Creating Sound Files With SoundEffects

To familiarize you with the process of audio editing, we're going to take you through the process creating, editing and formatting sound files with software provided on the Companion CD-ROM. We'll begin with the SoundEffects editor, but first you must make sure that your audio hardware is configured properly. To record a sample, you'll need to have an audio source plugged into the audio input jack (marked by a small microphone icon) on the back of your Mac. If your Mac doesn't have an audio input jack, you'll need to buy an audio input card mentioned in the previous section.

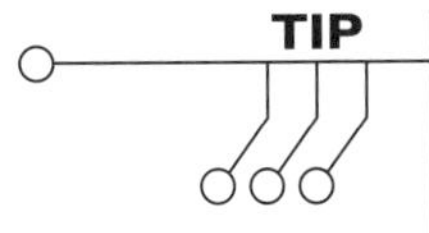

If you don't have an audio input card but you do have an AppleCD 300CD-ROM drive, you can convert audio tracks from an audio CD with any QuickTime-aware application, such as SoundEffects or SimpleText. Simply select Open from the File menu, find the file that you want to convert, double-click the filename, and select where you want to save the converted file. If you use SimpleText, be aware that you will need a large amount of disk space and be prepared to wait a while for the file to be converted.

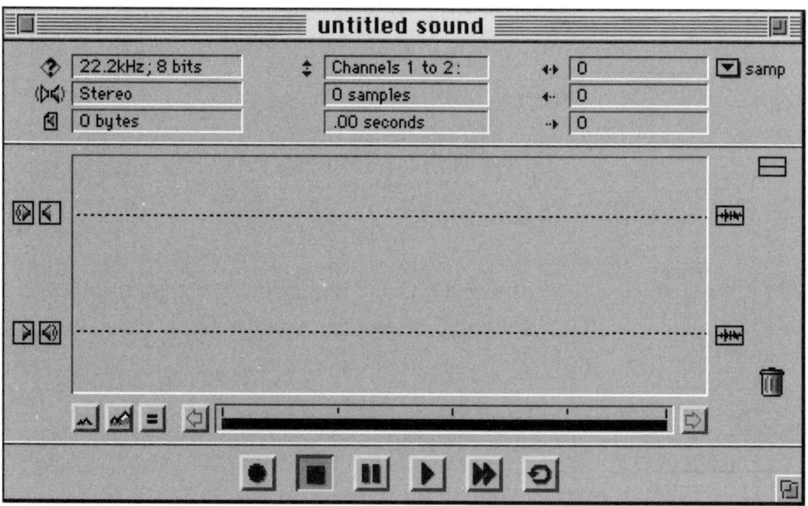

Figure 9-1: *The SoundEffects sound editor lets you create and edit AIFF sound files and Macintosh System sounds.*

Most Macs come with a microphone, so you could start by simply speaking into the microphone, or you could connect the output of a CD player or tape to the input. Once your hardware is configured, launch SoundEffects. When you're presented with the SoundEffects main window (Figure 9-1), click the record button to pull up the Record dialog box (Figure 9-2). Make sure that you've selected the correct sound input from the Sound control panel by opening the General Settings collapsible menu at the bottom of the Record dialog box. Click Device Settings to pull up the Input Source box and select External Audio and Playthrough (Figure 9-3). This will let you record and hear the signal coming in from your audio input jack.

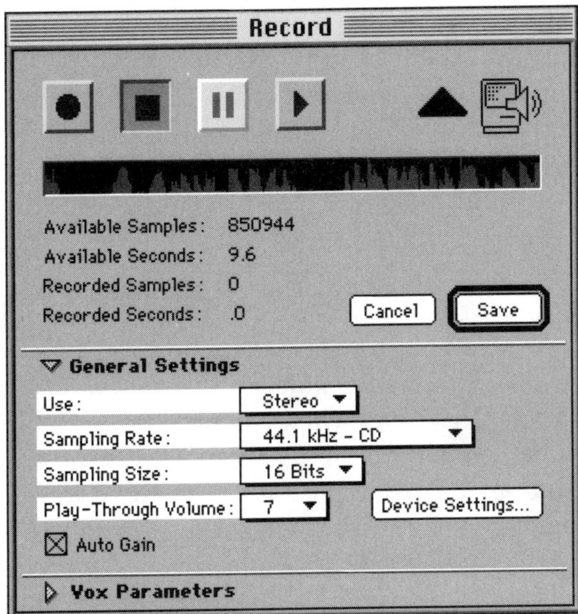

Figure 9-2: *The SoundEffects Record dialog box lets you easily adjust the recording settings.*

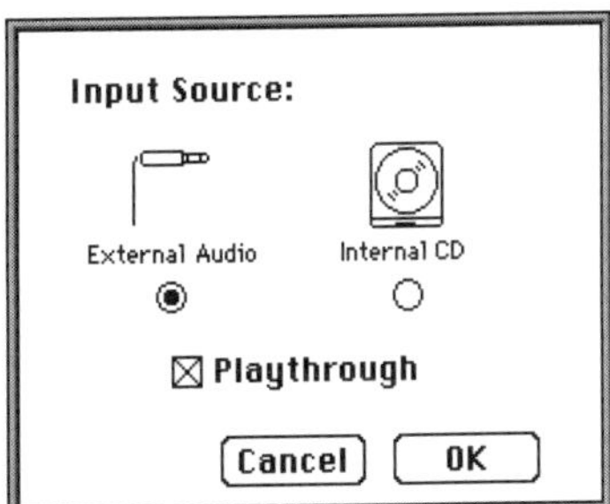

Figure 9-3: *The Device Settings button in the Record dialog box provides a shortcut to the Input Source dialog box.*

Next, you can adjust the audio recording settings. Select Stereo, 44.1 kHz - CD, 16 bits, and a Play-Through Volume of 7. Make sure that the Auto Gain box is checked, so the recorded signal won't be distorted. We're recording with these settings because we're going to need a high-quality sample to convert to MPEG later.

The amount you can record will be limited by the amount of memory you have allocated to SoundEffects, and since 16-bit, 44.1 kHz stereo samples require about 10 megabytes of space for every minute of audio, make sure you have made plenty of RAM available. If you have limited RAM, you can record in Mono mode or reduce the Sampling Rate and Sampling Size.

Now you're ready to record. When you click the Record button, the incoming waveform will turn red. Be sure to watch the continuous reading of the time left to record in the Available Seconds box. Click Save when you're done.

Now that you have a sample, you can manipulate it in many ways. You can select specific parts of the waveform by clicking and dragging over any area within the waveform display. The area you select will be the area affected by any special effects you apply to sample. One of the nicest things about SoundEffects is that the author invites programmers to develop plug-in effects for the application. Included on the Companion CD-ROM is one group of such plug-ins from gopher://gopher.archive.umich.edu:7055/00/mac/sound/soundutil/.

You can obtain information and help for individual effects at any time by holding down the Shift key and choosing the effect.

If you want the clip to fade in at the beginning, select the first few seconds of the sample and choose Effects>>Fade In. Make sure that you select both channels if you want the entire audio signal to fade smoothly. If you need a different view of the waveform, you can modify the display with the zoom-in and zoom-out buttons, or you can look at the entire waveform with the actual size button. You can also adjust other aspects of the waveform display from the File>>Preferences menu.

You can also add channels by dragging the New Channel icon to the right of the waveform, or you can delete channels by dragging the waveform icon next to the channel to the SoundEffects trash can.

Converting Sound Files

Since most audio archives on the Net contain samples in the MPEG and µ-law formats, you should become familiar with the steps necessary for converting recorded audio clips to these formats. We will illustrate this by exporting the audio clip you just prepared with SoundEffects and converting them with two separate applications.

Converting AIFF to MPEG Layer II

First, let's convert the 16-bit, 44.1kHz stereo sample to an MPEG Layer II (.mp2) file. Start by saving (File>>Save) the clip in SoundEffects as an AIFF file. Next, copy the MPEGAud application from the Companion CD-ROM to your hard drive and launch it. There are different versions of this program available for Macs with and without a floating point unit processor, so be sure to copy the one that's right for your machine. Open the AIFF file with MPEGAud (File>>Encode), and click Save when you see the dialog box showing the filename with the .mp2 extension. At this point you'll be given many options for how the sound file will be encoded (Figure 9-4). For now, leave the default settings as they are, and click OK. **Be Forewarned:** The MPEG Encoding process with MPEGAud is not real-time, and on some computers it takes quite a while. You may want to make sure that the selected file is only a few seconds long, unless you have time to wait. As MPEG-Aud is encoding the file, it will provide a status window reporting on the progress of the encoding (Figure 9-5).

EDialog

MPEG Audio Encoder Settings

Layer: ○ I BitRate: 448
◉ II BitRate: 384

Mode: ◉ Stereo
○ Joint Stereo
○ Dual Channel
○ Single Channel

Psychoacoustic Model: ○ 1 ◉ 2

De-emphasis: ◉ None
○ 50/15 microsecond
○ CCITT J.17

☐ Private Bit On ☐ Original
☐ Copyrighted ☐ Error Protection

Cancel OK

Figure 9-4: *The Device Settings button in the Record dialog box provides a shortcut to the Input Source dialog box.*

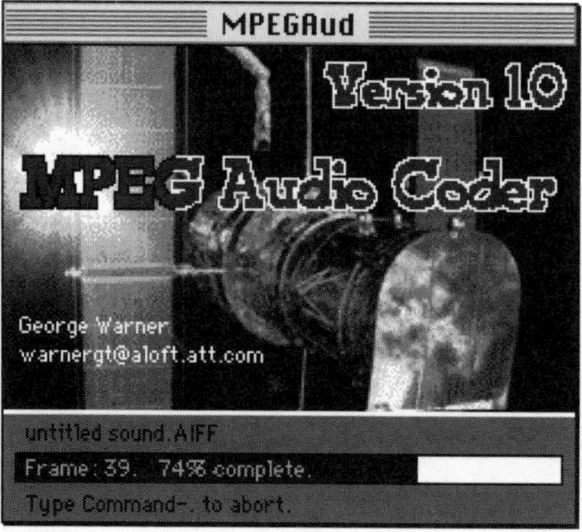

Figure 9-5: *The MPEGAud status window.*

When the MPEGAud is done, you can check to make sure it's encoded properly with the MPEG playback utility on the

CD-ROM called MPEG/CD. This program works with groups of .mp2 files called *lists*. To create a new list, choose File>>Add to List and select the file you just encoded. You could also select the demo file that comes with MPEG/CD if you think your file didn't encode correctly. To listen to the file, choose Audio>>Decode List. It will attempt to play the file back in real time, but if you don't have enough processing power, the audio signal may drop in and out. You can improve the playback by decoding only one channel at a time, which you can specify under Edit>>Decoder Preferences. The MPEG/CD Manual offers a number of tips about how to improve playback performance.

Preferences also gives you the option of decoding the audio clip to an AIFF file. This is handy if you're working on a lower-end Macintosh or if you want to edit the audio file. If you want to decode the file with full quality, duplicate the settings in Figure 9-6.

MPEG/CD Decoder Preferences

Subsampling Factor	None
Channel	Both
Prescan	On
Decompression Mode	Store To File
Output Buffer Size in Frames	40
Seconds of PlayTime	all

Cancel OK

Figure 9-6: *The correct MPEG/CD settings for converting an MPEG audio file to a high-quality AIFF file.*

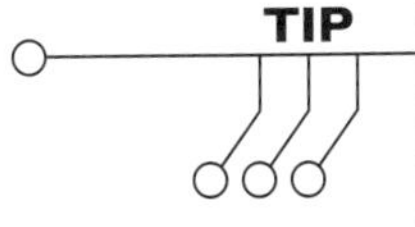

The makers of MPEG/CD, Kaua'i Media, sell a number of MPEG Audio encoding/decoding software solutions. You can check out their product specifications and compression statistics at http://www.kauai.com/~bbal/.

Converting AIFF to μ-law

To create μ-law files for Web site, you must convert the sample depth, sample rate and number of channels to be compatible with the existing standards on the Web. The conversion process will be different for every audio editor, but the process for SoundEffects described here should give you a pretty good idea of how to do it.

First, you need to convert the stereo file to mono. This isn't absolutely necessary, but since mono files are half the size of stereo files, and μ-law files are often used by people who don't have a stereo playback system, it's generally a good idea. From SoundEffects, choose Effects>>Quick Mix. Adjust your settings like those in Figure 9-7, and click OK. This will combine the stereo channels into a single channel, so you can drag the waveform icon to the right of the empty channel to the trash can. This will leave you will a single-channel sample.

Quick Mix

Mix to:
- ○ New Channel
- ◉ New Document

Use:
- ◉ Mono
- ○ Stereo

☐ Use each channel's pan

Cancel | OK

Figure 9-7: *The proper Quick Mix filter settings to convert a stereo file to mono.*

Next, you must change the sampling rate of the file by choosing Effects>>Resampling>>Resample Rate, manually entering 8000 Hz (since it's not a default option), and clicking OK. This is the standard sampling rate for μ-law files on the Net.

Finally, you need to downsample the sample depth by choosing Effects>>Resample>>Downsample Bits. Make sure that the dialog box displays "Downsample to 8 bits" and click OK. As you might have guessed, eight bits is the standard sample depth for µ-law files on the Net. Select File>>Save and save the modified file in the AIFF format.

To convert the 8-bit, 8 kHz mono AIFF to µ-law, you need to open it with SoundHack, the incredibly handy sound processing and conversion tool can be found on the Companion CD-ROM, as well as at ftp://music.calarts.edu/pub/SoundHack/. SoundHack reads and writes to .AIFF, .AIFC, .WAV and .AU sound files, as well as many others.

CD-ROM

When you open the file with SoundHack, it will display the file's properties, similar to the properties shown in Figure 9-8. To convert the file, choose File>>Save a Copy, set the File Type to NeXt • Sun and the Format to 8 Bit µ-law, and click OK. In the Save Soundfile As box, change the default .SND extension to .AU so that browsers at your site won't be confused. The amount of time SoundHack needs to convert the file will depend on the size of the input file and the speed of your computer.

Voilá! You now have a Net-compatible Sun/NeXT µ-law file.

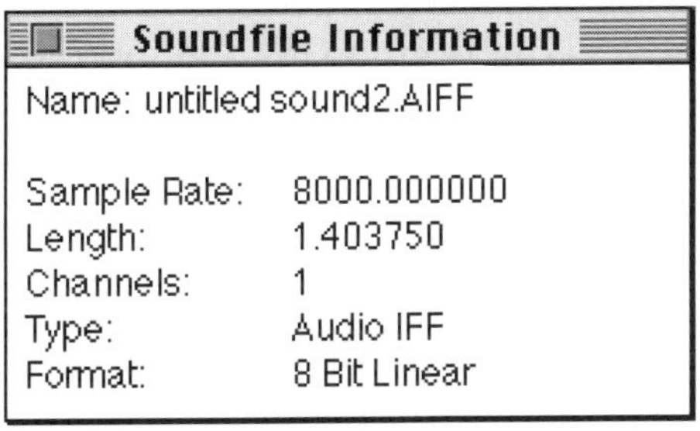

Soundfile Information

Name: untitled sound2.AIFF

Sample Rate:	8000.000000
Length:	1.403750
Channels:	1
Type:	Audio IFF
Format:	8 Bit Linear

Figure 9-8: *The SoundHack Soundfile Information dialog box.*

If this conversion process seems rather laborious to you, don't worry. Since Sound Manager 3.1 supports µ-law compression, and more Mac users are encountering 8-bit, 8kHz mono µ-law files, new conversion programs to automate the steps outlined here are sure to be introduced.

Converting to Other Formats

Since you may want to include other audio formats on your site, we've included a number of tools on the Companion CD-ROM that allow you to convert between numerous file types. Brian's Sound Tool is a handy utility that provides drag-and-drop conversion between Macintosh System sounds and .WAV files. It converts numerous non-Mac sound file formats (.WAV, .AU, .VOC and even .AIFF) into Mac System sounds and converts just about any files with Mac .SND resources in them to .WAV files. Besides letting you convert between numerous file formats, SoundHack allows you to apply gain changes, binaural filters, mutations, phase vocoders, and many other effects to audio files. Many of the settings on these effects are quite complex, but they can yield powerful and impressive results.

Publishing Video

Digital video has had an accelerated childhood and is quickly entering adolescence. In its current state, it's going through serious growing pains. It's awkward and unruly, but with a few preparatory measures, you'll see a world of promise for computer-based video editing and distribution. The following sections look at common digital video compression/decompression schemes and file format standards and explain what you need to create and publish video files at your Web site.

Video Codecs & File Format Standards

In discussions of digital video, you'll often come across references to "broadcast-quality" signals. This term refers to video signals that have been recorded at the National Television Standards Committee (NTSC) standard of 640 by 480 pixels at 30 frames per second (fps) in an interlaced fashion, with the odd and even horizontal lines alternating during each pass. This process divides each frame into two *fields*, thus producing 60 fields per second. Other video standards, such as PAL and SECAM, are used throughout the world, but NTSC is the most widely used.

For a video file to play smoothly, it needs to play back at 30 frames per second. A single frame of 24-bit video in its uncompressed state can require as much as a megabyte of disk space, *without* an audio track. That means that one second of uncompressed video is approximately 30MB. There are solutions to this heavy data load, such as reducing the number of colors or the size of the video, or even removing frames from the video, but all of these methods diminish the quality of the video signal. The need, then, is to find a standard codec that can compress the data to a manageable size so that it can be sent across the Internet without a noticeable loss in quality when decompressed and played back.

Luckily for Web publishers, no one really expects to find broadcast quality video files on the Internet . . . well, not yet anyway. While much of the hype about new media technologies has focused on high-definition television and increased resolution of images, the Internet community has come to expect less-than-perfect video quality. As computing technology evolves and bandwidth becomes more abundant, this is sure to change.

MPEG and QuickTime are the two most common video file formats found on the Internet. As more and more PCs have entered the Internet scene, the standard Windows AVI file format has also grown steadily in popularity. The following sections examine these file formats to help you decide which ones are most appropriate for your site. Like the audio file format descriptions, the video formats descriptions are preceded by their appropriate MIME types.

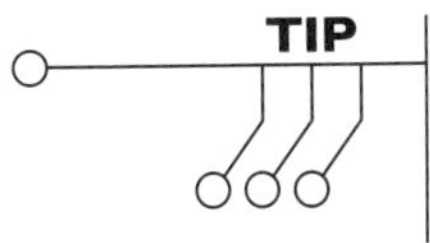

If you're interested in recording and working with broadcast-quality video, check out the Radius Digital Video Information Server. It includes information about everything from audio to setting up high-speed disk arrays to related Internet resources. The DV Information server is at http://research.radius.com/dv/maindv.html.

Occasionally you'll run across some video and animation file formats on the Internet that aren't used too often. Most of them are left over from days (and technologies) gone by, but you'll be able to view them with the MacAnim Viewer on the Companion CD-ROM. It will play GL, FLI, FLC, FLX, and DL animations, as well as display GIF, JPEG, PCX/PIC, and raw PPM image files. MacAnim will even automatically unzip PC zipped files.

The MPEG Video Format

video/mpeg mpeg mpg mpe

As discussed in the MPEG audio section of this chapter, MPEG compression is quickly becoming the preferred file format for the distribution of high-quality multimedia files online. While MPEG-2 is primarily used for high-end broadcast-quality video compression, MPEG-1 videos use a lower resolution of 352 x 240 pixels at 30 fps (in the U.S.). The MPEG codec takes advantage of *predictive calculation* for compression, which uses the current frame of video to predict what will be in the following frames. *This method of compression makes editing an MPEG video impossible.*

Speed and high compression ratios have made MPEG the format of choice for many video enthusiasts on the Internet. MPEG delivers decompressed data at 1.2 to 1.5MB per second and compresses data at a ratio of 50:1 or higher before you notice a degradation in video playback. Compression ratios as high as 200:1 are possible, but at such high compression rates, the images will be degraded unless you're using high-quality hardware. MPEG has the highest level of compression and delivers the best quality video when decompressed. Sounds great so far, but we've seen only one frame of the MPEG video picture.

Since A/V MPEG compression systems are typically hardware-based, it can be quite cost-prohibitive to produce interleaved audio/video MPEG files. Currently, there are no low-end MPEG interleaving packages available for the Mac, but numerous shareware and freeware QuickTime-to-MPEG, video-only encoding applications are available for both 680x0 and Power PC-based Macs. Most of them can be found on the MPEG server at ftp://ftp.crs4.it/mpeg/programs/. You can also get Sparkle, a popular MPEG and QuickTime playback application that's also a QuickTime to MPEG converter, at ftp://mirror.apple.com/mirrors/info-mac/_Graphic_%26_Sound_Tool/_Movie/sparkle-242.hqx. The latest version of Sparkle is also available on the Companion CD-ROM.

CD-ROM

If you need high-end MPEG encoding, or if you just want somebody else to digitize and encode videos for you, then service bureaus may be your solution. Most of these bureaus accept VHS,

Super-VHS, Beta, and 3/4-inch videotape or QuickTime and AVI files and convert it to MPEG format. The price can range from $30 to $300 a minute, so it pays to shop around. You'll find numerous service bureau listings in the back of magazines like *DV Digital Video, PC Graphics and Video* and *New Media*.

A new company called Duplexx Software has developed its own video file formats based on the MPEG codec. Identified with the .m15 and .m75 (15 and 7.5 fps, respectively), these files require an amazingly small amount of disk space, usually on the average of one megabyte for 30 seconds of 15fps video. Since this is a proprietary format, Duplexx has introduced the NET TOOB multimedia viewer for PCs. Even though the NET TOOB is not yet available for the Mac, they have an interim solution that works with Sparkle 2.4.2. To play synched audio and video, simply place the .m15 video and its corresponding audio file in the same directory.

The QuickTime Format

video/quicktime mov moov qt

Most Macintosh users are quite familiar with QuickTime format. It was the first immensely popular digital video format for the Mac, and Apple has since released QuickTime enablers for Windows-based PCs and Silicon Graphics computers. Since QuickTime supports video, audio and MIDI (control signals for electronic instruments that drastically reduce the necessary size for soundtracks), as well as numerous compression schemes, it has become the de facto standard for most digital video editing applications. QuickTime files are commonly identified by the .MOV, .MOOV and .QT extensions.

One of the most important things to remember when distributing QuickTime movies over the Internet is that when QuickTime movies are created on a Macintosh, they, like most Mac files, contain both a *data fork* and a *resource fork*. The resource fork contains small chunks of program code that describe various attributes of the file necessary for the Macintosh interface, while the data fork contains the actual numerical and textual data of the file. Since the HTTP does not provide support for transferring multi-forked files, it is necessary for QuickTime movies to be converted before they can be distributed over the WWW to be played on multiple platforms. The conversion process combines the resource and data forks into a single-forked file, commonly referred to as a "flattened" file. The resultant cross-platform QuickTime files can be stored on non-Mac file systems without loss of important data. To convert your QuickTime files, simply open them with the application flattenMOOV (included on the Companion CD-ROM) and save it as a flattened movie. Also, most digital video-editing systems let you export QuickTime clips as flattened MOOVs.

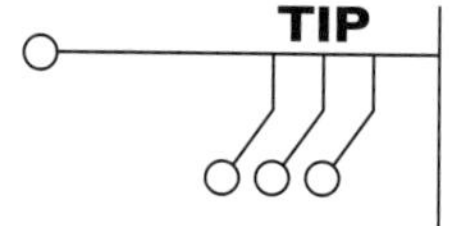

The QuickTime Continuum, Apple's Web server devoted to QuickTime-related information, is located at http://quicktime.apple.com/.

A technical overview of the QuickTime format, as well as the new QuickTime VR format (see the "Latest Developments" section later in this chapter), can be found at http://www.info.apple.com/dev/techqa/Main.html#quicktime.

The AVI Format

video/x-msvideo avi

The Audio/Video Interleaved (AVI) format is Microsoft's format for video and audio. As the name of the format implies, the video data is interleaved with audio data within the same file, so the audio portion of the movie is synchronized with the video portion. AVI uses Intel's Indeo and the Cinepack codecs, which have been getting a lot of publicity lately. AVI files typically play at about 15 frames per second in a small window (320 x 240 pixels).

With acceleration hardware or software, you can run AVI video sequences at 30 frames per second in a larger window or full screen. The AVI format accesses data from the hard disk without using a lot of memory. It's quick-loading and -playing, because only a few frames of video and a portion of audio are accessed at one time. AVI files are also compressed to boost the quality of your video sequences and reduce their size.

While AVI format is the standard Windows video file format, it's rare to find AVI files on the Internet. This is likely to change as the user base begins to reflect the huge number of Windows users jacking into the Internet.

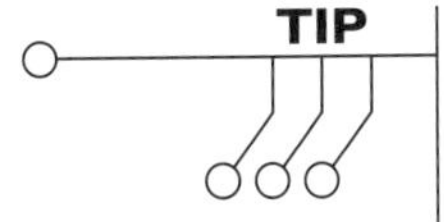

For a QuickTime-to-AVI and AVI-to-QuickTime converter, download the Video for Windows Macintosh Utilities at ftp://ftp.microsoft.com/developr/drg/Multimedia/VfW11-Mac/vfw11.sit.

Acquiring Video Files

The safest way to present a video file at your site is to create one yourself or use a royalty-free video clip. First Light Productions and Four Palms are two companies that sell royalty-free video clips. Both companies are included in the Resource section at the back of this book. There are also lots of video archives on the Internet. As with audio files, some problems arise when using video files on the Internet. For one, many video files are of poor quality. Another problem is that it's sometimes hard to tell which videos break copyright laws. Use videos from the Internet at your own risk. Of course, you can always create a link to a video in an archive. Table 9-2 lists and describes sites that include video clip files on the Web. As we mentioned in the section on sounds, just because we've listed these sites doesn't mean you can publish them at your Web site. However, you may want to experiment with videos, even if you don't add any of them to your Web pages.

URL	Contents
http://www.yahoo.com/yahoo/computers/multimedia/Movies/Archives	A listing of multimedia archives.
http://www.eeb.ele.tue.nl/mpeg/index.html	Lots of MPEG movies and animations. Several clips break copyright laws, such as videos of *The Simpsons* and popular movies. The list is broken into categories including supermodels, animations, music, space, racing and so on.
http://www.acm.uiuc.edu/rml/	Rob Malick's multimedia lab, sponsored by the Association for Computing Machinery at University of Illinois. Includes lots of movie clips in FLI and QuickTime format.
http://tausq.resnet.cornell.edu/mmedia.html	Randolph Chung's archive of movie clips, including such copyright breakers as Disney's *Aladdin*, *The Lion King* and *StarTrek*.
http://ice.ucdavis.edu/whimsy/fun_stuff/fun_stuff_movies.html	Sample movie clips and links to Harvey Chinn's movie archive list.
http://mambo.ucsc.edu/psl/thant/thant.html	Thant Nyo's huge list of links to computer generated animations, visualizations, movies and interactive images.
www.univ-rennes1.fr/ASTRO/anim-e.html	Astronomy clips, such as planets,eclipses, rocket launches, astronauts in orbit and clips from science fiction films.
http://wwwzenger.informatik.tumuenchen.de/persons/paula/mpeg/index.html	Andreas Paul's collection of various MPEG animations, such as a scene from Pink Floyd's *The Wall*, *Blade Runner* and *Psycho*. The site includes a disclaimer requesting the videos be used for personal use only.

Table 9-2: *URLs for video files.*

Including Video Files in a Web Page

To include a hyperlink to a video, use the same format you would use with a sound file. The only difference is the extension of the file that you are pointing to. For example, a link to a video file uses the following syntax:

```
<A HREF="URL/">hyperlink</A>
```

You may want to point to a video file that is published at some other site, because of space limitations on your host or other reasons. A little caution should be exercised if you decide to do this, because external files may be changed without your knowledge. If you include the link, check occasionally to make sure the video file is still available.

If you want to create an archive of video files, it's generally considered good form to identify the video file with an icon, such as a camera, a filmstrip or an eye, denoting the file type. The following is an example of a local video file named sample.mov in a directory named videos identified by an icon named camera.gif in the icons directory.

```
<IMG ALT="o" SRC="/icons/camera.gif"> <A HREF="/videos/
sample.mov"></A>
```

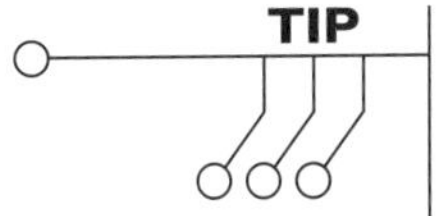

Make sure your intended audience has the necessary players. If you're not sure whether or not your audience can view your video files, refer them to the location of a player.

Video Capturing & Editing

With a properly equipped Mac and few preparatory steps, you can produce impressive digital video clips with fairly inexpensive hardware and software. This section provides you with some of the secrets for effective video capturing and editing.

The process of digitizing video signals, like the process of capturing audio, is called *sampling*. To sample a video, you'll need a video capture board. The AV line of Macs (660/AV, 840/AV and

AV Power Macs) comes equipped with the hardware necessary for capturing video, along with a copy of VideoFusion's Fusion Recorder. This software/hardware combination is sufficient for capturing medium-quality video files to put on your Web site. However, if you need high-quality video capture, check out Radius's SpigotPower AV ($999, 408-541-6100), which allows you to input and output broadcast-quality movies (640 x 480 pixel movies at 30 fps).

There are a few secrets to effective video capturing. These tips are applicable for just about any video recording hardware setup and video capturing program, including VideoFusion's Fusion Recorder and Adobe Premiere:

- Run just the Finder and the video capture application. This will free all available memory for the capturing process. Make sure you have allocated as much memory as possible (all but 2MB or so) to the video capturing applications from within the Get Info dialog box.
- Turn off AppleTalk and disable all nonessential extensions. Many times you can get away with running *only* the QuickTime extension and any enablers that might maximize the performance of your drive.
- Make sure the Monitors control panel is set to 256 colors or fewer to help conserve system resources.
- Set the Frames Per Second option within the Compression menu (which will differ between applications) to Best. This instructs the video capture hardware/software to save as many frames as possible.
- Set the Sound Settings to 22.05kHz, 8 bit, mono to help reduce the amount of storage space the movie will require.
- Capture the video uncompressed. Video compression takes up unnecessary processor time that could be devoted to writing the incoming video stream to disk.
- Use the Cinepak codec to post-compress the captured and edited video. Even though it takes quite a while to compress, the compression ratios and final quality are worth the wait. There's more information about various codecs in the FusionRecorder ReadMe file.

- If you have enough memory, record directly to RAM. Otherwise, make sure that your hard drive has been optimized so that the video stream can be written to a large, contiguous block of free space.

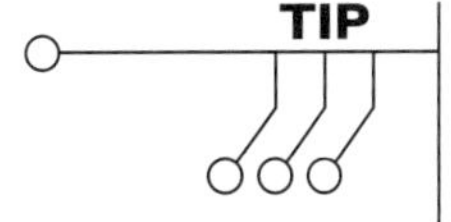

For more tips on effective video capturing techniques on the Mac, along with incredibly helpful tips on video output, see http://www.csua.berkeley.edu/~jwang/AV/AV_Video.html.

Adobe Premiere is an ideal solution for those who don't have thousands of dollars to invest in high-end video digital video editing systems. It presents a construction window in which you can easily edit multiple video tracks and add audio tracks. Working with multiple tracks simultaneously can be quite helpful, especially when working with transitions between two video clips (referred to as an *A/B roll*). Premiere includes numerous special effects that let you create smooth blends and transitions between scenes. It even includes *keying*, which lets you superimpose one video on top of another. Keying is the process used by your friendly TV weather reporter, who points out temperatures on a Chromakey weather map. Another powerful feature is *rotoscoping*, which lets you draw or paint on video frames to add animations to an existing video. You can also combine titles, sounds and graphic images. To learn more about Premiere, including key features, system requirements and production tips, visit http://www.adobe.com/Apps/Premiere.html.

Wondering about editing audio from within Premiere? A number of plug-ins that come with Premiere 4.0 allow you to modify the audio track from within the application. Also, third-party plug-ins, such as Plugged-In Software's Noise Gate, are becoming increasingly commonplace (see Figure 9-9). More plug-ins are sure to be introduced as desktop computers become better equipped for handling digital video and audio.

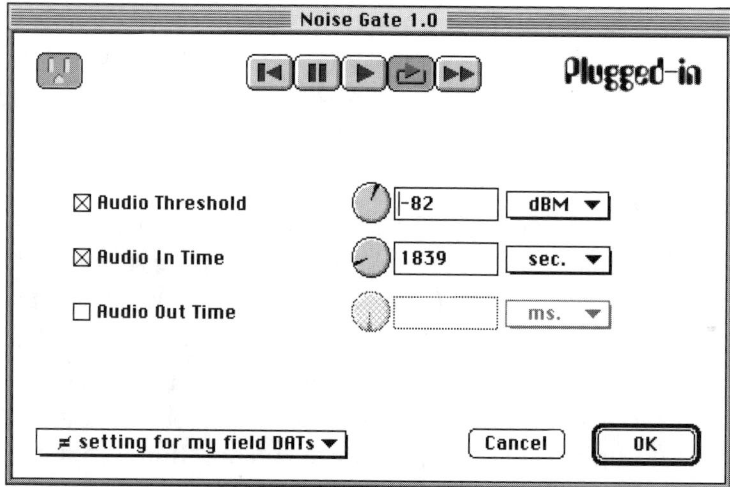

Figure 9-9: *The Noise Gate sound editing plug-in for Premiere.*

CD-ROM

Another option for users new to the world of digital video editing is QuickEditor, the shareware audio/video editor included on the Companion CD-ROM. For a $20 registration fee, Quick-Editor gives you many of the same effects and editing features as Premiere. QuickEditor even has an attractive, intuitive interface, with separate window regions for sound track editing, transitions, video effects and others, as seen in Figure 9-10. If you can't afford Premiere or other high-end video editing systems, we strongly suggest that you give QuickEditor a try. It's also available from ftp://mirror.apple.com/mirrors/info-mac/_Graphic_%26_Sound_Tool/_Movie/.

Figure 9-10: *The QuickEditor video editor is likely to be one of the most feature-packed pieces of shareware you'll ever find.*

Latest Developments

There's been a whirlwind of activity and hype surrounding the Web over the past year. The inevitable result has been a flood of new technologies that all promise to be the latest, greatest thing. Luckily, a number of the new technologies have proven quite useful, and many of them have shown enormous potential. This section gives you a brief introduction to some of the more promising multimedia technologies currently in use on the Internet.

Real-Time Audio & Video

For the past two years, researchers at Cornell have been pushing the envelope of audio/video transmissions over low-bandwidth networks with the CU-SeeMe project. The software developed by these researchers enables users to audio/video-conference over the Internet. Even though the video is black and white and is quite choppy (some users have coined the pixelated effect of the low-bandwidth video transmissions "Vannavision"), CU-SeeMe is giving lots of people their first taste of true teleconferencing.

To teleconference with numerous people simultaneously, a CU-SeeMe *reflector* must be set up on a UNIX workstation. There are many reflectors set up that are freely accessible by CU-SeeMe users, some of which are transmitting radio and TV stations 24 hours a day. Like its video counterpart, audio reception can be quite choppy, but this will improve as bandwidth limitations are improved. It's also possible to have one-on-one conferences without the use of a reflector simply by connecting to another Net-connected Mac or PC running the CU-SeeMe software.

URL	Description
http://cu-seeme.cornell.edu	Cornell's CU-SeeMe Welcome Page.
http://www.umich.edu/~johnlaue/cuseeme/default.htm	The CU-SeeMe event guide, which keeps track of special events taking advantage of CU-SeeMe.
http://sunsite.unc.edu/wxyc	The first 24/7 real-time Internet radio station, WXYC Online, courtesy of UNC-Chapel Hill's student-run radio station.
http://www.utexas.edu/depts/output/www/tstv.html	KVR-InterneTV, a real-time simulcast of the University of Texas's student-run television station.

Table 9-3: *CU-SeeMe URLs.*

The audio portion of CU-SeeMe is based on Charley Kline's Maven, an audioconferencing tool from the University of Illinois, Urbana-Champaign. Maven has numerous audio-encoding options, including support for GSM encoding, ideal for users of 14.4kb/s modems. The latest version of Maven is on the Companion CD-ROM, and updates are available from any Info-Mac mirror, including

ftp://mirrors.aol.com/pub/info-mac/comm/_MacTCP/

If you're interested in Internet-based audio-on-demand applications, you should definitely listen to RealAudio, a software package that allows you to receive real-time audio playback from digitized audio files on remote machines. RealAudio is unique in that it doesn't require you to download a large file before playback begins (unlike most audio file formats). You just need to download a small initialization file, which enables you to receive hours of audio transmissions off the network. Even though playback software is available for the Mac, Mac users can't yet serve on-demand audio from their site, because that requires a RealAudio server (which is only currently available for UNIX workstations and PCs). For more information, see the RealAudio home page at http://www.realaudio.com.

Macromedia Director

Another multimedia application that is receiving a lot of press and getting support on the Web is Director from Macromedia. This is an animation and multimedia program that has been fawned over by Macintosh multimedia authors for some time. Director is not a video editor; instead, it's a multimedia authoring package that lets you create stand-alone programs for multimedia presentations. It uses a metaphor of a stage where you work with text, sound, graphics and video clips. To add interactivity to a video, you use an English-like scripting language called Lingo. You can save your output as a video or a run-time module. There is no run-time royalty fee, although you need to let people know that it is a Macromedia file.

If you plan to include Director files on your Web site, you should link to the Windows Director Viewer, developed by Dave Walker, so that Windows users can view the files you have to offer. The viewer lets you view Director files, just like an MPEG viewer, off the Net. This viewer doesn't work with Windows NT. You can pick up the viewer at http://www.portal.com/~dwalker/dirhome.html. To visit a collection of Web pages devoted to Director, enter the URL: http://hakatai.mcli.dist.maricopa.edu/director/index.html.

The most important development for Director developers has been Netscape's announcement that it will incorporate Director playback software into the Netscape Navigator Web browsing software. To learn more about how Netscape and Macromedia plan to incorporate Director into Internet applications, see the Director-on-the-Internet White Paper at http://www.macromedia.com/Tools/Director/Shockwave/index.html. General Macromedia information is available at http://www.macromedia.com.

Virtual Reality

For the past few years, the term *virtual reality* (VR) has been thrown around quite a bit by the media and software companies. While many people still aren't sure exactly what VR is, most researchers agree that it's a collection of technologies that allow for the creation of computer-generated environments. Participants in these environments, or *virtual worlds*, can freely navigate and even manipulate their surroundings. Even though the most popular visions of VR include head-mounted displays and full-body input devices, a number of crafty developers have been working on ways to bring virtual reality technologies to the masses.

One of the VR technologies that has received quite a bit of press lately is the Virtual Reality Modeling Language. Based on Silicon Graphics's Open Inventor description language, VRML is a platform-independent language for three-dimensional scene design. It describes 3D objects and scenes in much the same way as the PostScript language describes images and text. Objects' descriptions, not their entire graphic representation, are transmitted between a client and server, reducing the bandwidth necessary for communication. These descriptions require that the client, not the server, render the 3D scenes. This approach not only speeds up the rendering process, it also reduces the amount of bandwidth necessary for distributing virtual worlds.

There are many 3D object file formats, but what sets VRML apart is its ability to incorporate hyperlinks for use with the World Wide Web. Any object in a VRML world can be defined as a *WWWanchor*, which will link the object to some URL on the Web. It is the dream of the VRML creators that much of the information

available on the Internet in the form of two-dimensional text and pictures will come to be represented by three-dimensional hyperlinked objects. And since VRML browsers are designed to work in conjunction with current Web browsers as helper applications, information providers don't have to worry about conflicts arising between HTML and VRML files distribution.

As of the writing of this book, no VRML browsers are available for the Mac, but a few software companies have promised that they will offer them soon, including Intervista Software and Template Graphics Software. In addition to these, the Virtus Corporation, already well-known for its architectural modeling program Virtus Walkthrough Pro, has recently announced that it will be offering a VRML export feature from within its applications. This means that Mac users will have access to an inexpensive modeling system for developing virtual worlds for distribution over the Net. Keep an eye out for the new book about VRML by Mark Pesce that will include a version of Virtus Walkthrough/Special Edition.

VRML	Description
http://www.sdsc.edu/vrml	The VRML Repository at the San Diego Supercomputer Center.
http://vrml.wired.com/vrml	The VRML Forum at *Wired*, including a Hypermail archive of the VRML mailing list and links to the VRML Technical Forum.
http://cedar.cic.net/~rtilmann /mm/index.html	Mesh Mart, a collection of 3D objects (including VRML files) for use by 3D modeling artists and developers.
http://www.virtus.com	The Virtus Corporation, with links to updates about their VRML export feature.
http://www.webmaster.com/ vrml/	Intervista Software's VRML browser for Mac.
http://www.cts.com/~template/	Template Graphics Software, soon to release a Mac VRML browser.
http://www.sgi.com/Products/ WebFORCE/WebSpace/ VRMLBackgrounder.html	Background on VRML by Mark Pesce.

Table 9-4: *URLs for more Virtual Reality Modeling Language information.*

Of particular interest to Macintosh users is the development of QuickTime VR, an extension of Apple's QuickTime format. Unlike VRML and most other computer-generated world-description formats, QTVR provides up to 360 degree panoramic views of real-world objects and spaces like the Beastie Boys's studio in Figure 9-11. This effect is achieved through the use of a panoramic photography technique developed by the QTVR development team. QTVR also allows you to incorporate digitally rendered and manipulated images into the panoramic scenes, thus giving you an amalgam of computer-generated and real-world objects. Also, like VRML's hyperlinkable objects, you can define *hot spots* for objects within the QTVR world that, when clicked, launch various forms of media, such as audio clips, video clips or other QTVR files.

There are a few major differences between QuickTime VR and VRML. VRML is a description language that can be exported from 3D modelers, so the average user will not have to learn the exact syntax of the language itself. The language is actually written by the modeling application when users export their creations as VRML. The most important prerequisite for VRML-world designers is proficiency with 3D-modeling software. QTVR authoring, however, requires a number of specialized skills, including photography experience, familiarity with Macintosh programming, and a working knowledge of Hypercard and/or Macromedia Director scripting.

The biggest difference between the two formats is that VRML was designed by a team of researchers from a number of private, academic and corporate backgrounds. It is intended to be a platform-independent description language that can be used with and seamlessly integrated into many of the existing technologies in use on the World Wide Web. QTVR, however, was developed solely by Apple as a proprietary file format. The ways in which QTVR can be incorporated into HTML and VRML-based technologies remain to be seen, but they are sure to be integrated as QTVR players become available for platforms other than the Macintosh.

As of the writing of this book, the QTVR viewer is only available for Macs (included on the Companion CD-ROM), but Apple promises that a Windows version will be available soon. If you're interested in learning more about QTVR, check out the QuickTime VR home page at http://quicktime.apple.com/qtvr.html and the QTVR White paper at http://quicktime.apple.com/qtvr/qtvrtech.html. You'll also find QTVR movies at http://quicktime.apple.com/archive/index.html.

Figure 9-11: *A QuickTime VR representation of the Beastie Boys's recording studio. You can rotate the horizontal view of the model 360 degrees by clicking and dragging the cursor to the left or right.*

While many of the new technologies are still in their infancy, they show great promise and will surely evolve into the distributed digital media communication systems of tomorrow. By familiarizing yourself with them now, you'll be well prepared for whatever lurks just around the technological corner.

Moving On

Multimedia is a newly formed world, filled with fascinating possibilities. Because multimedia is such a hotbed of activity, you'll need to keep up with the ways browsers add multimedia support and new multimedia authoring techniques. Several magazines, like *DV, New Media, PC Graphics and Video, MacWeek* and *Macworld* are great sources for keeping on top of new programs and following trends for publishing multimedia documents. Publishing multimedia files is a great way to entertain and involve the visitors to your site. The next chapter takes interactivity to another level by showing you how to create and publish interactive forms.

SECTION III

Putting the Pieces Together

10

Forms, Databases & CGI

Until now, you've been creating information for Web pages that go in one direction: from you to your reader. Through the use of forms, you can add two-way communication to your HTML pages. Forms allow a user to enter information, provide a method to supply that information to a "back-end" program of your choosing and creation, and return results to a user via regular HTML page construction. Forms were not part of the original HTML version 2 specification, but are so useful that most (if not all) Web broswers now support them. You can find many examples of forms on the Web. From these various examples you can pick and choose the features you want to use in your Web pages. In this chapter, you'll be introduced to the basics of form construction. We'll also learn more about the Common Gateway Interface (CGI), which was first introduced in Chapter 8, and how to create and identify programs that can interact with these forms by using CGI.

Using CGI With Your Web Page

Most HTML authoring is independent of the operating system running on the server. Once you venture into the realm of CGI and back-end processing, however, everything changes. Virtually anything you do relies heavily on the operating system and the HTTP server that you are running. In this book the discussion of forms is common across all operating systems. The CGI examples presented here focus on MacHTTP and WebSTAR, as indicated with each example. If you're using a Windows or UNIX-based server, the examples illustrate the techniques you need to use, but the code will not be very portable.

Unlike most other examples presented in this book, *the examples in this chapter using CGI require you to be running server software if you want to try them.* A demonstration version of the WebSTAR server program is included on the Companion CD-ROM. You can install this program to get started. There are several other servers currently available for the Macintosh: the predecessor to WebSTAR, MacHTTP, is less-expensive but is also less fully featured than the version of WebSTAR included here; other commerical and non-commercial servers are also available from various sources. For more information on servers, including details on acquiring these alternative servers, see Chapter 13, "Servers at Your Service."

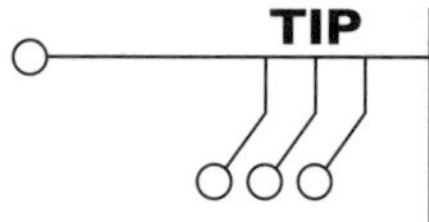

Perl users should be aware that there is a port of perl to Macintosh that offers a great deal of scripting power. So, if you currently use perl on UNIX, but want the simplicity of a Mac-based HTTP server, you should get a copy of MacPerl for your CGI back-ends. See Chapter 13 for details.

There's a lot of discussion in the Web community about the precise syntax and extensions of the forms under HTML, so some things may change. The syntax is certainly going to change in HTML version 3, so stay tuned. Also, the *official* documentation for HTML version 2 is the Internet RFC. At the time of this writing, it was just being submitted to the IETF for consideration as a proposed standard.

Understanding How Forms Are Submitted

Every form contains at least one element. If there is only a single text field on a form, the form is submitted when the user presses Return. On more complex forms there is a button or bitmap that triggers a submit operation. When a form is submitted, all the information entered in the fields is sent via HTTP to the server application. The information is sent in plain ASCII text, in a *name=value* format, with the name of the field sent first, followed by an equal sign, followed by the data that was entered in the field. Each *name=value* pair is separated with an ampersand (&). The way this information is sent to the server depends on the "method" used to send the form, which is described later in this chapter. The server application processes the information in some appropriate way, then returns a "results" page to the viewer. The results page can be anything you want, ranging from a simple "OK" to a complete database query result with multimedia elements. You can also create pages with CGI programs that are not related to specific database queries, but whose content (or address) changes on a regular basis.

As you look over the syntax for an HTML form you may wish to skip ahead to the "Common Gateway Interface" section to find out how the information entered by the user is processed.

Constructing a Form

In this chapter, you'll be creating elements that could make up a Customer Survey and Comment form to link to A Clean Well-Lighted Place for Books's home page that was constructed in the last few chapters. Figure 10-1 shows a comment form that illustrates all the elements you'll be working with in this chapter. Refer back to this figure to see how each element looks as rendered by Netscape.

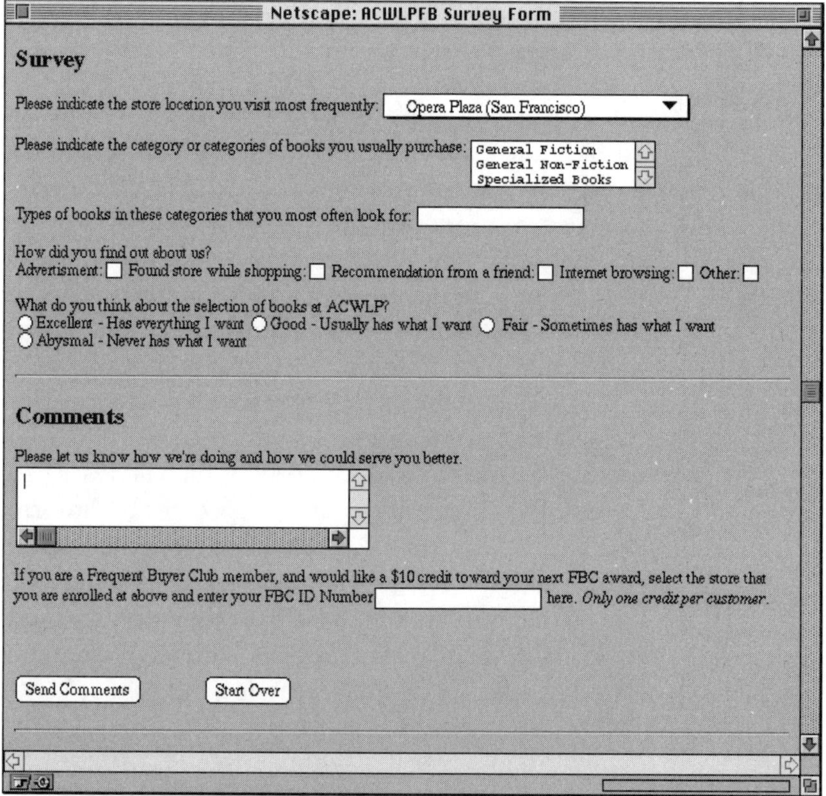

Figure 10-1: *The ACWLPFB Survey Form.*

A form is started and ended with the FORM tag and can contain a variety of fields and buttons. To get started, insert a FORM element, selecting from the HoTMetaL PRO Insert Element box or by selecting FORM from the Form button on the Other HTML palette. After you insert the FORM element, select Markup>>Edit SGML Attributes to enter an ACTION, METHOD and ENCTYPE. This is shown in Figure 10-2.

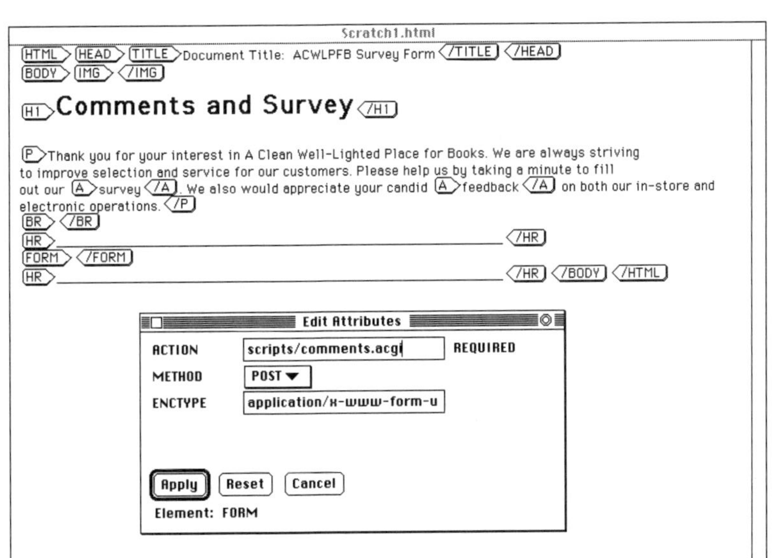

Figure 10-2: *Entering the FORM tag.*

For the ACTION attribute, enter **/scripts/comments.acgi**. This is the name of the program that will be executed when the form is submitted, and in this case the program comments.acgi is located in a folder called scripts. The name of the executable program or folder directory you use for your own forms depends on the server you are using; for example, some servers—notably UNIX—based servers-require that CGI applications all be stored in a specific directory on the server. This is not true for WebSTAR or InterServer Publisher. You could have entered a complete URL, host name and all. If you leave off the starting part of the URL, your Web browser will submit the form to the host that supplied the form. Since the ACTION attribute can be any URL, you could actually create a form that is submitted to a host that is not your own.

For METHOD, you have two choices: GET and POST. The METHOD you choose when you create your own forms will depend on how your server supports the protocols. Enter **POST** for now, since this is the recommended protocol.

For standard CGI, the GET method puts the information submitted by your users at the end of the URL that is submitted to your server. Since forms can be very large, the GET method can create huge URLs. For this reason, the GET method is discouraged for newly created forms. With the POST method, the information from the user is put into the data stream of the HTTP protocol, and your back-end program can read the input via the standard input data stream. For Macintosh CGI, both methods add the information to AppleEvents that your CGI program processes to obtain the data.

The last attribute, ENCTYPE, is always set to *application/x-www-form-urlencoded*. The HTML code for the form at this point might look like this:

```
<HTML><HEAD><TITLE>ACWLP Survey Form</TITLE>
</HEAD>
<BODY><H1>Comments and Survey</H1><IMG
SRC="file://images/survey.gif" ALT="Survey Logo">
<P>Thank you for your interest in A Clean Well-Lighted
Place for Books. We are always striving to improve selec-
tion and service for our customers. Please help us by taking
a minute to fill in our <A HREF="#survey">survey<A>.</
P><HR> <FORM ACTION="scripts /comments.acgi"
METHOD="POST"></FORM><HR>
</BODY></HTML>
```

Creating an Entry Field

Once the initial FORM tag is entered, you can start to enter the individual form elements. There are a variety of different form elements you can enter, including text fields, drop-down list boxes, scroll boxes, large text areas, buttons and boxes.

Creating a Drop-down List Box

A drop-down list box presents choices to a user. You have undoubtedly seen a drop-down list box in many Macintosh programs. The basic screen element is a box with a down arrow to the right of it. When the user selects the down arrow, a list of choices is presented. The following steps explain how to include a drop-down list box in a form:

1. Insert a Paragraph tag and enter the text introducing the drop-down list box. For this example, enter **Please indicate the store location you visit most frequently:**.
2. Insert a SELECT tag at the point in your page you want to position the list box. For this example, insert the SELECT tag between the beginning and ending paragraph tags. Position your cursor immediately after the first SELECT tag and choose Markup>>Edit SGML Attributes. The Edit Attributes dialog box appears, as shown in Figure 10-3.

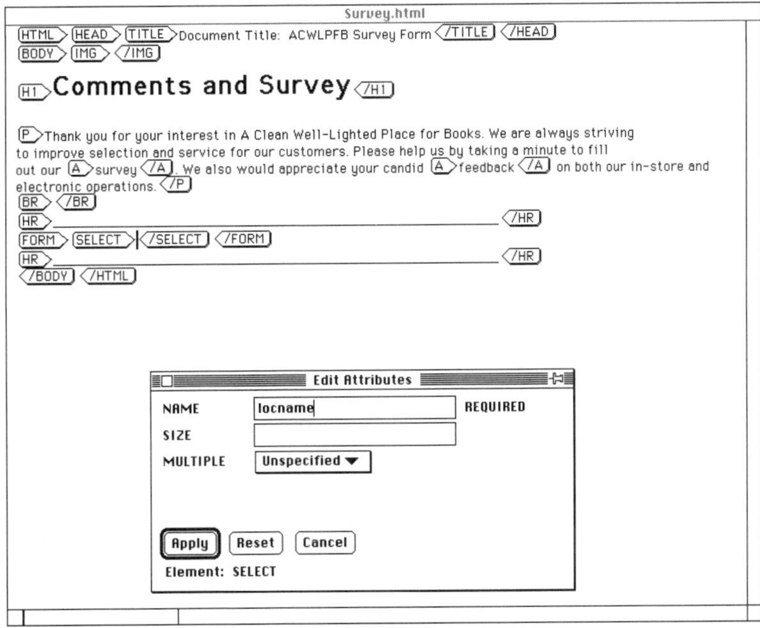

Figure 10-3: *Entering the SELECT tag.*

4. Enter a unique name in the NAME field. For this example, type **locname**. Every item on a form has a different name associated with it, so that when the data is submitted, each piece of user data has a unique identifier. For your own forms, you can use any name you wish. You don't need to use the SIZE and MULTIPLE options here; see Appendix C for a complete description of how these work.
5. Choose the Apply button to add the element to your form. The insertion point reappears after the SELECT tag.
6. Move the insertion point between the two OPTION tags. The OPTION tag identifies each choice.
7. Type the text for the first option; for this example, type **Opera Plaza (San Francisco)**. The insertion point is now between the OPTION and /OPTION tags.
8. Move the insertion point to between the /OPTION and /SELECT tags. Insert another OPTION tag after the close of the first OPTION tag by choosing OPTION from the Insert Element dialog box or by selecting OPTION from the FORM button's drop-down list of elements. Type the text for the next option.
9. Repeat step 8 to enter all five options shown in Figure 10-4.

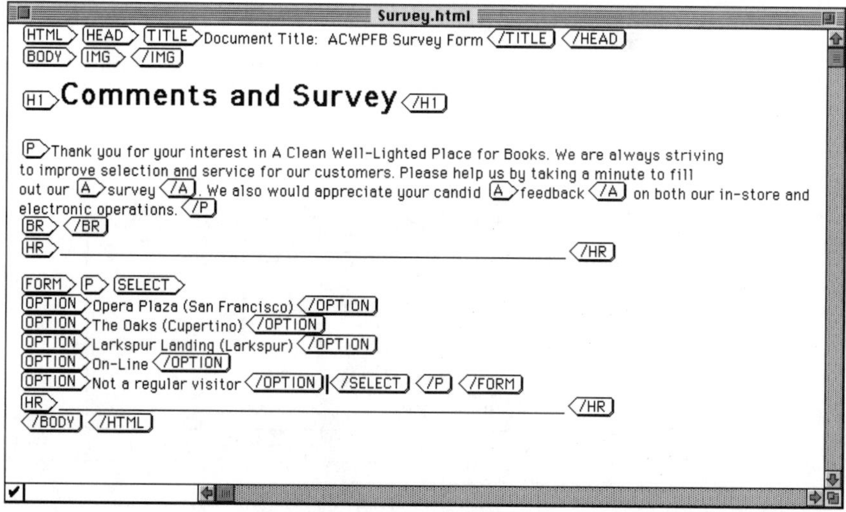

Figure 10-4: *Options for the SELECT field.*

The HTML code for the SELECT tag looks like this:

```
<P>Please indicate the store location you visit most fre-
quently: <SELECT NAME="locname">
<OPTION>Opera Plaza (San Francisco)</OPTION>
<OPTION>The Oaks (Cupertino)</OPTION>
<OPTION>Larkspur Landing (Larkspur</OPTION>
<OPTION>On-Line</OPTION>
<OPTION>Not a regular visitor</OPTION></SELECT></P>
```

Creating a Multiple Selection List Box

A multiple-selection list box is a variant on the drop-down list box. This type of list box allows the user to select more than one of the items on a list. The particular way a user selects the elements is dependent on the Web browser in use. The following steps explain how to include a multiple-selection drop-down list box in a form:

1. Insert a Paragraph tag after the previous example's ending paragraph tag and enter the text introducing the multiple-selection list box. For this example, enter **Please enter the category or categories of books you usually purchase:**.
2. Insert a SELECT tag at the point in your page you want to position the list box.
3. Choose Markup>>Edit SGML Attributes or press ⌘-]. The Edit Attributes dialog box appears, as shown in Figure 10-5.

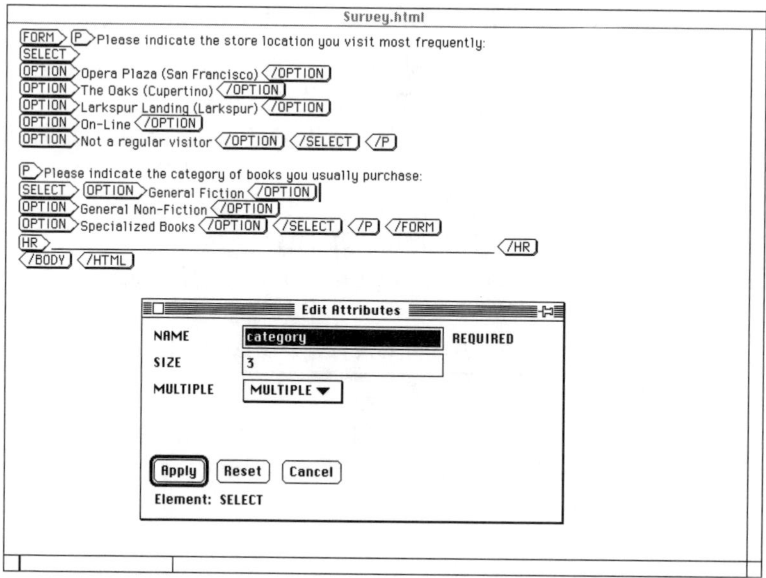

Figure 10-5: *Multiple Selection list box.*

4. Enter a unique name in the NAME field. For this example, type the name **category.**
5. Enter a SIZE of **3**, and choose the MULTIPLE option for the MULTIPLE attribute.
6. Choose Apply to add the element to your form.
7. Insert an OPTION tag. The OPTION tag identifies each choice.
8. Choose Markup>>Edit SGML Attributes or press ⌘-], enter a **1** for the first VALUE attribute and choose the Apply button. You'll need to increment the VALUE attribute for each option you add. The OPTION tag attributes are shown in Figure 10-6.

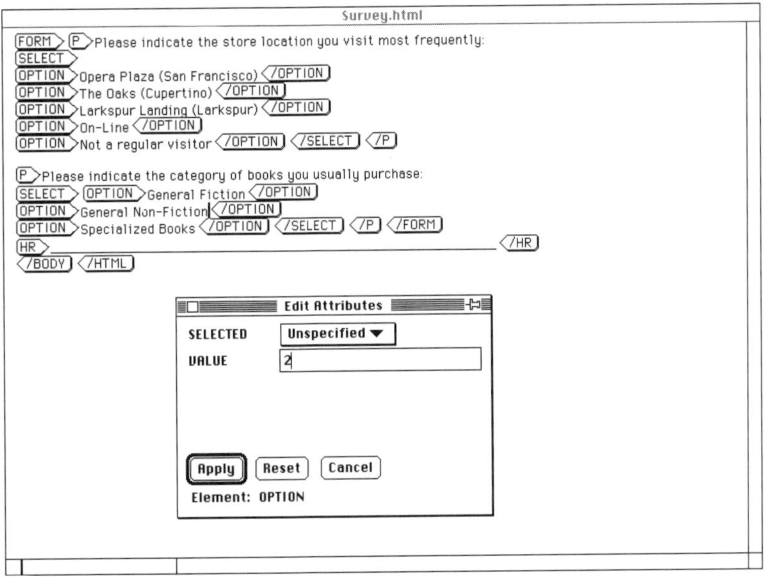

Figure 10-6: *Editing the OPTION tag.*

9. Type the text for the first option; for this example, type **General Fiction**. The insert point is now between the OPTION and /OPTION tags. Move the insert point between the /OPTION and /SELECT tags.
10. Repeat steps 7, 8 and 9 to enter all three options shown in Figure 10-6.

There are a few new items in the SELECT element that you may have noticed. In step 5, you entered a SIZE of 3 and specified the MULTIPLE option instead of leaving it as Unspecified. The SIZE indicates how many elements are to be expected in the list box. If the actual number of elements exceeds the number specified, a scroll bar on the right of the list box becomes active so that the user can scroll up and down to the desired entry. When there are the same number as or fewer elements than the SIZE parameter, the scroll bar is inactive.

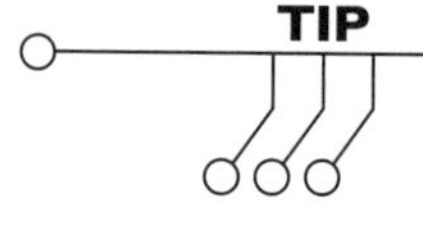

TIP

While you can use the Size parameter for any size list, if you have three items or fewer in the list, it's usually most attractive to allow all of them to show, as we do here. When there are multiple elements, and the Size is less than three, the arrows that allow scrolling may be obscured or difficult to activate in some browsers.

The MULTIPLE attribute specifies that more than one item in the list may be selected at a time. The user selects more than one element by holding down the Shift key while selecting. Figure 10-5 shows the screen for adding the Multiple Selection list box.

There was also a new element in the OPTION tag for this list box. In step 8, you entered a 1 for the VALUE instead of leaving it blank. This instructs a Web browser to use the 1 as the value of the field when it is submitted to your server *instead* of the text between the opening and closing option tags.

There are a few reasons you may want to do this. For starters, it may be more complex for a CGI program to parse out long text strings than shorter ones; many programming languages have special verbs for handling integer selection values. Or, if you are creating a form in multiple languages, the content of the list box may vary while the meanings do not. The VALUE attribute comes in handy in such cases. The HTML code for a multiple SELECT list box is shown here:

```
<P>Select one of more comment categories:
<SELECT NAME="category" SIZE="3"
MULTIPLE="MULTIPLE">
<OPTION VALUE="1">General Fiction</OPTION>
<OPTION VALUE="2">General Non-Fiction</OPTION>
<OPTION VALUE="3">Specialized Books</OPTION>
</SELECT></P>
```

Creating a TEXT Field

A TEXT field gathers a single line of text from a user and is one of the most common fields used on a form. A TEXT field is created by using an INPUT tag and applying one of the many options for the INPUT tag. To create a TEXT field:

1. Insert a Paragraph tag after the previous example's ending paragraph tag and enter the text introducing the text box. For this example enter **Types of books in these categories that you most often look for:**, as shown in Figure 10-7.

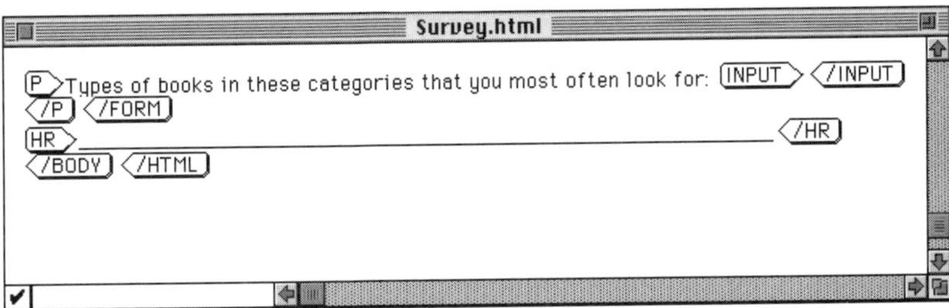

Figure 10-7: *A TEXT Field.*

2. Insert an INPUT tag at the point in your page you want to add a text field. The Input tags appear with the insertion point positioned between the opening and closing tags.
3. Choose the Markup>>Edit SGML Attributes, or use the ⌘-] shortcut key. Enter a unique name in the NAME field. For this example, enter **"types"**. The TYPE attribute defaults to TEXT, so you don't need to change it. Leave all the other attributes empty.
4. Choose the Apply button to complete the TEXT field.

There are a number of other options for INPUT fields that are discussed later in this chapter.

The HTML code for the TEXT field is shown here in:

```
<P>Types of books in these categories that you most often
look for: <INPUT NAME="types"></P>
```

Creating Check Boxes & Radio Buttons

Check boxes and radio buttons are an alternative way to collect one or more choices from a list of options. When *check boxes* are used, the user can select any, all or none of the choices. With *radio buttons*, only one of the choices in a group can be selected, and one is always selected. (Some of us can actually remember car radios with mechanical push buttons!) Radio buttons are *grouped together* by using the same NAME for each button. The VALUE of the button is sent to the server to distinguish it from the others.

Check Boxes

To enter a check box,

1. Insert a Paragraph tag after the previous example's ending paragraph tag and enter the text introducing the multiple-selection list box. For this example, enter **How did you find out about us?**
2. Type the text that will identify the first check box at the point in your page where you want to position the check box. In this example, enter **Advertisment:** before the area to display the first box.
3. Insert an INPUT element after the identifying text entered in step 1.
4. Choose Markup>>Edit SGML Attributes, or use the ⌘-] shortcut key. Enter a unique name in the NAME field. For this example, enter the name **ad**.
5. Select the value CHECKBOX for the TYPE attribute and choose the Apply button. This is shown in Figure 10-8.

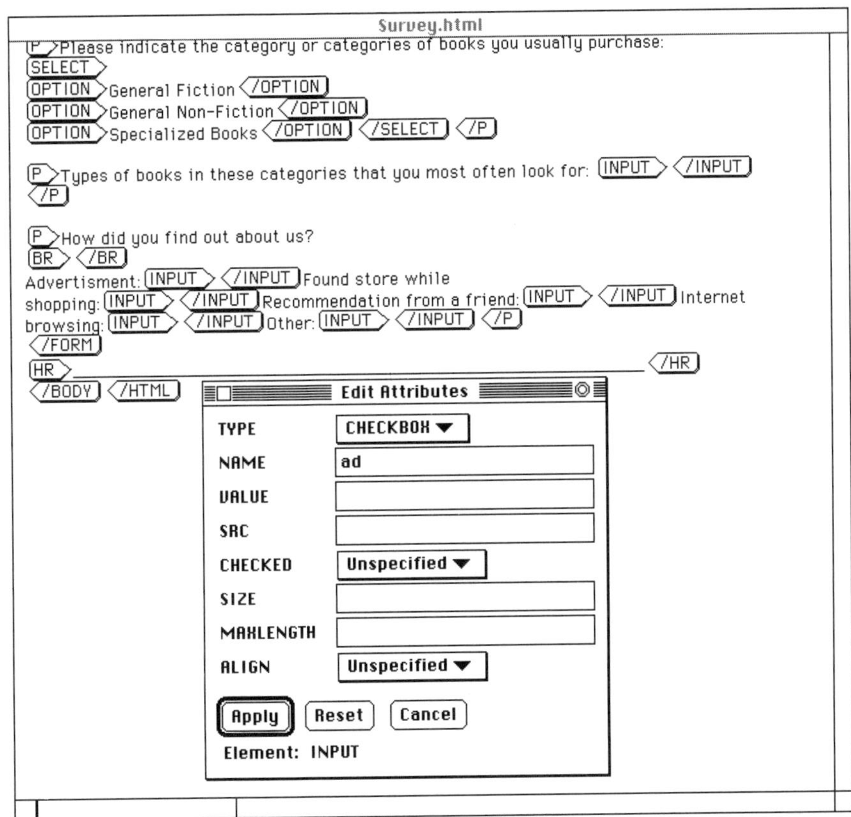

Figure 10-8: *CHECKBOX addition.*

6. Repeat steps 2 to 4 for every check box you wish to enter. For this example add four more check boxes, as shown in Figure 10-8.

For check boxes, the VALUE attribute specifies the text that should be sent to the server when the box is checked. If you leave the VALUE blank as we did in this example, the default is the text "on," which is usually okay. Unchecked check boxes send *no data* to the server instead of a value of "no" or "off."

The HTML for a CHECKBOX looks like this:

```
<P> How did you find out about us?
Advertisment: <INPUT TYPE="CHECKBOX" NAME="ad">
Found store while shopping: <INPUT TYPE="CHECKBOX"
NAME="shopping">
Internet browsing: <INPUT TYPE="CHECKBOX"
NAME="internet">
Recommendation from a friend:
<INPUT TYPE="CHECKBOX" NAME="recommendation">
Other: <INPUT TYPE="CHECKBOX" NAME="other">
</P>
```

Radio Buttons

Radio buttons are very similar to check boxes, except each button in a group has the same name, instead of unique names. The following steps explain how to include a set of radio buttons in a form:

1. Insert a Paragraph tag after the previous example's ending paragraph tag and enter the text introducing the radio buttons. For this example, type **What do you think about the selection of books at ACWLP?** and insert a Break tag.
2. Insert the INPUT element as you did for a check box at the point in your page you want to position the button.
3. Choose Markup>>Edit SGML Attribute and choose RADIO for the value of the TYPE attribute.
4. Enter the name of the push-button group in the NAME field in the Edit Attributes dialog box. For this example, type **select**.
5. Enter a unique value in the VALUE field and choose the Apply button.
6. Type the text that will identify the first radio button. For the first radio button, type **Excellent—Has everything I want**.
7. For the button in the group that you want to appear as the default, specify the CHECKED option. This creates a default push-button selection. For this exercise, no button is checked by default.

8. Repeat steps 2 to 5 for the remaining push-buttons in the group, as shown in Figure 10-9. Enter the same value for the NAME field in each case. Enter a different value for the VALUE field in each case.

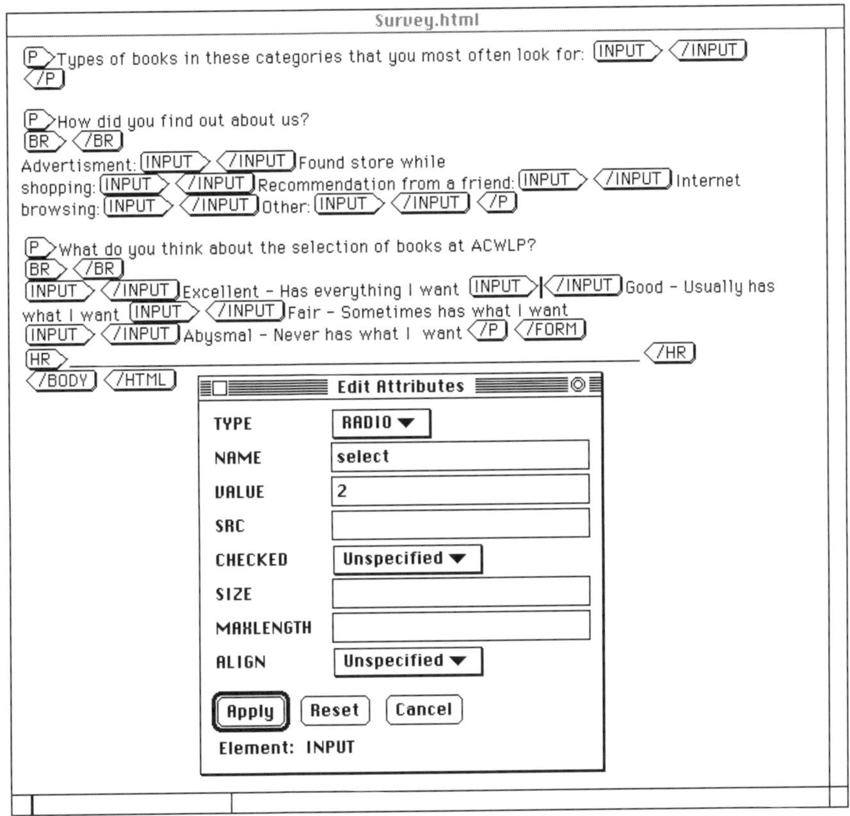

Figure 10-9: *RADIO button addition.*

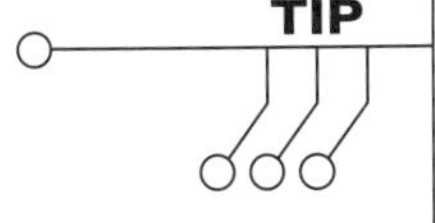

Note that you can place the button—or the check box, or whatever—either before or after the text that identifies it by where you position the <INPUT> tag. You can make the choice based on your decision about what looks best and seems most natural in your form.

You can have more than one radio button grouping on a form by using different names for the different groups. The HTML text for this radio button group looks like this:

```
<P>How is the selection of books at ACWLP?
<BR>
<INPUT TYPE="RADIO" NAME="select"
VALUE="1">Excellent - Has everything I want
nt<INPUT TYPE="RADIO" NAME="select" VALUE="2">Good
- Usually has what I want
<INPUT TYPE="RADIO" NAME="select" VALUE="3">Fair -
Sometimes has what I want
<INPUT TYPE="RADIO" NAME="select"
VALUE="4">Abysmal - Never has what I want
</P>
```

Creating Text Areas

Text areas are large "scratchpad" areas designed for free text entry that exceeds a single line. As the forms designer, you have the ability to choose the size of the text area by specifying the number of columns (of an average character width) and rows (lines) in the text area.

In the sample form, we have included a generic comments area and linked it back to the top of the form, so that users can send their comments without necessarily filling out the form. The code to do this is shown at the top of Figure 10-10. After the new heading, we have inserted a large text area where the user may enter any general comment.

To create a large text area,

1. Insert a Paragraph tag after inserting a new heading and anchor tag for the comments, and enter the text introducing the text area. For this example, type **Please let us know how we're doing and how we could serve you better.**
2. Insert a TEXTAREA tag at the point in your page you want to position the text input area. You will be presented with a dialog box that prompts you for the name and size of the text area.

3. Enter **textcomment** as the NAME, **3** for the ROWS and **40** for the COLUMNS and choose the Apply button.

Because some Web browsers use variable pitch fonts in TEXTAREA fields, the number of COLUMNS is just an estimate of how many characters will fit across the field. The text field has both vertical and horizontal scroll bars, so the user can actually enter any amount of text in this kind of field, up to the internal limits set by the Web browser. The attributes for a TEXTAREA element are shown in Figure 10-10.

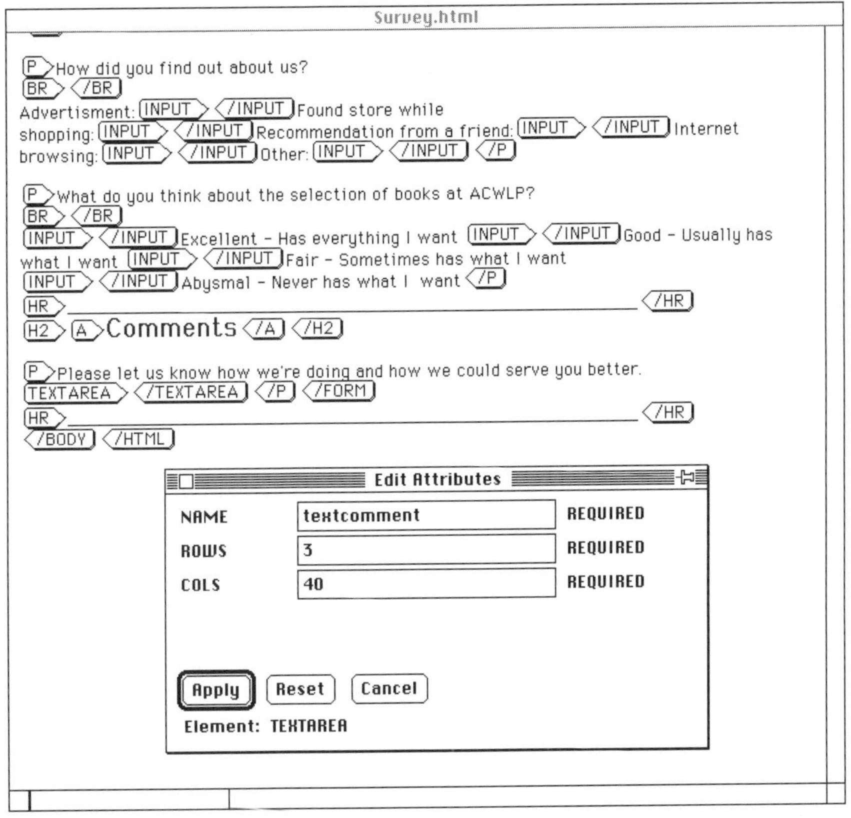

Figure 10-10: *TEXTAREA attributes.*

The HTML code for a TEXTAREA looks like this:

```
<P>Please let us know how we're doing and how we could
serve you better. <TEXTAREA NAME="textcomment"
ROWS="3" COLS="40"></TEXTAREA></P>
```

Using Other INPUT Field Attributes

There are a few other attribute choices for an INPUT field in addition to the ones you have seen so far. On the sample form, there is an entry for a Frequent Buyer Club identification number as a PASSWORD field, and a *hidden field* that reports the revision level of the form. Last, but not least, the INPUT field is used to create the required SUBMIT button, special submission buttons created from images, plus a RESET button that lets the browser clear the fields in a form without submitting the form.

As a trick to create spacing on a form, use a transparent IMAGE file to provide white space between the buttons that would normally be right next to each other.

PASSWORD Fields

Use a PASSWORD field for text input areas that should be kept private. This is useful only for protection from shoulder snoopers, because the text of the field is still sent across the network. On the Web browser's screen, asterisks appear instead of the text.

To create a PASSWORD field, enter the text that identifies the field, which in this case is "Frequent Buyer ID," and an INPUT field with the TYPE attribute set to PASSWORD. Figure 10-11 shows how this appears in HoTMetaL PRO.

To create a PASSWORD field,

1. Insert a Paragraph tag after the previous example's ending paragraph tag and enter the text introducing the password field. For this example, type **If you are a Frequent Buyer Club member and would like a $10 credit toward your next FBC award, select the store you're enrolled at above and enter your Frequent Buyer ID Number:**.
2. Enter the text that identifies the field in the NAME field, which in this case is **IDNumber**, and an INPUT field with the TYPE attribute set to PASSWORD. You can also enter a SIZE value, which sets the physical size of the password input box on the form, and a MAXLENGTH value. The browser will not allow the user to enter more characters than the number specified in MAXLENGTH. Together, these can guarantee that the user's password doesn't scroll off the end of the input area. For this example, enter **20** for the SIZE and **16** for MAXLENGTH.
3. Enter the remainder of the information that you want to present after the <INPUT> tag. For this example, enter **here. <EM>Only one credit per customer.</EM>**.

The HTML code for the PASSWORD field looks like this:

```
<P>If you are a Frequent Buyer Club member and would
like a $10 credit toward your next FBC award, select the
store you're enrolled at above and enter your Frequent
Buyer ID Number: <INPUT TYPE="PASSWORD" SIZE="20"
MAXLENGTH="16"> here.
<EM>Only one credit per customer.</EM>
</P>
```

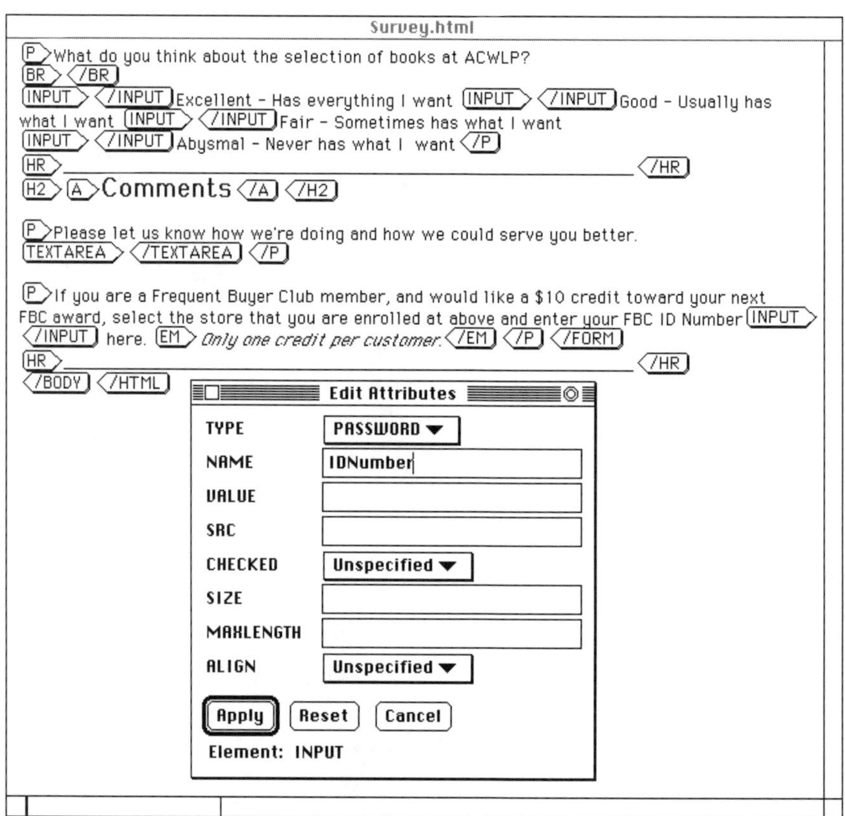

Figure 10-11: *The PASSWORD field.*

HIDDEN Fields

The HIDDEN type is useful for when you want to pre-load information in a field that will be sent to a server, but you would rather the user not see it. For example, if you have two forms identical in meaning but written in different languages, you may want to identify the language to the server when the form is sent. You could enter the language name (or some other identifier) in a HIDDEN field on the form, so the user is not distracted by it. Then when the form is sent to your server, the server program can identify the language of the form and possibly change how the form is processed or create a response in the appropriate language.

On the sample comment form, the HIDDEN field type is used to create a *revision number* field. This revision number will be sent to the server so that the revision number of the input form can be tracked. To create a HIDDEN field, add a paragraph tag and insert an INPUT field with the TYPE attribute set to HIDDEN. Enter revision for the NAME attribute and set the VALUE to 1.0. This value setting is sent to the server when the form is submitted. The HTML code looks like this:

```
<P><INPUT TYPE="HIDDEN" NAME="revision"
VALUE="1.0"></P>
```

Images as Part of an INPUT Field

You can use images as input fields as well. When you specify an IMAGE as the TYPE for an INPUT field, you also specify a .gif file in the SRC field. The image of the .gif file is what will be displayed to the user instead of a box or button. When the user clicks on the image, the form is *submitted*, and the coordinates of the mouse pointer are sent as *name*.x and *name*.y where *name* is the NAME of the image field. Note that if there is also a SUBMIT button on the form, and the user selects the SUBMIT button, *no* information about the image is submitted.

One example of an image field is to use it to display a number of different models of some product, so the user can select the model of product they are commenting on or requesting information about.

Using Standard IMAGE Fields

In addition to images as part of an INPUT button, you can also include standard images on a form. Since GIF images can be made transparent, as you learned in Chapter 8, you can create an image with no visible content at all, and then insert the image on a form to force the Web browser to insert space between your input fields and buttons. The transparent image used in this example is ½-inch wide, and is used to create a ½-inch blank space between buttons. Figure 10-12 illustrates what the form would look like without the IMAGE spacers inserted.

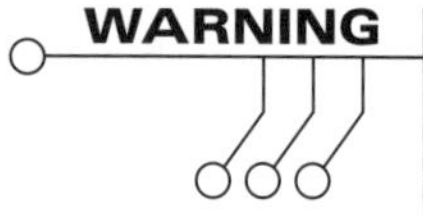

Be careful with this technique! If a Web browser has turned off inline images, the user will see the default image of the browser instead of your empty space.

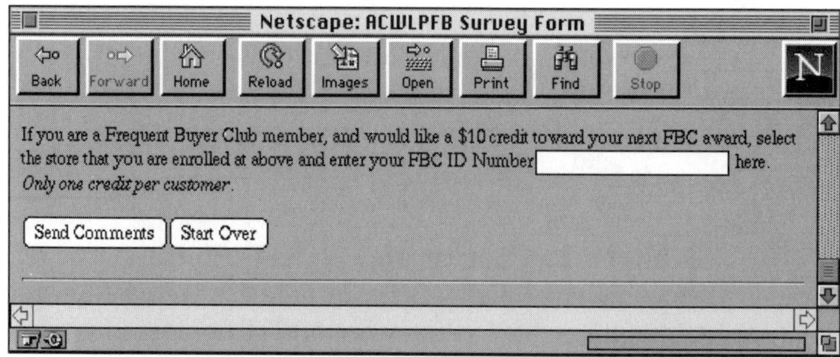

Figure 10-12: *Comment form without spacing.*

Images are entered as you learned in Chapter 8. As a review, the following steps show you how to enter a simple image:

1. Insert a Paragraph tag after the previous example's ending paragraph tag.
2. Insert an IMG tag at the point in your page where you want to position the blank space. You are presented with an Edit URL dialog box.
3. Choose file as the PROTOCOL attribute. The PROTOCOL field specifies how the image reference will be inserted into the HTML code. When you eventually publish the form, this file reference will be replaced with a URL reference that includes your system name instead of the FILE type.
4. Leave the HOST and PORT attributes blank, since you specified file for the protocol. Again, when this form is published, you could optionally include a host that was not your own, and a port that is not the standard port 80. If you leave these fields blank, the default is to use the host system that supplied the form originally—which is a very reasonable default.

5. Enter the name of the .gif file to be included in the Name field. For the sample, enter **images/spacer.gif**. This is shown in Figure 10-13. You can use the Choose File... button to search around on your system for an image if you don't know the complete file path name offhand.
6. Enter additional image fields if you want to insert additional space.

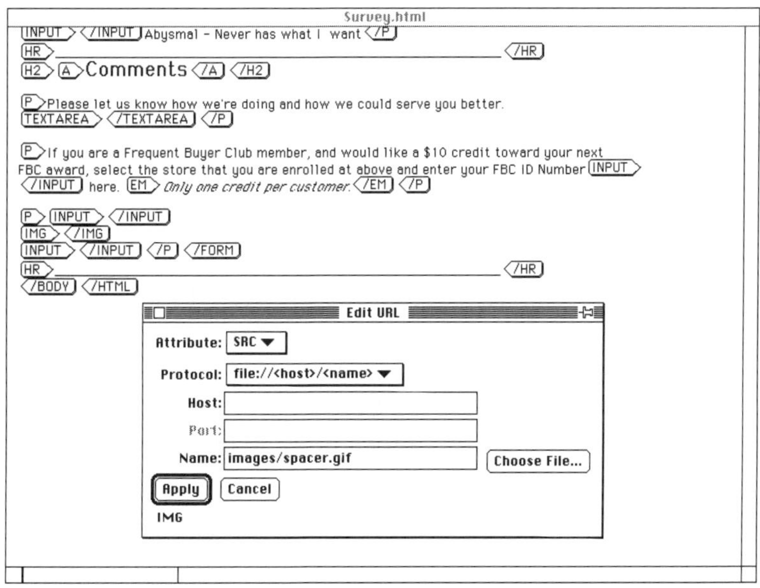

Figure 10-13: *URL dialog box for entering IMG elements.*

You can enter more than one IMG element if you want, for additional spacing.

```
<IMG SRC="file:///spacer.gif">
<IMG SRC="file:///spacer.gif">
```

Submit & Reset

Although last in this section, the final two possibilities for the TYPE attribute of an INPUT field are very important: SUBMIT and RESET. Every form that has more than one field *must* have a

SUBMIT button. The default text for a SUBMIT button is Submit Query. You can specify your own text for a SUBMIT button in the VALUE attribute. The resulting field on a form is a *push button* that is sized to the text you've specified. There is no NAME needed for a SUBMIT button, and when the SUBMIT button is selected, the contents of the form are transmitted to your server.

To add the SUBMIT button, enter an INPUT field with TYPE set to SUBMIT and the VALUE set to **Send Comments**.

The RESET button has a default text of "reset", and selecting a RESET button only clears the fields on the local form. The form is not submitted, and no other action is taken.

To add the RESET button, enter an INPUT field with TYPE set to RESET and the VALUE set to **Start Over**. The HTML code for submit and reset buttons looks like this:

```
<INPUT TYPE="SUBMIT" VALUE="Send Comments">
<INPUT TYPE="RESET" VALUE="Start Over">
```

You can have more than one RESET and SUBMIT button on a form, but remember that in many cases the user will not see the entire form at one time, so it is customary to place only a single SUBMIT button at the bottom of the form to ensure that a user scrolls all the way to the end of a form before sending it to the server.

Wrapping Up

In this part of the chapter you have seen all the elements you can use when creating a form. It's likely that the forms you create for your Web pages will not include every form element—as, for illustration purposes, this form does. In the following sections, we'll discuss the Common Gateway Interface and how to link forms and AppleScript CGI applications to process data supplied by your user.

Common Gateway Interface

The Common Gateway Interface (CGI) is a standard for external gateway programs to interface with HTTP servers. It's a very flexible way to process data sent from a Web browser and passed through the server, and is easily portable across multiple operating systems. The CGI was originally designed with UNIX-based operating systems in mind, so much of the data passing in the standard relies on "standard in," "standard out" and environment variables.

To get a feel for how information flows with the CGI, take a look at Figure 10-14, which shows a standard CGI interface, and Figure 10-15, which shows how WebSTAR uses AppleScript to process CGI data.

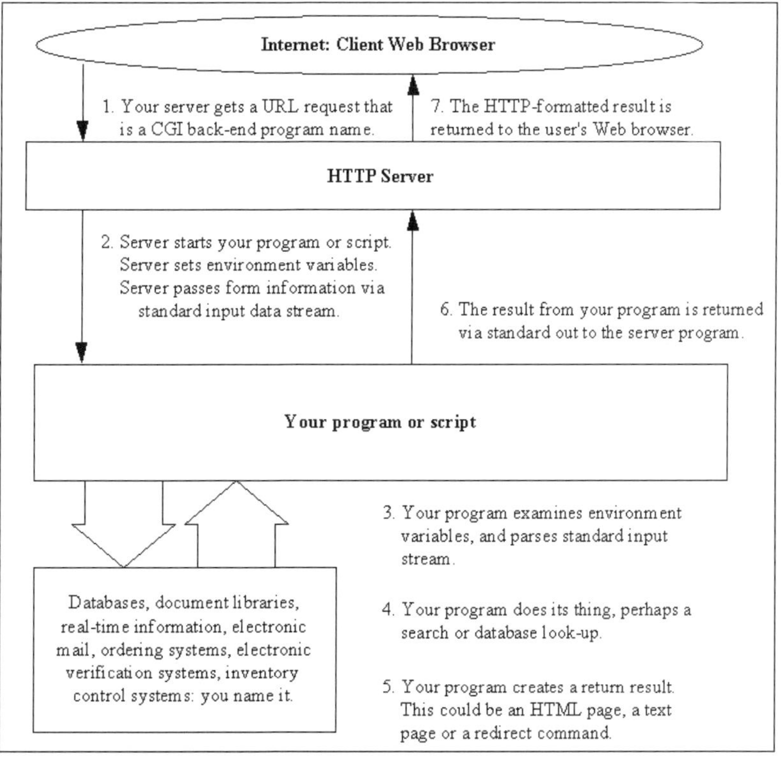

Figure 10-14: *CGI information flow.*

If you are working with a UNIX-based server, you'll find a broad variety of programs available to support development of CGI processing programs. (Check out the Web pages at http://hoohoo.ncsa.uiuc.edu/cgi/ for lots of great pointers.) Many of the same techniques can apply to the Macintosh environment, which is discussed later in this chapter. Due to the operating system-dependent nature of CGI processing, you should always check with the documentation and sample scripts that come with your HTTP server to see how it handles CGI.

The most significant difference between how you use CGI on a UNIX system and how you use CGI on a Macintosh system is that with UNIX you would very likely use shell programming and a parser such as perl to process almost all CGI requests. When you write programs that handle CGI for Macintosh, you'll find it much easier to use AppleScript or some equivalent event processing language, like Frontier. This is because UNIX has several very powerful and flexible command-shell processors available, and a tremendous assortment of command-line–oriented programs for processing "standard in" data. The Macintosh, on the other hand, is very much a graphically based system, with no attempt at command-line processing. However, the Macintosh OS has a full set of AppleEvents that can be passed between applications to start and control processing. As a result, the most powerful tools, such as AppleScript and Frontier, are not command-line programs, but instead process AppleEvents sent from the server.

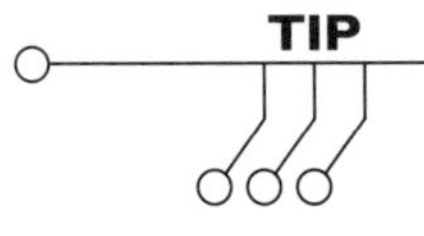

Even though the CGI interface is discussed in the chapter on forms, you can use CGI for anything you like! For example, you could have a hyperlink on a basic HTML page point to a CGI reference. The server will pass the URL to the specified back-end program, and your program could generate the jumped-to HTML page in real time. In fact, the sample script that comes with WebSTAR, newtest.acgi, does exactly that. This is useful for pages that change based on real-time data, or for pages that are completely generated from database references. Further, the CGI is also used with image maps, which were discussed in Chapter 8.

Processing CGI Data With AppleScript & WebSTAR

Data passed from an HTTP browser using the standard Common Gateway Interface is passed by MacHTTP or WebSTAR via custom Apple events. InterServer uses the same mechanism to process its data as well. This is described in more detail in the next section. Figure 10-15 illustrates how information flows from CGI in the Macintosh.

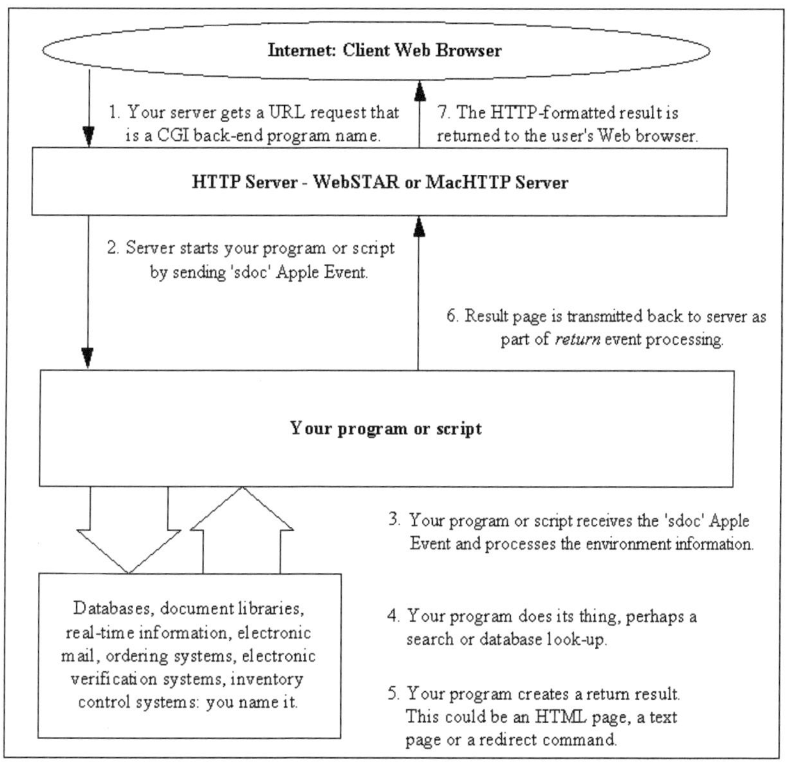

Figure 10-15: *CGI information flow using WebSTAR and Apple Events.*

You can also use Apple events to control WebSTAR's behavior. WebSTAR is completely scriptable and recordable. For example purposes, because of the limitations of the GET method, this section assumes that you are using the POST method exclusively.

With WebSTAR, you have a set of variables that are normally transmitted by the server itself, if they are available and appropriate. Command environment services are very similar to those of UNIX. The standard CGI interface generates a set of environment variables that contain information about the information being passed from the user. The following table is a list of the environment variables supported by the WebSTAR and MacHTTP servers.

Variable	Definition
path_args	The information in the URL after a $. The extra path information, as given by the client. In other words, scripts can be accessed by their virtual pathname, followed by extra information at the end of this path. The extra information is sent as PATH_INFO. This information should be decoded by the server if it comes from a URL before it is passed to the CGI script.
http_search_args	When the GET method is used (or with the ISINDEX form type) this is information that follows the ? in the URL that referenced this script. This is the query information. It should not be decoded in any fashion. This variable should always be set when there is query information, regardless of command-line decoding.
post_args	The information provided by forms, etc. when the POST method is used.
method	The method with which the request was made. For HTTP, this is GET, HEAD, POST, etc.
client_address	IP address or domain name of the remote client's host.
username	The authenticated user name.
password	The authenticated password.

Variable	Definition
from_user	The e-mail address of the remote user. Non-standard.
server_name	The server's hostname, DNS alias or IP address as it would appear in self-referencing URLs.
script_name	A virtual path to the script being executed, used for self-referencing URLs.
server_port	The port number to which the request was sent.
referer	This is the URL of the page that referenced this document. In other words, this is the URL of your original request, such as a form.
user_agent	The name and version of the WWW client software being used. The format is name/version.
content_type	When the input method is POST, this is the content type of the data. At this time there is only one type: **x-www-form-urlencoded.**
action	This is the name of the action (if any) that was requested.
action_path	This is the path specified in the HTML document for the script that is executed.
client_ip	The IP address of the remote host making the request.
full_request	This is the entire request information string, before formatting or other parsing has been done.

Table 10-1: *List of environment variables supported by the WebSTAR and MacHTTP servers.*

These variables are accessed by your CGI back-end program or script by a method that depends on the programming language you are using. For example, in C, the *getenv* function call is used to look up these parameters. In AppleScript, you use a rather strange syntax to extract this information from the Apple Event request, which is fully explained later in this chapter.

The way your back-end program collects data from the server depends on the method used to send the form. (Remember that you control the method when you set up your form, so you'll know in advance which to expect.) With the POST method (the recommended method), the data from the form is sent to your application as a stream named post_args. With the GET method, the data sent from the form will be in the http_search_args environment variable. In either case the data sent will be in the format:

name1=datastring1&name2=datastring2&name3=datastring3

Each piece of data (each field on the form) is identified with the *name=* part of the data stream, and the actual user data follows that up to the ampersand. Your program parses this data and takes whatever action is appropriate, such as performing a search or a database lookup. To create the result, your program generates the data to be displayed on the user's screen. While this is typically an HTML form (Content-type: text/html), it can also be a plain text display (Content-type: text/plain). The type of data returned is identified by your program to the server (and viewer) by the header information created by your program.

When returning the results page to the server, your program has the option of creating only the content of the return page, in which case the server adds HTTP headers, as shown in the following example:

```
Content-type: text/html
<HTML><HEAD><TITLE>Processed Return</TITLE>
</HEAD>
<BODY><H1>Processed Return</H1>
<P>This was processed by the server code to add HTTP
headers.</P>
</BODY></HTML>
```

This format is particularly useful for acknowledging receipt of information or sending error or status information back to your user. Alternatively, your program can create the entire return message, including the HTTP headers, as shown in the following example:

```
HTTP/1.0 200 OK
Server: Server-version-here
MIME-Version: 1.0
```

```
Content-type: text/html
<HTML><HEAD><TITLE>Transparent Return</TITLE>
</HEAD>
<BODY><H1>Transparent Return</H1>
<P>This was returned transparently.</P>
</BODY></HTML>
```

A third option for your program is to issue a two-line message that redirects the Web browser to yet another URL. The target URL could be any kind of document, including an HTML document or a plain text document. The two-line reply is shown in the following example:

```
Location: /mypath/my-document.html
[the second line is blank]
```

The document URL is typically another document on your own server, but could also be a full link to another site. This kind of a link can direct the Web browser to open a document that meets the criteria of a search, or direct a user to an instruction page if a query was done incorrectly.

Processing CGI Environment Data

All this is fairly theoretical at this point. Let's look at a simple example that just returns all the environment variables sent by WebSTAR. The example presented in this section is for WebSTAR 1.1, which can be found on the Companion CD-ROM, and uses a form bounce_info.html and a script, BounceInfo.acgi, which are also on the Companion CD-ROM. The sample simply constructs an HTML document that displays the environment variables you learned about earlier. To run this, you must have both WebSTAR and AppleScript installed. If you want to follow along with the example and build the sample yourself, you'll need a copy of AppleScript's Script Editor installed on your computer.

CD-ROM

Sample Program: Processing CGI Environment Data

The first thing to do is to create a simple CGI script that will process this data. The script here is derived from the sample newtest.acgi, which comes with your WebSTAR server software. This is the text listing for the BounceInfo.acgi script.

```
--this script must be compiled and saved as an application before running
--
-- Variables sent by WebSTAR that are available for use:
-- http_search_args - stuff in the URL after a ?
-- path_args - stuff in the URL after a $
-- post_args - stuff sent from forms, etc. when POST method is used
-- method - GET, POST, etc. Used to tell if post_args are valid
-- client_address - IP address or domain name of remote client's host
-- from_user - non-standard. e-mail address of remote user
-- username - authenticated user name
-- password - authenticated password
-- server_name - name or IP address of this server
-- server_port - TCP/IP port number being used by this server
-- script_name - URL name of this script
-- referer - the URL of the page referencing this document
-- user_agent - the name and version of the WWW client software being used
-- content_type - MIME content type of post_args
-- action
-- action_path
-- client_ip
-- full_request - the complete return generated by the remote client

--this builds the standard carriage return/line feed combination
property crlf : (ASCII character 13) & (ASCII character 10)

--this builds the normal HTTP header for regular access
property http_10_header : "HTTP/1.0 200 OK" & crlf & "Server: WebSTAR/1.1 ID/ACGI" & crlf & ¬
    "MIME-Version: 1.0" & crlf & "Content-type: text/html" & crlf & crlf

on «event WWWΩsdoc» path_args ¬
    given «class kfor»:http_search_args, «class post»:post_args, «class meth»:method, «class
addr»:client_address, «class user»:username, «class pass»:password, «class frmu»:from_user, «class
svnm»:server_name, «class svpt»:server_port, «class scnm»:script_name, «class ctyp»:content_type,
«class refr»:referer, «class Agnt»:user_agent, «class Kact»:action, «class Kapt»:action_path, «class
Kcip»:client_ip, «class Kfrq»:full_request
    -- What this really means is that you have the variables
    -- path_args, http_search_args, client_address, username, password, etc. to play with.
    -- They are all strings.

    try -wrap the whole script in an error handler
        set return_page to http_10_header ¬
            & ¬
            "<HTML><HEAD><TITLE>Test CGI</TITLE></HEAD>" & ¬
            "<BODY><H2>Test CGI</H2><U>CGI arguments sent:</U>" & ¬
            "<BR><B>path:</B> " & path_args & ¬
            "<BR><B>search:</B> " & http_search_args & ¬
            "<BR><B>post_args:</B> " & post_args & ¬
            "<BR><B>method:</B> " & method & ¬
            "<BR><B>address:</B> " & client_address & ¬
            "<BR><B>user:</B> " & username & ¬
            "<BR><B>password:</B> " & password & ¬
            "<BR><B>from:</B> " & from_user & ¬
            "<BR><B>server_name:</B> " & server_name & ¬
            "<BR><B>server_port:</B> " & server_port & ¬
            "<BR><B>script_name:</B> " & script_name & ¬
            "<BR><B>referer:</B> " & referer & ¬
            "<BR><B>user agent:</B> " & user_agent & ¬
```

```
            "<BR><B>content_type:</B> " & content_type & ¬
            "<BR><B>action:</B> " & action & ¬
            "<BR><B>action_path:</B> " & action_path & ¬
            "<BR><B>client_ip:</B> " & client_ip & ¬
            "<BR><B>full_request:</B><PRE> " & full_request & "</PRE>" & "</BODY></HTML>" & crlf
        -- return the page created. A return statement ends the
        -- processing of the Apple event
        return return_page

        -- This routine is called if an error occurs within the try
        -- errMsg contains the message sent by the System
        -- errNum contains the number of the error (negative for System, AE, or AS errors)
    on error errMsg number errNum
        -- create a page of HTML text to return
        set return_page to http_10_header ¬
            & ¬
            "<HTML><HEAD><TITLE>Error Page</TITLE></HEAD>" & "<BODY><H1>Error Report</
H1>" & return ¬
            & "An error was encountered while trying to run the script BounceInfo." & return
        set return_page to return_page ¬
            & "<H3>Error Message</H3>" & return & errMsg & return ¬
            & "<H3>Error Number</H3>" & return & errNum & return ¬
            & "<H3>Date</H3>" & return & (current date) & return
        set return_page to return_page ¬
            & ¬
            "<HR>Please notify Webmaster at " & ¬
            "<A HREF=\"mailto:webmaster@bookstore.com\">mailto:webmaster@bookstore.com</
A>" & " of this error." & "</BODY></HTML>"
        -- return the page created. The return statement ends the processing of the Apple event
        return return_page
    end try
end «event WWWΩsdoc»
```

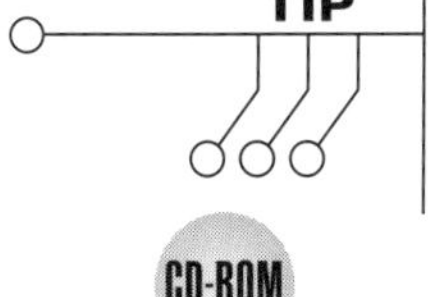

TIP

CD-ROM

The entire program is available on the Companion CD-ROM in AppleScript executable form as well as an editable text-only copy that you can print out and read. On the Companion CD-ROM the text-only file is called BounceInfo.acgi.text.

Since this isn't a book about AppleScript, we're not going to spend much time on the exact syntax of this application. The scripts provided here give you a good start on writing simple CGI applications. For more extensive stuff, get a good book on AppleScript and become familiar with its syntax and capabilities. Figure 10-16 shows you how this script looks in the Script Editor.

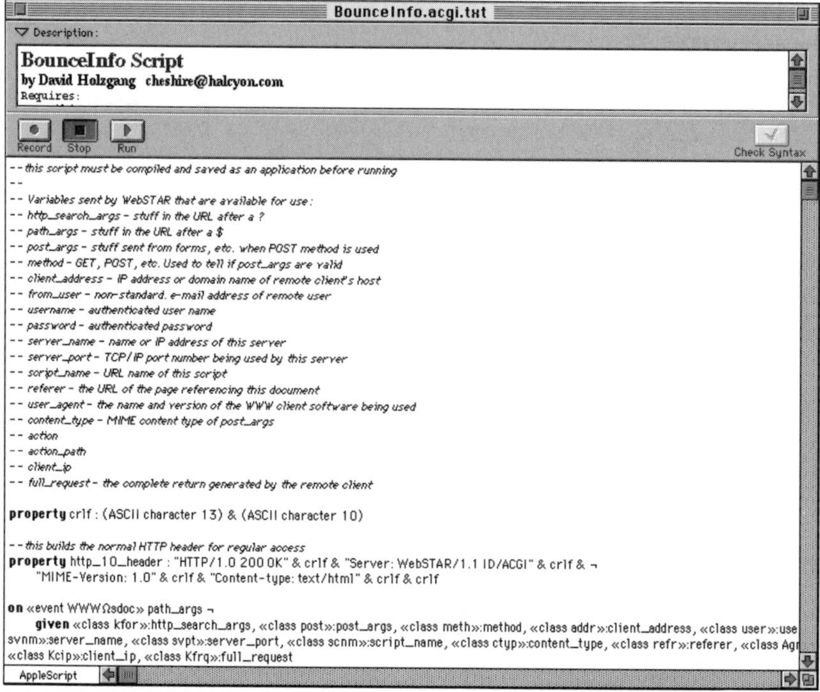

Figure 10-16: *The BounceInfo script in the Script Editor.*

Before looking at the actual script, however, you should note one important point about scripts. These scripts use characters that are not part of the standard ASCII sequence. Some of these are required by AppleScript generally and some by CGI applications in particular. In this script, these characters are « entered by pressing the Option and \ keys simultaneously; » entered by Shift-Option-\; ¬ entered by Option-l (that's a lower case L, not a 1); and capital omega, entered by Option-z. Because scripts require these special characters, they may not transmit successfully over standard telephone lines. So it's best not to try to load compiled scripts directly to your WebSTAR server. Instead, load the text versions of the scripts into the Script Editor and do a syntax check before storing them. This ensures that the scripts are complete and correct.

The script itself is fairly straightforward, as AppleScript scripts go. It begins with a series of comment lines—all lines beginning '--' are comments—which tell you something about the script and its processing. Next, you use the property command to build two permanent text elements for use in the script: *crlf*, a carriage return/line feed combination; and *http_10_header*, which defines the HTTP header for any document, as described earlier. The crux of the processing is in the *event* loop. WebSTAR sends a custom Apple event, called WWWΩsdoc, to set off the processing. When the script receives this event, it begins work. The basic processing is to take each element of the environment variables and echo it back in an appropriate HTML page. The HTML page simply consists of a series of lines, with one variable per line. Normal processing in the script finishes by returning the page that has been constructed to WebSTAR, which returns it to the sender.

The script has a short error handler at the end that returns an error page if anything goes wrong. Generally, you don't want to leave WebSTAR and your user hanging, waiting for some response.

Saving the CGI From AppleScript

Create the script presented earlier in the AppleScript Script Editor—or load from the Companion CD-ROM. Then follow these steps to turn your script into an AppleScript CGI application:

1. Click on the Check Syntax box at the top right of the Script Editor, as shown in Figure 10-16. This does two things: It checks the script for any errors, and it compiles the script for execution.
2. Select Save from the File menu to save the script in its present, text format, if you've made any changes.
3. Select Save As Run-Only... from the File menu. This saves the script in a run-only, compiled format, so you must be sure to save the script in an editable format as well.
4. This displays the dialog box shown in Figure 10-17.
5. Check both the Stay Open check box and the Never Show Startup Screen check boxes. It is *extremely* important that you check both boxes, or your application will not work.

6. Name the application BounceInfo.acgi. You must have the .acgi tag at the end so WebSTAR knows that this is a CGI application. Select the folder that you want for storing the application. It should be under the WebSTAR application somewhere. For these examples, we created a Scripts folder in the folder where WebSTAR resides, and placed all the scripts there.
7. Click on Save to save the application where you have selected.

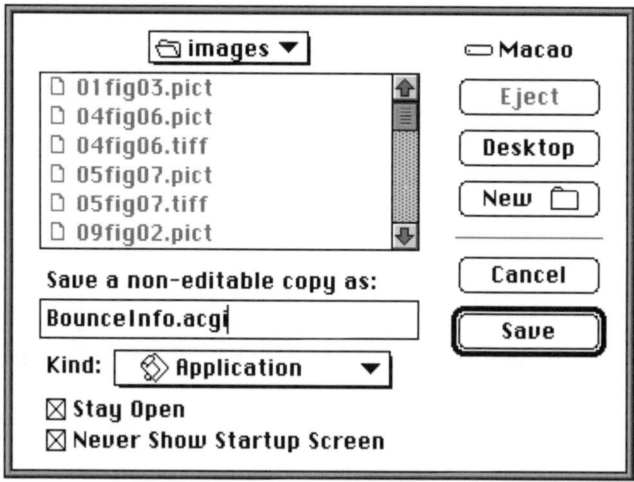

Figure 10-17: *Saving a compiled script from the Script Editor.*

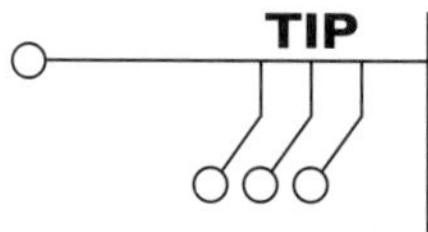

You could also save the script as a script or as an application that is not run-only. However, the method shown here provides the best performance and highest degree of safety. The only cost is the small inconvenience of having to store the text version of the script separately from the compiled version. (Hey, you need a backup anyway!)

Sample Form: Processing CGI Environment Data

The HTML form required to process this data is about the absolute minimum that you can build. Here is the entire form, which is on the Companion CD-ROM as bounce_info.html.

```
<HTML><HEAD><TITLE> Form Sample</TITLE></HEAD>
<BODY><FORM ACTION="scripts/BounceInfo.acgi"
METHOD="POST"> <INPUT TYPE="SUBMIT" VALUE="See
what you sent"> </FORM> </BODY></HTML>
```

This produces a page with a single button on it, as shown in Figure 10-18.

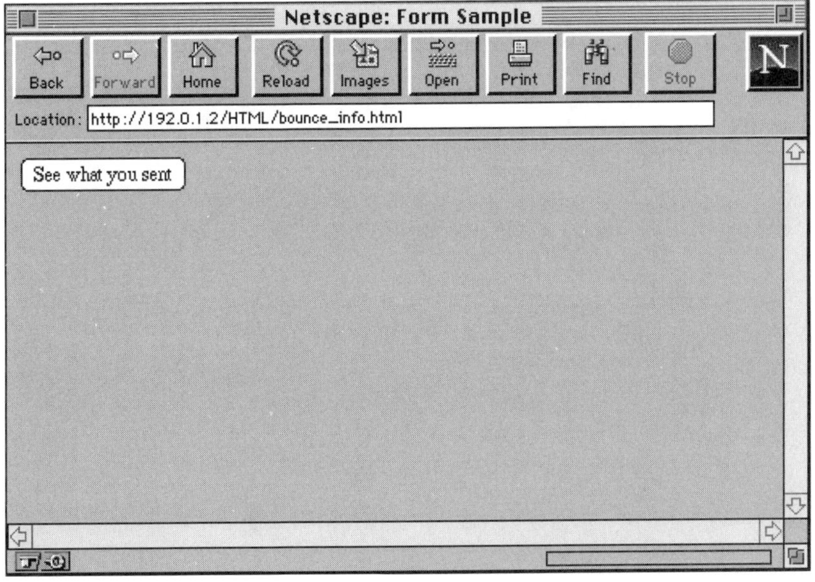

Figure 10-18: *The bounce_info document in the Netscape browser.*

Trying Out the Sample Program

Even if you don't have a full installation of AppleScript, you can test the example program. You'll need to install the WebSTAR server along with the basic AppleScript. This is discussed in Chapter 13, "Servers at Your Service." Spend some time with the server to understand how it works, then come back here to test this program.

Create a new folder in the same folder where you've installed WebSTAR, and call it *HTML*. This is where you'll store all the information related to your HTML documents. Copy the form bounce_info.html to the new *HTML* folder. Now create a new folder under the *HTML* folder called *scripts*. Compile and save the CGI script as described earlier and store it in the new *scripts* folder. (If you don't have the Script Editor, you can simply copy the program BrowseInfo.acgi from the Companion CD-ROM to the *scripts* folder.)

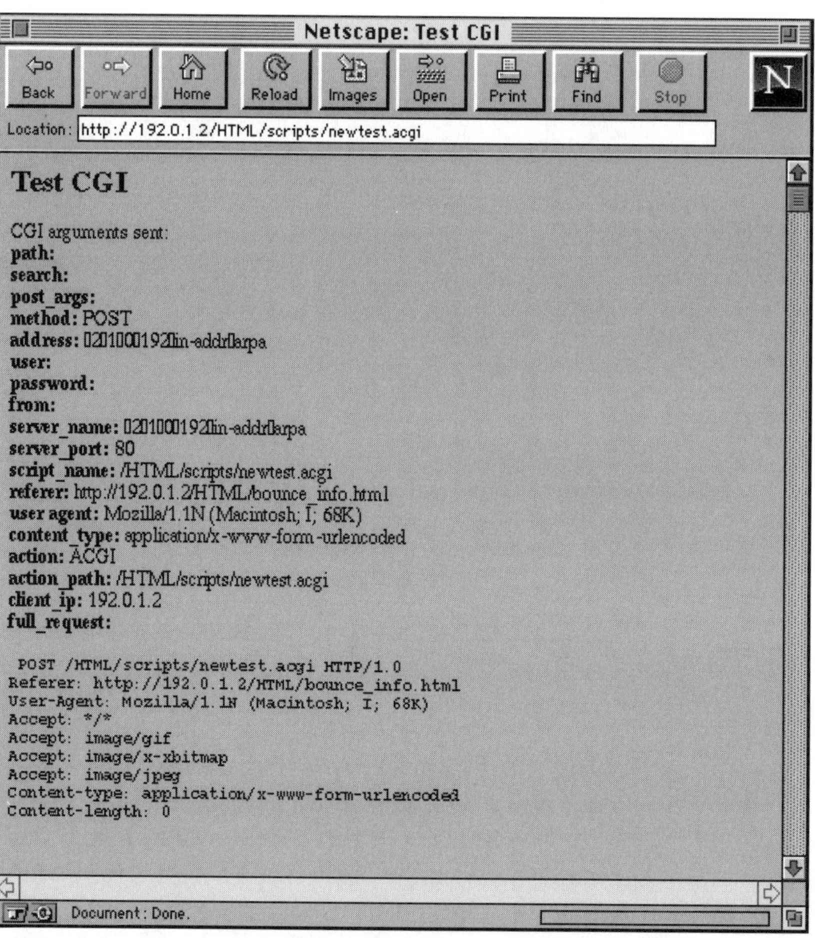

Figure 10-19: *The return page generated by the BounceInfo script.*

If you've set everything up correctly, you should now be able to connect to your WebSTAR server and request this document. If you're using the local connection described in Chapter 13, the Location URL for this document would be http://192.1.2.3/HTML/bounce_info.html. This will display the document as shown in Figure 10-18.

To exercise your new script, simply click on the button labeled "See what you sent". This calls up the BounceInfo script that should return a page that looks something like Figure 10-19.

And that's all there is to creating and retrieving the environment information that you're supplied with by WebSTAR.

Processing the Comments Form

In the first part of this chapter, you created a comments form that could be used to gather feedback from a user of your product or service. Now it's time to find out how to process that information at your server site. As already mentioned, the way that a CGI back-end program works and collects information relies on the specific operating system that is hosting the HTTP server. The example presented in this section is for WebSTAR 1.1, which can be found on the Companion CD-ROM and uses a simpler variant of the survey form survey.html and a script, BounceForm.acgi, which are also on the Companion CD-ROM. The sample application is a generic one that simply constructs an HTML document that displays the name and value of the form variables.

CD-ROM

To run this example, you must have both WebSTAR and AppleScript installed. This example also requires the Script Tools AppleScript extensions (OSAX) and the Parse CGI OSAX, which must be installed in the Scripting Additions folder in the Extensions folder in your System folder. These extensions are available on the Companion CD-ROM. If this isn't clear to you, consult the documentation that comes with these AppleScript extensions. As before, if you want to follow along with the example and build the sample yourself, you'll need a copy of AppleScript's Script Editor installed on your computer.

CD-ROM

Creating Survey Form Data

The HTML for the form processed by this example is a simplified version of the survey and comments form created at the beginning of this chapter. This code can be found on the Companion CD-ROM, so you don't need to type it all in. The following example shows the HTML code for the simplified form, and Figure 10-20 shows how it looks in Netscape. Note that the ACTION attribute of the FORM specification points to scripts/BounceForm.acgi.

```
<HTML><HEAD> <TITLE>ACWPFB Simple Survey Form</
TITLE> </HEAD>
<BODY><H1><IMG SRC="images/envquill.gif" ALT="Survey
Logo"
ALIGN="MIDDLE"> Comments and Survey</H1><P>Thank
you for your interest in A Clean Well-Lighted Place for
Books. We are always striving to improve selection and
service for our customers. Please help us by taking a
minute to fill out our <A HREF="#survey">survey</A>.
We also would appreciate your candid <A
HREF="#feedback">feedback</A> on both our in-store and
electronic operations.</P><BR><HR><H2><A
NAME="survey">Survey</A></H2> <FORM
ACTION="scripts/BounceForm.acgi" METHOD="POST">
<P>Please indicate the store location you visit most fre-
quently: <SELECT NAME="locname"> <OPTION>Opera
Plaza (San Francisco) </OPTION><OPTION>The Oaks
(Cupertino)</OPTION> <OPTION>Larkspur Landing (Lark-
spur)</OPTION> <OPTION>On-Line</OPTION>
<OPTION>Not a regular visitor</OPTION> </SELECT></P>
<P>Types of books that you most often look for: <INPUT
NAME="types"> </P><P>How did you find out about
us?<BR>Advertisment: <INPUT TYPE="CHECKBOX"
NAME="ad"> Found store while shopping: <INPUT
TYPE="CHECKBOX" NAME="shopping"> Recommendation
from a friend: <INPUT TYPE="CHECKBOX" NAME="friend">
Internet browsing: <INPUT TYPE="CHECKBOX"
NAME="internet"> Other: <INPUT TYPE="CHECKBOX"
NAME="other"> </P> <P>What do you think about the
selection of books at ACWLP?<BR><INPUT TYPE="RADIO"
```

```
NAME="select" VALUE="1">Excellent - Has everything I
want <INPUT TYPE="RADIO" NAME="select"
VALUE="2">Good - Usually has what I want <INPUT
TYPE="RADIO" NAME="select" VALUE="3">Fair - Some-
times has what I want <INPUT TYPE="RADIO"
NAME="select" VALUE="4">Abysmal - Never has what I
want </P><HR><H2> <A NAME="feedback">Comments
</A></H2><P>Please let us know how we're doing and how
we could serve you better. <TEXTAREA
NAME="textcomment" ROWS="3" COLS="40">
 </TEXTAREA></P> <P><INPUT TYPE="SUBMIT"
VALUE="Send Comments"><IMG SRC="images/
spacer.gif"><INPUT TYPE="RESET" VALUE="Start Over">
</P></FORM><HR></BODY></HTML>
```

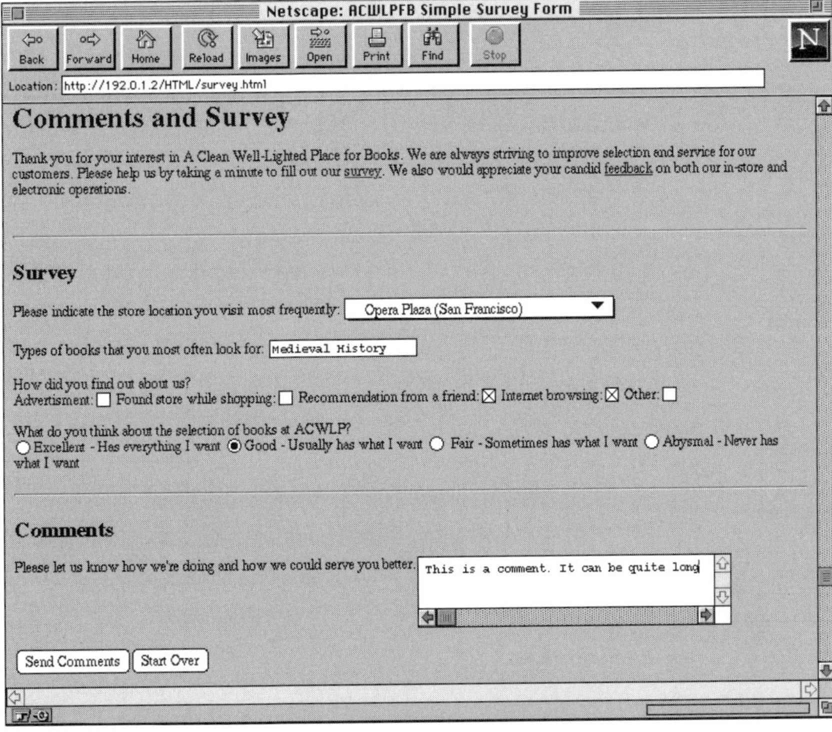

Figure 10-20: *How the survey form looks when filled in.*

This form will submit up to nine fields of information to the sample back-end program, depending on how many fields are filled out. (Remember that each check box is its own field and may be sent if checked.) The source code for this example is located on the Companion CD-ROM.

Processing Survey Form Data

There are a variety of ways to handle forms such as the survey form. For example, one useful way to handle comments from users would be to mail the survey and comment data submitted through the form to a system administrator. Since you are using AppleScript and Apple Events to handle your processing, you would need a scriptable mail application to act as the mail transport. Eudora 1.4.3 and later versions provide an excellent, scriptable mail application. Eudora is available on the Net at ftp://ftp.qualcomm.com/quest/mac/eudora/1.5/.

Jon Weiderspan has two sample CGI scripts that demonstrate how to format and transmit data from a form using AppleScript and Eudora. These are available, along with a lot of other useful utility applications and scripts, at ftp://ftp.uwtc.washington.edu/pub/Mac/Network/WWW. The specific file is LessonScripts1.8WebSTAR.sit.bin.

In this case, however, we are simply going to return the form data, parsed into field name and values. This script will actually work for any form that you create, and will echo back the names of your variables and the assigned values. This is a valuable debugging tool when creating and testing complex new forms.

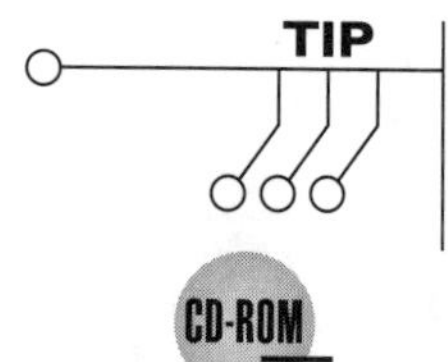

The entire program is available on the Companion CD-ROM in AppleScript executable form as well as a text-only copy that you can print out and read. On the Companion CD-ROM the text-only file is called BounceForm.acgi.text.

The script BounceForm.acgi takes advantage of a special AppleScript addition, called Parse CGI OSAX. This actually does the work of collecting the CGI data from the server. It puts the data you need in a number of data variables that you can use as you wish. Specifically, each variable is stored as a field name and a value. The Parse CGI OSAX is invaluable in handling form data. The OSAX comes with a description, in HTML, of how it operates and how to use it. Basically, it converts the data sent by the client browser into a series of string variables, each of which contains two elements: *field* contains the name of the field as entered in the form, while *value* contains the data the user entered in the corresponding field.

Here is the text script for BounceForm.acgi:

```
-- These properties are set only once each time the app is run
-- This is the carriage return/line feed combination (required for most text)
property crlf : (ASCII character 13) & (ASCII character 10)
--  This is a standard header for HTML files.
property http_10_header : "HTTP/1.0 200 OK" & crlf & "Server: WebSTAR/1.1 ID/ACGI" & crlf & ¬
    "MIME-Version: 1.0" & crlf & "Content-type: text/html" & crlf & crlf
--  Idletime is how many seconds you want this app to remain open to while waiting for the next
Apple Event
property idletime : 600 - set to 10 minutes
--  Datestamp will contain the current date. Initialize it here.
property datestamp : 0
set datestamp to current date
-- This is the handler that processes the WWWΩsdoc Apple events sent from WebSTAR.
on «event WWWΩsdoc» path_args ¬
    given «class kfor»:http_search_args, «class post»:post_args, «class meth»:method, «class
addr»:client_address, «class user»:username, «class pass»:password, «class frmu»:from_user, «class
svnm»:server_name, «class svpt»:server_port, «class scnm»:script_name, «class ctyp»:content_type,
«class refr»:referer, «class Agnt»:user_agent, «class Kact»:action, «class Kapt»:action_path, «class
Kcip»:client_ip, «class Kfrq»:full_request
    -- Variables used here:
    -- method - GET, POST, etc. Used to tell if post_args are valid
    -- http_search_args - the data from a GET. This is the stuff after a ?
    -- post_args - the data from a POST.
    -- client_address - IP address or domain name of remote client
    -- Using the "try" clause causes the "on error" routine to be run if an error occurs within the try
loop
    try
        -- save the current date and time to check later for automatic termination
        set datestamp to current date
        -- We only parse post_args, since this is the only
        -- data entered by the user (all else supplied by WebSTAR).
        set return_page to http_10_header ¬
            & ¬
            "<HTML><HEAD><TITLE>Survey Form Results</TITLE></HEAD>" & "<BODY><H1>Parsed
Survey Information</H1>" & return ¬
            & "<PAR>Method used for form is " & method & ".</PAR>" & return ¬
            & "<H4>http_search_args</H4>" & return ¬
            & http_search_args & return
        set return_page to return_page & "<H4>post_args</H4><PRE>" & return

        -- initialize postargtext in case the item is empty
        set postargtext to ""
```

```
        -- decode and parse all arguments, using parseCGI extension
        set formData to parse CGI arguments post_args

        -- traverse the list of records
        repeat with currField in formData
            set postargtext to postargtext & field of currField & " = " & value of currField & return
        end repeat

        set return_page to return_page ¬
            & postargtext & return & "</PRE>" & return ¬
            & "<H4>client_address</H4>" & return ¬
            & client_address & return
        set return_page to return_page ¬
            & "<HR><I>Results generated at: " & (current date) ¬
            & "</I>" & "</BODY></HTML>"
        -- return the page created. A return statement ends the
        -- processing of the Apple event
        return return_page

        -- This routine is called if an error occurs within the try
        -- errMsg contains the message sent by the System
        -- errNum contains the number of the error (negative for System, AE, or AS errors)
    on error errMsg number errNum
        -- create a page of HTML text to return
        set return_page to http_10_header ¬
            & ¬
            "<HTML><HEAD><TITLE>Error Page</TITLE></HEAD>" & "<BODY><H1>Error Report</
H1>" & return ¬
            & "An error was encountered while trying to run the script BounceForm." & return
        set return_page to return_page ¬
            & "<H3>Error Message</H3>" & return & errMsg & return ¬
            & "<H3>Error Number</H3>" & return & errNum & return ¬
            & "<H3>Date</H3>" & return & (current date) & return
        set return_page to return_page ¬
            & Â ¬
            "<HR>Please notify Webmaster at " & ¬
            "<A HREF=\"mailto:webmaster@bookstore.com\">mailto:webmaster@bookstore.com</
A>" & " of this error." & "</BODY></HTML>"
        -- return the page created. The return statement ends the processing of the Apple event
        return return_page
    end try
end «event WWWΩsdoc»
-- The idle function is run everytime the system sends an idle message.
-- If the current date is more than idletime seconds more than the last date
-- then it is time to quit.
on idle
    if (current date) > (datestamp + idletime) then
        quit
    end if
    return 5
end idle
on quit
    -- do any clean-up chores here
    continue quit
end quit
```

The first section of the code is similar to what you saw before. The major difference in this script is the central processing within the *try* block. Here there are the lines of code that actually do most of the work in the script.

```
-- decode and parse all arguments, using parse CDI extension
set formData to parse CGI arguments post_args
-- traverse the list of records
repeat with currField in formData
        set postargtext to postargtext & field of currField & ¬
        " = " & value of currField & return
end repeat
```

The Parse CGI OSAX takes the data from the post_args variable (remember that you set this form to use the POST method for data submission) and then converts it into a stream of arguments that is stored in formData. The repeat loop then extracts each argument out of formData into a variable, currField. This consists of a field name and a value. The set operation concatenates these text strings with some minimal formatting information and stores them into the postargtext variable. That's really the heart of the processing in this script. As before, there is an error-handling routine at the end of the event processing to handle any errors that occur within the try block. For brevity, most of the error cases have been removed.

This script has two new features that you'll probably want to use in your own work. First, it sets up a timing loop, based on the idle loop in the Macintosh system that checks to see if the application has executed in the last 10 minutes. If not, the application terminates. This is very useful since, once a CGI application has started, it won't stop of its own accord. Remember that you had to check the Stay Open box to create a valid CGI application; that means that the application, once launched, will not terminate automatically. Therefore, this script includes some code to test the time that has elapsed since the last time this application has been executed and terminate if it is longer than the value defined in the idletime variable. The script also has a clean-up section, where you can put any termination code that you want, such as logging information and other useful actions to be done just before the script terminates.

Trying Out the Survey Program

Copy the form survey.html to the server's *HTML* folder. Copy the program BounceForm.acgi from the Companion CD-ROM to the *scripts* folder or compile and store the text version, BounceForm.acgi.text. If you do not already have it in your System folder, copy the Parse CGI OSAX into the Scripting Additions folder in the Extensions folder. Finally, create a new *images* folder under the HTML folder and copy the file bell.gif to the new *images* folder.

Now open survey.html with Netscape. You should see the form as illustrated in Figure 10-20. Enter text in the various fields and select the Send Comments button. After a few seconds you will see either an error message, if you did something wrong, or a results page as shown in Figure 10-21.

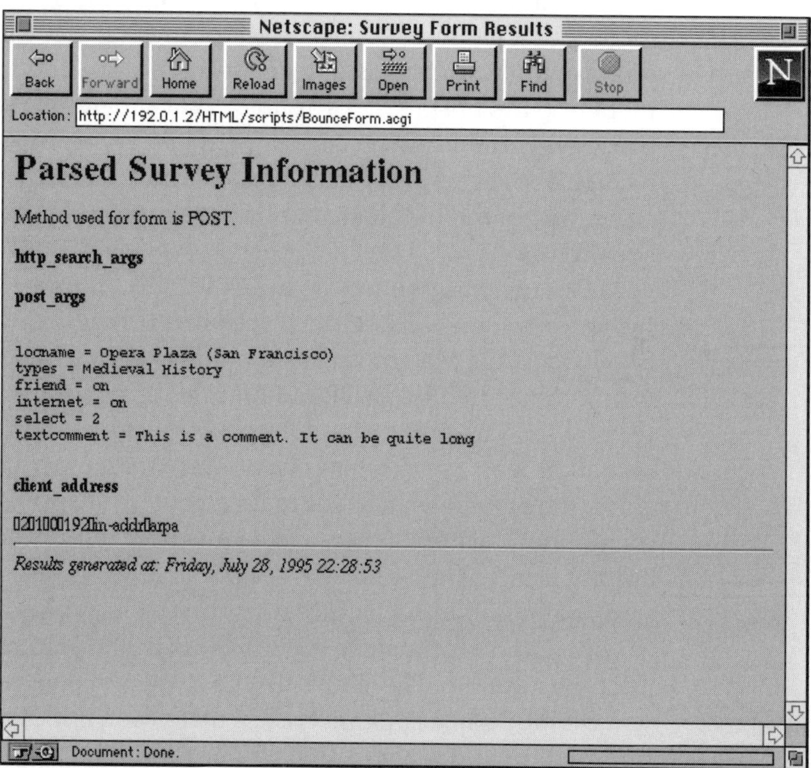

Figure 10-21: *Results page from the comment submission.*

Using an ISINDEX Tag

Using the ISINDEX tag is another way to gather input from a user. A page containing ISINDEX is generated by a CGI program so that when the user enters the information and presses Return, the resulting URL is sent back to the same CGI processing program that created the page.

When the user enters text in an ISINDEX field and presses the Return key, a special URL request is sent to the server. The URL is the original URL of the page, with the addition of a question mark and the text entered by the user. For example, if the URL of the HTML page with the ISINDEX tag were:

```
http://myhost.mycompany.com/scripts/specialpage.acgi
```

and the user entered:

```
aladdin lamp
```

then the resulting URL sent back to the server would be:

```
http://myhost.mycompany.com/scripts/
specialpage.acgi?aladdin+lamp
```

The server would send this command line to the program specialpage.acgi, which would parse the data "aladdin+lamp" and return the appropriate information, which would typically be the result of a search of files or a database lookup. This is a frequently used technique with UNIX-based Web servers.

Processing CGI Data With AppleScript & InterServer Publisher

InterServer Publisher uses the same basic Apple event mechanism to process its data. Everything you learned earlier about creating and using scripts with WebSTAR is equally applicable to InterServer. This should come as no surprise. MacHTTP and WebSTAR are the predominant servers in the Macintosh market today; it would be foolish, to say the least, for a new server to try to use a totally different processing concept without some extremely compelling reason.

In general, you can use the same scripts and scripting mechanisms to run InterServer that you use to run WebSTAR with only minor changes, as described below. As you will learn in Chapter 13, InterServer Publisher creates a new Web Sharing Folder that you must set in the preferences. This folder contains all the information that is available to Web clients; as a security precaution, they can't see or access anything outside of this folder. To make your documents available on InterServer, simply place your HTML documents inside the Web Sharing Folder. Here they can be referenced by any Web browsers simply by appending the name of the document to your address. For example, if you have a document named index.html in your Web Sharing Folder, then the URL for that document would be http://www.mycompany.com/index.html. To make your scripts work in the same way as they were described earlier, create a new scripts folder inside your Web Sharing Folder and place the scripts there. The URLs used in the earlier examples, you remember, used this method to keep the scripts available.

You can use Apple Events to control InterServer's behavior. InterServer seems fully scriptable and recordable; however, unlike WebSTAR, the documentation for doing this is rather sparse. If you were interested in scripting InterServer itself, look at the sample scripts provided in the Sample Configuration Scripts folder inside the Utilities folder.

With InterServer, as with WebSTAR, you have a set of variables that are normally transmitted by the server itself, if they are available and appropriate. The following table is a list of the environment variables supported by InterServer Publisher.

Name	Definition
http_search_args	When the GET method is used (or with the ISINDEX form type) this is information that follows the ? in the URL that referenced this script. This is the query information. For image maps, this is a point, presented as a (horizontal, vertical) coordinate pair. For a search, however, this will be a string.
post_args	The information provided by forms, etc. when the POST method is used.
method	The method with which the request was made. For HTTP, this is "GET," "HEAD," "POST," etc. This may be upper- or lowercase.
client_address	IP address or domain name of the remote client's host.
from_user	The e-mail address of the remote user. This is not necessarily provided by all Web clients.
username	The authenticated user name if available; blank otherwise.
password	The authenticated password.
server_name	The server's hostname, DNS alias or IP address as it would appear in self-referencing URLs.
script_name	A virtual path to the script being executed, used for self-referencing URLs.
server_port	The port number to which the request was sent.
referrer	This is the URL of the page that referenced this document. In other words, this is the URL of your original request, such as a form. Not all Web clients supply this information.
user_agent	The name and version of the WWW client software being used. The format is name/version.
form_item_list	This is the entire request information presented as a list of elements. Each element consists of two items: the variable name of the element, and the value of the element. This is unique to InterServer Publisher.

Table 10-2: *List of environment variables supported by InterServer Publisher.*

InterServer provides many basic variables that are identical to those supplied by WebSTAR and MacHTTP. However, there are several variables that are not supported: content_type; action; action_path; client_ip; and full_request. InterServer also provides an additional variable, called *form_item_list*, which is not available from other servers. This unique variable allows you access to fully decoded variable data without any additional processing. In the scripts you read earlier, you needed to use additional OSAXs to decode the variable data that is passed from the server. This data is encoded to eliminate characters that are not supported in HTML transmissions, such as the space, and special characters, like the backslash, pound sign and so on. In the scripts you read earlier, this decoding process was handled by the Parse CGI OSAX. InterServer Publisher provides this data fully decoded in the form_item_list; the encoded data is also provided in other variables so that you can still run your old scripts without any changes.

Working With InterServer Publisher

Because of the differences in the variables that are recognized and returned by the InterServer Publisher, you must make some modifications to both the scripts and documents presented earlier to allow them to work successfully in this environment. The primary change is in your CGI scripts. Since the server returns different variables, you need to make a change to tell AppleScript what variables to expect. As a second change, you must make a small change to some of the sample HTML documents shown earlier.

The change to the CGI scripts is the most important one, but is quite simple. Early in your script, you must change the section where you specify the variables that will be supplied. Every AppleScript CGI script that is prepared for WebSTAR or MacHTTP has the following section to set up the variable data:

```
on «event WWWΩsdoc» path_args ¬
	given «class kfor»:http_search_args, «class
post»:post_args, «class meth»:method, «class
```

```
addr»:client_address, «class user»:username, «class
pass»:password, «class frmu»:from_user, «class
svnm»:server_name, «class svpt»:server_port, «class
scnm»:script_name, «class ctyp»:content_type, «class
refr»:referer, «class Agnt»:user_agent, «class Kact»:action,
«class Kapt»:action_path, «class Kcip»:client_ip, «class
Kfrq»:full_request
```

As you saw in Table 10-2, some of these items are not available in InterServer, and if you include these items, your script won't run. So you must replace the above code with the following code in all your scripts.

```
on «event WWWΩsdoc» path_args ¬
        given «class kfor»:http_search_args, «class
post»:post_args, «class meth»:method, «class
addr»:client_address, «class user»:username, «class
pass»:password, «class frmu»:from_user, «class
svnm»:server_name, «class svpt»:server_port, «class
scnm»:script_name, «class refr»:referer, «class
Agnt»:user_agent, «class form»:form_item_list
```

This removes the CGI variables content_type, action, action_path, client_ip, and full_request, that are not supported by InterServer Publisher, and adds the one new variable, form_item_list that is supported.

Since InterServer reports different variables, you also will need to change the BounceInfo script to report the variables provided by InterServer. Besides changing the header shown here, you also need to remove the old variables from the report portion of the script and add the new form_item_list variable to the list. The sample BounceInfo script on the Companion CD-ROM has these changes already made.

CD-ROM

There are also some small changes that you need to make to your test HTML documents. If you remember, the simplest document that we created earlier has only a button to submit the form to the server. For InterServer, this approach causes severe problems. InterServer's special form_item_list variable is intended to return a list of variable names and values; if there is, in fact, no data, the server cannot do that, and it will fail. To get around this issue, simply add a text box to the form. You don't actually need to fill it out, the only requirement is that a form have at least one data element in it. In general, this isn't a problem because most forms do have one or more data items on them. The only problem here is that we have created a minimal form with only a SUBMIT button, and no data. Again, the bounce_info.html document for InterServer Publisher on the Companion CD has this change already provided.

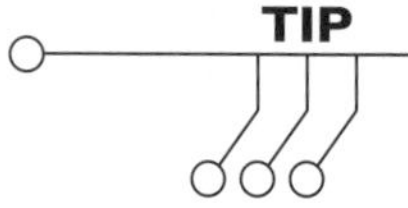

Remember that all these scripts and documents are on the Companion CD-ROM. Everything on the CD is duplicated, with one set for WebSTAR or MacHTTP and one set for InterServer Publisher, so you don't really need to worry about these changes as long as you use the scripts and documents provided. This information is primarily for use when you are converting other scripts that you have made from one server to the other. Most documents won't need to be converted to work on either system.

InterXTML HTML Extensions

InterServer Publisher has also developed some useful extensions to standard HTML codes that allow you to easily perform some common and desirable functions in your HTML documents. Some of the standard things that you may want to do on your server are provide a list of files in a certain folder, or count the number of times that you have had visitors to your page. All of these are tasks that require some programming on other servers, but InterServer has created new HTML extension tags, called InterXTML, that provide these services.

InterXTML is a server-side extension to HTML. This means that you can use these tags in your documents without worrying about whether the user's browser supports these tags. The tags are used by the server and transformed into standard HTML before the page is sent to the client. This means that these tags will be compatible with all current and future browsers.

InterXTML tags are really a kind of macro language. The server replaces the tag at the time it is executed with the appropriate information as requested by the tag, formatted in correct HTML tags. This makes the InterXTML tags dynamic, so you can use them for a variety of tasks that otherwise would require either some programming, or constant maintenance to your Web pages. InterXTML tags look very much like HTML tags: They are enclosed in angle brackets, use beginning and ending tags, and have attributes. InterXTML tags are also case-insensitive, like HTML. InterXTML tags differ from HTML tags by beginning with the character sequence "IX-", which allows the server to distinguish these tags from standard HTML tags.

You can use InterXTML tags in any place in a document where you can use a normal HTML tag. However, to inform the server that you are using the InterXTML extensions, you must insert the command <INTERXTML> somewhere within the first 100 bytes of your document file. This does not have to be within the <HTML> tags, so you can place it anywhere in the file.

Real-Time Page Creation & Other Tricks

The ability to have a back-end program create text or HTML pages is not limited to responses to database queries and comment forms. Here are just a few ideas to get you started.

Page Content Based on Client Address

One of the pieces of information your CGI program gets when called is the address of the remote host. If you parse the remote host address, you could provide different information to different people. For instance, you may have a database of information that contains some sensitive information, so only certain users get the full information. Everyone in a group, however, should have access to the basic database information. Still others—not in the group—should be presented with a screen that invites them to subscribe to your database service. By reading the IP address that is requesting the information, you can create customized pages based on IP addresses.

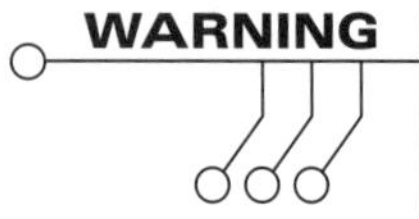

Hackers almost always access their targets through systems that appear legal. You should only use this technique for systems that are secure, or isolated from the Internet. You could, however, combine this technique with the basic authentication provided by many of the servers to create an additional layer of security.

Master Pages That Point to Dynamic Addresses

The information on the World Wide Web is becoming increasingly commercial, and you may want to prevent others from linking to any page on your Web (or a part of your Web) other than your home page. For instance, you might want to have a significant copyright notice on your Web document, but not want to repeat it on every page. By making the top page of your document a CGI reference, you can have a CGI program generate your home page with internal links that change daily (or hourly) and have a coordinated program change the names of your internal pages at the same time. This way, if someone does establish a link directly to a subpage, the link won't be good for very long. Again, this is not a way to secure your server, but only to guide most users through a top page before accessing a lower-level page.

Creating a Game Web

You could create an entire Web page that's a game—with links that change randomly or according to what others are doing on your server at the same time. This is particularly interesting when used with image maps that just pass back the coordinates a user clicked. The CGI back-end could select different destinations at different times. Also, the images that are returned to a user could change, based on various factors. Two good examples of this are the Stolichnaya home page (http://www.stoli.com/) and the University of Kansas' URouLette page (http://kuhttp.cc.ukans.edu/cwis/organizations/kucia/uroulette/uroulette.html). Both of these are featured in Chapter 11, Looking Good on the Net.

Moving On

With the addition of forms and the CGI interface, your formal introduction to the pieces of HTML authoring is complete. Now it's time to move on to putting together what you've learned in a series of examples in Part 3, "Putting the Pieces Together." Additional examples of CGI interface programs for various Macintosh-based HTTP servers are provided in Chapter 13, "Servers at Your Service."

11

Looking Good on the Net

The Web is a unique new media venue that brings with it new ways to present information and market products. The layout possibilities for an HTML document are fairly limited, but the Web is teeming with creativity. Looking good on the Net is its own reward. Unlike typical advertising, the Web is its own vehicle for publicity. If I like your Web page, I can, in turn, become a publicist for your site and include a link to your site in a list of sites that I recommend. And because the Web thrives on sharing information and recommendations, presenting a well-designed, good looking page encourages others to promote your Web site. The cycle continues and soon your site is caught in the Web. This chapter shows different ways to present Web pages and shares some sites that exploit the power of Web publishing.

Guidelines for Internet Publishing

In Chapter 3, "Structuring Information in Web Documents," we stressed the importance of structuring information and defining your document's goal to capture your audience. The following sections build on the skeletal outline of your Web site. The main concerns addressed are: making sure your Web documents match the reader's needs and creating pages that look good on the Net, regardless of who is accessing your site.

Present Content-Rich Web Pages

Web publishing is an extension of other publishing media; it complements rather than replaces traditional publishing. The Web is still somewhat of a grassroots publishing movement centered around current, off-the-cuff information. For the most part, people searching the Web are looking for information that is specific, detailed and comprehensive. They also may want to be entertained or amused, but they don't want to be bombarded by advertising hype. The key to successful Web publishing is to take a unique approach to publishing visually appealing pages and presenting content-rich messages that others will appreciate.

Look Beyond Web Browsers & Fast Connections

Anyone can access Web pages, how they access them can determine how well your Web pages appear onscreen. One reader may have an ISDN connection and another may connect using a 9600 baud modem. It's important to make the size of inline image files as small as possible, yet maintain a professional quality, or include two presentations of your site: one for graphics-based browsers and the other for text-based browsers. Whenever possible be sure to include the ALT attribute, to address people using text-based browsers.

If you want to make files available to the widest audience, you'll want to add other Internet services to capture Internet users that don't have access to the World Wide Web. FTP and Gopher are two text-based methods of sharing files and information that can also be accessed on the World Wide Web. Setting up an FTP server is a fairly simple operation. Most service providers, companies that sell Internet connections and provide server services, and server services, companies that sell space or Net publishing services, will set up an FTP site for a small charge. Once you've set up an FTP site, you can add a link to the FTP site in your World Wide Web page. Setting up a Gopher site at a service provider or server service is usually a little more difficult and expensive.

Address Security Issues

Security is a major issue if you're selling a product or service online. If potential customers don't feel that ordering from your site is safe, you're not going to succeed. Some people are reluctant to use their credit card to place an order over the Internet, even if you're using a secure server. Therefore, it's important to give your readers an alternative to sending their credit card information over the Net, such as publishing an 800 number or including a fax order line. Some sites let users set up credit card accounts over the phone and then let users send in orders via e-mail. This ensures that the credit card information isn't intercepted over the Net.

If you're creating Web documents to be published on a UNIX-based server, you may want to search out a service provider or server service that provides a secure server. Netscape Communications and NCSA both offer secure servers and Web browsers. You also may want to check out some of the toolkits for conducting business on the Net. OpenMarket, for example, provides a StoreBuilder toolkit that works with existing Web clients and uses a payment URL that encodes the price and date in the information sent to the client program. You can find out more information about StoreBuilder and other OpenMarket products and services at http://www.openmarket.com/about/ProdBackground.html.

Terisa Systems, a joint venture between RSA Data Security and Enterprise Integration Technologies (EIT) has announced a suite of client and server tools called SecureWeb Toolkit that incorporates a variety of encryption schemes to enable you to perform secure transactions over the Net. Digital signatures, which can be used to verify the identity of someone over the Net, are also supported.

If you use a secure server, such as Netscape's commercial secure server, or an alternative method of security, inform your readers. Many people want to be reassured or will want to know just how safe your system is. The more comfortable a customer feels, the more likely he or she is to purchase your product online.

Pretty Good Privacy (PGP)

If you want to share private documents with other users, check out PGP (Pretty Good Privacy). PGP is available as freeware for non-commercial users. Version 2.6.2 is the safest version. Version 2.3a is more popular, but there are some patent issues that have yet to be resolved. PGP lets you generate public and private keys for encrypting and decrypting documents. Some Web sites, such as CD*now!* (http://cdnow.com/), use PGP to perform business transactions. If you want to buy a license for PGP, contact Via Crypt at (800) 536-2664.

Let Readers Respond

Be sure to include a link to a form for reader feedback. Many sites also include a guest book for readers to include comments. Letting readers respond shows that you care about what your readers have to say about your product, service or site. If you choose not to include a comments form, at the very least include an e-mail address. Publishing a Web document without an e-mail address connotes that the information is wanting, and will likely receive the same attention given an unsigned form letter. Not only does omitting an address frustrate readers, it also short circuits the power of the Web, cutting you off from individuals who may have valuable input.

Validate Your Web Document

HoTMetaL PRO is a rules-based HTML editor. If you create your document with HoTMetaL PRO, you can choose the Special>>Validate Document command to make sure that your document conforms to the standard HTML rules. Most Web browsers are very forgiving right now about bad HTML coding, but this is expected to change. The more HTML tools that enter the arena, the greater the need to write HTML code that conforms to the HTML standard.

HTML validation services exist on the Web that can check the validity of an HTML document. Some can even point out common HTML authoring mistakes. For example, Weblint is a perl script written by Neil Bowers and is presented as a public service of UniPress. The Weblint form lets you enter your URL to check the validity of your Web document. It also checks for any anchor text that uses the word "here", such as the phrase "click here", a common Web publishing faux pas. The Weblint form is available at http://www.unipress.com/weblint/.

Another HTML validation site is available at HAL Computer Systems. Presented by Mark Gaither, this service lets you specify the level of HTML conformance, including Strict, Level 0 through Level 3, and a Mozilla option for testing HTML documents with Netscape extensions. To use the HTML Validation Service, enter http://www.halsoft.com/html-val-svc.

Provide Portable Document Alternatives

Not all information lends itself to short Web pages. In some cases, you may want to present a brochure that has high-quality images and extensive formatting, but you want to make them available to users of different platforms online. Some readers are paying for connection time and may want to download the document to save money and read the document off-line.

The answer to presenting a formatted document is to create a portable document using a program like Acrobat or Common Ground. This way you can have control over the output of the document. Adobe's Acrobat and No Hands Software's Common Ground are both trying to become the standard multiplatform publishing tool. Acrobat's PDF format supports hypertext links that start and load the Web page in your Web browser when you click a Web-based hyperlink. Both Acrobat and Common Ground viewers are free. Acrobat is the defacto standard. Common Ground 2.0 uses a proprietary format called Digital Paper. Digital Paper uses TrueDoc technology to convert TrueType and PostScript Type 1 fonts into compressed scaleable fonts.

Creating an Adobe Portable Document File requires that you purchase Acrobat Exchange, which includes the Acrobat PDF writer. To create a portable document, choose the Acrobat printer driver and print the document to a file. Creating a Digital Paper document is done in a similar manner. You purchase the Common Ground program and use a printer driver to print the file in the Digital Paper format.

Common Ground also gives you the option of embedding the viewer and the document into a single executable file. So unlike Acrobat files, the reader does not have to have the Common Ground viewer to read the file. This is really a moot point since the Acrobat Reader is free. It is also possible to print a document to a PostScript file and include a hyperlink to the PostScript file, but this is fast becoming an outdated method. Acrobat and Common Ground include many features, such as adding hypertext links that can't be done with a PostScript file. Soon we can expect to see a Web browser that includes the capability to read PDF or Digital Paper files. In fact, Netscape and Adobe have already announced that a future version of the Netscape browser will include a capability to read PDF files from within Netscape.

The Acrobat Reader and Common Ground Viewer are both included on the Companion CD-ROM. As of this writing, Common Ground was not available on the Net. However the Acrobat Reader is. If you like, you can include a link to Adobe's FTP site for users to download the Acrobat Reader. The URL for the Adobe Acrobat Reader is ftp://ftp.adobe.com/pub/adobe/Applications/Acrobat/Macintosh/2.0.1/AcroRead.mac.sit. Note, however, that the Acrobat Reader requires the presence of ATM (Adobe Type Manager) software on your computer to run. ATM is not available on the Net at this time, but is available direct from Adobe, and comes free as part of several of Adobe's popular software applications, such as Illustrator, Photoshop, Premiere and others.

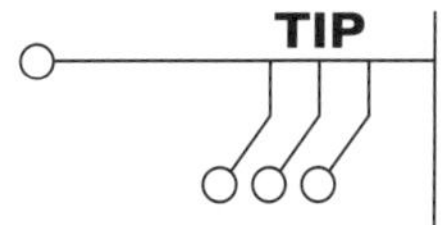

Adobe has done a great job of including a list of hyperlinks to sites that produce exemplary PDF documents. You can check out these PDF documents by visiting Adobe's site at http://www.adobe.com/.

Take a Unique Approach

One way to look good on the Net is to take a unique approach or offer a superior service to other Web sites. Just about anyone who has spent any amount of time surfing the Net has come across CyberSight. CyberSight's popularity is credited to its great graphics and unique interactive approach to presenting entertaining information. If you haven't seen CyberSight, enter the URL: http://cybersight.com/. CyberSight's home page is shown in Figure 10-1. Taking an innovative approach to your site is sure to draw a crowd. The following sections include several examples of sites taking unique approaches to Web publishing.

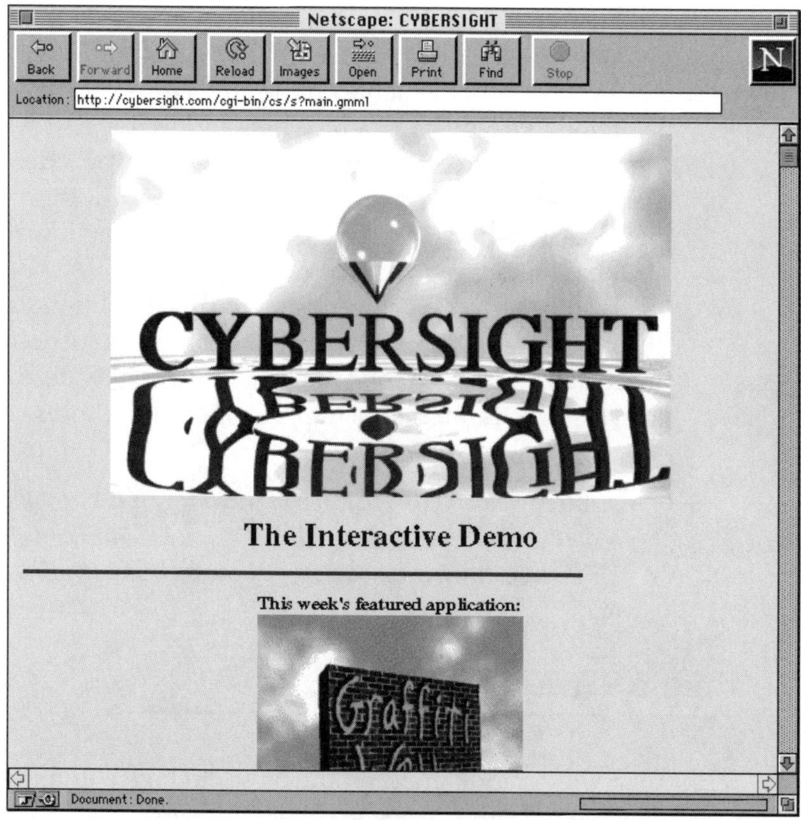

Figure 11-1: *CyberSight is popular for having a sense of humor and for its unique interactive approach.*

Offer Contests, Games & Freebies

Contests, games and freebies have long been a staple of TV and print advertising. A Clean Well-Lighted Place for Books uses exactly this mechanism to interest and involve readers in its server. ACWLP has a monthly "mystery quotation" contest, where readers are invited to identify a (more or less obscure) quotation. All those who correctly identify the quotation are placed in a drawing to win their choice of one of the staff's favorite books listed on the ACWLP Staff Favorite's page.

Internet Marketing Incorporated, the same people who brought you CyberSight, created a site for Stolichnaya Vodka that includes an interactive puzzle, an interactive painting and a random Web site game. Figure 11-2 shows the interactive puzzle on the Stoli Cipher page. You can visit Stolichnaya's home page at http://www.stoli.com/.

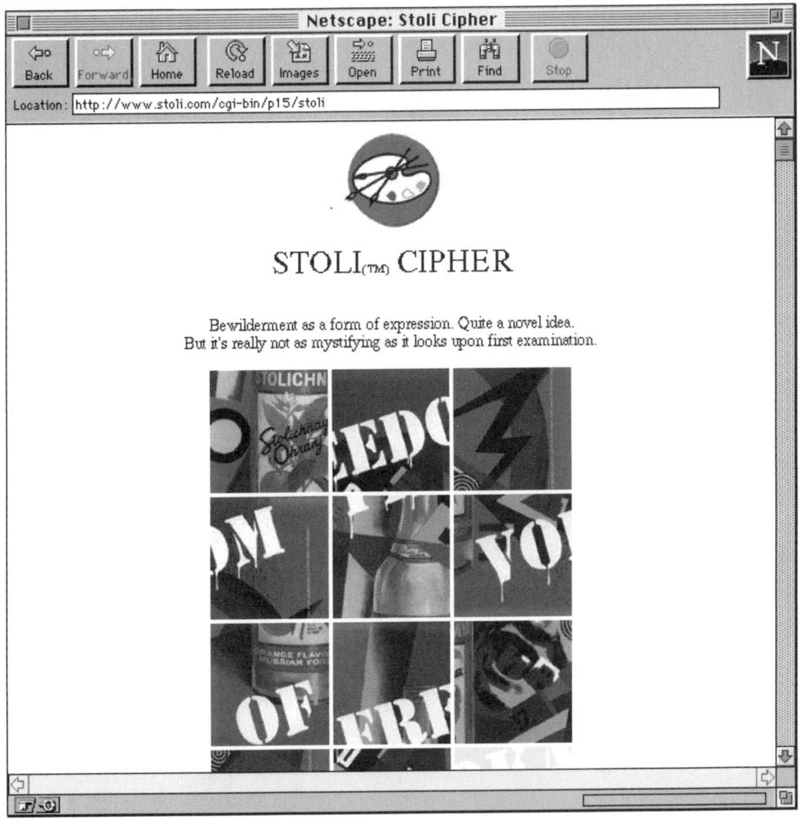

Figure 11-2: *Stolichnaya presents Stoli Cipher, an interactive puzzle.*

Another way to catch readers' interest is to offer freebies, such as drawings for a free T-shirt. Some companies offer free items for anyone purchasing over a certain amount of merchandise. We looked up the word "contest" at Yahoo and found over 50 companies that offered free prizes for drawings or correct submissions that solved an online puzzle. While the idea of a drawing for a freebie is not unique, many sites add their own twist by presenting unique contests. For example one site offered prizes to the winner of a Web scavenger hunt.

Provide a Service

Some sites draw attention to themselves by offering a unique service. Depending on the type of service, this approach can sometimes require some programming expertise. Many large universities and companies have gained notoriety by offering searching services and subject listings. For example Stanford University, EINet, and O'Reilly and Associates, all have received accolades for their search facilities and well-organized subject listings of hyperlinks to Web sites. One of the most popular sites is Yahoo, which stands for Yet another hierarchical officious oracle. Figure 11-3 shows the Yahoo list of Web sites. You can visit Yahoo at http://www.yahoo.com/yahoo/.

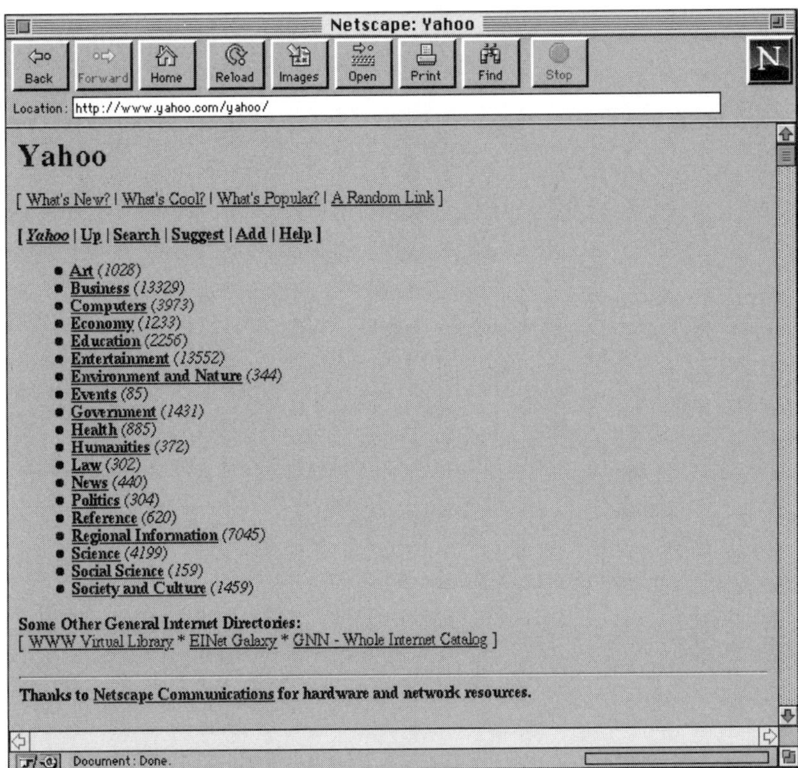

Figure 11-3: *Yahoo is a huge hierarchical listing of Web sites organized by subject.*

Computer Literacy is the largest computer bookstore in the world. A practical service Computer Literacy Bookshops brings to the Web is their database of computer books. Not only does this service provide information on computer-related books, but obviously is helpful for their mail-order business. The search form lets you search for books by author, title, ISBN or subject. Figure 11-4 shows Computer Literacy Bookshops's database search form. You can visit the database page directly by entering the URL: http://www.clbooks.com/cgi-bin/browsedb.

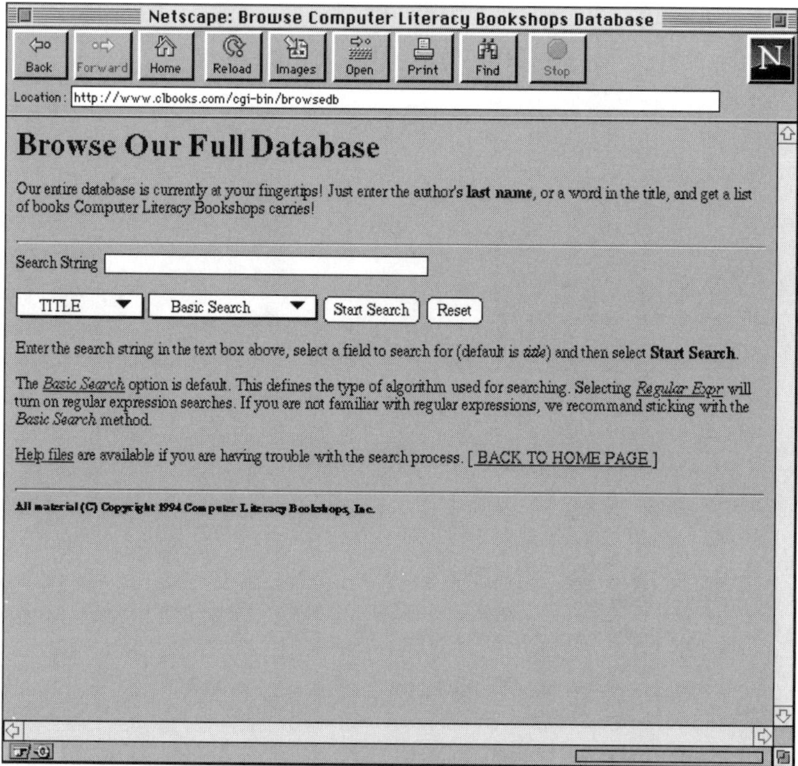

Figure 11-4: *Computer Literacy Bookshops's database lets readers look up books by author, title, ISBN or subject.*

David Koblas is well known for his Currency Converter Web page. This page is a part of O'Reilly and Associates's Web site. It presents the value of a nation's currency relative to another nations. You can try out the Currency Converter at http://gnn.com/cgi-bin/gnn/currency/. Koblas is also the author of the giftool application, a DOS tool for handling GIF images.

Taxing Times is a service provided by the S-Cubed Division of Maxwell Labs. The page presents U.S. and Canadian tax information. The primary service is an extensive archive of Federal and State tax forms and instructions in different formats, such as Adobe Acrobat's PDF format. You can even download the entire tax code, if you want to. Many of the forms can be downloaded and legally used for submitting your taxes. Taxing Times resides at http://inept.scubed.com/tax/tax.html.

Kansas University Campus Internet Association came up with an innovative idea that has generated a lot of links and publicity. URouLette is a Web page that uses an image map of a roulette wheel to send visitors to a completely random Web site. Figure 11-5 shows the URouLette Web page. You can try out URouLette by entering http://kuhttp.cc.ukans.edu/cwis/organizations/kucia/uroulette/uroulette.html.

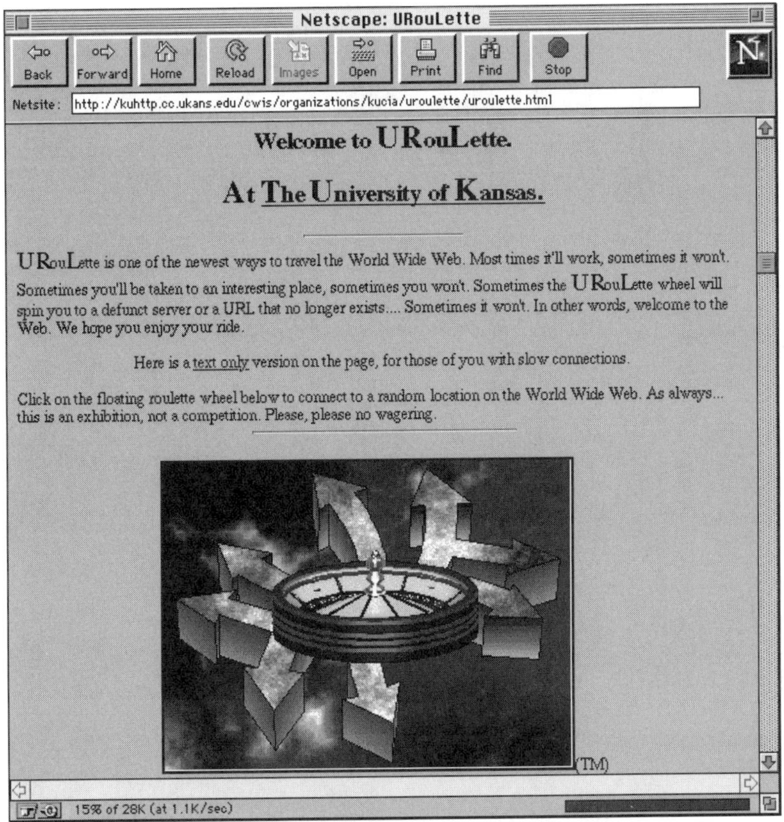

Figure 11-5: *The URouLette Web page presents an image map of a roulette wheel that when clicked sends visitors to a completely random Web site.*

Thomas Boutell is a savvy programmer who is responsible for the Mapedit program used for creating image maps. Tom also came up with the idea to present an interactive form that tells you who was born on the current day's date. It also provides links to that person's home page. Figure 11-6 shows Thomas Boutell's birthday server. You can register your birthday and include your e-mail address so others can send you birthday e-mail. Boutell's Web page is at http://sunsite.unc.edu/btbin/birthday/.

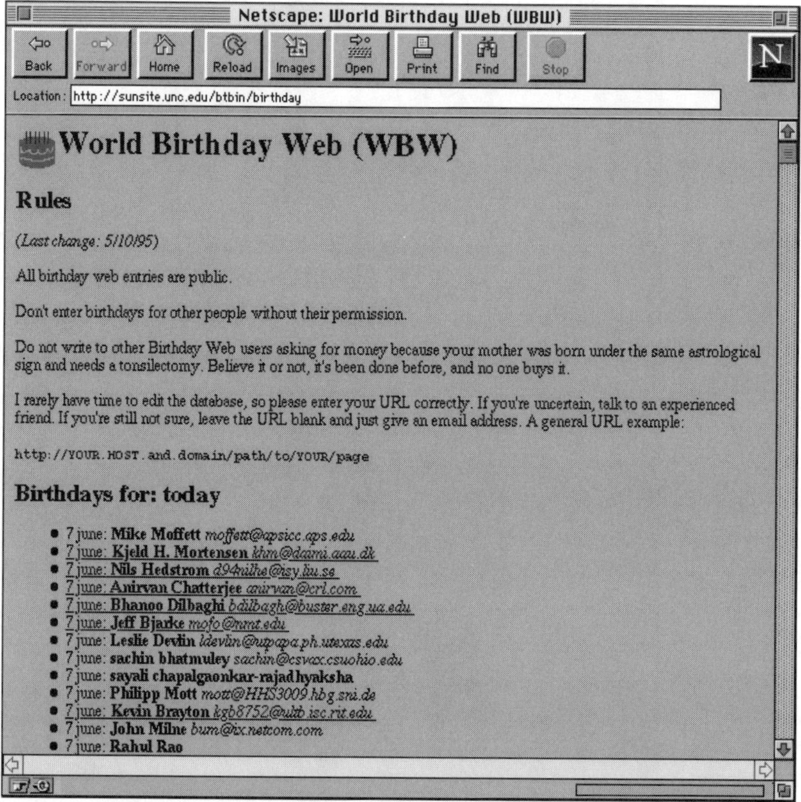

Figure 11-6: *Thomas Boutell's birthday server.*

Just about every appliance imaginable has been hooked up to the Internet and received Net coverage, including aquariums, coke machines, coffee pots, hot tubs, toasters and wine cellars. The latest trend is sites that let you remotely operate a robot's arm. You may want to be careful what object you connect to the Net or what you point your video camera at. One site that made the "Useless WWW Pages" list was a camera focused at one person's toilet. Hey you can publish just about anything on the Net. If you want to take a look at interactive sites, check out Mark's List of Internet Interactivity at http://www.eia.brad.ac.uk/mark/fave-inter.html.

Another approach is to cover a subject you believe people are dying to know about. For example, at Christmastime many people use a Web searching facility using the keyword "Christmas" to locate sites offering Christmas-related information. Centering a page around a seasonal holiday is a short-lived attraction, but it does attract attention. At Christmastime, anyone who looked up the word "Christmas" was bound to come across the Cygnus Christmas tree, which presented an image of the company Christmas tree. A questionable service, but one that got a fair amount of attention on the Web and in the press. You certainly are not limited to a holiday. If you can't find a subject you're interested in, you may want to do some additional homework and create your own page that addresses the subject.

Interactive Multimedia Publishing

While the Net chokes a little when distributing large sound and video files, Web publishers get a lot of attention for presenting multimedia files. Carl Malamud has garnered quite a following by publishing audio files as a part of the Internet Multicasting Service and his Internet Talk Radio broadcasts. One feature that has been widely publicized is the "Geek of the Week," which is a weekly interview with a popular figure in the technical community. This type of publishing is fairly advanced and resource intensive, making it fall outside the realm of most Web publishers. You can check out the archives of interviews and Internet-related news at http://www.ncsa.uiuc.edu/radio/radio.html.

Another multimedia centered Web site is the Internet Underground Music Archive (IUMA). IUMA is a well-designed, popular Web site that delivers a variety of free music. Rob Lord bills IUMA as "the Net's first free hi-fi music archive." Many of the pages include large, impressive inline images. The songs are high-quality (44.1kHz) and files are compressed and stored in the MPEG audio format. Readers can submit instant reviews and comments. An interactive form lets you set up a personalized view of the archive by choosing the artists and songs you're most interested in. Several record labels have home pages at IUMA, including Warner Brothers. Figure 11-7 shows the home page for IUMA. You can visit IUMA by entering http://www.iuma.com/.

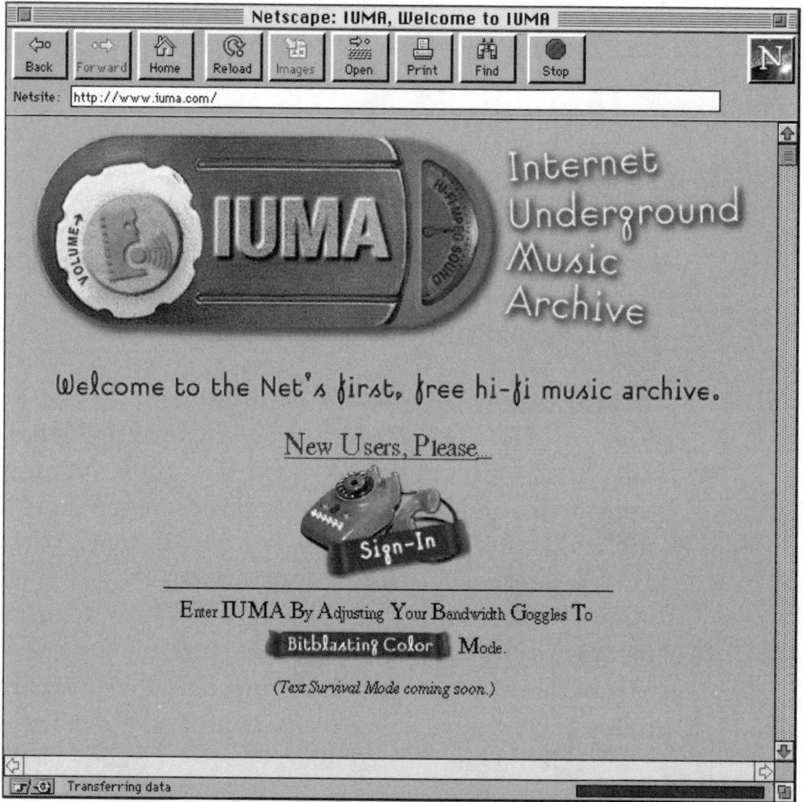

Figure 11-7: *IUMA is one of the most popular multimedia Web sites.*

Artist-In-Residence

Kaleidospace is an online gallery of independent artists. Artists provide samples of their works and Kaleidospace showcases them in a Web page. In order to look good on the Net and help promote the Web site, Kaleidospace employed a method of improving their recognition that has been used by many universities. They asked respected science fiction writer David Brin and graphic novelist P. Craig Russell to be artists-in-residence. This proved to be a great way to help promote the artists and the site. At the time we were writing this book, renowned horror author and film director Clive Barker was the artist-in-residence and was scheduled to share some of his original art. A behind-the-scenes interview with the cast and crew of the movie *Candyman* was also available, along with a related QuickTime film clip. You can visit Kaleidospace at http://www.kspace.com/.

Virtual Reality & Web Publishing

Virtual Reality environments are one of the newest trends in Web publishing. A language known as VRML (Virtual Reality Markup Language) is hovering on the horizon of Web publishing that will allow Web authors to create multidimensional documents. However, visitors of VRML Web sites will require a special browser. One of the first attempts at creating a virtual reality Web site using HTML is WAXweb. WAXweb marries David Blain's award-winning film, *WAX or Discovery of TV among the Bees*, with the interactivity of a game, called a MOO (Multi-user Object-Oriented environments). The site embeds over one thousand images, hundreds of video clips and two thousand audio clips into the site. WAXweb lets readers interact by inserting comments and creating their own pages. Figure 11-8 shows the WAXweb home page. You can visit WAXweb at http://bug.village.virginia.edu/.

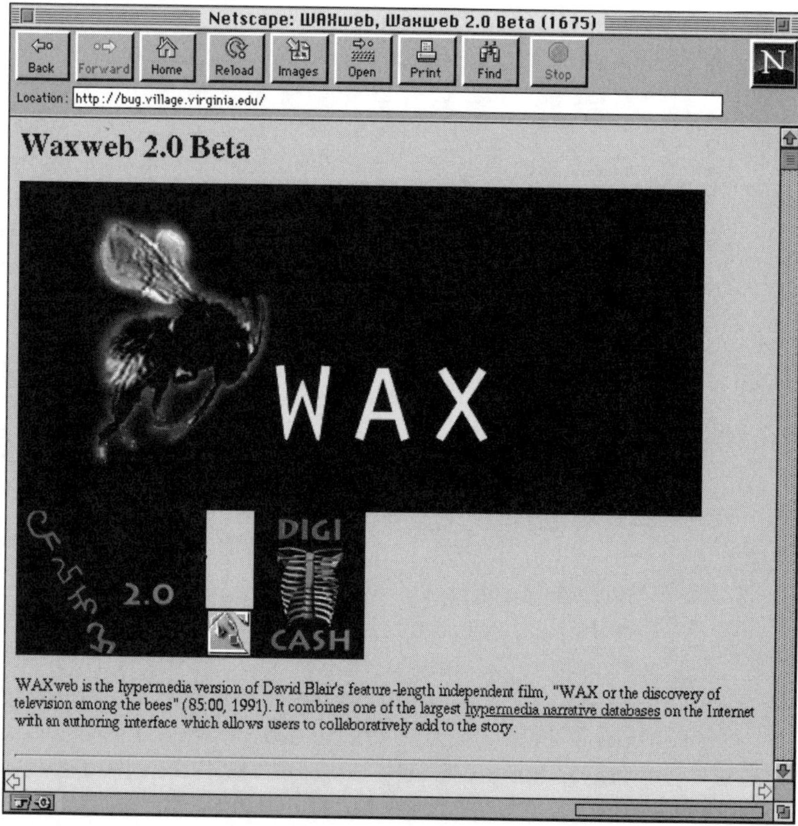

Figure 11-8: *WAXweb marries Web publishing with a MOO.*

Another multimedia MOO Web site that has received a lot of press is SenseMedia Publishing's ChibaMOO—The Sprawl. (The names are a nod toward the seminal novel, *Neuromancer*, by William Gibson, which introduced the idea of "cyberspace.") The Sprawl presents a virtual world that lets users interact and create objects and Web pages. Figure 11-9 shows the home page for the Sprawl. You can visit the Sprawl by entering http://sensemedia.net/sprawl/.

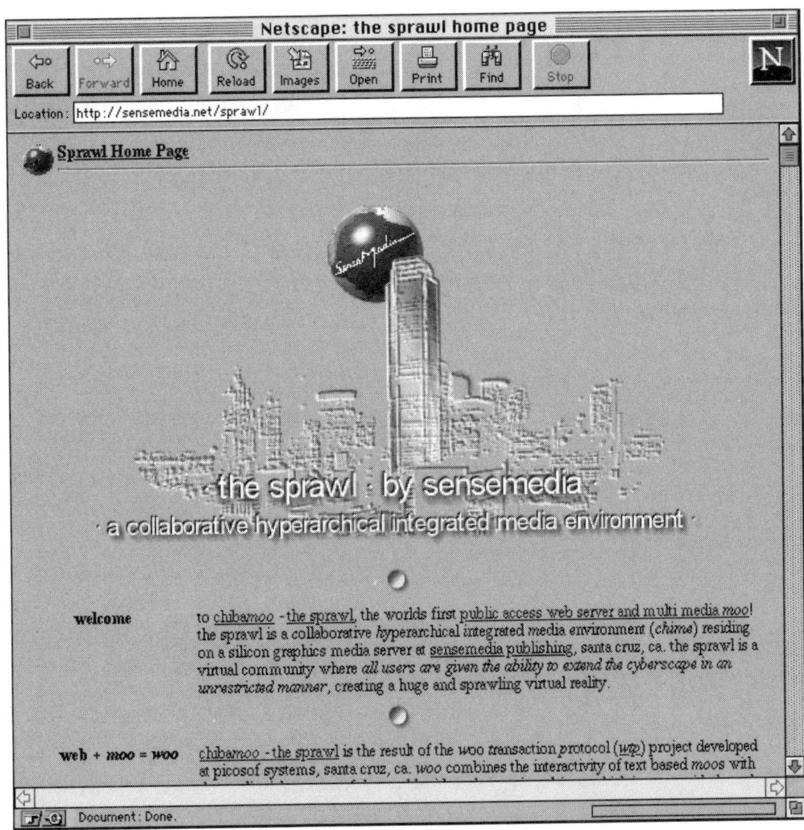

Figure 11-9: *SenseMedia Publishing's ChibaMOO—The Sprawl is an interactive cyberworld.*

Promote Your Site

In order to look good on the Net, people have to be able to find you. There are a few ways you can promote your site. You can announce your presence using other Web sites, such as NCSA's What's New page, the OpenMarket commercial sites' index and the Net-Happenings' mailing list and newsgroup. Some sites that include search facilities, such as Stanford University's Yahoo, are interactive and let you add your own home page to the list.

Wired, *Internet World*, *NetGuide*, *.net* and other Internet-related publications are always looking for well-designed Web pages that take a unique approach to delivering information. Ventana has two titles, *Internet Roadside Attractions* and *Walking the World Wide Web*, which list and describe interesting Web sites. These periodicals and books are only the tip of the iceberg. More important resources, however, are the numerous Web sites, such as Netscape Communications, NCSA, GNN and so on, that include lists of "new" and "cool" Web sites for people to visit.

Use a Design Checklist

Here are some pointers for designing a successful Web site. Some of these have been mentioned in this chapter and in previous chapters. This list is by no means complete, but it's a good place to start.

- Let readers know who you are. Be sure to sign your Web pages and provide an e-mail address.
- Use headings as headings. Don't use a heading for a note or warning just because of the formatting. New HTML tools and Web browsers promise to take advantage of HTML coding; using headers incorrectly would create an outline or table of contents that was unusable.
- Give readers a way to go home again. Every subsequent page should include a link back to the home page.
- Don't use the phrase "click here." This not only insults the intelligence of your reader but it is a non-descriptive way of presenting information.
- Organize your pages so they are independent of each other. If you need to present a long document, such as documentation or a manual, include a link to the file in a portable document format.
- Copyedit and spell check your document. Grammatical errors and misspellings are annoying and can confuse your reader. Publishing a Web page filled with errors also affects your credibility.

- Don't use too many links and emphasis tags. This can make your page dark and difficult to read.
- Be consistent with the design of your Web pages. For example, don't mix two disparate types of images, such as color digital photos and black-and-white clip art. Note that some of the scripting languages, like Frontier, can help you maintain a consistent appearance.
- Inform your readers if you're using Netscape extensions. If you think that your readers will be confused include a link to the Netscape browser.
- Publish two presentations of your site if your site includes more than a couple of inline images. Create one that takes advantage of graphics for users with fast connections and another that is primarily text-based. This way you address anyone using a text-based browser as well as the person who wants to get the information quickly without having to wait for the graphics to download.
- Interlace your inline images. This lets users start viewing your page quickly without having to wait for images to download.
- Keep in mind text-based browsers by including the Alternate text attribute and alternate text.
- Keep your images small—up to about 50k. Large images can be time-consuming to download and may frustrate readers with slow modem connections.
- Use thumbnails for large images. This lets readers decide which images they want to view in a larger size.
- Include the size of the file in the text if you include links to a large file, such as an image, sound or video file. This gives users some idea of how long it will take to download the file.
- Test your links to other Web pages. Many Web publishers have the best intentions when publishing a Web page, but don't take the time to ensure that the links work and are up-to-date.

- Provide access to a sample, rather than an actual product, you want to sell. Putting a product online at an unsecured site is one way to invite trouble. Some hackers may take this as a challenge.
- Include a table of contents, indexes or cross references for long Web documents. You want readers to be able to go directly to the page or section that contains the information they want.
- Give readers a reason to come back. Present a service, such as up-to-date information on a unique topic, an online comic, a contest or something that will give readers an incentive to return.
- Validate your Web pages before you publish them to make sure you haven't broken any HTML coding rules or overlooked any design mistakes.

Web Publishing Examples

Most Web documents fall into at least one of eight main categories: a home page, brochure, catalog, press release, zine, information center, virtual storefront or cybermall. The following are examples of well-designed Web pages from each of these categories. If you like, visit these sites and take a look at their source code. If you're using Netscape, choose the View>> Source command. If you want, you can use Netscape Navigator's File>>Save command to save the HTML source and modify portions of the HTML source code to meet your needs. Don't copy the site's code verbatim. Most pages are copyrighted material. The Web has always been a place where people share information and, often, their code. In this environment, copying someone else's code may not be taken very seriously. However, as the Web becomes more widespread and commercial, you should be aware that directly copying code is a copyright violation, and might result in problems. Besides, originality counts for a lot on the Web. If a page or site design inspires you, look at their code and then use that as an example for your own work.

Home Pages

No matter what your goal, the place to start is your home page. First impressions count. If a person is not impressed with your home page, chances are they will not read on. We have chosen a couple of impressive personal home pages as examples. The first comes from Justin Hall, who publishes "Links from the Underground," an entertaining and enlightening information site that is a little on the edge. Justin is always improving his site by adding links and testing Netscape extensions. His home page shows off some of Netscape's newest extensions, such as the table's embossed border around links to the site's main attractions. If you visit, be sure to check his great hotlist. Figure 11-10 shows Justin's home page. You can visit Justin's "Links from the Underground" by entering http://www.links.net/.

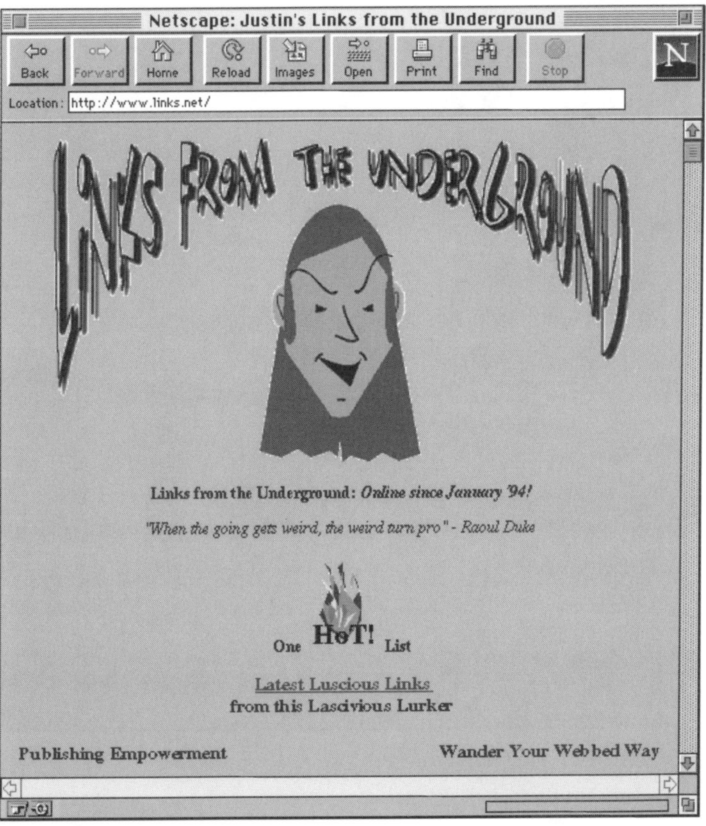

Figure 11-10: *Justin's "Links from the Underground" home page.*

Another well-designed personal Web page is brought to you by author and visionary Howard Rheingold. Figure 11-11 shows Howard Rheingold's home page. The page is fairly simple with eye-catching, transparent, interlaced graphic images strategically placed. The text is not overcrowded. The site is also divided into sections with graphic rainbow-colored horizontal rules. A few links point to pages that take advantage of the graphic and multimedia nature of the Web, including Rheingold's art, images of his painted shoes and an animation in the QuickTime format. The site also includes a link to a collection of Rheingold's popular "Tomorrow" column. This inviting home page is at once personal and professional. You can visit Howard Rheingold's home page at http://www.well.com:80/www/hlr/.

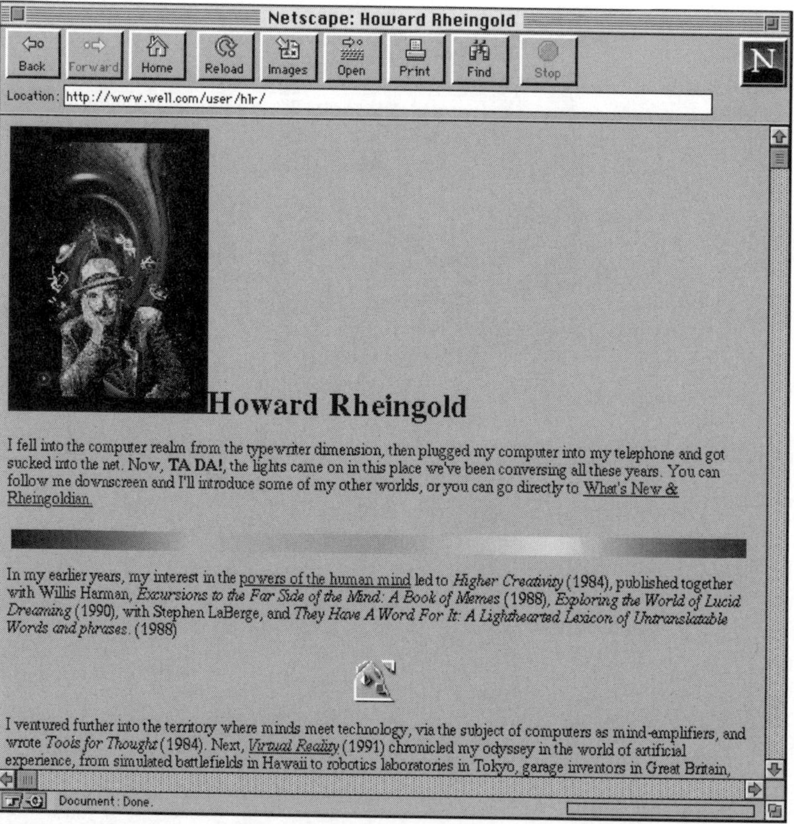

Figure 11-11: *Howard Rheingold's home page.*

Brochures

A brochure is used to describe a company's or individual's goals and is typically targeted to inform prospective customers about individual products or services. Brochures should be simple and concise. CyberSight publishes a good example of a simple Web brochure. Figure 11-12 shows some of the text used to describe CyberSight's services. You can view Internet Marketing Incorporated's brochure for creating Web sites by entering http://cybersight.com/cgi-bin/imi/s?main.gmml.

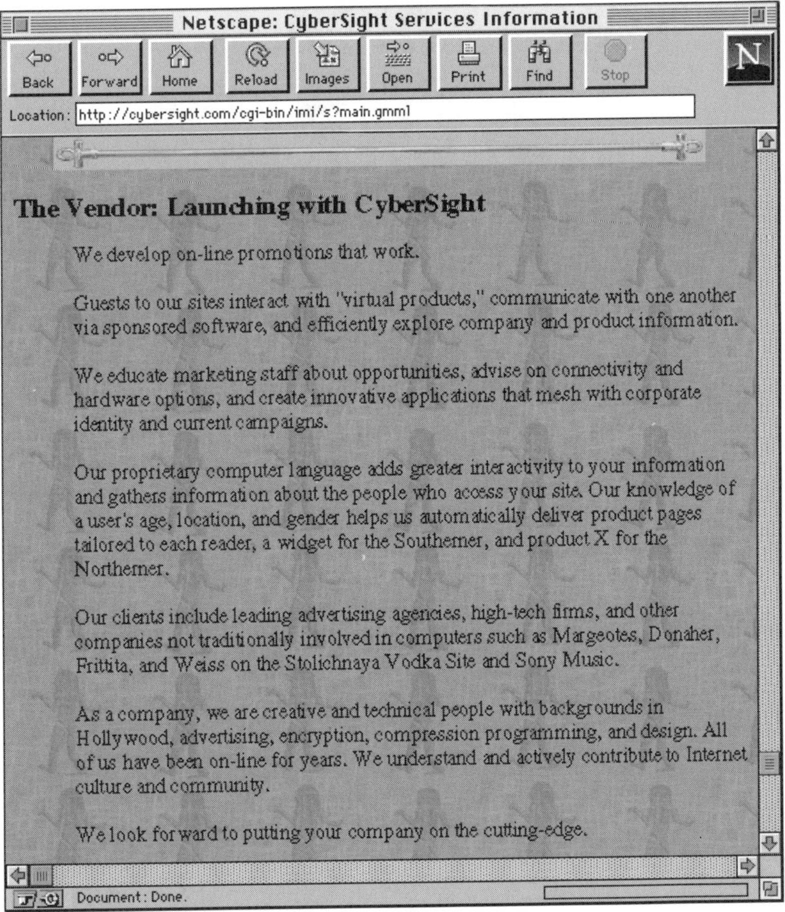

Figure 11-12: *CyberSights's brochure.*

Catalogs

A catalog is the next step beyond a brochure. Like a traditional catalog, an online catalog lists information about a product or service. Most Web catalogs include a link to an order form. A catalog may appear as a hypertext listing. One of the most comprehensive and impressive catalogs on the Net is CD*now!*'s listing of videos and compact disks. Figure 11-13 shows one screen of CD*now!*'s catalog. You can visit CD*now!* at http://cdnow.com/.

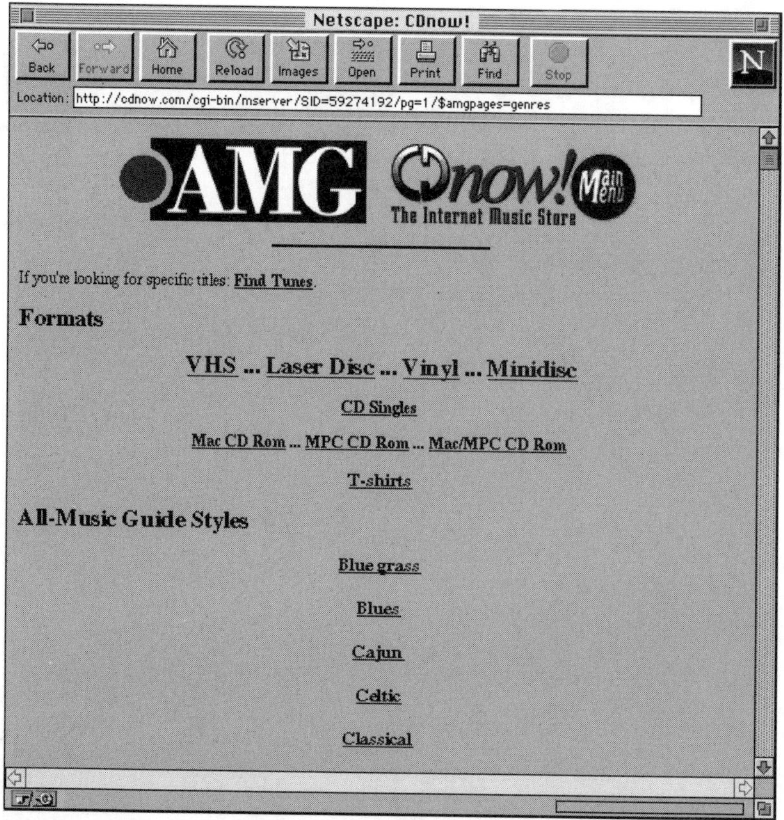

Figure 11-13: CDnow! *includes an impressive catalog of compact disks and videos.*

Press Releases

Press releases follow the lead of their paper-based counterparts. In most cases, a press release appears exactly as it was sent out to the press. Currently only a few press releases include hyperlinks. Hyperlinks in press releases will become more prevalent as companies become more comfortable with the idea of hypermedia. Feel free to include a link at the bottom of the press release to an order form or back to the home page. Figure 11-14 shows Netscape Communication's original press release for Netscape Navigator 1.1. You can display this press release by entering http://home.netscape.com/info/newsrelease16.html.

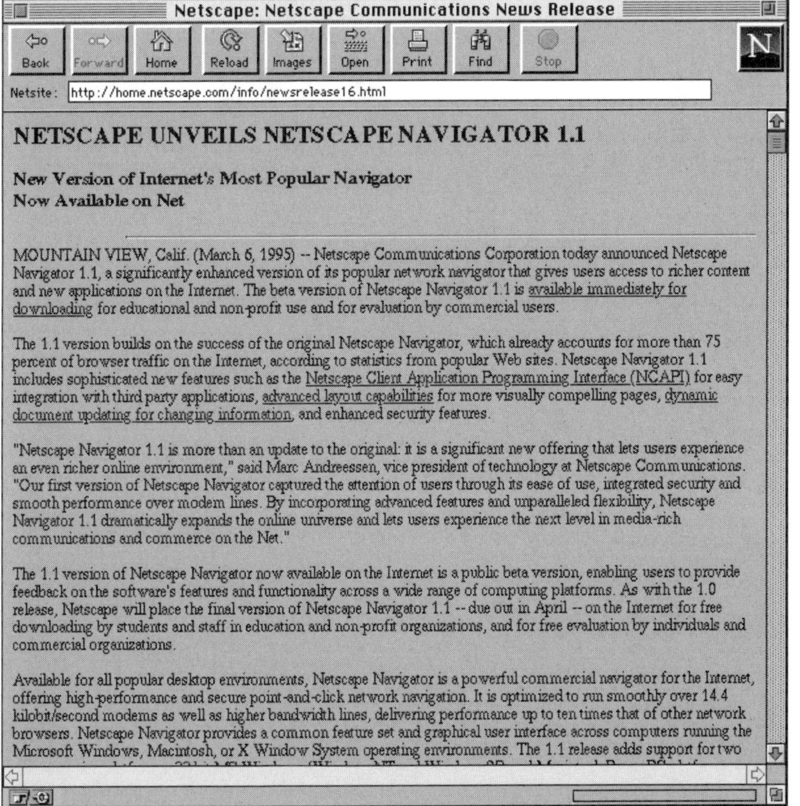

NETSCAPE UNVEILS NETSCAPE NAVIGATOR 1.1

New Version of Internet's Most Popular Navigator Now Available on Net

MOUNTAIN VIEW, Calif. (March 6, 1995) -- Netscape Communications Corporation today announced Netscape Navigator 1.1, a significantly enhanced version of its popular network navigator that gives users access to richer content and new applications on the Internet. The beta version of Netscape Navigator 1.1 is available immediately for downloading for educational and non-profit use and for evaluation by commercial users.

The 1.1 version builds on the success of the original Netscape Navigator, which already accounts for more than 75 percent of browser traffic on the Internet, according to statistics from popular Web sites. Netscape Navigator 1.1 includes sophisticated new features such as the Netscape Client Application Programming Interface (NCAPI) for easy integration with third party applications, advanced layout capabilities for more visually compelling pages, dynamic document updating for changing information, and enhanced security features.

"Netscape Navigator 1.1 is more than an update to the original: it is a significant new offering that lets users experience an even richer online environment," said Marc Andreessen, vice president of technology at Netscape Communications. "Our first version of Netscape Navigator captured the attention of users through its ease of use, integrated security and smooth performance over modem lines. By incorporating advanced features and unparalleled flexibility, Netscape Navigator 1.1 dramatically expands the online universe and lets users experience the next level in media-rich communications and commerce on the Net."

The 1.1 version of Netscape Navigator now available on the Internet is a public beta version, enabling users to provide feedback on the software's features and functionality across a wide range of computing platforms. As with the 1.0 release, Netscape will place the final version of Netscape Navigator 1.1 -- due out in April -- on the Internet for free downloading by students and staff in education and non-profit organizations, and for free evaluation by individuals and commercial organizations.

Available for all popular desktop environments, Netscape Navigator is a powerful commercial navigator for the Internet, offering high-performance and secure point-and-click network navigation. It is optimized to run smoothly over 14.4 kilobit/second modems as well as higher bandwidth lines, delivering performance up to ten times that of other network browsers. Netscape Navigator provides a common feature set and graphical user interface across computers running the Microsoft Windows, Macintosh, or X Window System operating environments. The 1.1 release adds support for two

Figure 11-14: *Netscape Communications's press release for Netscape Navigator 1.1.*

Hypermedia Zines

Zines are electronic magazines and are a popular forum for self-expression on the Net. A zine can come in many different formats, such as ASCII text, hypertext, PostScript or Adobe's Portable Document Format. Hypermedia zines include many elements that are found in traditional magazines, such as a masthead, table of contents and list of contributors.

One exemplary hypermedia zine is *Urban Desires: A Magazine of Metropolitan Passion.* It is an online culture magazine covering topics such as art, film, music, food and erotica. *Urban Desires* takes a highly interactive approach. For example, one Web page titled "Pocketful of Posies" includes a "Replant" button that when clicked rearranges the images on the page. It also includes pages that take advantage of Netscape's background and table extensions. *Urban Desires* is brought to you by a group of talented Web authors at agency.com, who are also responsible for *Vibe Online*, another zine. Figure 11-15 shows the front page of *Urban Desires*. To check out *Urban Desires*, enter http://desires.com/.

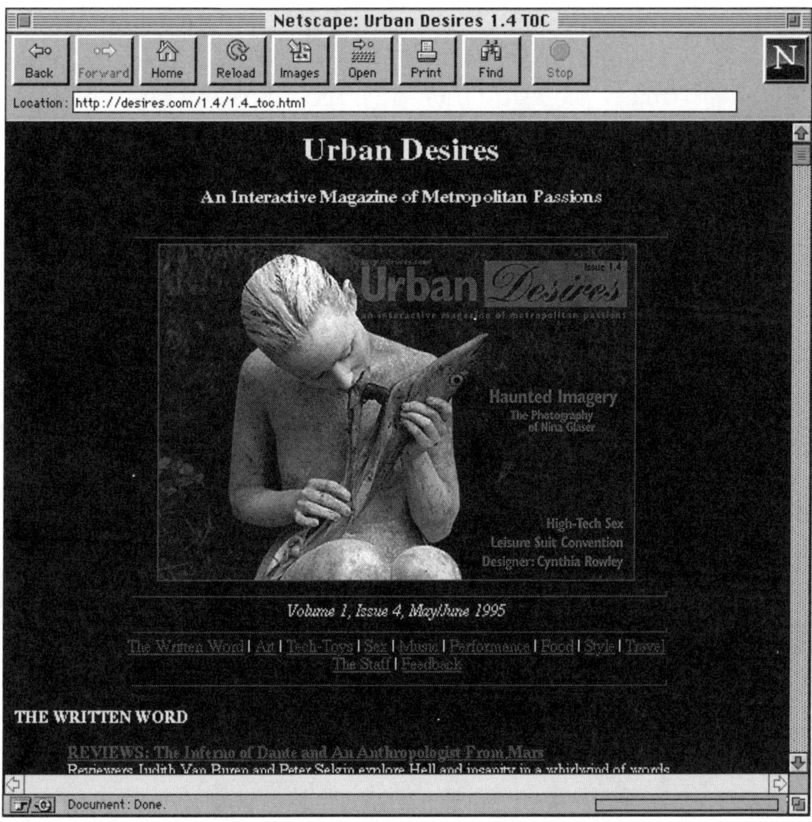

Figure 11-15: Urban Desires: An Interactive Magazine of Metropolitan Passion *is a well-laid-out interactive culture zine.*

Melvin is the zine brainchild of Matt Nolker at New Media. It has been chosen by several sites, including Netscape Communications, as one of the best zines on the Net. This irreverent, humorous zine is strongly reminiscent of *National Lampoon*'s glory days, back when Doug Kenny, Michael O'Donohue, Tony Hendra, Gerald Sussman and John Hughes were writing. *Melvin* takes a unique design approach. It delivers some formatted pages as inline GIFs. This looks gorgeous, but it does have the drawback of possibly losing readers with slow connections. The images are created with a couple of Macintosh graphic programs (Adobe's

Illustrator and Photoshop) and a UNIX layout program. Only a few of the pages use inline graphics to present formatted text, but many pages do include large inline images. The final production is very slick. Figure 11-16 shows the feature story presented as an inline image. You can out check out *Melvin* at http://www.melvin.com/.

Figure 11-16: Melvin *takes a unique approach using GIFs to present two-column text and graphics.*

Urban Desires and *Melvin* are two unique Web zines, but there are several other sites that are Web counterparts to traditional magazine publishing. HotWired is *Wired* magazine's foray into the Web zine scene and is one of the most popular zines on the Net. HotWired takes advantage of the Web medium to add interactive capabilities that Web publishing brings, rather than just trying to convert the text from the current issues of *Wired* magazine. You can visit HotWired at http://www.hotwired.com/. Figure 11-17 shows HotWired's home page.

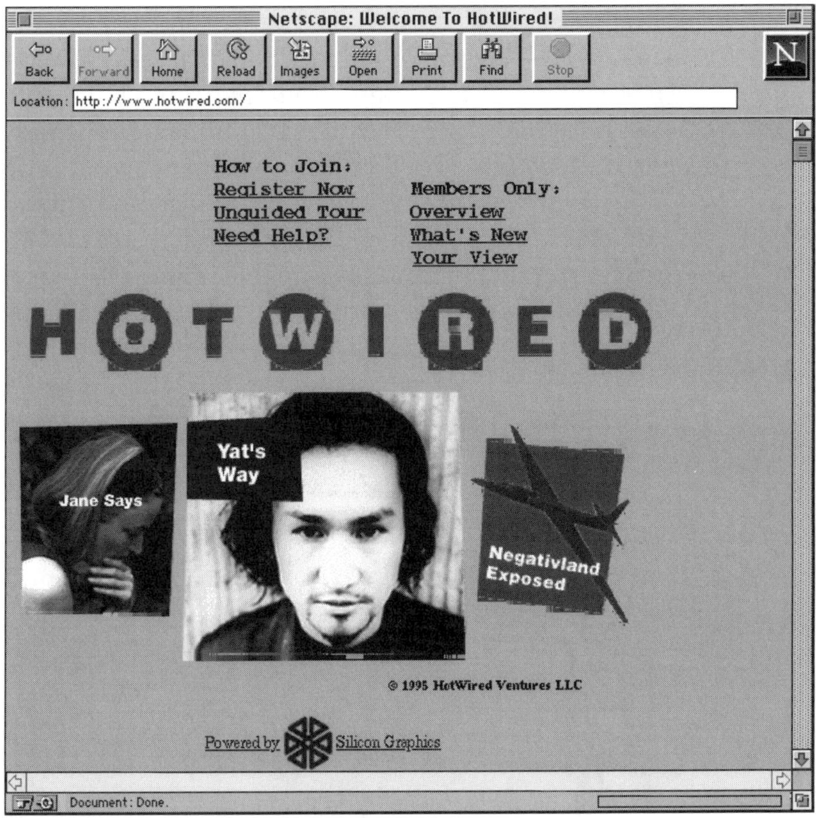

Figure 11-17: *HotWired's home page.*

Some magazines simply mirror portions of their paper-based counterparts; for example Time Warner has a site that includes links to *Time* and *People* magazine (http://www.pathfinder.com/) and Ziff Davis has a site, named Ziff Net (http://www.ziff.com/), that includes links to online versions of *PC Magazine, PC Computing, Windows Sources, Computer Shopper* and more. In addition to magazines, newspapers are also appearing on the Web. One example of a newspaper on the Web that is exceptionally well designed is the *San Jose Mercury News*. You can read the *San Jose Mercury News* by entering http://www.sjmercury.com/.

Information Centers

An information center is the closest type of Web site to a virtual storefront. The only difference is that an information center doesn't take orders online from the Web site. Information centers can be set up to accept orders by phone or fax. Many companies set up accounts over the phone and then accept orders via e-mail. The majority of businesses on the Net are information centers. For example, Apple, Adobe, Claris and Microsoft are all business sites that currently fall into this category. Figure 11-18 shows Claris' home page, which is made up of a large image map. You can visit Claris at http://www.claris.com/WelcomeMap.html.

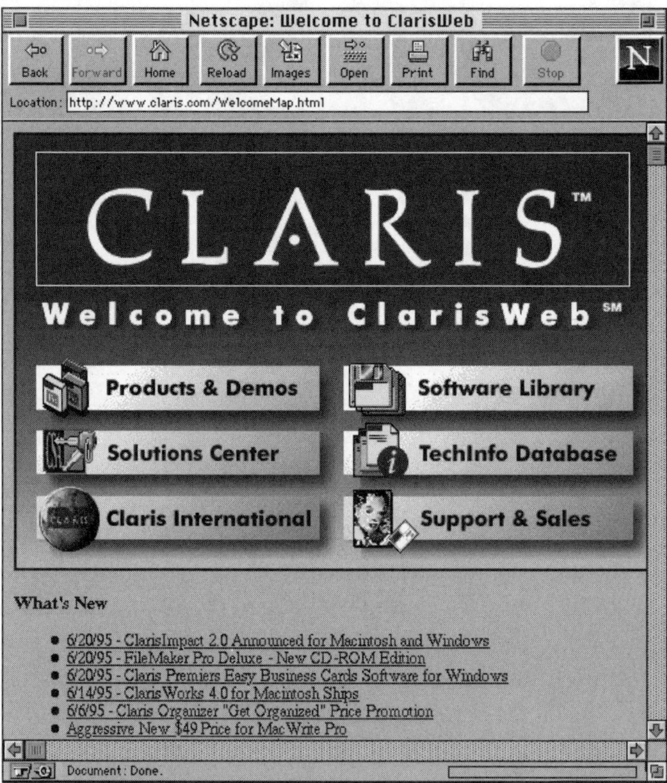

Figure 11-18: *Claris is an example of an information center.*

To contrast two information centers, take a look at Adobe's Web site, shown in Figure 11-19. Notice that the icons are consistently designed and are fairly small in size. You can visit Adobe directly at http://www.adobe.com/.

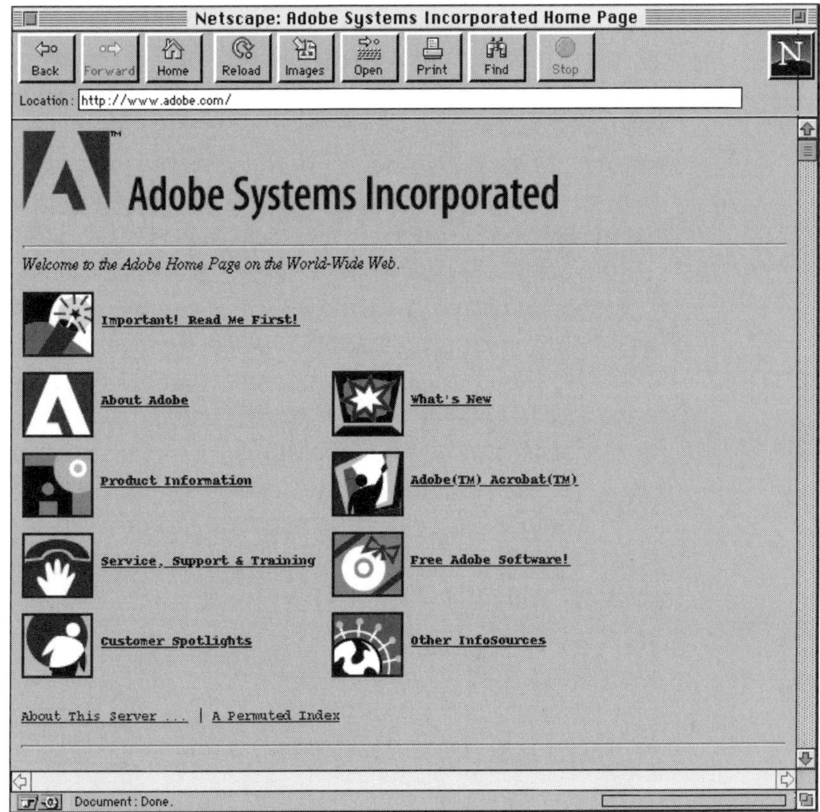

Figure 11-19: *Adobe Systems is another example of an information center.*

Virtual Storefronts & Cybermalls

A virtual storefront can be a part of a cybermall or can stand alone on a server. A virtual storefront, like an information center, presents products and services, but is also set up to accept credit cards online. A good example of a virtual storefront is software.net. This exceptionally well-presented site sells and ships shrink-wrapped software in addition to selling selected software programs online. The use of consistent graphics is pleasing to the eye and helps meet the site's objective. It includes all the Web pages required to inform the reader about the products and services and make the customer feel secure about ordering. This site includes the right mix of Web pages, such as a what's new page, a catalog of products indexed by subject or company, a customer support page and an online forum for sending feedback. It also has several draws, including the full text of *PC World* magazine, giveaways (at the time the site was offering free tickets to Internet World) and a drawing for a free T-shirt for readers from the pool of readers that leave feedback. Software.net is the one site that others should look to as the premiere example of a virtual storefront. Figure 11-20 shows the home page for software.net. To visit software.net enter https://www.software.net.

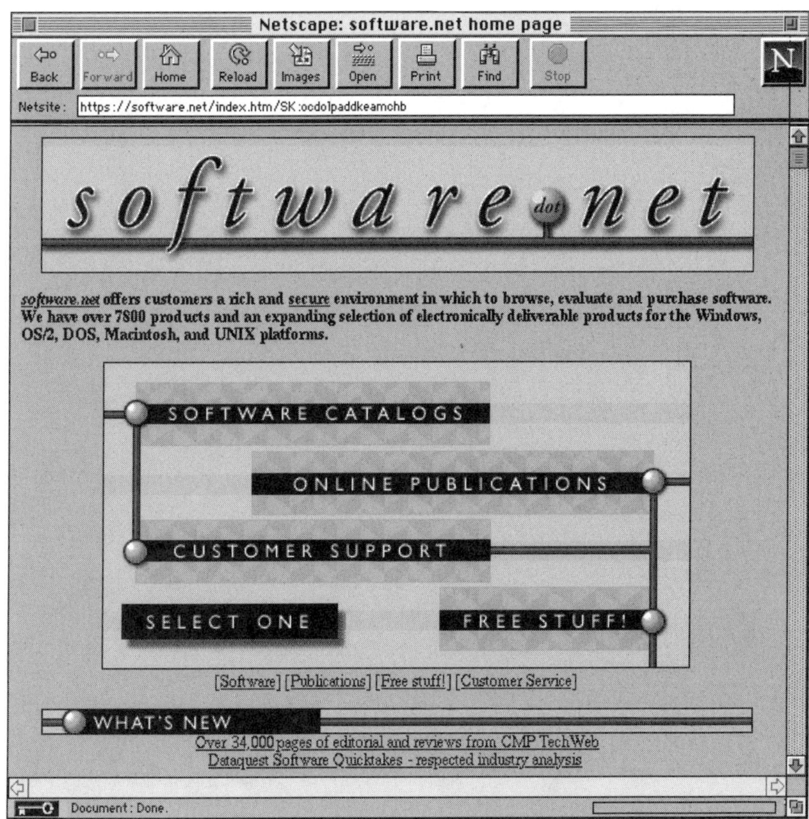

Figure 11-20: *Software.net is the premiere example of a virtual storefront.*

Another exceptional example of a virtual storefront is the Internet Shopping Network (ISN). ISN started as a part of Commerce Net, a non-profit consortium funded in part by a grant from the U.S. government's Technology Reinvestment Project. ISN was recently purchased by the Home Shopping Network. Like the Home Shopping Network, ISN presents numerous companies' products and makes it possible to order them online. ISN presents both a text-based and graphics-based version of the site. It includes one of the best online catalogs on the Web, including over 10,000 software- and electronic-based products. Pages can present products sorted either by subject or company. There is also a search facility. Figure 11-21 shows a page that allows users to take a guided tour of the Internet Shopping Network. As a draw, ISN includes online issues of *InfoWorld* and *Computer Currents* magazine for registered users. You can take a tour on your own by entering http://www.internet.net/.

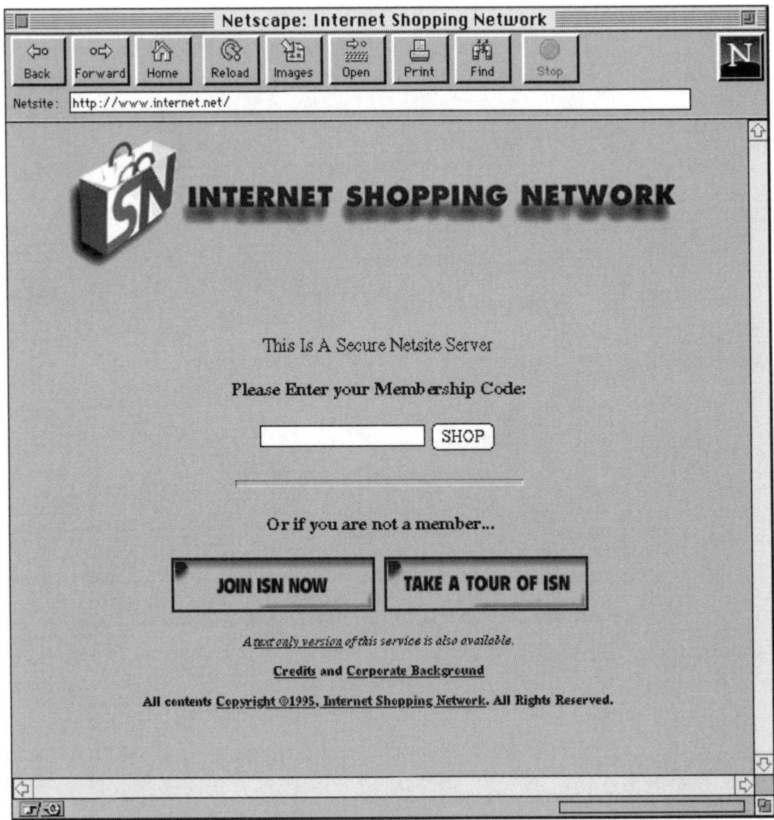

Figure 11-21: *The Internet Shopping Network.*

ISN is slowly making the transition from virtual storefront to cybermall and has recently included two companies at its site. A cybermall is a Web site that includes a collection of virtual storefronts. Cybermalls are typically presented by server services, companies that sell space or Net publishing services. Some service providers, companies that sell Internet connections, also provide server services. InterNex, for example, is both a service provider and a server service. Typically the Web documents that make up the virtual storefronts are stored at the server service's or service provider's site, but they can also be links to other sites. An exceptional cybermall is Branch Mall, which is located at http://www.branch.com. The brainchild of Jon Zeeff, Branch Mall was one of the first, if not the first, cybermall on the Net. Figure 11-22 shows Branch Mall's home page.

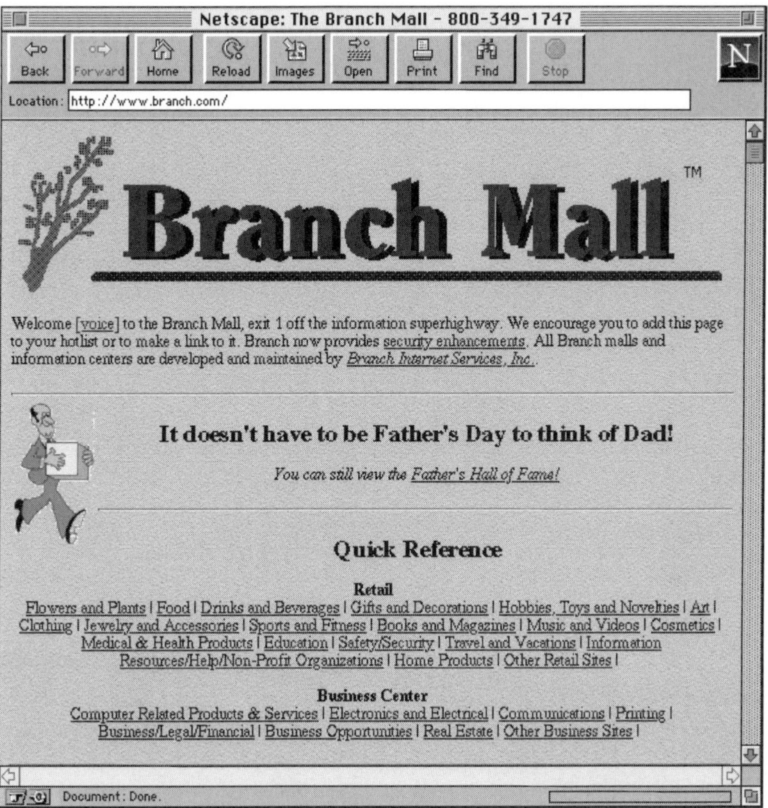

Figure 11-22: *Branch Mall was one of the first cybermalls on the Net.*

Moving On

Looking good on the Net means effectively communicating with your reader. If the reader is put off by your presentation or if you fail to meet his or her needs, the communication is lost. If the reader connects, chances are he or she will return. This chapter presented several techniques for connecting with readers and gave examples of different types of Web documents. The following two chapters take the next step by giving you the information you need to publish Web pages using a service provider, server service or setting up an HTTP server and publishing on your own.

12

Service Providers & Server Services

Now that you've created your HTML-based Web masterpiece, the only remaining question is how to bring your work to the international Internet. For some, this may not be an issue—particularly if you're developing an internal corporate server and already have a network set up. For many, however, the issue of getting a server onto the Internet is a big decision: Should I run my own server and have my own connection to the Internet, or should I rent space on someone else's server and just look like I have a direct connection?

This chapter provides the information you need to weigh the options of sharing space on a server service—a service that provides Internet publishing services such as Web servers, FTP servers and virtual storefronts; services dedicated to commercial trade; or sharing space on a multipurpose host at a service provider. Service providers typically provide dial-up Internet access in addition to Web services. Which option you choose depends to a large degree on what you're trying to accomplish.

Understanding the Services Available

Before you choose your commercial service provider, you need to define the services you want to provide to the readers of your Web pages. A broad range of services is available. The most basic Web server might just deliver your HTML pages with no additional services, no CGI and no image maps. On the other hand, the most sophisticated Internet shopping center server might support secure transactions, credit cards, advertising and perhaps provide you with your own unique URL. Although the range of options is fairly continuous from the simple to the sophisticated, there are three basic types of commercial services: sharing a server, using the services of a virtual storefront, or sharing a server without appearing to. The first type, sharing space on a commercial Internet service, is where you are one of many people who use that service and share space on that server. This is the most appropriate choice for a casual Web publisher, or someone with information to share, but who doesn't need a high profile or have a great interest in developing a unique identity. This option is discussed later in this chapter in "Sharing Space."

A second option is to use the services of a virtual storefront, or mall. Typically, these services cater to the needs of a business with a product or service to sell, and want a way to sell it on the Internet. These services may also provide you with advertising and are more aggressive in promoting you and other companies on their server. A final type of server service is one in which you appear to have your own server and identity. With this kind of service, the fact that you share your service is not apparent, allowing you the freedom to develop your own home page with its own unique look and feel. Often, though, these services won't be able to provide the credit card and security services provided by a virtual storefront.

Finally, you need to consider any additional Internet service you may want to provide to your customers or readers. For example, do you distribute software and need an anonymous FTP capability? Or perhaps you want to allow text searching of your pages. Also, almost every image map or CGI interface requires adjustments and configuration on the Web server. Is your service provider willing to do this for you? At the end of the chapter is a list of questions you may want to ask your service provider when shopping for a server to publish your Web pages. As you read through the chapter, decide which features are important to you so that when you start researching service providers, you're armed with a ready list of requirements.

Deciding Between Service Providers & Going it Alone

Without a doubt, you can get the most control over your World Wide Web pages and other Internet services if you run your own server. For most individuals and many companies, however, this option is an economic impossibility. Although providing your own Web server is covered in detail in Chapter 13, "Servers at Your Service," this is a good time to stop and examine your options.

Connections to the Internet at this time are the single biggest expense when you consider ongoing maintenance of a directly connected Web site. For decent commercial-grade performance, you'll want at least a 56,000 bit-per-second link (56 kbps) and a full-time link so that people can reach you any time of the night or day. While the cost of a link like this from your business or home to the closest Internet service provider varies widely, you should figure you won't get away for less than $200–$400 dollars per month. It doesn't take much more calculation than that to realize a private Internet connection is out of the question for most people. And, unfortunately, even though you are paying for this line 24 hours a day, the actual amount of time you have data going over the line is far, far less—unless, of course, you have a very popular site or have more activity than just your Web server. By using the services of a commercial Internet provider, the costs of the lines to the Internet are spread out over many, many users. Remember, although you are sharing your Internet connection, the average load on the service provider's Internet line still permits your customers to retrieve information from your pages very rapidly. Most of the time Internet providers have line speeds of a T-1 (1.544 megabits per second) or greater. Of course, if the service provider has *too* many customers, the average link load goes up—and your individual performance goes down.

Perhaps one of the biggest advantages for having your Web pages on a commercial service is that it doesn't matter where the service provider is located. You can be in California, but you could use a service provider in Chicago, if it has the price and services you want.

Sharing Space

Many companies and individuals get by just fine with the simplest of options. The idea of sharing space on a provider's computer is very simple: you have your own "home" directory, and you put your HTML pages in that directory or in subdirectories of your home directory. The most rudimentary service of this type is found on many UNIX-based systems, where there are many individuals who have accounts on the system, and any of the users can add Web pages directly in their own account's space. Each user can have an HTML link to the master home page of the service provider simply by putting an HTML file with a specific name, such as index.html, in his or her home directory. The service provider then scans the users' home pages on a regular basis and creates a list of everyone who has an HTML page in his or her home directory.

How Much Does it Cost?

Sharing space on a service is about the cheapest option for having a Web presence. A typical charge is $65 per quarter with a 10-megabyte disk space limit. You can fit a *lot* of Web pages into 10 megabytes of disk, too.

What Does My Address Look Like?

In most cases, when sharing space, the URL to your HTML page would look something like this:

http://www.servprovidr.com/~yourlogin/index.html

The important issues to remember about this URL are that (1) the name of the system is *your service provider's name*, and (2) people reach you through a reference to your login: *~yourlogin*. If you just want to get information to the Internet community, this may be the fastest and cheapest way to do it. The drawbacks for a company, however, are that it is unlikely a casual browser would stumble across your latest sales brochure, or that someone who knows your company's name would think to look on the system owned by your service provider.

On the other hand, there are many Web searching programs and indexes available to the Internet community, and these programs will eventually find you and your home page. If you've chosen the words used in page titles and text carefully, you can ensure that people who are interested in the product you're selling or service you're providing can find you. Also, there are ways you can specifically seed search databases with your URL and inform the Internet community about your site. For example, the Lycos search engine at http://lycos.cs.cmu.edu/ has a form you can fill out that lets their search engine know about your site. The Yahoo directory will accept candidates to be included in its list, which is arranged by category. This directory is indexed as well. Go to http://www.yahoo.com/yahoo/bin/add/ and fill out a form requesting placement on their lists. For general advertising to the Internet community, you can send information about new sites to the moderated USENET newsgroup comp.internet.net-happenings.

What Other Services Can I Get?

You may be interested in Internet services besides a basic Web server, such as anonymous FTP and USENET news. If you are distributing software, for example, you could use anonymous FTP as a way to distribute shareware or software updates. In some cases, you might want customers to upload files to you. You should ask your service provider if it can make an anonymous FTP service available to your customers.

Having the ability to access USENET newsgroups is very common and can be a great benefit if you want to scan the newsgroups for topics that concern your business or interest. Often, you can find people who are inquiring about some product or service you offer and can reply to them via e-mail.

Handling Image Maps & CGI Interfaces

When you share a server, you also share the HTTP server and its associated services. If you want to use an image map, for example, you'll need to add information about your specific image map to a configuration file on the shared server. The configuration file contains information about the "hot" areas on your images, so that when a browser clicks on an image, the server will know what to do. Find out if this is something you can do yourself, or if you need to have your service provider add the information.

Forms require the use of back-end CGI programs. Find out if your service provider will allow you to create your own CGI programs, or if they must be installed in a protected area that only the service provider can access. Many service providers offer consulting and programming services to help with the creation of CGI back-ends, so even if you are allowed to write your own programs, you may not want to.

Cybermalls

Being part of a collection of companies on a commercial system, often called a *cybermall*, is another way to bring your pages to the Internet. In this model, you are one of many companies that share space on a Web server that is specifically set up to house many "stores." In this storefront or mall analogy, a person interested in buying something or learning about your product would first enter the "mall" by going to the main home page for the service provider. From that point, the browser is led to your page by lists or a directory of stores on that server. Once at your home page, the user can look at whatever materials you've put on display. Very often, the service provider for the mall will also provide a way for people to pay for merchandise you have for sale.

As a small business, this is a great way to get started. The service provider takes care of setting up the server, creates a front-end for the mall that will attract people to browse, and provides you with a way to actually make sales over the Internet. Since the service provider is responsible for the security and authentication of the consumer, you're off the hook for the use of credit card numbers or setting up customer accounts. Some of the Web servers now on the market offer encrypted transaction protocols and offer a secure way to conduct business on the Internet. Security on the Web is a tricky business—especially when financial transactions are involved—and your customers will always expect you to bear the ultimate responsibility for the privacy of their information. You should always be familiar with the security techniques used by your provider.

Similar to the previous example of sharing space on a commercial Web site, the various Web indexes will eventually pick up trails to your pages; it's also likely that your mall service provider will make an effort to link its storefront to as many other Web pages as possible. Also, security remains the job of the Internet provider, but in this case since the entire mission of the service provider is commercial, it is likely that it will be running with a high degree of emphasis placed on privacy and security.

How Much Does it Cost?

The cost of being part of a cybermall can vary widely depending on the level of service provided by the mall owner, but as an example, the introductory pricing for the service provider Open Market (http://www.openmarket.com/) is $75 per month for up to 5MB of storage (about 100 pages), a $500 setup fee, plus per-transaction fees (for when your customers actually buy something) of between 3 and 7 percent. Another provider, First Virtual, offers an information-selling service with service charges of between 2 and 10 percent based on the way the service is configured, plus a $10 setup fee. This server is focused on information that can be transmitted electronically.

What Does My Address Look Like?

Just as if you were in a real mall, people find you by going to the virtual mall site first. You can still be reached directly, however, by using a full URL that points straight to your page. For example, Lexis/Nexis has a storefront, and their "direct" address is http://www.openmarket.com/lexis-nexis/. While it's the responsibility of the mall operator to properly advertise their site, you can still get listed on Web search sites and directories by listing your direct URL.

National Public Radio, which uses First Virtual as a service provider, offers their transcripts for sale at http://www.infohaus.com/access/by-seller/National_Public_Radio/. NPR is an example of an organization that actually has their own Web server (at http://www.npr.org/) but is getting help from First Virtual to handle the sales of transcripts, because they don't want to get into the business of handling the sales themselves.

Having Your Own Server—Without Your Own Server

This kind of service is fairly new to the Internet and is perfect for the company or person who wants an identity on the Internet, but still doesn't want to go through the expense and bother of running a site. Basically, this consists of sharing a server among several clients that the service provider actually owns and operates. The server is configured, by special programming, to look like each client has their own server—in particular, each client has their own address of the form: http://www.*mycompany*.com/.

How Much Does it Cost?

The cost for this service is comparable to that of the virtual storefront, at under $100 per month, plus a $150 setup charge, with no usage fees. This compares favorably with the cost of a private 56 kbps private line, which *starts* at over $100 month and can be many times more expensive, depending on how far you live from the telephone company's switching office and what your local telephone company charges for private lines.

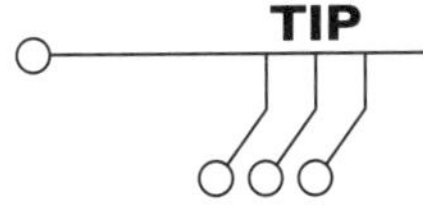

Be careful when shopping for a service provider. Some service providers charge you based on how many bytes are transmitted for you over the Internet, which in turn depends on how complicated your pages are and how many people access your Web pages. Since the number of accesses cannot be predicted, you leave yourself open for a huge end-of-the-month bill!

What Does My Address Look Like?

In this case, the service provider still shares a common system among many users, but through some clever programming of the HTTP server, you can actually support multiple IP addresses on one host. In this way, you get your own unique IP address and name, such as www.*mycompany*.com, but when people connect to this computer, they are actually connecting to a computer that has many identities on the Internet. In this way, your small company can have the same Internet name stature as AT&T, DEC or IBM, without actually having its own computer on the Web!

For many Web users, a common way to locate a company they're interested in is to create a URL that starts with "www," put your company's name or initials in the middle and end with ".com". When you establish your service, work with your Internet service provider to pick a name that people would think of when trying to find you. You may find that your perfect name is already taken, so be prepared with a few additional options.

An excellent example of a service provider that can support multiple IP addresses on a single host is Best Internet Communications (http://www.best.com) located in Mountain View California. Best uses a virtual service program called WWWDirect to provide individual accounts with IP addresses and names. For example, the company A Clean Well-Lighted Place for Books, the main example in this book, is one of numerous accounts located on a computer at Best, but it has the unique name www.bookstore.com and the IP address 204.156.147.35.

Another prime example of a virtual server is Macro Computer Solutions, a commercial provider located in Chicago (http://www.mcs.com/vserv/index.html). In their offering, called VSERVE for Virtual Service, they currently have The Underground Network (http://underground.net/), Internet Training and Consulting Services (http://www.itcs.com/), IT Solutions (http://www.its.com/) and Cybersight (http://cybersight.com/cgi-bin/cs/s?main.gmml/).

There's no way for anyone to tell if these four companies are on four different systems, or all on the same system. With a shared service such as this, you're still left with the problems of setting up your own way of selling products and conducting secure transactions. If, however, you aren't trying to conduct actual business transactions over the Internet just yet, the Virtual Presence solution may be perfect for you.

One particular benefit of this approach is that your clients access you by your company name, which is registered on the Internet for you alone. In this way, when and if you are ever ready to go to your own dedicated server, your customers never have to change their Net address for you. Although the Internet is electronic, changing addresses is just as much trouble here as actually moving your business, so this can be important to you if you plan growth in the future.

Server Services & Web Pages

Although this book is mostly about creating your own HTML pages, you may decide that you don't want to go it completely alone. Many server services have close relationships with consultants willing to help with almost any aspect of HTML page creation. For example, if you're not artistically inclined, a server service can direct you to an HTML design service. Most service providers can also hook you up with local programming talent if you don't want to create your own HTML pages, or need help with a back-end CGI program.

Going Shopping

Now that you've read about the different options available when choosing a provider, here's a list of questions to ask when shopping for a service provider or server service.

The Basics

- Do you offer a Web server, and can I control my own Web pages? How do people find me on your server?
- What is the cost of this account? Is there a time limit that I have to watch out for? If so, how do I know what I've already used?

- What services do you offer to the public? Can I have anonymous FTP space that anyone can read from? Is there a place for "incoming" files, and is it visible or hidden? Do you limit the size of files placed in an "incoming" anonymous directory?
- Can I also send and receive electronic mail? What about USENET newsgroups? Can you alias my e-mail account to use a more personal system name?
- How fast is your link to the Internet? How fast is your equipment? Do you measure the load on your links, and when do you add capacity?
- How do you handle disk storage? What's my limit, and is it advisory or enforced?
- How much experience does your system administration staff have, and how do I reach you?
- How secure is my data? What's your policy on backups?

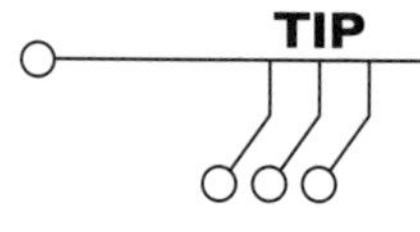

Even though your data may be backed up by your service provider, you should always keep a copy of your Web pages on your own computer, and on your own backup media. This way, you can be sure the pages will never be destroyed.

- How often do system outages or partial outages occur? Do you have records, and can I look at them? What is your policy on repairing the system during off-hours? Can I report system problems 24 hours a day?
- What billing methods do you support? Can I use a credit card? Will you bill me?
- Do you keep credit card numbers on the computers that are connected to the Internet?
- Can I create and manage my own image maps? How quickly can I make changes if I need to ask you to update your server?
- Can I create CGI programs and control them myself?

- What kind of Web server hardware and software are you using? (If you plan on writing your own CGI scripts, this can be very important!)

For Virtual Storefronts

- What methods are available for collecting money from my customers? Credit cards? Individual accounts?
- What is your charge for purchase transactions?
- What is your security scheme? Do clients need a special Web browser to conduct secure transactions?
- Do you provide an alternate way to accept orders if a customer doesn't want to leave a credit card number?
- Do you keep my customers' credit card numbers on an Internet-connected system, or do you transmit them to a protected system?

For Private Rented Systems (Virtual Servers)

- Do I get to pick my own URL name? Do I use a standard IP port number for my Web server?
- Do I share hardware with others, or is this my own machine? If I share space, can others measure the volume of information being offered by my Web server?
- Do you charge me a flat rate? Or do you measure the amount of information sent over the Internet?

Moving On

Using a commercial service provider for your Web pages has many advantages over using your own server, particularly if you have no other reason to have a full-time connection to the Internet. Based on your needs and budget, there are several options you can choose from, and a wide variety of commercial service providers available. See Appendix D, "Resources," for a listing of numerous service providers and server services. For a comprehensive listing of Internet service providers in the United States and many other countries, check out http://www2.celestin.com/pocia/index.html.

If you have other reasons to be connected to the Internet that would justify the cost of a private line, or if you want to selectively share HTML documents with friends or other people on the Internet with a modem dial-up line, read the next chapter about setting up your own Web server. Using your own server provides you the ultimate amount of control and privacy over your small part of the Web, and can be lots of fun. With a Macintosh and System 7.1 or later, you have several choices of servers, and a variety of ways to provide information to the Internet community. With the information in the next chapter and the servers provided on the Companion CD-ROM, you can get started today!

13

Servers at Your Service: Publishing on Your Own

Just as there are instances when you would want to use the services of a commercial Internet provider, there are very good reasons for running your own server. Setting up a server on your computer not only lets you publish Web documents for the general public, it gives you more flexibility for controlling access to your system. Maybe you have sensitive information that you don't want to share. By setting up a server on your own, you can selectively share Web documents with friends and business associates without a dedicated (24-hour) connection. This chapter describes setting up and working with two servers: WebSTAR (formerly MacHTTP), which is the main Macintosh HTTP server; and InterServer Publisher, which is an excellent new server, recently released by InterCon Systems. Either of these fine servers is able to give you complete control over the way your information is presented to selected readers or the entire world. The chapter also briefly discusses other servers, which may suit your needs.

Providing Your Own Server

What do you need to get started? If you expect to publish Web pages for the general public to read, you will need a full-time connection to the Internet plus a computer to host your Web server. A full-time connection can come in a variety of speeds, ranging from a slow 14.4kb/s leased line through the more common 56kbps lines up to T-3 (45MB/s) lines. As you would expect, the faster the line, the more expensive the monthly charge. It's almost impossible to quote rates for leased lines on a national basis, because every telephone company prices the lines differently, and the price you pay will also depend on how far you are from the central telephone switching office. The best way to determine the cost of a line is to contact several Internet service providers in your area and ask them to help you get rates from the phone company. Your service provider can tell you exactly where you will need to connect, and will either set you up or put you in touch with the right person at the phone company.

Of course you can also publish your Web pages without a dedicated connection. This is especially helpful in the process of creating and testing Web pages or sharing information with selected individuals. In order for the person to view your Web pages, you must have your Web server set up, be connected to your service provider and have your Web server turned on.

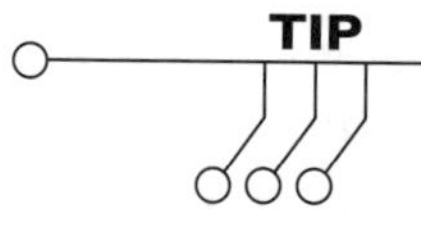

Look for the introduction of a new kind of Internet service in the near future: a dial-out *ISDN connection. With this service, you would have a regular dial-up ISDN line, and you would use it only when you need it. The key to this service is that your Internet service provider knows* your *ISDN number, and when someone tries to contact your system, the service provider automatically dials you up to complete the connection. This way, you are paying for the connection only when you need to dial out* or *someone is trying to reach you.*

If you are connected to the Internet through your business or school, all of this may be taken care of already. All you will need is a connection to your local area network and a computer that supports a Web server. Web servers are often called HTTP servers, since HTTP (HyperText Transfer Protocol) is the name of the protocol used primarily on the World Wide Web. You have a number of choices of operating systems, including most UNIX-like variants, Windows 3.1, Windows 95, Windows NT and Macintosh. The primary focus of this book is Macintosh systems, so this chapter discusses servers that are available on the Macintosh.

In this chapter, you will learn about WebSTAR, formerly called MacHTTP, which is the most popular server on the Macintosh. A demonstration version of this full-featured server is included on the Companion CD-ROM. The complete server setup is provided, along with several useful utilities, so you can try everything out for yourself. You will also learn about the new InterServer Publisher server. A demonstration version of this server, which includes FTP and Gopher access as well as Web access, is also provided on the Companion CD-ROM. The installation also includes utilities for monitoring and controlling the server and sample documents and scripts. In addition to these servers, there are a few other fine Macintosh-based servers that you can look into, and which are described later in this chapter.

CD-ROM

CD-ROM

Each of the available servers provides basic Web server services. Where you have a choice in the Macintosh servers, you'll probably wind up making a decision based on a particular feature you want, or a level of documentation or support you need. As this book was being written, several commercial server releases were still in development. Because it is unfair to compare performance of beta products, or pick out specific bugs in developing products, the coverage of these products is limited to the features and benefits of each. For the most up-to-date information, check in the USENET newsgroup comp.infosystems.www.providers, or get demonstration copies from the publishers.

WebSTAR & MacHTTP

WebSTAR is the commercial successor to the very popular MacHTTP, which was the first server written for the Macintosh system. Both servers were written by Chuck Shotten of Biap Systems and are now both sold by StarNine Technologies, which also provides service and support.

The full list of features for this server is impressive. The most interesting and important are:

- Multiple simultaneous transfers, using threaded connection processing.
- CGI interface using standard GET and POST methods.
- Controlled site access based on IP address or DNS name.
- Password controlled access to specific pages or folders.
- Automatic pre- and post-processing of HTTP protocol MIME types.
- Fully scriptable and recordable.
- Real-time display of server activity.
- Configurable log data file that can be set for either text or database output or both.
- Large integrated set of HTML documentation, including authoring and administration references and primers.

WebSTAR uses the same approach and user interface as MacHTTP—which is not surprising, since they share a large amount of code—but is faster and has more features than MacHTTP. This product offers a fully functional Web server for a very reasonable price. It has all of the more sophisticated features of the professional UNIX servers that you may be familiar with, including access control, remote server management and proxy server capabilities. The most recent information about WebSTAR and MacHTTP can be found at http://www.starnine.com.

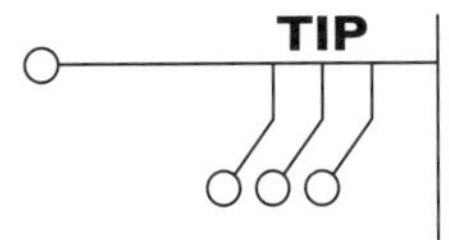

In addition to the WebSTAR server, the full version of WebSTAR comes on a CD-ROM that includes FTP and Gopher servers for sharing files across the Internet. It also contains a demonstration version of ListSTAR, a WebSTAR companion product that allows you to add automated mailing lists and e-mail to your WebSTAR server. And it has additional sample scripts and information to help you develop your site.

This Web server is simple to install, using the installer application provided with it. It comes with a getting started home page and complete online documentation in HTML format, so you don't necessarily need to jump right in and start creating your own pages.

The WebSTAR server also comes with a sample CGI host program (written in AppleScript) to get you started. The server is designed to use AppleEvents to communicate with your CGI applications. This allows WebSTAR to handle maps, forms, mailings and so on. You can use any language to write the CGI programs as long as they handle AppleEvents, which most languages do on the Macintosh. The sample applications are written in AppleScript, which is widely available and easy to learn (well, relatively easy as programming languages go). However, there are many alternative sources for CGI programs in a variety of languages, including MacPerl, a port of the perl language to the Macintosh; Frontier, a scripting language similar to AppleScript, but more powerful; C and C++; and so on. You can find a comprehensive listing of a variety of CGI applications on Jon Wiederspan's Macintosh WWW development guide at http://www.uwtc.washington.edu/Computing/WWW/ Lessons/START_HERE.html.

Installing the WebSTAR Server

The demonstration version of WebSTAR is included on the Companion CD-ROM. You can use this to install the WebSTAR server and use it for evaluation purposes for thirty days. If you don't need the full features of WebSTAR, you can still download MacHTTP Version 2.2 from http://www.biap.com/machttp/ftp/machttp.sit.hqx. This is slower and has fewer features than the commercial WebSTAR server, but it is also much less expensive. Like WebSTAR, you can download this and use it for evaluation purposes for thirty days.

What You'll Need Clearly, you'll need a Macintosh computer, running System 7.0 or later. You will also need MacTCP and the basic AppleScript system extensions, which are included on the Companion CD-ROM as a part of the WebSTAR installation. If you want to create any CGI applications for WebSTAR, you'll need a full AppleScript installation, including the Script Editor, as well. The full AppleScript software development environment is a commercial product available from APDA (an Apple division that supplies software and other tools for developers). Information on APDA is available at http://www.info.apple.com/dev and the latest tools and developer information is on their ftp site at ftp://ftp.info.apple.com/Apple.Support.Area/Developer_Services.

WebSTAR requires at least 1MB of available memory for 12 simultaneous connections, and 3MB for a more reasonable 25 connection maximum. Other than that, there are no hard-and-fast rules for memory requirements or system speed, so you'll have to judge for yourself if the response time you get from the server is OK. Although you can run WebSTAR on as small a computer as a Mac Plus, you will probably need at least a Mac SE/30 for testing and development. For a real Web site, of course, you will need a more powerful computer; ideally, this would be a 6100 or faster PowerMac. As with any HTTP server, if you want to provide a public service, you'll need a full TCP/IP Internet connection, and you'll probably need the help of your service provider in setting up the connection.

Getting Started Installing WebSTAR is quite simple. Just launch the WebSTAR Installer application and choose Easy Install. The Installer determines from your system what components need to be installed and places the necessary elements into the active System folder. In particular, if you don't already have AppleScript and MacTCP installed, it installs them for you. Then it creates a new WebSTAR folder and installs the WebSTAR application and documentation into that folder, along with some useful additional

information. Although the basic WebSTAR installer places the new folder on your desktop, you can place it anywhere you like once the installation is complete.

If you have installed MacTCP and AppleScript, you need to restart your computer to make these new system extensions become active. In addition, you may need to set MacTCP for the appropriate access, especially if you want to test your server using local access before you "go public" as it were. These issues are discussed in the following section on testing your server.

In addition to the WebSTAR application itself, you will get a WebSTAR Admin application, which allows you to change WebSTAR configuration information while WebSTAR is running.

Testing the Installation

Once you've installed your WebSTAR server correctly, you need to connect it to the Net to allow others to use it. To do this, you must have a full TCP/IP connection to the Net. If you are already using Netscape and other network tools to get information from the Net, then you probably have such a connection.

Launch WebSTAR in the usual way, by double-clicking on the application or by choosing File>>Open. When WebSTAR starts for the first time, you'll have to enter the demo serial number provided in the ReadMe file on the Companion CD when requested to activate WebSTAR—this is only required the first time you run WebSTAR.

You can run your browser software, such as Netscape Navigator, on the same system that is running the WebSTAR server. This requires at least 2MB of free memory (for both products) and is likely to slow down WebSTAR's performance. We recommend that you use another system to access your server if possible. Remember that the server itself can be run on fairly simple Macintosh systems. So, if you have an extra, older system available, you may use that for the server and do your browsing and document preparation and testing from your usual computer.

Once WebSTAR is up and running and connected to the network, you should perform a test access to ensure that you are really connected to the Net. To do this, launch your browser and connect to your server for a test access. If you are using Netscape

Navigator, then use the Open Location command from the File menu and enter your domain name as http://myname.com/. If you don't have a domain name—which is most of us the first time around, anyway—then use the actual IP address for your server in the Open Location dialog box, as http://192.7.8.9/. Note that there is no "www" in front of the name, nor any other fancy address segmentation. This is just a simple test access.

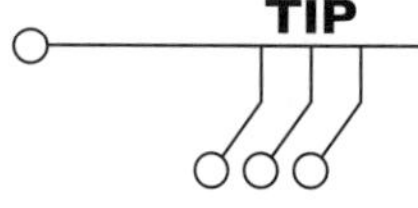

If you are using MacTCP with a commercial service provider, you may not know your actual IP address. You can determine what IP address WebSTAR is using when it runs, by launching the WebSTAR Admin application after you have successfully started WebSTAR itself. This shows you the current IP address for the running copy of WebSTAR along the top of the Admin screen. Use this as the address in your browser.

Connecting Locally Without a Network If you are working on creating and publishing a Web site, you will find it much more satisfactory if you can build and test your site information without actually being connected to the Net. You can do this, but it requres some fancy footwork. Basically, what you need to do is set up MacTCP to use your built-in LocalTalk system as its network. Setting that up allows two applications in the same machine—your server and your network browser—to communicate.

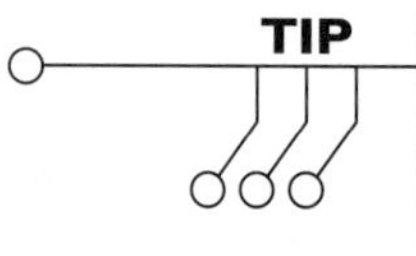

To do this, you'll need to reset MacTCP. If you are presently connected to a network, you don't want to lose the current settings, since you'll have to restore them to get back on the Net. Before making any changes to MacTCP, be sure to write down the exact settings that are currently being used and save these. Then you can re-enter them into the MacTCP Settings dialog box when you are ready to go back on the Net. Alternatively, you can use MacTCP Switcher, a utility application included on the Companion CD, to save the current settings as described later.

To set MacTCP to work without a Net connection, you can follow these steps: First, open the MacTCP Control Panel by selecting MacTCP from the Control Panel display and click on the More button at the bottom of the MacTCP control panel. This displays the MacTCP settings dialog box shown in Figure 13-1.

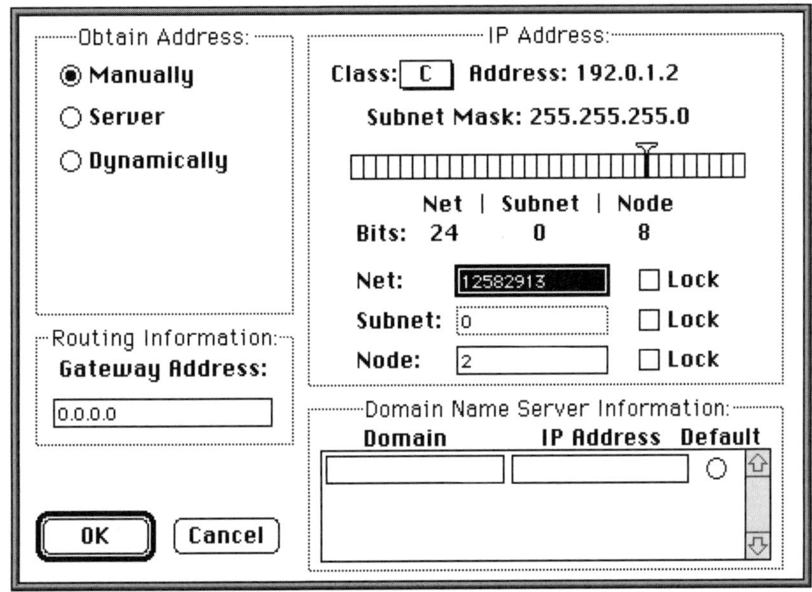

Figure 13-1: *The MacTCP Settings dialog box.*

As you can see, this dialog box is divided into four sections: Obtain Address, Routing Information, IP Address and Domain Name Server Information. Each one of these needs to be set correctly for you to connect directly from your browser to your WebSTAR server.

1. Set Obtain Address to Manually.
2. Set the Gateway Address in Routing Information to 0.0.0.0.
3. Set the IP Address to Class C. Don't bother setting anything else in this section of the dialog box.
4. Clear out all information in the Domain Name Server Information box or boxes.

When this is done, click on OK to return to the MacTCP control panel display shown in Figure 13-2.

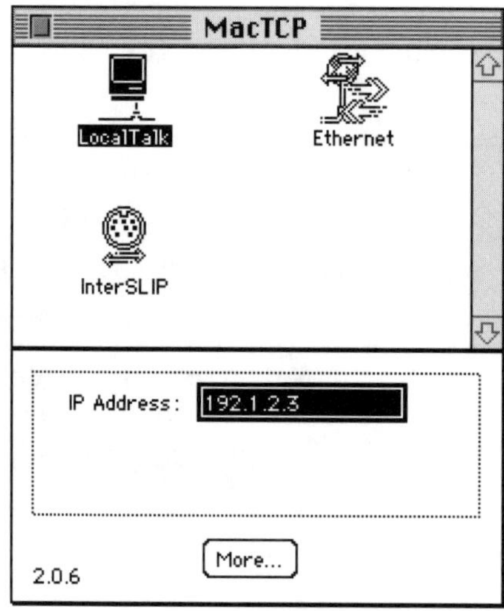

Figure 13-2: *The MacTCP Control Panel display.*

If you've changed the settings as described above, you will now be able to enter a new IP address in the small box in the bottom of the control panel. Enter the value 192.1.2.3 as the IP address. (The first number must be 192; the rest can be anything you want.) Also click on the LocalTalk icon in the top section of the display to set MacTCP to use LocalTalk instead of any other communication method. When you're done, click on the close box to dismiss MacTCP. Now you need to restart your Macintosh to use these new settings.

Once you've restarted your Mac, the new MacTCP settings are in effect. Now start WebSTAR and be sure that it's running and ready to accept connections. Next, launch Netscape Navigator (or your own favorite browser) and enter the IP address you chose as the address in the Open Location dialog box. The actual address will be http://192.1.2.3/ if you are using the same number mentioned earlier. You should immediately connect to your WebSTAR server, which will display the default home page.

Connecting Over a LocalTalk Network It's also possible to connect two Macs over a standard LocalTalk network. This has worked fine in our offices, but postings on the Net suggest that this may not always work. Nevertheless, it's worth a try because it allows you to develop and test pages and scripts on one machine while running the server on a different machine. This is quite useful when you are developing new material for the Net. Obviously, for this to work, you must have two Macintosh systems connected by a working LocalTalk network. If you're not sure how to do that, check your Macintosh system documentation. All Macs come with LocalTalk built in, so you can do this very easily.

The basic mechanism is the same as that described earlier for connection within a single Macintosh. Change MacTCP to use the LocalTalk connection and define your own IP address on the server machine. Then, on the client machine (the one where you want to run your browser) set MacTCP in the same way, except choose an IP address that is one greater than the address you used on the server. In our example, if you use 192.1.2.3. for the server, use 192.1.2.4 for the client. Then launch Navigator on the client system and connect as described earlier. This should take you across the LocalTalk network to the server machine.

Setting Options You set options for WebSTAR from the WebSTAR Admin application. To use Admin, WebSTAR must be running. When WebSTAR is running, you can launch Admin and see the current settings and values in the server itself. You must also have AppleScript installed and running for the Admin application to report the server activity correctly.

When you launch the Admin application, you are given a choice of all the servers running on your network. Once you are connected to the server, you have the ability to completely configure it as it is running, including accepting or rejecting new logins, setting the status and format of the log message file, and other useful utility functions. You can also close the server down from the Admin application if you wish. This gives you complete, interactive control of server processing.

Additional HTTP Utilities

MacTCP Switcher The single most useful tool for running WebSTAR that we've found is MacTCP Switcher. This handy little utility allows you to set up several different MacTCP settings and save each one under a name. Then, simply by clicking on the desired saved setting, you can change MacTCP to the saved values. This is ideal if you are using MacTCP in a local mode, as described earlier, for testing, and then want to switch back to your regular settings for full network access. This also allows you to avoid writing down the MacTCP setting for later re-installation. Note however that this doesn't remove the requirement that you restart your Macintosh for the settings to become effective—this simply makes it easier for you to reset MacTCP to the correct values.

MacTCP Switcher is so simple that it really doesn't require much documentation. However, it does come with a brief description of how to work it, which also describes exactly what the application does. If you're interested, the actual source code and additional documentation, along with the latest version of the application itself, are available at ftp://ftp.acns.nwu.edu/pub/jlnstuff/mactcp-switcher/.

InterServer Publisher

InterServer Publisher is a full-featured Macintosh server from InterCon, the folks who created and supply the TCP/IP II commercial system extension and the InterSLIP and InterPPP freeware system extensions that allow your Macintosh to communicate with the Internet. As you would expect, their server is a solid and effective performer.

The full list of features for this server is impressive. The most interesting and important are:

- Gopher and FTP processing as integrated features of the server.
- Special CGI interface that automatically decodes incoming data in addition to all standard CGI processing.

- Controlled and configurable site access based on a variety of factors.
- Built-in support for forms and clickable maps.
- FTP server, which supports different access levels, from secure to anonymous.
- Is fully scriptable and recordable.
- Server administration from a single application.
- Real-time display of server activity.
- Special server-side HTML extensions, called InterXTML, to make many standard and useful server functions almost automatic.

With some minor changes, InterServer is fully compatible with WebSTAR and MacHTTP scripts and functions. This product offers a fully functional Web server for a reasonable price. The most recent information about InterServer Publisher can be found at http://www.intercon.com/newpi/InterServerP.html.

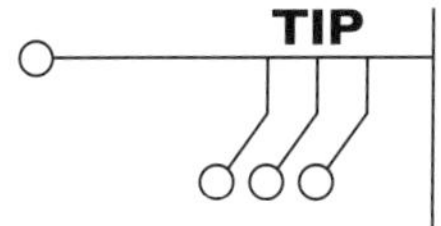

In addition to InterServer Publisher, the software comes with a Utilities folder that includes sample configuration scripts and controlling applications. It also contains a version of HTML Pro, an HTML editor. And it has additional sample documents and information to help you develop your site.

This Web server is simple to install, using the installer application provided with it. It comes with a Getting Started home page, which points to a series of example documents, so you don't necessarily need to jump right in and start creating your own pages.

Installing InterServer Publisher

The demonstration version of InterServer Publisher is included on the Companion CD-ROM. You can use this to install the server and use it for evaluation purposes for thirty days. Once you install the server, you must contact InterCon to get a working demo key. This is required before you can run or configure the server software. You can get a demo key by sending e-mail to demo@intercon.com or by calling 1-800-INTRCON (1-800-468-7266). Users outside the United States can call the main InterCon telephone at (703) 709-5500.

What You'll Need Clearly, you'll need a Macintosh computer, running System 7.0 or later. You will also need MacTCP and the basic AppleScript system extensions, which are included on the Companion CD-ROM, if you want to run any scripts. If you want to create any CGI applications for InterServer Publisher, you will require a full AppleScript installation, including the Script Editor, as well. The full AppleScript software development environment is a commercial product available from APDA (an Apple division that supplies software and other tools for developers). Information on APDA is available at http://www.info.apple.com/dev and you can access the latest tools and developer information is on their ftp site at ftp://ftp.info.apple.com/Apple.Support.Area/Developer_Services.

InterServer Publisher loads as a system extension to your Macintosh, and will expand the memory required for your system by about 2MB. Other than that, there are no hard-and-fast rules for memory requirements or system speed, so you'll have to judge for yourself if the response time you get from the server is OK. As with any HTTP server, if you want to provide a public service, you'll need a full TCP/IP Internet connection, and you'll probably need the help of your service provider in setting up the connection.

Getting Started Installing InterServer Publisher is quite simple. Just launch the InterServer Publisher Installer application and choose Install. The Installer will determine from your system what components need to be installed and will place the necessary elements into the active System folder. In particular, it will install the InterServer Publisher system extension in the Extensions folder for you. Then it will install the InterServer Publisher Setup application and the Web Sharing Folder, which includes sample scripts and documentation, along with some useful additional information.

Besides running the InterServer Publisher Installer, you should copy the Utilities folder that is stored with it onto your hard disk. This folder contains utility scripts and software that are not required to run InterServer Publisher, but which can be very useful.

If you want to use InterServer Publisher in local mode, you may need to set MacTCP for the appropriate access, especially if you want to test your server using local access before you "go public" as it were. These issues are discussed in the following section on testing your server.

Testing the Installation

Once you have installed your InterServer Publisher server correctly, you need to connect it to the Net to allow others to use it. To do this, you must have a full TCP/IP connection to the Net. If you are already using Netscape and other network tools to get information from the Net, then you probably have such a connection.

InterServer Publisher is automatically started when you start your Macintosh. In this it differs significantly from WebSTAR, where you control the startup. It will automatically try to establish an active network connection when it starts. If you are on a dial-up network, you will need to ensure that the modem is on and available before starting your Mac. Even though InterServer Publisher is running, you will not be able to use it until you've run the InterServer Setup application and provided a demo key to activate the software.

Once you are up and running, you can use the two supplied utilities, StartServer and StopServer to control whether the server software is active on your system. However, since InterServer Publisher is a system extension, it starts automatically when you start your Macintosh. If you have a problem with this, you should restart your Mac while holding down the Shift key. This restarts with all system extensions turned off except those needed for operation.

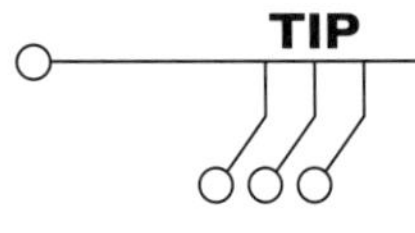

This automatic startup can be quite annoying if you're not ready for it. Once you have correctly installed and set up InterServer, you can adjust this to ensure that the server doesn't keep you out of business when you start your Mac because you don't have your modem on or connected.

You can run your browser software, such as Netscape Navigator, on the same system that is running the InterServer Publisher server. This requires at least 2MB of free memory and is likely to slow down the server's performance. We recommend that you use another system to access your server if possible. Remember that the server itself can be run on fairly simple Macintosh systems. So, if you have an extra, older system available, you may use that for the server and do your browsing and document preparation and testing from your usual computer.

Once InterServer Publisher is up and running and connected to the network, you should perform a test access to ensure that you are really connected to the Net. To do this, launch your browser and connect to your server for a test access. If you are using Netscape Navigator, then use the Open Location command from the File menu and enter your domain name as http://myname.com/. If you don't have a domain name—which is most of us the first time around, anyway—then use the actual IP address for your server in the Open Location dialog box, as http://192.7.8.9/. Note that there is no "www" in front of the name, nor any other fancy address segmentation. This is just a simple test access.

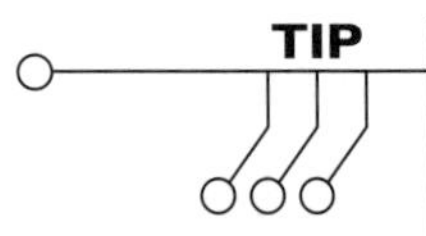

If you are using MacTCP with a commercial service provider, you may not know your actual IP address. Unfortunately, there is no easy way to determine the current IP address from InterServer Publisher, as there is with WebSTAR. If you don't know the number, you will have to contact your service provider for guidance.

Connecting Locally Without a Network If you are working on creating and publishing a Web site, you will find it much more satisfactory if you can build and test your site information without actually being connected to the Net. You can do this, but it requires some fancy footwork. Basically, what you need to do is set up MacTCP to use your built-in LocalTalk system as its network. Setting that up allows two applications in the same machine—your server and your network browser—to communicate.

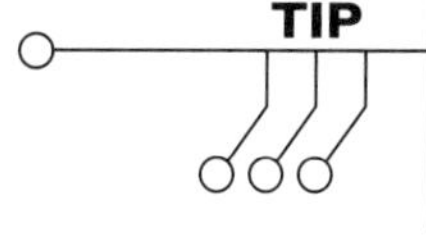

To do this, you will need to reset MacTCP. If you are presently connected to a network, you don't want to lose the current settings, since you will have to restore them to get back on the Net. Before making any changes to MacTCP, be sure to write down the exact settings that are currently being used and save these. Then you can re-enter them into the MacTCP Settings dialog box when you are ready to go back on the Net. Alternatively, you can use MacTCP Switcher, a utility application included on the Companion CD, to save the current settings as described later.

The steps required to set MacTCP to work without a Net connection were detailed earlier for use with WebSTAR. Use these same steps to set MacTCP for local access with InterServer Publisher. However, that's only half the story for InterServer Publisher.

Next, you need to add a domain name for MacTCP to use. InterServer Publisher will not run if the domain name isn't correctly set. To set a domain name,

1. Open your System folder and find the file named Hosts. This is a configuration file used by MacTCP to set domain names. Normally, you don't need to monkey with this, but it's essential to get InterServer Publisher to run in local mode.
2. Open the file with a simple text editor, like SimpleText. You will see something like Figure 13-3.

```
Hosts
; Hosts
; This file is parsed by the MacTCP domain name resolver and the resource records
; are loaded into the resolver's cache.
;
; The Hosts file follows a SUBSET of the Master File Format (see rfc1035 pg 33).
; Each line in this file has the form: <domain-name> <rr> [<comment>]
; <domain-name> is an absolute domain name (see rfc1034 pg 11).
; <rr> = [<ttl>] [<class>] <type> <rdata> OR [<class>] [<ttl>] <type> <rdata>
; A comment starts with ";" or by a line begining with a " ".
;
; NOTES:
;   $INCLUDE is not implemented
;  Class is always IN, ttl is in seconds, type can be A, CNAME or NS.

; Examples

;knowAll.apple.com.  A      128.8.1.1            ; address of host knowAll.apple.com.
;
;apple.com.     NS     knowAll.apple.com.        ; apple.com name server
;.        NS     knowAll.apple.com.        ; root name server
;
;myHost.apple.com.  IN  604800  A  128.8.1.2        ; ttl of 1 week
;JohnS.apple.com.  A       128.8.1.3
;Sculley.apple.com.  CNAME    JohnS.apple.com.        ; canonical name for alias Sculley.apple.com
```

Figure 13-3: *The basic Hosts file used by MacTCP.*

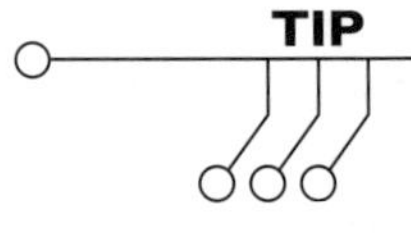

All lines beginning with a ';' are comments. As you can see, the basic Hosts file actually doesn't have any executable lines in it; it's all comments. You can eliminate these if you choose to simplify the file; we left them in as a reminder of how to format and edit entries for the file.

3. At the bottom of the file, enter your new domain name. The format is "domain.name A 192.1.2.3" with a single space between the domain name, the character *A*, and the IP address that you are using. This entry allows MacTCP to change your requested domain name into an IP address for use over the Net.
4. You can also add additional aliases to distinguish your World Wide Web server, your FTP server and so on. Figure 13-4 shows you all of these entries for our test server, cheshire.com.

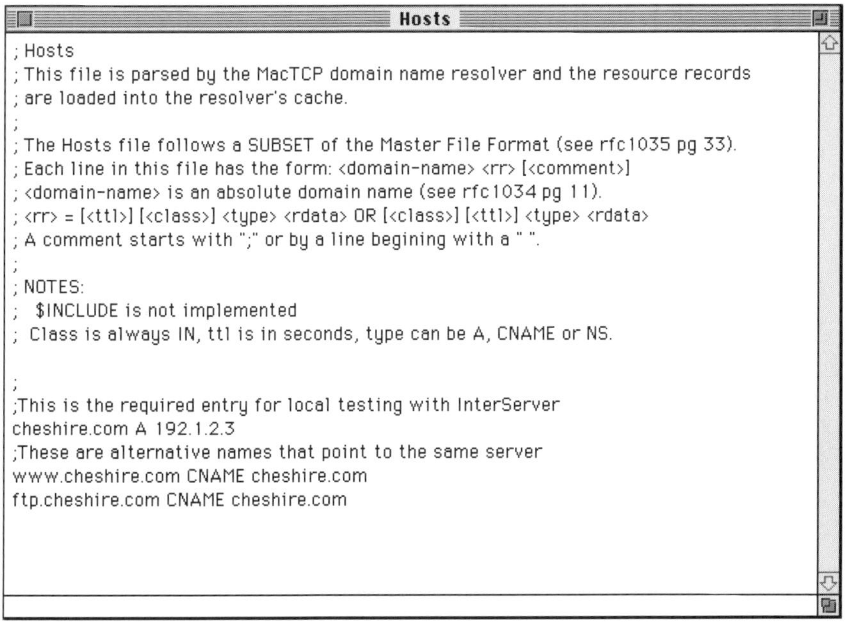

Hosts

```
; Hosts
; This file is parsed by the MacTCP domain name resolver and the resource records
; are loaded into the resolver's cache.
;
; The Hosts file follows a SUBSET of the Master File Format (see rfc1035 pg 33).
; Each line in this file has the form: <domain-name> <rr> [<comment>]
; <domain-name> is an absolute domain name (see rfc1034 pg 11).
; <rr> = [<ttl>] [<class>] <type> <rdata> OR [<class>] [<ttl>] <type> <rdata>
; A comment starts with ";" or by a line begining with a " ".
;
; NOTES:
;   $INCLUDE is not implemented
;  Class is always IN, ttl is in seconds, type can be A, CNAME or NS.

;
;This is the required entry for local testing with InterServer
cheshire.com A 192.1.2.3
;These are alternative names that point to the same server
www.cheshire.com CNAME cheshire.com
ftp.cheshire.com CNAME cheshire.com
```

Figure 13-4: *The Hosts file with the new local domain name and standard aliases for World Wide Web and FTP servers.*

Now you need to restart your Macintosh to use these new settings.

Once you have restarted your Mac, the new MacTCP settings are in effect. Be sure that InterServer Publisher is running and ready to accept connections. You can determine its status by running the InterServer Log Viewer, which will show you the startup information. Next launch Netscape Navigator (or your own favorite browser) and enter the domain name you chose. You should immediately connect to your InterServer Publisher server, which will display the default home page.

Setting Options You set up and configure InterServer Publisher from the InterServer Publisher Setup application. To use Setup, you must have configured the MacTCP Hosts file as described earlier.

The first time you run Setup, you will be asked to identify yourself, your company, and to provide the demo key that you received from the InterCon sales staff. After you have entered and validated the demo key, or when you launch the Setup application after the first time, you are given a variety of items to configure.

In particular, you will want to set which servers are automatically activated: World Wide Web, FTP, and Gopher. Also you should set the location of your server folders at the same time. The Setup application provides clear information about how to set and use these functions.

Connecting Over a LocalTalk Network It's also possible to connect two Macs over a standard LocalTalk network. This technique was described earlier and works equally well (or poorly) with InterServer Publisher as with WebSTAR.

The basic mechanism is the same as that described earlier for connection within a single Macintosh. Change MacTCP to use the LocalTalk connection and define your own IP address on the server machine. Then, on the client machine (the one where you want to run your browser) set MacTCP in the same way for local connection, except choose an IP address that is one greater than the address you used on the server. In our example, if you use 192.1.2.3. for the server, use 192.1.2.4 for the client. Then launch Navigator on the client system and connect as described earlier. This should take you across the LocalTalk network to the server machine.

Other Macintosh Servers

If WebSTAR or InterServer Publisher doesn't seem to fill your exact needs, there are indeed some alternatives that you may wish to consider. Although WebSTAR and MacHTTP are the most common and widely supported servers available for the Macintosh, each of the the following alternative servers offers something special.

Netwings 1.0

The Netwings server is a full HTTP server built using the 4D database system. In addition to the usual requirements for any server, such as MacTCP, Netwings also recommends nothing less than a Power Macintosh as a host. The server itself is very expensive, but has many integrated features that require additional applications on other servers. In addition, there is an annual renewal fee.

Netwings supports the full HTTP 1.0 standard, including CGI applications. It provides full site protection, will retrieve documents for the server from any accessible drive on the network, and can serve documents or files built on-the-fly. Netwings, unlike WebSTAR, has full list server processing built into it, with access both from mail clients and from WWW pages. One of its main features is an automated setup and support mechanism, which allows you to set up and control your server with very little experience in HTML or CGI applications. You can get more information and download a demo copy of Netwings from the Netwings home page at http://netwings.com.

httpd4Mac

httpd4Mac is a real, bare-bones HTTP server for the Macintosh, created by Bill Melotti. It does not support maps or CGI applications, but it will run with the latest versions of the Macintosh operating system. Its great attraction, however, is that it's freeware. To find out more, check out the home page at http://130.246.18.52 or contact the author at bill.melotti@rl.ac.uk. This site is a public server and should only be used outside of normal business hours in the UK, 0830-1700 BST (British Standard Time, which is 1 hour later than GMT).

MacCommon LISP Server

Folks that think that LISP is the greatest innovation in programming languages since APL will love this server. This LISP server supports HTTP 1.0 and HTML 2.0 and allows you to publish LISP programs on the Net. The server comes with source code, so you can see exactly how it does what it does. The server requires MCL (Macintosh Common Lisp) version 3.0 to run in a multithreaded mode, but will run under MCL 2.0.1 as a single thread. The server is available at ftp://ftp.ai.mit.edu/pub/users/jcma/cl-http/.

If you are interested in LISP and the World Wide Web, you may want to subscribe to the listserve that supports this topic at www-cl@ai.mit.edu. You subscribe by sending an e-mail message to www-cl-request@ai.mit.edu with the line

```
subscribe www-cl
```

in the body of the message.

NetSite Communication Server

Nescape Communications, which brought you the great Netscape Navigator browser, is also in the process of providing servers for the WWW community. They have introduced the NetSite Communications Server, which is currently available for UNIX systems, with a version for Macintosh and Windows systems to follow in the future. Their server comes in two versions, a secure and nonsecure version. Find out how they're doing on a Mac version by checking their Web site at http://home.netscape.com.

CGI Server Programs

AppleScript

To create a shell script for the WebSTAR server, first create a form that will call your script. The text of a simple script to display a few environment variables is shown in Chapter 9.

Once you've created the script, you need to save it as a CGI AppleScript application and store it in the folder hierarchy that WebSTAR uses—that is, either in the same folder as WebSTAR itself, or in a folder under the WebSTAR folder. WebSTAR will send an AppleEvent to the AppleScript application, which will then process the event and return a message by AppleEvent to WebSTAR for retransmission to the client.

This script doesn't do anything but echo the environment variables, so the form that invokes it can be pretty much anything you want. The important aspect of the form is the FORM tag, which must use the following structure:

```
<FORM METHOD=POST  ACTION="folder-name/
yourscript.acgi">
```

The folder name refers to the subfolder, relative to the root of the WebSTAR directory, that contains the scripts. To make this work, you must have compiled *yourscript*.acgi with the Script Editor (as described in Chapter 10) and placed it in the designated folder. Note that this is not a complete HTML document; the minimum document to access your script would look like Figure 13-5. See Chapter 10 for a detailed description of how to create and use AppleScript CGI scripts.

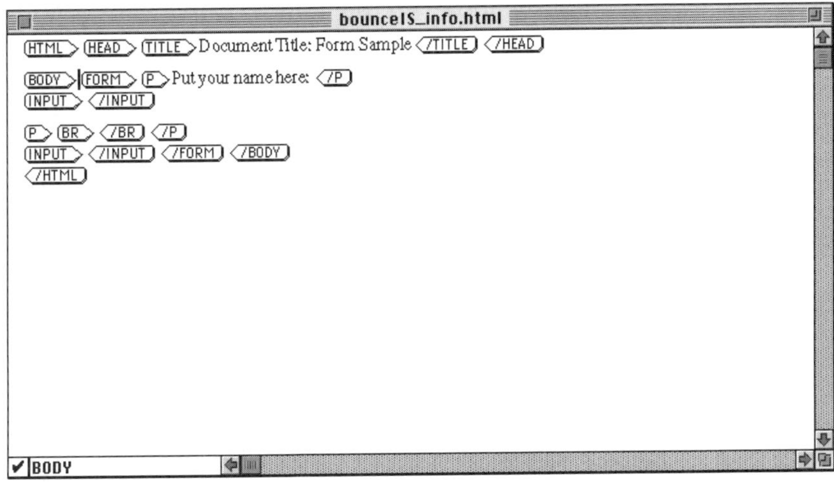

Figure 13-5: *A simple HTML form to execute a script.*

The key issues to note are:

1. You must compile and save your script from the Script Editor with the correct settings: No Startup Screen and Stay Open.
2. The script must be stored within the folder hierarchy of WebSTAR.
3. Your HTML document must insert the script name and path in the ACTION URL within the FORM tag.

Frontier & Aretha

Frontier is a very powerful scripting language for the Macintosh built around a custom database mechanism. Many Mac scripters feel it is more powerful and more flexible than AppleScript. In addition, early in 1995, UserLand, the creators of Frontier, changed their license policy from shareware to freeware and made the latest version of Frontier, codenamed Aretha, freely available. This release of Frontier has many new features, including the ability to create CGI scripts that work with WebSTAR. For complete current information about Aretha, look at http://www.hotwired.com/userland/aretha/.

Up to now, most CGI scripts running on the Macintosh with WebSTAR have been written in AppleScript for two reasons. First, this is a fairly easy way to perform the required actions—compared to C++, for example. Second, this was the way that most of us learned about writing CGI scripts, and most of the tutorial and example information on the Net about CGI Mac scripting uses AppleScript. Now, however, you can use Frontier's UserTalk scripting language to create CGI scripts. This is a real improvement for several reasons:

1. Frontier allows many scripts to run concurrently inside the Frontier application. In AppleScript, as you may have noticed if you ran many of the sample scripts in Chapter 9, the AppleScript applications each run separately.
2. Frontier scripts can share information across scripts as well as having their own data.
3. Frontier has a more complete set of actions, called *verbs*, than AppleScript. Frontier has verbs that allow you to perform the most common operations, which require AppleScript extensions (OSAX) for running in the AppleScript environment.
4. Frontier has a built-in debugger for UserTalk scripting.
5. Frontier allows you to run AppleScript CGI applications as well as its own UserTalk applications with minimal conversion.

To run Frontier, you must set up WebSTAR by using the Admin application. The basic idea is to have WebSTAR run Frontier whenever a request is made for a script with an .fcgi extension. To do this, you need to take three steps:

1. Make an alias to the Frontier application and store it in WebSTAR's scripts folder as *frontier.acgi*.
2. Use the Admin application to define a new action, called FRONTIER, that points to the frontier.acgi file.
3. Use the Admin application to map the suffix .fcgi to the FRONTIER action.

Now you can use Frontier scripts as CGI applications. To call a Frontier script, simply change your URL to call the script using the suffix .fcgi. For example, if you rewrite your BoundInfo script from Chapter 9 as a UserTalk script, you would call it as <FORM ACTION="scripts/BounceInfo.fcgi" METHOD="POST">. Of course, Frontier must be installed on your system and the script must be defined in the Frontier database. More information about CGI scripting with Frontier is available at http://www.webedge .com/frontier, which is a site dedicated to Frontier scripting and is full of useful information.

Perl Scripts

For many users of UNIX-like operating systems such as Solaris, perl is a familiar and very powerful script programming language. If you are such a person, you'll be happy to find that there is a version of perl that works with the Macintosh, called, reasonably enough, MacPerl. MacPerl and the PCGI extension is the work of Matthias Neeracher. You can get MacPerl at ftp://ftp.share.com/ pub/macperl/. The latest version as of Fall 1995 is version 4.1.8; the stand-alone application version of this is Mac_Perl_418_appl.bin. A better way to find out all about MacPerl is to read the information from the MacPerl Q&A form at http://err.ethz.ch/members/ neeri/macintosh/perl-qa.html. This site has questions and answers about using MacPerl and links to sites providing the most current versions of source code, MPW format and stand-alone application for free. To use MacPerl, you will also need the MacHTTP CGI Script extension, called PCGI, which is available from ftp://err.ethz.ch/pub/neeri/MacPerlBeta/. The latest version as of Fall 1995 is PCGI_20Feb95.sit.hqx, but you should check for the latest version before downloading.

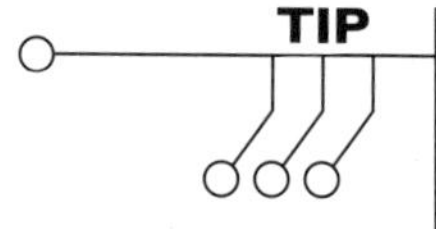

Note that the version of 20Feb95 is a complete rewrite of the original PCGI files. If you find any earlier versions on the Net, don't use them. The earlier versions don't come with any documentation, and they don't work as described here. Get the current version directly from the ftp site mentioned earlier.

Using perl scripts is very easy, once you have the required extension. The MacPerl CGI files include all you'll need to get started, including an example script. To make the CGI extensions work, you must copy the file "MacHTTP CGI Script" to the MacPerl Extensions folder in your MacPerl folder. Once this is installed, you can open or create scripts that will become CGI applications. To make a perl script into a suitable CGI application, just select "MacHTTP CGI Script" from the Type box at the bottom of the dialog box. This saves your MacPerl script in a format that can be run as a CGI application. A good method of tying the script and the application together is to use the same name with an appropriate extension. Here, we have used a script named PCGItest.perl and saved it as PCGItest.pcgi. In this way, the .perl extension tells you that this is the perl script, and the .pcgi extension tells you that this is the converted CGI application, generated by MacPerl.

When you create forms, using perl scripts as CGI applications is very similar to using AppleScript scripts. As with other scripts, the FORM tag must be set up correctly:

```
<Form METHOD=POST  ACTION="/folder-name/
PCGItest.pcgi">
```

where *folder-name* is the folder (or path) from the WebSTAR or MacHTTP folder. To make this work, you must have a copy of MacPerl installed and operating on your system.

The shell script itself must return the HTML or plain text page. In this case the content of PCGItest.perl appears as follows:

```
#!./perl
print "Content-type: text/html\n";
print "\n";
print "<HTML><HEAD><TITLE>Perl CGI Test</TITLE>
</HEAD>\n";
print "<BODY><H1>Perl CGI Test</H1>\n<HR>Environment
Variables:<PRE>\n";
foreach $var (sort keys(%ENV)) {
	print $var, ": ",$ENV{$var},"\n";
}
print "</PRE><HR></BODY></HTML>\n";
&MacPerl'Quit(1);
```

There are many perl scripts written as CGI scripts, but remember that most of them are UNIX scripts, so you may need to make changes to them to adapt them to MacPerl.

Moving On

Currently there are several choices for servers on Macintosh-based systems. Each of them is a product worth considering for commercial Web server operation. The increasing speed of Macintosh hardware, combined with the natural ease of operation and ease of management of the Macintosh operating system makes the use of a Macintosh server or series of servers extremely attractive, even though various kinds of UNIX operating systems have been the proving ground in the past. If one of the programs described in this chapter doesn't meet your needs, keep checking around. With the tremendous growth in the World Wide Web, there will certainly be more HTTP servers to come. Also, the servers described in this chapter are new and are undergoing continuing development. Always check with the manufacturer for the latest price, feature and availability information.

Although we've finished our discussion of publishing on the Internet, this is in no way the last word on Web publishing. As you continue to traverse the Web, you are bound to come upon many exciting, new Web publishing features and vehicles. The more you continue to explore the possibilities of Internet publishing, the greater the rewards. The next move is up to you, but fortunately you have the Web publishing world at your fingertips and the next step is only a hyperlink away.

SECTION IV

Appendices

About the Online Companion

Create your own Web pages! The *HTML Publishing on the Internet Online Companion* is your one stop location for Web publishing resources on the Internet. It serves as an informative tool as well as an annotated software library aiding in your exploration of the World Wide Web and HTML publishing.

The *HTML Publishing on the Internet Online Companion* links you to available newsgroups, Web pages and e-mail discussion groups. So you can just click on the reference name and jump directly to the resource you are interested in.

Perhaps one of the most valuable features of the *HTML Publishing on the Internet Online Companion* is its Software Archive. Here, you'll find and be able to download the lastest versions of all the software mentioned in *HTML Publishing on the Internet for Macintosh* that are freely available on the Internet. This software ranges from HTML editors to graphics and sound tools to CGI scripting applications. Also, with Ventana Online's helpful description of the software, you'll know exactly what your getting and why. So you won't download the software just to find you have no use for it.

The *HTML Publishing on the Internet Online Companion* also links you to the Ventana Library where you will find useful press and jacket information on a variety of Ventana Press offerings. Plus, you have access to a wide selction of exciting new releases and coming attractions. In addition, Ventana's Online Library allows you to order the books you want.

The *HTML Publishing on the Internet Online Companion* represents Ventana Online's ongoing commitment to offering the most dynamic and exciting products possible. And soon Ventana Online will be adding more services, including more multimedia supplements, searchable indexes and sections of the book reproduced and hyperlinked to the Internet resources they reference.

To access the *HTML Publishing on the Internet Online Companion*, connect via the World Wide Web to http://www.vmedia.com/hpim.html.

About the Companion CD-ROM

The CD-ROM included with your copy of *HTML Publishing on the Internet for Macintosh* contains a wealth of valuable software, including Netscape Navigator, HoTMetaL LITE from SoftQuad and numerous tools and utilities to make publishing on the Internet easier than ever. These tools can be divided into the following groups: graphics tools and images, HTML editors, movie utilities, server software and utilities, and sound utilities. In short, this CD offers virtually everything you'll need to start publishing on the Internet today.

To install the CD-ROM, load the CD and double-click on the icon that appears on your desktop. The setup routine creates an icon called Internet Publishing. You'll see a menu screen offering several choices. Click on the appropriate menu item to explore the contents of the CD-ROM.

To install specific programs or utilities, see the accompanying README files for instructions. Each product or program has a separate folder with a document that describes how to install and use that software. For the latest information on the software products and other topics related to this book, please refer to the *HTML Publishing on the Internet for Macintosh Online Companion.*

Below is a list of the programs included on the *HTML Publishing on the Internet* CD-ROM.

Program Name	Description
Stuffit Expander	Expansion tool
Images	Graphics files
Photos	Graphics files
WebMap	Graphics imagemapper
GifConverter 2.3.7	Graphics tool
CLIPGIF	Graphics tool
Transparency	Graphics tool
GraphicConverter 2.1.2	Graphics tool
JPEGView	Graphics viewer
MacAnimViewer 1.1	Graphics/Animation viewer
ARACHNID	HTML design tool
HoTMetaL LITE	HTML editor
BBEDIT Lite	HTML editor
Sample files	HTML files
BBEDIT HTML Tools	HTML tools
QuickEditor 3.6	Movie utility
QuickTime VR	Movie utility
sparkle	MPEG player
flattenMOOV	MPEG tool
Acrobat Reader	PDF viewer
Common Ground	PDF viewer
RTF2HTML	RTF converter
WebSTAR	Server software
InterServer Publisher	Server software
Mail File	Server utility
Netcloak	Server utility
Netforms	Server utility
Webstat	Server utility
Frontier Aretha	Server utility
Filemaker PRO-CGI	Server utility/CGI database
Brian's Sound Tool 1.3	Sound utility
SoundApp	Sound utility
SoundHack	Sound utility
µ-law	Sound tool

Program Name	Description
Plugged-In 0.5.2a	Sound utility
SoundEffects 0.9.2	Sound utility
MPEGAud FPU 1.08a	Sound utility
MPEG/CD	Sound utility
Sound Machine 2.1	Sound utility
Mac TCP Switcher	TCP/IP tool
Maven 2.0a37	Video conferencing tool
Netscape Navigator	Web browser

APPENDIX C

An Illustrated HTML Reference

The HyperText Markup Language (HTML) is composed of a set of elements that define a document and guide its display. This appendix presents a concise reference guide to HTML, listing almost all of the elements and giving a brief description and illustration of each one.

You should be aware that HTML is an evolving language, and different World Wide Web browsers may recognize slightly different sets of HTML elements. In particular, the Netscape browser included on the Companion CD-ROM uses an extended set of HTML codes. These codes are indicated in this list by N **Netscape Extensions:** after the section heading where the new extension tag information is located.

HTML markup elements fall into two classes: *markup tags* and *character entities*. Markup tags define elements of the document that require special display or presentation. Character entities define special characters that are used within the document. The list here is divided into three sections. The first section displays all the standard document markup tags and extended tags. The second section lists the special markup tags that are used in HTML forms. The third section lists all the character entities. Within each section, the items are listed alphabetically by tag for easy reference. This means, for example, that the Anchor tag <A> comes before the Address tag <ADDRESS>.

Uniform Resource Locator

The URL (Uniform Resource Locator) is not a tag, but is a standard method for inserting document linking information into an HTML document. The structure of a URL may be expressed as: resource_type://host.domain:port/pathname where the possible resource types include: file, http, news, gopher, telnet, ftp and wais, among others. Each resource type interprets the pathname in its own way. Note that each resource type relates to a specific server type. The domain name may be optionally followed by a colon, followed by an integer TCP port number, used when a server is listening on a non-standard port. If the port number is absent, the standard port number is used. The standard port for WWW servers is :80. Most URLs don't require a port number.

For example, a link to the home page for the National Center for Supercomputing Applications at the University of Illinois (home of the Mosaic network navigator) is given by:

```
http://www.ncsa.uiuc.edu/SDG/Software/Mosaic/
NCSAMosaic.html
```

To point to a local home page on the C drive in the http directory, a system would use the following URL:

```
file://HardDisk/http/home.html
```

Notice that the URL section containing the host and domain name is missing in this reference, since this file is located on the local host. In this case, the two forward slashes separating the host and domain name section from the pathname are directly before the single forward slash marking the beginning of the pathname.

Markup Tags

An HTML markup tag may include a name, some attributes and some text or hypertext. Each markup tag has a specific name and is bracketed by the < (less than) and > (greater than) symbols. Tag names are not case sensitive, so that the tag <DL COMPACT>, for example, is exactly the same as <dl compact>. For ease of reading, all tags presented here will be in capital letters.

The tag will appear in an HTML document in one of three formats, depending on the type of the tag:

<tag_name>
<tag_name>. . .</tag_name>
<tag_name attribute_name="argument">. . .</tag_name>

The first type of tag indicates a tag that stands alone and affects the information that follows in some way. For example, the <DD> tag marks the following item in the document as a definition description.

The second type of tag encloses some portion of the document, which may consist of text, graphics, or other HTML commands—or all of these. For example,

<TITLE> My Home Page </TITLE>

creates a title element in a document.

The last type of tag also encloses some portion of the document but also includes attribute information within the tag itself. Attributes may be used in either of two formats. The first format is simply the attribute name itself, like this:

<tag_name attribute_name>

For example, the tag <DL COMPACT> defines a definition list that is presented in a compacted form, as indicated by the attribute COMPACT.

In the second format, the attribute has an argument associated with it, like this:

< tag_name attribute_name="argument">

For example, the anchor tag <A NAME="Tag1"> defines an anchor tag that marks a location that is named "Tag1". Arguments that are text information usually must be enclosed in double quotation marks; attributes that are numbers usually may be inserted without quotations. However, most browsers will accept quotation marks around any argument, so inserting them, even if they are not required, is usually acceptable.

Because HTML is an evolving standard, not all documents will use all these tags or follow all these rules. In a similar way, not all browsers or servers will understand and present information with all of these tags. The listings here will give you a way to determine the use and visual presentation of most standard HTML tags for your documents. In particular, to allow older HTML documents to remain readable, the <HTML>, <HEAD> and <BODY> tags are optional within HTML documents.

ANCHOR TAG

<A>. . .</A>

A [HREF:] /A

Purpose

Defines an anchor tag. An anchor is either the origin or destination of a hyperlink within the document.

Syntax

```
<A NAME="Anchor_Name" | HREF="URL|#Anchor_Name |
URL?search_word+search_word"  REL="relationship"
|REV="relationship" |
TITLE="HREF_document_name"  >Hypertext</A>
```

Attributes & Their Arguments

The Anchor tag has two attributes: HREF and NAME. An anchor must include either a NAME or an HREF attribute, and may include both.

NAME="anchor_name"
The "anchor_name" defines a target location in a document. This target location can be referenced by other anchors in the document by using the "anchor_name" as part of an HREF attribute within another anchor tag.

HREF="#anchor_name"
Links to a location in the same document.

HREF="URL"
Links to another file or resource.

HREF="URL#anchor_name"
Links to a target location in another document.

HREF="URL?search_word+search_word"
Sends a search string to a server. Different servers may interpret the search string differently. In the case of word-oriented search engines, multiple search words might be specified by separating individual words with a plus sign (+).

In addition to these, there are three optional attributes: REV, REL and TITLE. However, these attributes are not widely used in the Anchor tag.

REL="relationship"
Defines the relationship between this document and the link URL given in the HREF attribute.

REV="relationship"
Defines the relationship between the link URL given in the HREF attribute and this document. This is the reverse of the specification provided by the REL attribute.

TITLE="HREF_document_name"
Indicates the document title of the document pointed to by the HREF attribute. This is not used much by current browsers. It is most useful when the link is to a document, such as a Gopher menu, that does not have an internal name. By using this, the menu can be displayed on the browser window with a name.

Examples

A link to a page at another location

The following includes an HREF that links to Ventana Media's home page.

```
<A HREF="http://www.vmedia.com/">Ventana Media
Online</A>
```

A local link to a file

The HREF points to the local file product.zip in the files directory.

```
<A HREF="/files/product.zip">Our Product listing</A>
```

A link within a page

The following example includes the HREF attribute to specify the destination anchor named end.

```
<A HREF="#end">Jump to Conclusions</A>
```

In order to move to the destination labeled end, the document must also include the anchor with the NAME attribute set to end.

```
<A NAME="end"></A>
```

A link to a target location in another document

Similar to a link within a page, this link must also include the HREF attribute to specify the document (order.html) as well as the destination anchor (feedback).

```
<A HREF="order.html#feedback">Place an order</A>
```

In order to move to the destination, the document order.html must exist and must include an anchor with the NAME attribute set to feedback.

```
<A NAME="feedback"></A>
```

See Also

LINK, URL, IMG and FORM

Address Tag

<ADDRESS> . . . </ADDRESS>

ADDRESS /ADDRESS

Purpose
Defines a signature or address. This tag is normally used at the bottom or top of a page to provide address, signature or other author information.

Syntax

<ADDRESS>Signature</ADDRESS>

Attributes & Their Arguments
None.

Example
The following would insert the author's name and e-mail address on two separate lines.

<ADDRESS> Brent Heslop
bheslop@isdn.bookware.com </ADDRESS>

See Also
BLOCKQUOTE, BODY, BR and FORM

Bold Tag

<B> . . . </B>

B /B

Purpose
Presents the text within the tags in boldface type. The Strong tag is preferred.

Syntax

<B>Text</B>

Attributes & Their Arguments

None.

Examples

The following markup defines the enclosed text to be displayed in a bold font.

<B>Ventana Media Online</B>

See Also

EM, I, STRONG and TT

Base Tag

<BASE>

BASE [HREF:] /BASE

Purpose

Specifies the pathname to be used to resolve relative addresses within the document. This is useful when link references within the document do not include full pathnames (i.e., are relative pathnames).

Syntax

<BASE HREF="URL">

Attributes & Their Arguments

The Base tag has one required HREF attribute.

HREF="URL"

Links to another server or system.

Examples

A pointer to a remote server or system
Generally, all pointers used in a document for local links use relative addressing. This means that the links within the document will work even when the document and its associated files are moved to a different location. However, if the server cannot find a link, the Base tag provides a pointer to the original location of the links. For example, this HREF points to the files directory at Ventana Media's server.

```
<BASE HREF="http://www.vmedia.com/files">
```

With this as a base, all relative anchor references in the document would use this as a base when accessing relative file information if a reference could not be found on the local server. For example, an HREF that points to the local file product.zip would be inserted into the document as:

```
<A HREF="product.zip">Our Product listing</A>
```

The server would first look for this file in the current directory that holds the document; if it was not found there, the server would concatenate the anchor tag and the base information to access the following reference:

```
http://www.vmedia.com/files/product.zip
```

See Also
A and HEAD

BASEFONT TAG (NETSCAPE EXTENSION)

```
<BASEFONT>. . .</BASEFONT>
```

BASEFONT /BASEFONT

Purpose
Defines the size of the base font used in the document. All subsequent font changes are based on this size. Note that Netware does not require the ending </BASEFONT> tag, but does allow it. If

the ending tag is present, the basefont setting applies only to text within the tags. If the ending tag is absent, the setting applies to all the remaining fonts used in the document.

Syntax

```
<BASEFONT SIZE=number >Text</BASEFONT>
```

Attributes & Their Arguments

```
SIZE=number
```

Establishes the desired size for the font used to display the document. The number argument must be between 1 and 7; the default value is 3.

Example

The following defines the basefont for the enclosed text to be slightly larger than the standard size.

```
<BASEFONT SIZE=4><P>This is larger type for easier read-
ing.</P></BASEFONT>
```

See Also

FONT

BLINK TAG (NETSCAPE EXTENSION)

```
<BLINK>. . .</BLINK>
```

BLINK /BLINK

Purpose

Causes the text within the tags to blink when displayed.

Syntax

<BLINK>Text</BLINK>

Attributes & Their Arguments

None.

Example
The following displays the text within the tags as a blinking element in the same font as the body text.

```
<P>One portion of this sentence is <BLINK>blinking text
</BLINK> to create emphasis.</P>
```

See Also
EM, STRONG, I and B

Block Quote Tag

```
<BLOCKQUOTE> . . . </BLOCKQUOTE>
```

BLOCKQUOTE /BLOCKQUOTE

Purpose
Includes a section of text quoted from some other source.

Syntax

```
<BLOCKQUOTE>Block of text</BLOCKQUOTE>
```

Attributes & Their Arguments
None.

Examples
The following block quote displays as an indented, single-spaced block of text, which is separated from the body text by a paragraph break.

```
<BODY>A recent press release from Canyon software tells
you about their new software.
<BLOCKQUOTE><I>Drag And Zip</I>, Drag And File's built-
in Zip Manager, links directly to Internet World Wide Web
browsers including Mosaic and Netscape. Drag And Zip
also supports files compressed with PKZIP, LHA and GZIP
programs and has a built-in virus scanner.
</BLOCKQUOTE></BODY>
```

See Also
BODY, P and PRE

BODY TAG

<BODY>. . . </BODY>

BODY > < /BODY

Purpose
Defines the part of the document that represents the actual document contents. Distinguished from the Head section of the document.

Syntax

```
<BODY>Text of document, including additional HTML tags
if desired</BODY>
```

Attributes & Their Arguments
None.

Examples
The Body tag defines the display elements of the document. For example,

```
<BODY>This is a minimum of text to be inserted into the
body of a document. It will display as a single paragraph
</BODY>
```

N Netscape Extensions:

Syntax

```
<BODY BACKGROUND="image_URL" BGCOLOR="#rrggbb"
TEXT="#rrggbb" LINK="#rrggbb" VLINK="#rrggbb"
ALINK="#rrggbb" >
```

Attributes & Their Arguments

BACKGROUND="image_URL"

Allows you to specify a URL that points to an image to be used as background for the body of the document. The image is tiled to fill the background viewing area.

BGCOLOR="#rrggbb"

Allows you to specify a background color for the body of the document. The argument "#rrggbb" is a set of three hexadecimal numbers that specify the color that you wish displayed.

TEXT="#rrggbb"

Allows you to specify the color of all text in the document that is not specially colored to indicate a link or other special attribute. The argument "#rrggbb" is a set of three hexadecimal numbers that specify the color that you wish displayed.

LINK="#rrggbb"

Allows you to specify a color for body text that gives link information. The argument "#rrggbb" is a set of three hexadecimal numbers that specify the color that you wish displayed. The default color is blue (#0000FF).

VLINK="#rrggbb"

Allows you to specify a color for body text showing a link that has already been visited. The argument "#rrggbb" is a set of three hexadecimal numbers that specify the color that you wish displayed. The default color is purple (#FF00FF).

ALINK="#rrggbb"

Allows you to specify a color for body text showing a link that is currently activated. The argument "#rrggbb" is a set of three hexadecimal numbers that specify the color that you wish displayed. The default color is red (#FF0000).

See Also

HEAD and HTML

BREAK TAG

BR > < /BR

Purpose
Forces a line break immediately and retains the same style.

Syntax

Attributes & Their Arguments
None.

Examples
The following would insert the author's name and e-mail address on two separate lines. The Break tag forces a new line immediately after the name, but retains the Address tag style for the e-mail address.

```
<ADDRESS> Brent Heslop <BR> bheslop@bookware.com
</ADDRESS>
```

N Netscape Extensions:

Syntax
<BR CLEAR="keyword" >

Attributes & Their Arguments
CLEAR="keyword"
Allows you to specify how to insert the break after a floating image. The CLEAR attribute specifies whether to take floating images into account when producing a break. Possible keyword entries are: ["left" | "right" | "all"]. CLEAR="left" inserts a line break in the text and moves vertically down until the left margin is clear . CLEAR="right" inserts a line break in the text and moves vertically down until the right margin is clear. CLEAR="all" inserts a line break in the text and moves vertically down until both margins are clear.

See Also
P and PRE

Center Tag (Netscape Extension)

<CENTER>. . .</CENTER>

CENTER /CENTER

Purpose
Centers the enclosed text.

Syntax

```
<CENTER>Text</CENTER>
```

Attributes & Their Arguments
None.

Example
The following shows an example of centered text.

```
<CENTER>This text will be centered on the document
line.</CENTER>
```

See Also
IMG and TABLE

Citation Tag

<CITE>. . .</CITE>

CITE /CITE

Purpose
Style tag for display of a citation. Text is typically displayed in italics or underlined.

Syntax

<CITE>Citation text</CITE>

Attributes & Their Arguments

None.

Example

The following shows a typical citation as it might appear in a document:

<CITE>Caesar: The Gallic War; English Translation by H. J. Edwards, C.B.; Loeb Classical Library, Cambridge, MCMLXXIX </CITE>

See Also

B, EM, IT, STRONG and TT

CODE TAG

<CODE>. . .</CODE>

CODE /CODE

Purpose

Defines a text element to be rendered in a format suitable for computer program text. Text is usually rendered in a monospaced font.

Syntax

<CODE>code_text</CODE>

Attributes & Their Arguments

None.

Example

The following is a sample of computer code rendered in a Code tag.

<CODE>class CErectorView : public CView</CODE>

See Also
PRE and TT

DEFINITION TAG

<DFN>. . .</DFN>

Not supported by HoTMetal PRO

Purpose
Provides a definition of a term or phrase within a text block. Similar to the Strong tag. This is a new tag and may not be supported by all browsers.

Syntax

```
<DFN>Text</DFN>
```

Attributes & Their Arguments
None.

Example
The following includes a definition item within a normal text paragraph.

```
<P>In Windows, <DFN>resources</DFN> are user-interface
items, such as menus, icons, dialog boxes, and so on, that
are used to interact with the user. </P>
```

See Also
VAR, STRONG, DL, B, I and U

DIRECTORY LIST TAG

<DIR>. . .</DIR>

Purpose
Defines a list of directory items. A directory list is an unordered list consisting of one or more List Item tags. List items in this type of list should be less than 24 characters long. The intention is to generate a short, concise list. This limit is not generally enforced by browsers. If you exceed this limit, however, the displayed list may not look as you intended. Note that directory lists should not be nested.

ASSOCIATED TAG: LIST ELEMENT TAG

<LI>. . .

Purpose
Defines an element in a list. Note that this tag should never be used outside a list definition tag as it may not be correctly displayed by a browser. Also notice that this tag does not have a matching termination.

Syntax

```
<DIR><LI> List_element</DIR>
```

Attributes & Their Arguments
None.

Example
The following displays a directory list with three entries.

```
<DIR> <LI>First Directory Entry <LI>Second Directory Entry
<LI>And so on... </DIR>
```

See Also
DL, MENU, OL and UL

Definition List Tag

<DL>. . .</DL>

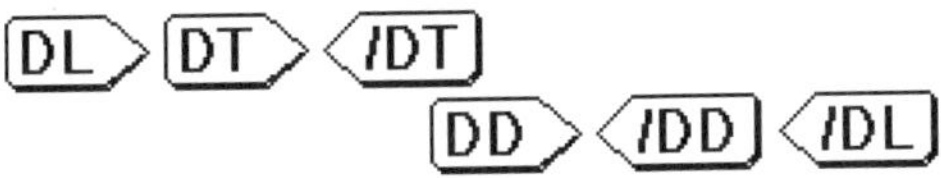

Purpose
Presents a list of items and their definitions; it may also be used to present a glossary. A definition list is an unordered list consisting of one or more Definition Term tags and an associated Definition Description tag. These tags always occur together in the list, and each list element is composed of one set of tags.

Associated Tag: Definition Term Tag

<DT> . . .

Purpose
Marks a term to be defined within a Definition List. Note that this tag should never be used outside a Definition List tag as it may not be correctly displayed by a browser. Also notice that this tag does not have a matching termination. It must be followed by a Definition Description tag.

Associated Tag: Definition Description Tag

<DD>. . .

Purpose
Provides the definition text for the associated Definition Term tag within a Definition List. Note that this tag should never be used outside a Definition List tag as it may not be correctly displayed by a browser. Also notice that this tag does not have a matching termination. It must be preceded by a Definition Term tag.

Syntax

<DL [COMPACT]> <DT>Defintion_term <DD>Definition_text </DL>

Attributes & Their Arguments

The Definition List tag has one optional attribute.

COMPACT

This attribute presents a definition list or glossary that uses a minimum amount of indentation and white space when displayed.

Example

The following displays a definition list with two entries.

<DL> <DT>First Term <DD>Definition of First Term <DT>Second Term <DD>Definition of Second Term </DL>

The same list can be compressed for display by using the following argument.

<DL COMPACT> <DT>First Term <DD>Definition of First Term <DT>Second Term <DD>Definition of Second Term </DL>

See Also

DIR, MENU, OL and UL

EMPHASIS TAG

<EM> . . . </EM>

Purpose

Presents the text within the tags in emphasized format. This is usually underlined, but may appear in italics. The important point is that the emphasized text be noticeably different from the surrounding normal text.

Syntax

<EM>Text</EM>

Attributes & Their Arguments

None.

Examples

The following markup creates a text element that is emphasized (usually in italic font).

```
<EM>Ventana Media Online</EM>
```

See Also

BOLD, I, STRONG and TT

FONT TAG (NETSCAPE EXTENSION)

```
<FONT>. . .</ FONT>
```

FONT /FONT

Purpose

Changes the size of the enclosed text from the size set by the Basefont tag (or from the default size if no Basefont tag has been set).

Syntax

```
<FONT SIZE=number>Text</FONT>
```

Attributes & Their Arguments

SIZE=number

Establishes the desired size for the font used to display the document. The number argument may be an integer between 1 and 7 that sets the font to the new size. The number may be preceded by + or – to indicate a relative change to the basefont size. The default basefont size is 3.

Example

The following defines the font for the enclosed text to be slightly larger than the current basefont size.

```
<FONT SIZE=+2><P>This is larger type for easier reading.
</P></FONT>
```

See Also
BASEFONT

HEADER TAGS

<H1> . . . </H1> Most prominent header
<H2> . . . </H2>
<H3> . . . </H3>
<H4> . . . </H4>
<H5> . . . </H5>
<H6> . . . </H6> Least prominent header

H1 /H1
H2 /H2
H3 /H3
H4 /H4
H5 /H5
H6 /H6

Purpose
Defines the data contained between the tags as a text header. The headers are defined in six descending categories. The first Header tag, <H1>, is the most prominent header, with each successive level being less prominent but still distinct from the normal text and from each other. Headings are generally distinguished by size and bold type, but a browser may use another method of display if required.

Syntax
<H*n*>Header_text</H*n*>

Attributes & Their Arguments
None.

Examples

The following shows a series of headers.

```
<H1>Major Heading</H1>
<H2>First sub-heading</H2>
<H3>Minor heading</H3>
<H3>Another minor heading</H3>
<H2>Final sub-heading</H2>
```

See Also

BODY and HEAD

HEAD TAG

```
<HEAD>. . . </HEAD>
```

HEAD /HEAD

Purpose

Defines the part of the document that contains general data about the page. Distinguished from the Body section of the document.

Syntax

```
<HEAD>Header information</HEAD>
```

Attributes & Their Arguments

None.

Examples

The Head tag defines the page description and information elements of the document. These are placed ahead of the body of the document. For example:

```
<HEAD><TITLE>Minimum Page</TITLE></HEAD>
<BODY>This is a minimum of text to be inserted into the
body of a document. It will display as a single paragraph
</BODY>
```

See Also

BODY and HTML

Horizontal Rule Tag

<HR>

HR /HR

Purpose
Draws a horizontal rule across the width of the document. The individual browser controls the size and presentation of the line, and some browsers may render a line of fixed length.

Syntax

```
<HR>
```

Attributes & Their Arguments
None.

Example
The following would insert a horizontal line the width of the browser window between the two paragraphs of text.

```
<P> This is two paragraphs of text divided by a single,
horizontal line. </P> <HR> </P> This is the second para-
graph of text. </P>
```

N Netscape Extensions:

Syntax

```
<HR ALIGN="keyword" NOSHADE SIZE=number
WIDTH=value >
```

Attributes & Their Arguments

ALIGN="keyword"

For rules that are not the full document width, the ALIGN attribute specifies where the rule is to be placed. Possible keyword entries are: [“left” | “right” | “center”].

NOSHADE

Specifies that you want a solid rule instead of the default Netware horizontal rule, which is a shaded, engraved line.

SIZE=number

Defines the vertical size of the rule in pixels.

WIDTH=value

Specifies the width of the rule. The default rule is automatically the width of the page. The value argument is [number | percent], which allows you to specify the width of the rule in pixels or as a percentage of the document width.

See Also

BR and P

HTML TAG

<HTML>. . . </HTML>

HTML /HTML

Purpose

Defines the data contained between the tags to be in HTML format.

Syntax

```
<HTML>Document_data</HTML>
```

Attributes & Their Arguments

None.

Examples

The HTML tag defines entire document. These tags are placed around the contents of the document. For example,

```
<HTML>
<HEAD><TITLE>Minimum Page</TITLE></HEAD>
<BODY>This is a minimum of text to be inserted into the
body of a document. It will display as a single paragraph
</BODY>
</HTML>
```

See Also
BODY and HEAD

ITALIC TAG

<I> . . . </I>

Purpose
Presents the text within the tags in italic type.

Syntax

<I>Text</I>

Attributes & Their Arguments
None.

Examples
The following markup defines the enclosed text to be displayed in an italic font.

```
<I>Looking Good in Print, R. Parker, Ventana Press</I>
```

See Also
B, EM, STRONG and TT

IMAGE TAG

<IMG>. . .</IMG>

IMG [SRC:] /IMG

Purpose
Embed a graphic image in the document.

Syntax

```
<IMG SRC="URL" ALT="textstring" ALIGN="keyword"
ISMAP >
```

Attributes & Their Arguments

The Image tag has one required attribute: SRC, and three optional attributes: ALT, ALIGN and ISMAP.

SRC="URL"

Specifies the location of the image that is to be rendered by the browser in the document at the point where the Image tag is located.

ALT="textstring"

Allows a text string to be put in place of the image in browsers that cannot display images.

ALIGN="keyword"

Specifies a position relationship to surrounding text. Possible keyword entries are: "top" | "middle" | "bottom".

ALIGN="top" aligns the image with the top of the tallest element in the line of surrounding text.

ALIGN="middle" aligns the center of the image with the baseline of the line of surrounding text.

ALIGN="bottom" aligns the base of the image with the baseline of the surrounding text.

ISMAP

If ISMAP is present and the image tag is within an anchor, the image will become a "clickable image." The pixel coordinates of the cursor will be appended to the URL specified in the anchor if the user clicks within the ISMAP image. The resulting URL will take the form "URL?*m*,*n*" where *m* and *n* are integer coordinates.

Examples

A simple image

The following is a typical Image tag that might be used to display a picture of the author of a page.

```
<H3> <IMG HREF="author.gif" ALIGN="top" ALT="Brent
Heslop"> My Picture </H3>
```

An image within an anchor tag

A better way to use the image might be to link the Image tag to an Anchor tag that references a resumé, for example.

```
<A HREF="bio.html"> <IMG HREF="author.gif" ALIGN="top"
ALT="Brent Heslop"> My Resum$eacute; </A>
```

Netscape Extensions:

Syntax

```
<IMG SRC="URL" ALT="textstring" ALIGN="keyword"
ISMAP BORDER=value HSPACE=value VSPACE=value
WIDTH=value HEIGHT=value >
```

Attributes & Their Arguments

ALIGN="keyword"

Specifies a position relationship to surrounding text. Possible keyword entries are: "left" | "right" | "top" | "texttop" | "middle" | "absmiddle" | "baseline" | "bottom" | "absbottom" .

ALIGN="left" defines a floating image. The image is rendered at the left margin and subsequent lines of text are wrapped around the right side of the image.

ALIGN="right" defines a floating image. The image is rendered at the right margin and subsequent lines of text are wrapped around the left side of the image.

ALIGN="top" aligns the top of the image with the top of the tallest element in the line of surrounding text. This is the same as the standard behavior.

ALIGN="textop" aligns the top of the image with the top of the tallest text in the line of surrounding text. This is usually, but not always, the same as ALIGN="top".

ALIGN="middle" aligns the center of the image with the baseline of the line of surrounding text. This is the same as the standard behavior.

ALIGN="absmiddle" aligns the center of the image with the center of the surrounding text line.

ALIGN="baseline" aligns the base of the image with the baseline of the surrounding text line. This is the same as ALIGN="bottom".

ALIGN="bottom" aligns the base of the image with the baseline of the surrounding text line. This is the same as the standard behavior.

ALIGN="absbottom" aligns the base of the image with the bottom of the surrounding text.

BORDER=value

The integer value argument defines the thickness of the border around the image. The value argument may be 0, indicating no border. Note that BORDER=0 on images that are also part of an Anchor tag may confuse users who are accustomed to seeing a colored border around active images.

HSPACE=value

For a floating image, the integer value argument defines the amount of space to be allocated between the alignment margin and the image and between the image and the text adjoining it.

VSPACE=value

For a floating image, the integer value argument defines the amount of space to be allocated between the bottom of the text line and the top and bottom of the image.

WIDTH=value HEIGHT=value

Both attributes take an integer value that indicates the width and height of the image. These values are provided to speed up the display. They allow the browser to allocate the image area and calculate its size while the image is still being loaded.

See Also

URL, A and FORM

INDEXED TAG

<ISINDEX>

ISINDEX /ISINDEX

Purpose
Specifies that the current document describes a database that can be searched using the index search method appropriate for whatever client is being used to read the document. This tag occurs in the Head section of the document. This tag is meaningful only if the document resides on a server that provides indexing services. For this reason, you should be careful about adding this tag manually. Most servers that support searching will add this element automatically to the document when they send it.

Syntax

```
<ISINDEX>
```

Attributes & Their Arguments
None.

Examples
The following markup defines an indexable document:

```
<HEAD> <TITLE>An Indexable Document</TITLE>
<ISINDEX></HEAD>
```

N Netscape Extensions:

Syntax

```
<ISINDEX PROMPT="text" >
```

Attributes & Their Arguments

PROMPT="keyword"

Specifies the message that should appear in front of the search window. The default message (used by the standard Search tag) is "This is a searchable index. Enter search keywords:"

See Also
HEAD and TITLE

KEYBOARD INPUT TAG

<KBD>. . .</KBD>

KBD /KBD

Purpose
Defines a text element that defines a sequence of characters to be entered by the user from a keyboard. This is intended for use in instructional or other text as a distinctive graphic element to show users what to enter. This is not a fill-out section of a form. Text is usually rendered in a monospaced font.

Syntax

```
<KBD>user_entry_text</KBD>
```

Attributes & Their Arguments
None.

Example
The following is a sample of keyboard code rendered in a Keyboard Input tag.

```
<P>When requested, enter your user name at the login:
prompt, like this <KBD>login: dh</KBD></P>
```

See Also
FORM and PRE

LINK TAG

<LINK>

LINK [HREF:] /LINK

Purpose

Defines a link with another document. The link tag allows you to define relationships between the document containing the link tag and the document specified in the HREF attribute. A link tag must contain an HREF attribute.

Syntax

```
<LINK HREF="URL" [ REL="relationship" |REV="relationship"
|
TITLE="HREF_document_name" ] >
```

Attributes & Their Arguments

The link tag has one required attribute: HREF, and three optional attributes: REL, REV and TITLE.

HREF="URL"

Defines the link between this document and another entity, usually specified by the REL or REV attributes.

REL="relationship"

Defines the relationship between this document and the link URL given in the HREF attribute.

REV="relationship"

Defines the relationship between the link URL given in the HREF attribute and this document. This is the reverse of the specification provided by the REL attribute.

TITLE="HREF_document_name"

Indicates the title of the document pointed to by the HREF attribute. This is not used much by current browsers. It is most useful when the link is to a document, such as a Gopher menu, that does not have an internal name. This lets you display the menu on the browser window with a name.

Example

A simple link

The following includes an HREF that points to Ventana Media's home page and indicates that Ventana Media was the maker of this document.

```
<LINK HREF="http://www.vmedia.com/" REL="made">
```

A link within a series

The following example shows links for a document that represents Chapter 2 (chapt2.html) in a series of chapters.

```
<HEAD> <TITLE>Chapter 2: How I grew up</TITLE> <LINK
HREF="http://www.myserver.com/Bio/chap3.html"
REL="precedes" <LINK HREF="http://www.myserver.com/
Bio/chap1.html" REV="supercedes" </HEAD>
```

See Also

A, URL and FORM

LISTING TAG

```
<LISTING> . . . </LISTING>
```

LISTING /LISTING

Purpose

Example computer listing; similar to the Preformatted Text tag except that no embedded tags will be recognized. To preserve formatting, the text is displayed in a monospaced font. This is an obsolete tag; the Preformatted Text tag is preferred.

Syntax

```
<LISTING>Text</LISTING >
```

Attributes & Their Arguments

None.

Examples

The following shows how you may use text in a listing text block.

<LISTING>This is sample listing text</LISTING>

See Also

XMP and PRE

MENU TAG

<MENU>. . .</MENU>

MENU LI /LI /MENU

Purpose

Defines a list of menu items. A menu list is an unordered list consisting of one or more List Item tags. Each item in this type of list should be a single line. The list generated on a browser may be rendered more compactly than an Unordered List. Note that menu lists should not be nested.

ASSOCIATED TAG: LIST ITEM TAG

<LI>

Purpose

Defines an element in a list. Note that this tag should never be used outside a list definition tag as it may not be correctly displayed by a browser. Also notice that this tag does not have a matching termination.

Syntax

<MENU><LI> List_element</MENU>

Attributes & Their Arguments

None.

Example
The following displays a menu list with three entries.

<MENU> <LI>First Menu Item <LI>Second Menu Item <LI>Third Menu Item </MENU>

See Also
UL, OL, DL and DIR

Nobreak Tag (Netscape Extension)

<NOBR>. . .</NOBR>

NOBR /NOBR

Purpose
Forces enclosed text to stay together, without any line breaks.

Syntax
<NOBR>Text</NOBR>

Attributes & Their Arguments
None.

Examples
The following shows a single line of text that will be kept together on one line by use of the Nobreak tag.

<NOBR>This text must stay together on one line. </NOBR>

See Also
BR and WBR

Ordered List Tag

<OL>. . .</OL>

Purpose
Defines an ordered (numbered) list consisting of one or more List Item tags.

Associated Tag: List Item Tag

<LI>

Purpose
Defines an element in a list. Note that this tag should never be used outside a list definition tag as it may not be correctly displayed by a browser. Also notice that this tag does not have a matching termination.

Syntax

```
<OL><LI> List_element</OL>
```

Attributes & Their Arguments
None.

Example

A simple ordered list
The following displays an ordered list with three entries.

```
<OL> <LI>First List Item <LI>Second List Item <LI>And so
on... </OL>
```

An ordered list nested with other lists
The following list has three items, with the first item being a sub-list with two items. The numbers start over for each nested list.

```
<OL> <LI>First List Item <OL> <LI>First Sub-Entry Item
<LI>second Sub-Entry Item </OL> <LI>Second List Item.
This is a long entry to show how the browser handles list
elements that are longer than a single line. In fact, a list
element may be a significant block of text. <LI>And so on...
</OL>
```

Netscape Extensions:

Syntax

<OL TYPE="keyword" VALUE=number > <LI TYPE="keyword" VALUE=number> List_element</OL>

Attributes & Their Arguments

TYPE="keyword"

Allows you to specify how you want list items marked. Use of the TYPE attribute in the List tag affects the entire list. Use of the attribute in a List Item tag affects that tag and all subsequent tags. Possible keyword entries are: "a" | "A" | "i" | "I" | "1".

TYPE="a" uses small letters for list elements.
TYPE="A" uses capital letters for list elements.
TYPE="i" uses small Roman numerals for list elements.
TYPE="I" uses capital Roman numerals for list elements.
TYPE="1" uses numbers for list elements. This is the default.

VALUE=number

Allows you to specify an index number that should be used when starting the list. The index number specifies the starting point of the list elements in the sequencing method selected by the TYPE attribute. For example, using VALUE=3 will start the list at c, C, iii, III or 3 depending on the setting of TYPE.

See Also

UL, DL, DIR and MENU

PARAGRAPH TAG

<P> . . . </P>

Purpose

Presents the text within the tags as a single paragraph. In an obsolete form, this tag might be used alone (as </P>) to mark the end of a paragraph; preferred usage is to include the paragraph text within the tags.

Syntax

<P>Text</P>

Attributes & Their Arguments

None.

Examples

The following displays two separate paragraphs of text, divided by a horizontal rule.

<P> This is two paragraphs of text divided by a single, horizontal line. </P> <HR> <P> This is the second paragraph of text. </P>

See Also

BR and PRE

Preformatted Text Tag

<PRE> . . . </PRE>

PRE /PRE

Purpose

Identifies text that has already been formatted (preformatted) by some other system and must be displayed as is. Preformatted text may include embedded tags that will be interpreted for rendering, but not all tag types are permitted. The Preformatted Text tag can be used to include tables in documents. To preserve formatting, the text is displayed in a monospaced font. The Preformatted Text tag is preferred to the obsolete Listing <LISTING> and Example <XMP> tags.

Syntax

<PRE>Text</PRE>

Attributes & Their Arguments

The Preformatted Text tag has one optional attribute.

WIDTH="value"

This attribute tells a browser the maximum width to be expected in the block of preformatted text. This allows the browser to adjust the window, and perhaps the font and size of the displayed text, to improve rendering.

Examples

The following shows how you may use text in a preformatted text block.

```
<PRE>
        Act Three, Scene Two
<I>Antony:</I> Friends, Romans, countrymen, lend me your
ears;
            I come to bury Caesar, not to praise him.
            The evil that men do lives after them,
            the good is oft interred with their bones.
</PRE>
```

See Also

BR, P, CODE, LISTING and XMP

SAMPLE TAG

<SAMP>. . .</SAMP>

SAMP /SAMP

Purpose

Defines a text element that represents a series of literal characters. Text is usually rendered in a monospaced font.

Syntax

```
<SAMP>sample_text</SAMP>
```

Attributes & Their Arguments
None.

Example
The following is a sample of sample text.

```
<SAMP>This is a sequence of sampled characters</SAMP>
```

See Also
CODE, KBD and PRE

STRIKEOUT TAG

```
<STRIKE> . . . </STRIKE>
```

not supported by HoTMetaL PRO

Purpose
Presents the text within the tags in strike-out format (with a line through the text). This is a common style used in legal documents and in revisions and editing of text. This is a new tag and not supported by all browsers. If a browser does not support this tag, the text is generally rendered just like normal text.

Syntax

```
<STRIKE>Text</STRIKE>
```

Attributes & Their Arguments
None.

Examples
The following markup creates a display with the text enclosed by the tags with a line through it.

```
<P>You can use type-specific tags to show edits by
<STRIKE>striking out</STRIKE> text rather than removal.
</P>
```

See Also
EM, STRONG, I and B

STRONG TAG

<STRONG> . . . </STRONG>

STRONG /STRONG

Purpose
Presents the text within the tags with a stronger emphasis than the Emphasis tag. Usually, the text is displayed in bold. This tag is preferred to the Bold tag.

Syntax
<STRONG>Text</STRONG>

Attributes & Their Arguments:
None.

Examples
The following markup displays the enclosed text in a very different manner than the body text (usually in bold font).

<STRONG>Pay Attention. This is important.</STRONG>

See Also
B, EM, I and TT

TABLE TAG (NETSCAPE EXTENSION)

<TABLE>. . .</TABLE>

not supported by HoTMetaL PRO

Purpose
Defines a table. A table is an ordered set of data presented in rows and columns. Tables may be nested.

Associated Tag: Table Row Tag

<TR>. . .</TR>

Purpose
Defines a row of a table. This tag should never be used outside a table definition tag. The number of rows in a table is equal to the number of Table Row tags that it contains.

Associated Tag: Table Data Tag

<TD>. . .</TD>

Purpose
Defines a data cell in a table. Table data must appear within a table row. Each row need not have the same number of data cells; short rows are padded with empty cells to the right.

Associated Tag: Table Header Tag

<TH>. . .</TH>

Purpose
Defines a header cell in a table. Header cells are identical to data cells except that text or data in header cells is presented in a bold font. Table headers must appear within a table row.

Associated Tag: Caption Tag

<CAPTION>. . .</CAPTION>

Purpose
Defines the caption for the table. Caption tags are optional. If used, they must appear between the Table tags but outside of table rows or cells. Captions are horizontally centered with respect to the table.

Syntax

<TABLE BORDER | BORDER=value | CELLSPACING=value | CELLPADDING=value | WIDTH=value>
<CAPTION ALIGN="keyword"> Caption_text </CAPTION>
<TR ALIGN="keyword" | VALIGN="keyword">
<TH | ALIGN="keyword" | VALIGN="keyword" | NOWRAP | COLSPAN=value | ROWSPAN=value | WIDTH=value>
Table_heading_text </TH>
</TR>
<TR ALIGN="keyword" | VALIGN="keyword">
<TD | ALIGN="keyword" | VALIGN="keyword" | NOWRAP | COLSPAN=value | ROWSPAN=value | WIDTH=value>
Table_element </TD>
</TR>
</TABLE>

Attributes & Their Arguments

Many attributes are available in several different tags used in tables. Each attribute listed below describes any special effects that depend on the tag it is associated with. The general rule is that attributes at a lower level override any previous attribute settings. For example, the default alignment of a table is ALIGN=:"left". This is overridden for any given row by specifying the ALIGN attribute for that row. Within a row, the ALIGN attribute specified for a cell or header overrides the alignment for that row.

ALIGN="keyword"

Sets the alignment of the data controlled by the tag. For the <CAPTION> tag, the ALIGN attribute specifies where the caption text is to be placed. Possible keyword entries are: "top" | "bottom". The default setting is ALIGN="top". For the <TR>, <TH> or <TD> tags, the ALIGN attribute specifies where the data is to be placed. Possible keyword entries are: "left" | "right" | "center". The default setting is ALIGN="left".

BORDER=value

Specifies that you want a border around the table and all table cells. If absent, the table is drawn without borders, but space is allocated for the border by default. This means that a table without the BORDER attribute will occupy the same space as one with the BORDER attribute but without a value argument. The optional value argument allows you to specify the size of the border. If a value of 0 is used, the table will not have a border and no space will be saved for the border, making the table more compact than simply eliminating the BORDER attribute.

CELLPADDING=value

Controls the padding around the data in a cell. The cell padding is the space between the borders of the cell and the contents of the cell. The default CELLPADDING is 1. Note that using CELLPADDING=0 in a table with visible borders is not recommended, as the data in the cells may touch the border.

CELLSPACING=value

Controls the spacing between cells of the table. The default CELLSPACING is 2.

COLSPAN=value

Specifies how many columns of the table this cell should span. The default COLSPAN is 1.

NOWRAP

Prevents the data within the cell from being broken to fit the width of the cell. The resulting cell may be larger than a standard cell to accommodate the data.

ROWSPAN=value

Specifies how many rows of the table this cell should span. The default ROWSPAN is 1. The rows spanned must be defined by Table Row tags. An attempt to extend a cell into a row not specified with a <TR> tag will be truncated.

VALIGN="keyword"

Sets the alignment in the vertical direction within the cell for the data controlled by the tag. Possible keyword entries are: "top" | "middle" | "bottom" | "baseline". The default setting is VALIGN="middle".

WIDTH=value

Specifies the width of the overall table or of a specific cell within a table. The default width for tables and cells is determined by complex algorithms within the browser. The value argument is number | "percent" which allows you to specify the width of the element in either pixels or as a percentage of the document width (for a table) or of the table width (for cells).

Example

The following displays a three-column table with two rows and a caption.

```
<TABLE BORDER>
<CAPTION>A Table</CAPTION>
<TR><TH> Heading 1 </TH> <TH COLSPAN=2> Heading 2
</TH></TR>
<TR><TD>Item Name</TD> <TD ALIGN="center"> 100
</TD> <TD ALIGN="center"> 200 </TD> </TR> </TABLE>
```

See Also

OL, UL and PRE

TITLE TAG

```
<TITLE> . . . </TITLE>
```

TITLE Document Title: /TITLE

Purpose

Specifies a title for an HTML document. This tag occurs in the Head section of the document and is required by HTML standards. Note that the title will not appear directly on the document as is customary on printed documents; instead, it will usually appear in a window bar identifying the contents of the window where the document information is displayed. HTML Header tags perform the functions usually reserved for titles in printed documents.

Syntax

```
<TITLE>Text</TITLE>
```

Attributes & Their Arguments

None.

Examples

The following markup defines a title for an HTML document.

```
<TITLE>Sample Document</TITLE>
```

See Also
HEAD and BODY

TYPEWRITER TAG

<TT> . . . </TT>

Purpose
Presents the text within the tags in a monospaced font (usually Courier) that looks like a typewriter.

Syntax

```
<TT>Text</TT>
```

Attributes & Their Arguments
None.

Examples
The following markup displays the enclosed text in a monospaced font (usually Courier or a variant of that font).

```
<TT>This is simple, monospaced text that looks like a
typewriter.</TT>
```

See Also
B, EM, I and STRONG

UNDERLINE TAG

<U> . . . </U>

not supported by HoTMetaL PRO

Purpose
Presents the text within the tags underlined.

Syntax

<U>Text</U>

Attributes & Their Arguments

None.

Examples

The following markup defines the enclosed text to be displayed underlined.

```
<P>You can use type-specific tags to force
<U>underlining</U> when you require that and nothing
else.</P>
```

See Also

B, I, EM and STRONG

UNORDERED LIST TAG

<UL>. . .</UL>

Purpose

Defines an unordered (bulleted) list consisting of one or more List Item tags.

ASSOCIATED TAG: LIST ITEM TAG

<LI>

Purpose

Defines an element in a list. Note that this tag should never be used outside a list definition tag as it may not be correctly displayed by a browser. Also notice that this tag does not have a matching termination.

Syntax

<UL><LI> List_element</UL>

Attributes & Their Arguments

None.

Example

A simple unordered list

The following displays an unordered list with three entries.

```
<UL> <LI>First List Item <LI>Second List Item <LI>And so
on... </UL>
```

An unordered list nested with other lists

The following list has three items, with the first item being a sub-list with two items. Many browsers will show different bullet types to indicate the level of indentation within an unordered list.

```
<UL> <LI>First List Item <UL> <LI>First Sub-Entry Item
<LI>second Sub-Entry Item </UL> <LI>Second List Item.
This is a long entry to show how the browser handles list
elements that are longer than a single line. In fact, a list
element may be a significant block of text. <LI>And so on...
</UL>
```

N Netscape Extensions:

Syntax

<UL TYPE="keyword"> <LI> List_element</UL>

Attributes & Their Arguments

TYPE="keyword"

Allows you to specify how you want list items marked. Use of the TYPE attribute in the List tag affects the entire list; use of the attribute in a List Item tag affects that tag and all subsequent tags. Possible keyword entries are: "disc" | "circle" | "square".

TYPE="disc" uses the default solid round bullet for list elements.
TYPE="circle" uses an open circle bullet for list elements.
TYPE="square" uses a square bullet for list elements.

See Also

UL, DL, DIR and MENU

Variable Tag

```
<VAR>. . .</VAR>
```

VAR /VAR

Purpose
Provides a variable term or phrase within a text block. Similar to the Emphasis tag.

Syntax

```
<VAR>Variable_text</VAR>
```

Attributes & Their Arguments
None.

Example
The following includes a variable item within a normal text paragraph. The variable term is displayed with emphasis within the text.

```
<P>In C++, <VAR>variables</VAR> may be private, public,
or protected. </P>
```

See Also
DFN, STRONG, DL, B, I and U

Word Break Tag (Netscape Extension)

```
<WBR>
```

WBR /WBR

Purpose
Allows Netscape to break a word or text block at the tag if necessary.

Syntax

```
<NOBR>Text el<WBR>ement</NOBR>
```

Attributes & Their Arguments

None.

Examples

The following shows a single line of text that will be kept together on one line by use of the Nobreak tag but may be broken at the Word Break tag if necessary.

```
<NOBR>This text must stay together <WBR>
on one line if possible.</NOBR>
```

See Also

BR and NOBR

EXAMPLE TEXT TAG

```
<XMP> . . . </XMP>
```

XMP /XMP

Purpose

Similar to the Preformatted Text tag, except that no embedded tags will be recognized. To preserve formatting, the text is displayed in a monospaced font. This is an obsolete tag; the Preformatted Text tag is preferred.

Syntax

```
<XMP>Text</XMP>
```

Attributes & Their Arguments

None.

Examples

The following shows how you may use text in an example text block.

```
<XMP>This is sample example text</XMP>
```

See Also
LISTING and PRE

COMMENT TAG

<!-- . . . -->

not supported by HoTMetaL PRO

Purpose
Allows you to insert comment data into the HTML document without displaying it on the screen. Often used to provide information about the author, revision data and so on. Some browsers have problems with comments that are longer than a single line. For best compatibility, you should make multiline comments into several comment lines.

Syntax

```
<!-- Text -->
```

Attributes & Their Arguments
None.

Examples
The following shows a typical use of comments. Note that the comment has been broken into several different lines, with each line an individual comment.

```
<!-- Created by: David Holzgang -->
<!-- using HoTMetaL Pro 1.0 -->
<!-- on 23 February 1995 11:22 -->
<!-- Revised: dh 1 Mar 95 16:35 -->
```

See Also
HEAD and TITLE

HTML Forms

The HTML forms interface allows document creators to define HTML documents containing information to be filled out by users. When a user fills out the form and presses a button indicating the form should be "submitted," the information on the form is sent to a server for processing. The server will usually prepare an HTML document using the information supplied by the user and return it to the browser client for display.

A form may contain any of the standard HTML tags. In addition, forms have certain special tags that are only used, and recognized, within a form document. The following tags define and implement the forms interface:

```
<FORM>...
<INPUT>
<SELECT>...</SELECT>
<OPTION>
<TEXTAREA>...</TEXTAREA> </FORM>
```

The last four tags are only valid within a Form tag.

Form Tag

<FORM>. . .</FORM>

FORM [ACTION:] /FORM

Purpose
Defines a form within an HTML document. A document may contain multiple Form tags, but Form tags may not be nested. Note that non-form tags can be used within a Form tag.

Syntax
<FORM ACTION="URL" METHOD=[GET|POST]> Text of form, including additional standard HTML tags and form tags if desired </FORM>

Attributes & Their Arguments

Forms have two required arguments.

ACTION="URL"

The URL location of the program that will process the form.

METHOD=method

The method may be either GET or POST. This is the method chosen to exchange data between the client and the program started to process the form.

Example

The is an example of how a Form tag might be used to define a registration form for a university.

```
<FORM ACTION="http://kuhttp.cc.ukans.edu/cgi-bin/
register" METHOD=POST> . . . </FORM>
```

See Also

URL and BODY

INPUT TAG

<INPUT>

INPUT [SRC:] /INPUT

Purpose

Defines an input field where the user may enter information on the form. Each input field assigns a value to a variable that has a specified name and a specified data type.

Syntax

```
<INPUT TYPE="keyword" NAME="textstring"
|VALUE="textstring"|CHECKED|SIZE=number|
MAXLENGTH=number">
```

Attributes & Their Arguments

TYPE="keyword"

Specifies the data type for the variable. Possible values for keyword are ["text" | "password" | "checkbox" | "radio" | "submit" | "reset"].

TYPE="text" and TYPE="password" accept character data.

TYPE="checkbox" is either selected or not.

TYPE="radio" allows selection of only one of several radio fields, if they all have the same variable name.

TYPE="submit" is an action button that sends the completed form to the query server.

TYPE="reset" is a button that resets the form variables to their default values.

NAME="textstring"

where textstring is a symbolic name (not displayed) identifying the input variable.

VALUE="textstring"

where the function of textstring depends on the argument for type as follows:

TYPE="text" or TYPE="password"

textstring is the default value for the input variable.

TYPE="checkbox" or TYPE="radio"

textstring is the value of the input variable when it is "checked".

TYPE="reset" or TYPE="submit"

textstring is a label that will appear on the submit or reset button in place of the words "submit" and "reset".

CHECKED

No arguments. For TYPE="checkbox" or TYPE="radio", if CHECKED is present the input field is "checked" by default.

SIZE=number

where number is an integer value representing the number of characters allowed for the TYPE="text" or TYPE="password" input fields.

MAXLENGTH=number

where number is an integer value representing the number of characters accepted for TYPE="text" or TYPE="password". This attribute is valid only for single line "text" or "password" fields.

Examples

A simple text input area

The following provides an input area for entering a user's name.

```
<P>Please enter your name:</P> <INPUT TYPE="text"
NAME="username" SIZE=30 >
```

Using input for submission of data

These two Input tags add the necessary buttons to submit data accumulated in the form or cancel it.

```
<INPUT TYPE="submit" VALUE="Send Form">
<INPUT TYPE="reset" VALUE="Clear Form">
```

Using radio buttons as input

The following example defines four radio buttons. The third button is checked by default when the form is first displayed.

```
<P> Please select one of these destinations:
<INPUT TYPE="radio" NAME="S1" VALUE="CANADA">
Canada
<INPUT TYPE="radio" NAME="S1" VALUE="GB"> Great
Britian
<INPUT TYPE="radio" NAME="S1" VALUE="USA"
CHECKED> United States of America
<INPUT TYPE="radio" NAME="S1" VALUE="AUS">
Australia</P>
```

See Also

FORM

Select Tag

```
<SELECT>. . .</SELECT>
```

Purpose

Defines and displays a set of optional list items from which the user can select one or more items. This element requires an <OPTION> element for each item in the list.

ASSOCIATED TAG: OPTION ITEM TAG

<OPTION>

Purpose

Defines an element in a selection list. Within the Select tag the Option tags are used to define the possible values for the select field. Note that this tag should never be used outside a Select tag as it may not be correctly displayed by a browser. Also notice that this tag does not have a matching termination.

Syntax

```
<SELECT NAME="textstring" [SIZE=value MULTIPLE]
<OPTION [SELECTED]>Option_item </SELECT>...
```

Attributes & Their Arguments

NAME="textstring"

where textstring is a symbolic name (not displayed) identifying the input variable.

SIZE=value

The argument for SIZE is an integer value representing the number of <OPTION> items that will be displayed at one time.

MULTIPLE

If present, the MULTIPLE attribute allows selection of more than one <OPTION> value.

SELECTED

If this attribute is present, then the option value is selected by default.

Example

In the following example all three options may be chosen but bananas are selected by default.

```
<SELECT MULTIPLE>
<OPTION>Apples
<OPTION SELECTED>Bananas
<OPTION>Cherries
</SELECT>
```

See Also
FORM

TEXTAREA TAG

<TEXTAREA>. . .</TEXTAREA>

TEXTAREA /TEXTAREA

Purpose
Defines a rectangular field where the user may enter text data. If a default text element is present, it will be displayed when the field appears. Otherwise the field will be blank.

Syntax

```
<TEXTAREA NAME="textstring" ROWS=value
COLUMNS=value >default_text</TEXTAREA>
```

Attributes & Their Arguments

NAME="textstring"

where textstring is a symbolic name (not displayed) identifying the input variable.

ROWS=value COLS=value

Both attributes take an integer value that represents the lines and number of characters per line in the text area to be displayed.

Example
The following demonstrates the use of a Textarea tag.

```
<P>Please enter your comments below:<BR> <TEXTAREA
NAME="tree_data" ROWS=5 COLUMNS=40>I like trees
because...</TEXTAREA></P>
```

See Also
FORM

Character Entities

One problem that occurs when transmitting text across computer systems is the problem of how to represent punctuation marks, accented characters and other characters that may be commonly used in one language or system and not in another. Each computer system has some method for handling these problems. For example, on the Macintosh, you can generate an e with an acute accent—the last é in the word resumé—by pressing the Option key and the "e" key, followed by the "e" key again. However, the character generated in this way cannot be displayed correctly on any system that isn't a Macintosh, so if you use this character within an HTML document, the recipient will probably not see the correct character. This is one type of character display problem.

Another problem is how to display certain punctuation marks. For example, the HTML language uses the characters "<" (the less-than sign) and ">" (the greater-than sign) to signal HTML commands within a document. For obvious reasons, you cannot insert these same characters in the text of the document without causing problems when the document is displayed. You need another method for displaying these characters in your text.

To solve this problem when using an HTML document, the HTML language defines character entities that are used instead of these special characters. These may take one of two formats.

&keyword;

Displays a particular character identified by a special keyword. For example the entity *&* displays the ampersand character, (&), and the entity *<* displays the less than (<) character. Note that the semicolon following the keyword is required, and the keyword must be one from Table A-1 shown below. The definitive list of acceptable keywords is presented at http://info.cern.ch/hypertext/WWW/MarkUp/Entities.html.

&#ascii_equivalent;

Uses a character from the ISO Added LATIN I character set identified by the decimal integer ascii_equivalent. Again note that the semicolon following the ASCII numeric value

is required. Table A-2 shows the character and gives the ascii_equivalent value for all the characters in the ISO Added LATIN I character set that are not available from the keyboard and do not have a character keyword. Note that Table A-1 shows the integer ascii_equivalent for the characters as well as the keyword. You can use either method (keyword or ascii_equivalent) to insert these into your text; however, the keyword is considered the better alternative.

When using HoTMetaL PRO , you can insert any of these characters without worrying about how to encode them. HoTMetaL PRO allows you to simply insert most special character entities that you want by using the Insert Character Entity command in the Markup menu (⌘-E). This displays a HoTMetaL Insert Entity dialog box that shows you the most common characters that you might want to use in your text as keys. Simply press the key for the character that you want and HoTMetaL PRO inserts the correct encoding for that character entity in your text. HoTMetaL PRO also automatically supplies the correct encodings if you type either of the special characters "<" or "&" from the keyboard, as these cannot be allowed in any HTML text, for obvious reasons. For all other character entities, you need to use the Insert Entity dialog box as described here or type the entity directly into the text.

Mnemonic	As Displayed	Description	Decimal ASCII Equivalent
AElig	"Æ"	capital AE diphthong (ligature)	#198
Aacute	"Á"	capital A, acute accent	#193
Acirc	"Â"	capital A, circumflex accent	#194
Agrave	"À"	capital A, grave accent	#192
Aring	"Å"	capital A, ring	#197
Atilde	"Ã"	capital A, tilde	#195
Auml	"Ä"	capital A, dieresis or umlaut mark	#196
Ccedil	"Ç"	capital C, cedilla	#199
Eth	"_"	capital Eth, Icelandic	#208
Eacute	"É"	capital E, acute accent	#201
Ecirc	"Ê"	capital E, circumflex accent	#202

Mnemonic	As Displayed	Description	Decimal ASCII Equivalent
Egrave	“È”	capital E, grave accent	#200
Euml	“Ë”	capital E, dieresis or umlaut mark	#203
Iacute	“Í”	capital I, acute accent	#205
Icirc	“Î”	capital I, circumflex accent	#206
Igrave	“Ì”	capital I, grave accent	#204
Iuml	“Ï”	capital I, dieresis or umlaut mark	#207
Ntilde	“Ñ”	capital N, tilde	#209
Oacute	“Ó”	capital O, acute accent	#211
Ocirc	“Ô”	capital O, circumflex accent	#212
Ograve	“Ò”	capital O, grave accent	#210
Oslash	“Ø”	capital O, slash	#216
Otilde	“Õ”	capital O, tilde	#213
Ouml	“Ö”	capital O, dieresis or umlaut mark	#214
Thorn	“_”	capital Thorn, Icelandic	#222
Uacute	“Ú”	capital U, acute accent	#218
Ucirc	“Û”	capital U, circumflex accent	#219
Ugrave	“Ù”	capital U, grave accent	#217
Uuml	“Ü”	capital U, dieresis or umlaut mark	#220
Yacute	“Y”	capital Y, acute accent	#221
aacute	“á”	small a, acute accent	#225
acirc	“â”	small a, circumflex accent	#226
aelig	“æ”	small ae diphthong (ligature)	#230
agrave	“à”	small a, grave accent	#224
amp	“&”	ampersand	#38
atilde	“ã”	small a, tilde	#227
auml	“ä”	small a, dieresis or umlaut mark	#228
ccedil	“ç”	small c, cedilla	#231
eacute	“é”	small e, acute accent	#233
ecirc	“ê”	small e, circumflex accent	#234
egrave	“è”	small e, grave accent	#232
eth	“∂”	small eth, Icelandic	#240
euml	“ë”	small e, dieresis or umlaut mark	#235
gt	“>”	greater than	#62
iacute	“í”	small i, acute accent	#237
icirc	“î”	small i, circumflex accent	#238
igrave	“ì”	small i, grave accent	#236

Mnemonic	As Displayed	Description	Decimal ASCII Equivalent
iuml	“ï”	small i, dieresis or umlaut mark	#239
lt	“<“	less than	#60
ntilde	“ñ”	small n, tilde	#241
oacute	“ó”	small o, acute accent	#243
ocirc	“ô”	small o, circumflex accent	#244
ograve	“ò”	small o, grave accent	#242
oslash	“ø”	small o, slash	#248
otilde	“õ”	small o, tilde	#245
ouml	“ö”	small o, dieresis or umlaut mark	#246
quote	“‘“	single quote	#62
szlig	“ß”	small sharp s, German (sz ligature)	
thorn	“_”	small thorn, Icelandic	#254
uacute	“ú”	small u, acute accent	#250
ucirc	“û”	small u, circumflex accent	#251
ugrave	“ù”	small u, grave accent	#249
uuml	“ü”	small u, dieresis or umlaut mark	#252
yacute	“y”	small y, acute accent	#253
yuml	“ÿ”	small y, dieresis or umlaut mark	#255

Table A-1: *Character keywords in HTML.*

Number	As Displayed	Description
#161	"¡"	inverted exclamation mark
#162	"¢"	cent sign
#163	"£"	pound sign
#164	"¤"	general currency sign
#165	"¥"	yen sign
#166	"¦"	broken (vertical) bar
#167	"§"	section sign
#168	"¨"	umlaut
#169	"©"	copyright sign
#170	"ª"	ordinal indicator, feminine
#171	"«"	angle quotation mark, left
#174	"®"	circled R/registered sign
#175	"¯"	macron
#176	"°"	degree sign
#177	"±"	/pm B: plus-or-minus sign
#178	"²"	superscript two
#179	"³"	superscript three
#180	"´"	acute accent
#181	"µ"	micro sign
#182	"¶"	pilcrow (paragraph sign)
#183	"·"	/centerdot B: middle dot
#184	"¸"	cedilla
#185	"¹"	superscript one
#186	"º"	ordinal indicator, masculine
#187	"»"	angle quotation mark, right
#188	"¼"	fraction one-quarter
#189	"½"	fraction one-half
#190	"¾"	fraction three-quarters
#191	"¿"	inverted question mark

Table A-2: *ISO Added LATIN 1 character entities with only a numeric representation.*

APPENDIX D

Resources

This appendix lists Internet publishing related programs and periodicals. The topics include TCP/IP software, Web browsers, HTML editors and converters, portable document viewers, graphic editors, 3D rendering applications, clip art, multimedia applications, Web servers, CGI programs and utilities. This resource guide also lists some Web design companies and server services as well as service providers who will let you publish your pages at their site.

If you don't find what you're looking for here, we recommend you use a Web directory or a Web searching facility. You can use the Yahoo directory or search program by entering the URL:

http://www.yahoo.com

Another popular directory is Trade Wave from EINet. To check out Trade Wave, enter the URL:

http://www.einet.net/galaxy.html

One of the best and more advanced Web searching facilities is Carnagie Mellon's Lycos Catalog of the Internet. Lycos catalogs over five and half million Web pages. To scour the Internet using Lycos, enter the URL:

http://lycos.cs.cmu.edu/

The WWW Virtual Library has long been a standard searching facility. To use the WWW Virtual Library, enter the URL:

http://www.w3.org/hypertext/DataSources/bySubject/Overview.html

TCP/IP Software

Internet Membership Kit
Ventana Communications Group, Inc.
P.O. Box 13964
Research Triangle Park, NC 27709-3964
Voice: (919) 544-9404
Fax: (919) 544-9472
URL: http://www.vmedia.com
E-mail: help@vmedia.com

Internet Valet
Software Ventures
2907 Claremont Avenue
Berkeley, CA 94705
Voice: (510) 644-3232
Fax: (510) 848-0885
URL: http://www.svcdudes.com
E-mail: valet-info@svcdudes.com

InterPPP
InterCon Systems Corporation
950 Herndon Parkway, Suite 420
Herndon, VA 22070
Voice: (800) 468-7266
Voice: (703) 709-9890
Fax: (703) 709-5555
URL: http://www.intercon.com
E-mail: comment@intercon.com

InterSLIP
Freeware
InterCon Systems Corporation
950 Herndon Parkway, Suite 420
Herndon, VA 22070
Voice: (800) 468-7266
Voice: (703) 709-9890
Fax: (703) 709-5555
URL: http://www.intercon.com
E-mail: comment@intercon.com

MacTCP
APDA (Apple Programmers and Developers Association)
P.O. Box 319
Buffalo, New York 14207
Voice: (800) 282-2732
Voice: (800) 767-2775 (Tech Support)
Fax: (716) 871-6511
URL: http://www.info.apple.com/dev/apda.html
E-mail: apda@applelink.apple.com

MacPPP
Freeware
Author Larry Blunk
URL: www.merit.edu/pub/ppp/mac
E-mail: ljb@merit.edu

MacSLIP
TriSoft
1825 E. 38 1/2 Street
Austin, Texas 78722
Voice: (800) 531-5170
Voice: (512) 472-0744
Fax: (512) 473-2122
URL: http://www.zilker.net/~hydepark
E-mail: trisoft@bga.com

TCP/Connect II
InterCon Systems Corporation
950 Herndon Parkway, Suite 420
Herndon, VA 22070
Voice: (800) 468-7266
Voice: (703) 709-5500
Fax: (703) 709-5555
URL: http://www.intercon.com
E-mail: comment@intercon.com

VersaTerm with VersaTilities
VersaTilities
Synergy Software
2457 Perkiomen Avenue
Reading, PA 19606
Voice: (800) 876-8376
Voice: (610) 779-0522
Fax: (610) 370-0548
E-mail: maxwell@sales.synergy.com

World Wide Web Browsers

Enhanced NCSA Mosaic for Macintosh 2.0
OEM licences to commercial firms
Spyglass Inc.
1800 Woodfield Drive
Savoy, IL 61874
Voice: (217) 355-6000
Fax: (217) 355-8925
URL: http://www.spyglass.com/

MacWeb
Commercial
TradeWave Corporation
3636 Executive Center Drive
Suite 100
Austin, TX 78731
Voice: (800) 844-4638
URL: http://galaxy.einet.net/EINet/MacWeb/MacWebHome.html
E-mail: macweb@tradewave.com

NCSA Mosaic for Macintosh
National Center for Supercomputing Applications
University of Illinois at Urbana-Champlain
NCSA Documentation Orders
152 Computing Applications Building
605 East Springfield Avenue

Champaign, IL 61820-5518
Voice: (217) 355-6000
URL: http://www.ncsa.uiuc.edu/SDG/Software/MacMosaic/MacMosaicHome.html
E-mail: mosaic-mac@ncsa.uiuc.edu

Netscape Navigator for Macintosh
Shareware/Commercial
Netscape Inc.
501 East Middlefield Road
Mountain View, CA 61874
Voice: (415) 254-1900
URL: http://home.netscape.com/

NetShark
InterCon Systems Corporation
950 Herndon Parkway, Suite 420
Herndon, VA 22070
Voice: (800) 468-7266
Voice: (703) 709-9890
Fax: (703) 709-5555
URL: http://www.intercon.com
E-mail: comment@intercon.com

HTML Editors & Convertors

Arachnid
Robert McBurney
Second Look Computing
Weeg Computing Center
University of Iowa
Iowa City, IA 52242
Voice: (319) 335-5596
URL: http://sec-look.uiowa.edu/about/projects/arachnid-page.html
E-mail: info@sec-look.uiowa.com

BBEdit HTML Extensions
Freeware
Carles Bellver
Grupo de Sistemas de Información
Universitat Jaume I
Castelló, Spain
URL: http://www.uji.es/bbedit-html-extensions.html
URL: ftp://ftp.uji.es/pub/uji-ftp/mac/util/
E-mail: bellverc@si.uji.es

BBEdit HTML Tools
Freeware
Lindsay Davies
URL: http://www.york.ac.uk/~ld11/BBEditTools.html
URL: ftp://ftp.york.ac.uk/pub/users/ld11/BBEdit_HTML_Tools.sea
E-mail: Lindsay.Davies@sheffield.ac.uk

BeyondPress (Quark XPress)
Commercial
Astrobyte LLC
1800 15th Street
Suite 104
Denver, CO 80202
Voice: (303) 534-6344
Fax: (303) 534-6557
URL: http://www.astrobyte.com/astrobyte/BeyondPressInfo.html
E-mail: info@astrobyte.com

HoTMetaL
Shareware version
URL: http://www.sq.com/
E-mail: hotmetal@sq.com

HoTMetaL PRO
Commercial version
SoftQuad Inc.
56 Aberfoyle Crescent
Toronto, Ontario M8X 2W4
Canada
Voice: (416) 239-4801
Fax: (416) 239-7105
URL: http://www.sq.com/
E-mail: hotmetal@sq.com

HTML Editor
Shareware
Rick Giles
Box 207
Acadia University
Wolfville, N.S. B0P 1X0
Canada
URL: http://dragon.acadiau.ca/~giles/HTML_Editor/Documentation.html
E-mail: rick.giles@acadiau.ca

HTML Pro
Shareware
Nicklas Frykholm
Rothoffsv. 37 A
903 42 Umeå
Sweden
URL: http://www.ts.umu.se/~r2d2/shareware/htmlpro_help.html
E-mail: nisfrm95@student.umu.se

HTML Web Weaver
Shareware
Robert C. Best III
118 Leroy Street
Apt. N2
Potsdam, NY 13676
URL: http://www.potsdam.edu/Web.Weaver/About.html
URL: ftp://ftp.potsdam.edu/pub/HTML_Web_Weaver/
E-mail: Robert.Best@potsdam.edu

MSWToHTML (MS Word 6.0)
Shareware
Dan Berrios
3145 Geary Boulevard
Suite 413
San Francisco, CA 94118
URL: http://dreyer.ucsf.edu/mswtohtml.html
E-mail: dan@dreyer.ucsf.edu

NaviPress
Commercial
NaviSoft Inc
(America Online subsidiary)
Vienna, VA 78731
Voice: (800) 879-6882
Voice: (703) 918-2137
URL: http://www.navisoft.com/
E-mail: interest@navisoft.com

RTF to HTML
Freeware
Chris Hector
URL: ftp://ftp.cray.com/src/WWWstuff/RTF/latest/binaries/macintosh.sit.hqx
E-mail: cjh@cray.com

WebDoor
Commercial
Open Door Networks, Inc.
110 Laurel Street
Ashland, OR 97520
Voice: (503) 488-4127
Fax: (503) 488-1708
URL: http://www.opendoor.com/WebDoor/WebDoor.html
URL: ftp://ftp.opendoor.com/pub/webdoor/
E-mail: info@opendoor.com

WebSucker (PageMaker)
Freeware
Mitch Cohen
URL: http://www.iii.net/users/mcohen/websucker.html
E-mail: mcohen@media.iii.net

Webtor
Jochen Schales
Fraunhofer Institute for Computer Graphics
Wilhelminenstrasse 7, D-64283
Darmstadt, Germany
Voice: +49 (0) 6151 155-133
URL: http://www.igd.fhg.de/~neuss/webtor/webtor.html
E-mail: schales@igd.fhg.de

WebWorks Publisher (FrameMaker)
Commercial
Quadralay Corporation
3925 West Braker Lane
Suite 337
Austin, TX 78759-5321
Voice: (512) 305-0240
Fax: (512) 305-0248
URL: http://www.quadralay.com/products/WebWorks/Publisher/index.html
E-mail: info@quadralay.com

World Wide Web Weaver
(successor to HTML Web Weaver)
URL: http://www.northnet.org/best/home.html
E-mail: Best@northnet.org

Portable Document & Other Document Viewers

Adobe Acrobat Reader, Exchange and Network Distiller
Adobe Systems Incorporated
1585 Charleston Road
P.O. Box 7900
Mountain View, CA 94039-7900
Voice: (800) 862-3623
Voice: (800) 833-6687
Fax: (415) 961-3769
URL: http://www.adobe.com
URL: ftp://ftp.adobe.com/pub/adobe/Applications/Acrobat

Common Ground 2.0
Common Ground Software
1301 Shoreway Road #220
Belmont, CA 94002
Voice: (800) 598-3821
Voice: (415) 802-5800
Fax: (415) 593-6868
URL: http://www.commonground.com/

Envoy
Novell Inc.
2180 Fortune Drive
San Jose, CA 95131
Voice: (800) 526-5011
Voice: (801) 429-7000
URL: http://wp.novell.com/
E-mail: info@novell.com

Replica

Farallon Computing, Inc.
2470 Mariner Square Loop
Alameda, California 94501
Voice: (510) 814-5100
Fax: (510) 814-5020
URL: http://www.farallon.com/www/product/rep/repmac.html
E-mail: info@farallon.com

GRAPHIC APPLICATIONS & UTILITIES

Adobe Dimensions

Adobe Systems Incorporated
1585 Charleston Road
P.O. Box 7900
Mountain View, CA 94039-7900
Voice: (800) 862-3623
Voice: (800) 833-6687
Fax: (415) 961-3769
URL: http://www.adobe.com

Adobe Illustrator

Adobe Systems Incorporated
1585 Charleston Road
P.O. Box 7900
Mountain View, CA 94039-7900
Voice: (800) 862-3623
Voice: (800) 833-6687
Fax: (415) 961-3769
URL: http://www.adobe.com

Adobe Photoshop
Adobe Systems Incorporated
1585 Charleston Road
P.O. Box 7900
Mountain View, CA 94039-7900
Voice: (800) 862-3623
Voice: (800) 833-6687
Fax: (415) 961-3769
URL: http://www.adobe.com

clip2gif
Freeware
Yves Piguet
Institut d'automatique
EPFL
1015 Lausanne
Switzerland
Voice: +41 21 693-3834
Fax: +41 21 693-2574
URL: ftp://ftp-2.amug.org/info-mac/gst/grf/
E-mail: piguet@ia.epfl.ch

Fractal Design Painter
Fractal Design Corporation
335 Spreckels Drive
Aptos, CA 95003
Voice: (408) 688-5300
Fax: (408) 688-8836
URL: http://www.fractal.com

Freehand
Macromedia
600 Townsend Street
San Francisco, CA 94103-9632
Voice: (800) 288-4797
Voice: (415) 252-2000
Fax: (415) 626-0554
URL: http://www.macromedia.com/Tools/Freehand/

Graphic Converter
Shareware
Thorsten Lempke
Lemke Software
Insterburger Strasse 6
31228 Peine
Germany
Fax: +49 (0) 5171-72920
URL: ftp://ftp.uwtc.washington.edu/pub/Mac/Graphics/
E-mail: 100102.1304@compuserve.com

Kai's Power Tools
HSC Software
6303 Carpinteria Avenue
Carpinteria, CA 93013
Voice: (805) 566-6200
Fax: (805) 566-6385

Transparency
Freeware
Aaron Giles
URL: ftp://ftp.uwtc.washington.edu/pub/Mac/Graphics/
E-mail: giles@med.cornell.edu

Clip Art & Digital Photography

ClickArt Studio Series
T/Maker Company
1390 Villa Street
Mountain View, CA 94041
Voice: (415) 962-0195
Fax: (415) 962-0201

CMCD
CMCD Inc.
600 Townsend Street, Penthouse
San Francisco, California 94103
Voice: (800) 664-2623
Fax: (415) 703-0711
URL: http://www.cmdesign.com

Corel Professional Photos
Corel Corporation
1600 Carling Avenue
Ottawa, Ontario CANADA K1Z 8R7
Voice: (800) 772-6735
Voice: (613) 728-3733
Fax: (613) 761-9176
URL: http://www.corelnet.com

Image Club Graphics Inc.
729 24th Avenue Southeast
Calgary, Alberta CANADA T2G 5K8
Voice: (800) 387-9193
Fax: (403) 261-7013
URL: http://www.adobe.com/imageclub/
E-mail: imageclub@aol.com

Instant Buttons & Controls
stat Media
7077 East Shorecrest Drive
Anaheim Hills, CA 92807-4506
Voice: (714) 280-0038
Fax: (714) 280-0039

Multimedia Applications & Utilities

Adobe Premiere
Adobe Systems Incorporated
1585 Charleston Road
P.O. Box 7900
Mountain View, CA 94039-7900
Voice: (800) 833-6687
Fax: (415) 961-3769
URL: http://www.adobe.com

Avid's VideoShop
Avid Technology
1 Metropolitan Park West
Tewksbury, MA 01876
Voice: (800) 949-2843
Voice: (508) 640-6789
Fax: (508) 640-1366
URL: http://www.avid.com
E-mail: info@avid.com

Brian's SoundTool
Brian Scott
2 Pascoe Road
Boronia 3155 Australia
E-mail: bscott@ironbark.ucnv.edu.au
plug-ins from: gopher.archive.umich.edu.7055/00/mac/sound/sound util/

Cambium Sound Choice
Cambium Development
P.O. Box 296-H
Scarsdale, NY 10583-8796
Voice: (800) 231-1779
Voice: (914) 472-6246
Fax: (914) 472-6729

Digidesign's Sound Designer II
Digidesign's Pro Tools
Sound Tools
URL: http://www.digidesign.com

Elastic Reality
Transjammer
Avid Technology
1 Metropolitan Park West
Tewksbury, MA 01876
Voice: (800) 949-2843
Voice: (508) 640-6789
Fax: (508) 640-1366
URL: http://www.avid.com
E-mail: info@avid.com

flattenMoov
Freeware
Author: Robert Hennessy
URL: ftp://mirror.apple.com/mirrors/info-mac/_Graphic_&_Sound_Tool/_Movie/flatmoov.hqx
E-mail: 70363.2164@compuserve.com

InterActive
Kai's Power Tools
KPT Convolver
HSC Software
6303 Carpinteria Avenue
Carpinteria, CA 93013
Voice: (800) 472-9025
Voice: (805) 566-6200
Fax: (805) 566-6385
URL: http://www.hsc.com
E-mail: hscsales@aol.com

MacroMedia Director
Macromedia
600 Townsend Street
San Francisco, CA 94103-9632
Voice: (800) 288-4797
Voice: (415) 252-2000
Fax: (415) 626-0554
URL: http://www.macromedia.com

Maven QTR viewer
Freeware
Authors: Charley Kline and Eric Scouten
URL: ftp://mirrors.aol.com/pub/info-mac/comm/_MacTCP/maven-20d37.hqx
E-mail: kline@uiuc.edu and scouten@uiuc.edu

MPEGAud
George Warner
E-mail: warnergt@aloft.att.com

MPEG/CD
Kaua'i Media
URL: http://www.kauai.com/~bbal/
E-mail: bbal@kauai.com

Multimedia Utilities
CamraMan
PROmotion
Motion Works International
330 Townsend Street, Suite 123
San Francisco, CA 94107
Voice: (415) 541-9333
Fax: (415) 541-0555
URL: http://www.mtw.com
E-mail: info@motionworks.com

MusicBytes
Prosonus
2820 Honolulu Avenue, Suite 268
Verdugo City, CA 91046
Voice: (800) 999-6191
Voice: (818) 766-5221
Fax: (818) 248-9417

Opcode Systems' DigiTrax
Opcode Systems' Inc.
3950 Fabian Way
Palo Alto,CA 94303
Voice: (415) 856-3333
Fax: (415) 856-0777
URL: http://www.opcode.com
E-mail: info@opcode.com

QuickEditor
Author: Mathias Tschoop
13 Troupe
CH-1253 Vandoeuvres
Geneva Switzerland
Fax: (41-22) 348.33.28
URL: ftp://mirror.apple.com/mirrors/info-mac/_Graphic_&_Sound_Tool/_Movie/quick-editor-361.hqx
E-mail: mtschopp@perokcity.net.ch

QuickTime for Windows & QuickTime Development Kit (APDA, #R0453LL/B)
APDA Apple Computer, Inc.
P.O. Box 319
Buffalo, NY 14207-0319
Voice: (800) 282-2732
Voice: (800) 637-0029 Canada
Voice: (716) 871-6555 Intl
URL: http://www.apple.com
E-mail: APDA@applelink.apple.com

Radius Spigot Power AV and Spigot Pro
215 Moffet Park Drive
Sunnyvale, CA 94089
Voice: (408) 541-6100
Fax: (408) 541-6150
URL: http://www.radius.com

SoundEdit 16
Macromedia
600 Townsend Street
San Francisco, CA 94103-9632
Voice: (800) 288-4797
Voice: (415) 252-2000
Fax: (415) 626-0554
URL: http://www.macromedia.com

Sound Effects
Author: Alberto Ricci
Corso De Gasperi 45
10129 Torino
Italy
URL: ftp://ftp.alpcom.it/software/mac/Ricci
E-mail: ricci@pmn.it

Sound Hack
Author: Tom Erbe
Frog Peak Music (A Composers' Collective)
Box 1052
Lebanon, NH 03766
URL: ftp://music.calarts.edu/pub/SoundHack/
E-mail: tre@music.calarts.edu

Sound Manager
URL: ftp://ftp.info.apple.com/Apple.Support.Area/Apple.Software.Updates/US/Macintosh/System/Other_System/Sound_Manager_3.1.sea.hqx

SoundTrack
Access Softek
2550 Ninth Street, Suite 206
Berkeley, CA 94710
Voice: (800) 386-4272
Voice: (510) 848-0606

Sparkle
Freeware
Author: Maynard Handley
ftp://mirror.apple.com/mirrors/info-mac/
Graphic&_Sound_Tool/_Movie/sparkle-245.hqx
E-mail: maynardh@apple.com

Web Servers, CGI Programs & Utilities

Aretha/Frontier
Freeware
UserLand Software, Inc.
400 Seaport Court
Redwood City, CA 94063
Voice: (415) 369-6600
Fax: (415) 369-6618
URL: htpp://www.hotwired.com/userland/aretha/

InterServer Publisher
Commercial
Intercon Systems Corporation
950 Herndon Parkway
Suite 420
Herndon, VA 22070
Voice: (800) 468-7266
Voice: (703) 709-9890
Fax: (703) 709-5555
URL: http://www.intercon.com
URL: ftp://ftp.intercon.com/public
E-mail: comment@intercon.com

MacCommon LISP Server
Freeware
John C. Mallery
Artificial Intelligence Laboratory
Massachusetts Institute of Technology
Cambridge, MA 02139-4301
Voice: (617) 253-5966
Fax: (617) 253-5060
URL: ftp://ftp.ai.mit.edu/pub/users/jcma/cl-http/
E-mail: JCMa@AI.MIT.edu

MacHTTP Server
Shareware
Chuck Shotten
Biap Systems
URL: ftp://ftp.uwtc.washington.edu/pub/Mac/Network/WWW/MacHTTP2.2.sit.bin

MacPerl & MacPerl CGI Extensions
Freeware
Matthais Neeracher
URL: http://err.ethz.ch/members/neeri/macintosh/perl-qa.html
E-mail: neeri@iis.ee.ethz.ch

MacTCP Switcher
Freeware
John Norstad
Academic Computing and Network Services
Northwestern University
URL: ftp://ftp.acns.nwu.edu/pub/jlnstuff/mactcp-switcher/
E-mail: j-norstad@nwu.edu

Netscape Communications Server
Commercial
Netscape Inc.
501 East Middlefield Road
Mountain View, CA 61874
Voice: (415) 254-1900
Fax: (415) 528-4124
URL: http://home.netscape.com/
E-mail: info@netscape.com

Parse CGI OSAX
Shareware
Mark Kriegsman & Alex Powers
Document Directions, Inc.
131 State Street
Boston, MA 02109
Voice: (617) 227-2100
URL: ftp://ftp.uwtc.washington.edu/pub/Mac/Programming/AppleScript/
E-mail: ddi@document.com

Script Tools OSAX
Freeware
Mark Alldritt
1571 Deep Cove Road
North Vancouver, BC V7G-1S4
Canada
URL: ftp://gaea.kgs.ukans.edu/applescript/osaxen/
E-mail: alldritt@wimsey.com

WebMap
Shareware
Rowland Smith
City Net Express
3531 SE 11th Avenue
Portland, OR 97202
URL: http://www.city.net/cnx/software/webmap.html
E-mail: rowland@city.net

WebSTAR Server
Commercial
StarNine Technologies
2550 Ninth Street
Suite 112
Berkeley, CA 94710
Voice: (510) 649-4949
Fax: (510) 548-0393
URL: http://www.starnine.com/webstar.html
E-mail: info@starnine.com

Compression Utilities

Compact Pro
Shareware
Bill Goodman
Cyclos
P.O. Box 31417
San Francisco, CA, 94131-0417
URL: ftp://ftp.uwtc.washington.edu/pub/Mac/CompEnc/

MacBinary II +
Freeware
Peter Lewis
10 Earlston Way
Booragoon, WA, 6154
Australia
URL: ftp://ftp.uwtc.washington.edu/pub/Mac/CompEnc/
E-mail: peter@cujo.curtin.edu.au

Stuffit Deluxe
Commerical
Aladdin Systems, Inc.
165 Westridge Drive
Watsonville, CA 95076
Voice: (408) 761-6200
Fax: (408) 761-6206
E-mail: aladdin@well.com

Stuffit Expander
Freeware
Aladdin Systems, Inc.
165 Westridge Drive
Watsonville, CA 95076
Voice: (408) 761-6200
Fax: (408) 761-6206
URL: ftp://ftp.uwtc.washington.edu/pub/Mac/CompEnc/
E-mail: aladdin@well.com

SunTar 2.0.2
Freeware
Sauro Speranza
via Cappuccini 18
40026 Imola
Italy
URL: ftp://ftp.uwtc.washington.edu/pub/Mac/CompEnc/
E-mail: speranza@cirfid.unibo.it

Web Document Design Services

@design
Alan Eyzaguirre
979 Dolores Street
San Francisco, CA 94110
Voice: (415) 824-4611
Fax: (415) 648-8917
URL: http://www.atdesign.com/
E-mail: ake@atdesign.com

American Information Systems Inc.
911 North Plum Grove Road, Suite F
Schaumburg, IL 60173
Voice: (708) 413-8400
Fax: (708) 413-8401
URL: http://www.ais.net
E-mail: info@ais.net

Audio Online Inc.
8672 Heritage Road
Norval, Ontario CANADA L0P 1K0
Voice: (905) 451-2804
URL: http://www.audio-online.com/ao/
E-mail: dave@audio-online.com

Best Internet Communications
Jan Herzog
421 Castro Street
Mountain View, CA 94041
Voice: (415) 964-2378
Fax: (415) 691-4195
URL: http://www.best.com
E-mail: webmaster@best.com

Beverly Hills Software
469 S. Bedford Drive
Beverly Hills, CA 90212
Voice: (310) 843-0414
Fax: (310) 843-9917
URL: http://netwizards.com/
E-mail: sales@bhs.com

Bonsai Software
2582 Old First Street
Livermore, CA 94550-3155
Voice: (510) 606-5701
Fax: (510) 606-5702
URL: http://www.bonsai.com
E-mail: ksedgwic@bonsai.com

EPublish
2806 Union St.
Madison, WI 53704
Voice: (608) 243-8000
URL: http://www.fullfeed.com/epub/index.html
E-mail: office@epublish.com

Free Range Media, Inc.
117 South Main, Suite 400
Seattle, WA 98104
Voice: (206) 340-9305
Fax: (206) 340-0509
URL: http://www.freerange.com/
E-mail: info@freerange.com

Internet Design Group
Kenneth Li
745 Stanford Avenue
Palo Alto, CA 94306
Voice: (415) 424-0747
Fax: (415)424-0751
URL: http://www.mall.net/homepage.htm
E-mail: idg@mall.net

The Internet Group
305 South Craig Street
Pittsburgh, PA 15213
Voice: (412) 688-9696
FAX: (412) 688-9697
URL: http://www.tig.com/
E-mail: info@tig.com

Internet Outfitters
Chris Paine
12335 Santa Monica Blvd. #445
Los Angeles, CA 90025
Voice: 310-395-3003
Fax: 310 395-3923
URL: http://www.netoutfit.com/
E-mail: cpaine@netoutfit.com

Internet Technologies Group
59 Sparks St.
P.O. Box 714, Station B
Ottawa, Ontario
K1P 5P8
Voice: (613) 720-0293
URL: http://www.magi.com/itg/
E-mail: itg@magi.com

Knossopolis
John Maxwell
Box 65789 Station F
Vancouver, Canada V5N 5K7
Voice: (604) 988-4770
Fax: (604) 873-5786
URL: http://www.knosso.com/
E-mail: knossopolis@wimsey.com

Lara Consulting Group
188 North Street, Suite 43
Boston, Massachusetts 02113
Voice: 617/248-6999
Fax: 617/248-6898
URL: http://www.lara.com/
E-mail: info@lara.com

MachNet Internet Services
14510 Big Basin Way Suite 180
Saratoga, CA 95070
Voice: (408) 985-2616
Fax: (408) 985-2441
URL: http://www.machnet.com
E-mail: info@machnet.com

MacVantages
Colin Enger
Voice: (703) 739-2671
Fax: (703) 739-2671
URL: http://www.macvantages.com/
E-mail: postmaster@macvantages.com

Michele~Shine Media
1800 Market Street, Suite 204
San Francisco, CA 94103
Voice: (415) 621-0299
Fax: (415) 621-5023
URL: www.internex.com/MSM/home.html
E-mail: crmk@netcom.com

NetMind Media
713 Sutter Avenue
Palo Alto, CA 94303
Voice: (415) 323-8125
Fax: (415) 626-1226
URL: http://www.mindnet.com/
E-mail: info@mindnet.com

NEW GENISYS
Voice: (510) 277-7726
Fax: (510) 743-4531
URL: http://www.intellisoft.com/newgenisys/
E-mail: ngenisys@ix.netcom.com

NPiX Interactive Web Marketing
Voice: (404) 892-1971
URL: http://www.com/npix
E-mail: info@npixi.com

Phaedrus Company
63 Prospect St. Suite 2B
Waltham, MA 02154
Voice: Phone: (617) 899-9056
Fax: (617) 899-9428
URL: http://www.thinkthink.com/phaedrus/
E-mail: postmaster@phaedrusco.com

Tecnation Digital World
555 Bryant Street #257
Palo Alto, California 94301
Voice: (415) 327-4332
Fax: (415) 327-1910
URL: http://www.tecnation.com/tecnation/
E-mail: hello@tecnation.com

Thunderstone Software — EPI, Inc. (Information Retrieval)
11115 Edgewater Drive
Cleveland, Ohio 44102
Voice: (216) 631-8544
Fax: (216) 281-0828
URL: http://www.thunderstone.com
E-mail: info@thunderstone.com

UniPress W3 Services Division
UniPress Software, Inc.
W3 Services Division
2025 Lincoln Highway
Edison, NJ 08817
Voice: (800) 222-0550 x922 (Clay Webster)
Voice: (908) 287-2100
URL: http://www.unipress.com/w3/
E-mail: w3@unipress.com

Virtual Marketing, Inc.
7229 W Franklin
Boise, ID 83709
Voice: (208) 377-1380
Fax: (208) 377-9150
URL: http://www.vmis.com/
E-mail: info@www.vmis.com

Webvertising
2727 Nasha Road 1, Suite 615
Seabrook, TX 77586
Voice: (713) 326-4886
Fax: (713) 326-3952
URL: http://www.sccsi.com/welcome.html
E-mail: whitney@sccsi.com

Xynergy
ElectoMedia Interactive Web Design
136 Piedra Loop
Los Alamos, NM 87504
Voice: (505) 470-2589
Voice: (505) 982-8383, ext. 20
URL: http://www.nets.com/xynergy.html
E-mail: electromedia@nets.com

Young Ideas
207 2nd Street, Suite B
Sausalito, CA 94965
Voice: (415) 331-3128
Fax: (415) 331-9620
URL: http://www.slip.net/~indi/
E-mail: indi@bonsai.com

Macintosh, Internet & Web Related Publications

Boardwatch Magazine
Newstand/Subscription
8500 W. Bowles Avenue, Suite 210
Littleton, CO 80123
Voice: (303) 973-6038
Fax: (303) 973-3731
URL: http://www.boardwatch.com
E-mail: jack.rickard@boardwatch.com

Digital Video Magazine
Newstand/Subscription
80 Elm Street
St. Peterborough, NH 03458
Voice: (800) 441-4403
Voice: (603) 924-0100
Fax: (516) 562-7406
Subscriptions: (800) 998-0806
E-mail (subscriptions): subs@dv.com

Internet Business Journal
Strangelove Internet Enterprises, Inc.
208 Somerset Street East, Suite A
Ottawa, Ontario Canada K1N 6V2
Voice: (613) 565-0982
Fax: (613) 569-4432

The Internet Letter
NetWeek LLC
1294 National Press Building
Washington, DC 20045
Voice: (202) 638-6020
Fax: (202) 638-6019
URL: http://www.infohaus.com/access/by-seller/Internet_Letter
E-mail: info@netweek.com

Internet World
Newstand/Subscription
Mecklermedia Corporation
20 Ketchum Street
Westport, CT 06880
Voice: (203) 226-6967

MacUser
Newstand/Subscription
P.O. Box 56986
Boulder, CO 80322-6986
Phone: (800) 627-2247
Voice: (303) 665-8930
Fax: (303) 604-7455
E-mail: faq@macuser.ziff.com (enter sub-faq in the subject line)

Macworld
Newstand/Subscription
501 Second Street
San Francisco, CA 94107
Voice: (800) 288-6848
Fax: (415) 442-0766
E-mail: 70370.702@compuserve.com

Matrix News
Matrix Information and Directory Services
1106 Clayton Lane, Suite 500W
Austin, TX 78723
Voice: (512) 451-7602
Fax: (512) 452-0128

NetGuide
Newstand/Subscription
600 Community Drive
Manhasset, NY 11030
Voice: (516) 562-5000
Fax: (516) 562-7406
URL: http://wais.wais.com:80/techweb/ng/current/
E-mail: netmail@netguide.cmp.com

Net Week Inc.
220 National Press Building
Washington, DC 20045
Voice: (202) 638-6020
Fax: (202) 638-6019
E-mail: netweek@access.digex.net

New Media
Newstand/Subscription
901 Mariner's Island Boulevard, Suite 365
San Mateo, CA 94404
Voice: (415) 573-5170
Fax: (415) 573-5131

ONLINE ACCESS
Newstand/Subscription
900 N. Franklin, Suite 310
Chicago, IL 60610
Voice: (312) 573-1700

Publish
Newstand/Subscription
501 Second Street
San Francisco, CA 94107
Voice: (415) 978-3280
Fax: (415) 975-2613
E-mail: 76127.205@compuserve.com

WIRED
Newstand/Subscription
544 Second Street
San Francisco, CA 94107
Voice: (415) 904-0660
Fax: (415) 904-0669
URL: http://www.wired.com
E-mail: info@wired.com

SERVICE PROVIDERS & SERVER SERVICES

Allied Access Inc.
Areas Code(s): 800, 618, 217, 314
1002 Walnut Street
Murphysboro, IL 62966
(800) 463-8366
Voice: (618) 684-2255
Fax : (618) 684 5907
URL: http://www.intrnet.net/
E-mail: sales@intrnet.net

American Information Systems Inc. (Server Service)
Area code(s): 312, 708, 800, 815
911 North Plum Grove Road, Suite F
Schaumburg, IL 60173
Voice: (708) 413-8400
Fax: (708) 413-8401
URL: http://www.ais.net
E-mail: info@ais.net

Automatrix, Inc. (Server Service)
P.O Box 196
Rexford, NY 12148
Voice: (518) 372-5791
Voice: (518) 877-7270
URL: http://www.automatrix.com

BBN Planet
3801 East Bayshore Road
Palo Alto, CA 94303
Voice: (800) 662-4770
Voice: (415) 934-2655
Fax: (415) 934-2665
URL: http://www.bbnplanet.com
E-mail: info@bbnplanet.com

Best Internet Communications Inc.
421 Castro Street
Mountain View, CA 94041
Voice: (415) 964-2378
Fax: (415) 691-4195
URL: http://www.best.com
E-mail: info@best.com

BizNet Technologies (Server Service)
Corporate Research Center
1872 Pratt Drive, Suite 1725
Blacksburg, VA 24062
Voice: (703) 231-7715
URL: http://www.BizNet.com.blacksburg.va.us/index.html
E-mail: biznet@bevnet

Branch Information Services (Server Service)
2910 Hubbard
Ann Arbor, MI 48105-2467
Voice: (313) 741-4442
Fax: (313) 995-1931
URL: http://branch.com:1080
E-mail: jon@branch.com

CCI Networks
Area code(s): 403
4130 95th Street
Edmonton, Alberta Canada T6E 6H5
Voice: (403) 450-6787
URL: http://www.ccinet.ab.ca
E-mail: info@ccinet.ab.ca

CCnet Communications
Area code(s): 510
Voice: (510) 988-0680
190 N. Wiget Lane, Suite# 291
Walnut Creek, CA 94598
Voice: (510)988-0680
URL: http://www.ccnet.com
E-mail: info@ccnet.com

CERFnet
Area code(s): 619, 510, 415, 818, 714, 310, 800
P.O. Box 85608
San Diego, CA 92186-9784
Voice: (800) 876-2373
Voice: (619) 455-3900
URL: http://www.cerfnet.com
E-mail: sales@cerf.net

CICNet
Area code(s): 217, 309, 312, 313, 708, 800
2901 Hubbard Drive
Ann Arbor, MI 48105
Voice: (800) 947-4754
Voice: (313) 998-6703
Fax: (313) 998-6105
URL: http://www.cic.net
E-mail: info@cic.net

Clark Internet Services, Inc. (Server Service)
Area Codes: 202, 310, 410, 703
10600 Route 108
Ellicottt City, MD 21042
Voice: (800) 735-2258
Fax: (410) 730-9765
URL: http://www.clark.net
E-mail: info@clarknet

Cloud 9
Area code(s): 914
15 Lake Street
White Plains, New York 10603-3851
Voice: (914) 682-0626
Fax: (914) 682-0506
URL: http://www.cloud9.net/
E-mail: info@cloud9.net

Colorado SuperNet
Area code(s): 303, 719, 800
One Denver Place
999 18th Street
Denver, CO 80202
Voice: (303) 296-8202
Fax: (303) 296-8224
URL: http://www.csn.org
E-mail: info@csn.org

Computing Engineers (Server Service)
P.O. Box 285
Vernon Hills, IL 60061
Voice: (708) 367-1870
Fax: (708) 367-1872
URL: http://www.wwa.com/
E-mail: info@wwa.com

Concentric Research Corporation
10590 N. Tantau Ave.
Cupertino, CA 95014
Voice: (517) 895-0500
Fax: (517) 895-0529
URL: http://www.cris.com/
E-mail: support@concentric.net

CRL
Area code(s): 213, 310, 404, 415, 510, 602, 707, 800
Box 326
Larkspur, CA 94977
Voice: (415) 837-5300
Voice: (415) 381-2800
Fax: (415) 381-9578
URL: http://www.crl.com
E-mail: info@crl.com

CTS Network Services (Server Service)
Area code(s): 619
4444 Convoy Street, Suite 300
San Diego, CA 92111
Voice: (619) 637-3637
Fax: (619)637-3630
URL: http://www.cts.com
E-mail: support@cts.com

CyberGate
Area code(s): 305
662 South Military Trail
Deerfield Beach, FL 33442
Voice: (305) 428-4283
Fax: (305) 428-7977
URL: http://www.gate.net
E-mail: info@gate.net

Cyberius Online Inc.
Area Code(s): 613, 800
99 Fifth Avenue, Unit 406
Ottawa, Ontario K1S 5P5 Canada
Voice: (613) 233-1215
Fax: (613) 233-0292
URL: http://www.cyberus.ca/
E-mail: info@cyberus.ca

Cybersight (Server Service)
2162 NW Everett, Office #2
Portland, OR 97210
Voice: (503) 228-4008
Fax: (503) 224-1749
URL: http://cybersight.com
E-mail: imi@cybersight.com

Cyberspace
Area code(s): 206
300 Queen Anne Avenue North, Suite 396
Seattle, WA 98109-4599
Voice: (206) 505-5577
URL: http://www.cyberspace.com/
E-mail: support@cyberspace.com

Cyberspace Development (Server Service)
3700 Cloverleaf Drive
Boulder, CO 80304
Voice: (303) 938-8684
Fax: (303) 546-9667
URL: http://marketplace.com
E-mail: office@marketplace.com

DATABANK, Inc.
1473 Hwy 40
Lawrence, KS 66044
Voice: (913) 842-6699
Fax: (913) 843-8518
URL: http://www.databank.com
E-mail: info@databank.com

Digital Express: Group, Inc.
Area code(s): 301, 410, 609, 703, 714, 908, 909
6006 Greenbelt Road, Suite 228
Greenbelt, MD 20770
Voice: (800) 969-9090
Voice: (301)220-2020
URL: http://www.digex.net
E-mail: info@digex.net

EarthLink Network Inc.
Area Code(s): 213, 310, 714, 800, 805, 818
3171 Los Feliz Blvd., Suite 203
Los Angeles, CA 90039
Voice: (213) 644-9500
Fax: (213) 644-9510
URL: http://www.earthlink.net/
E-mail: info@earthlink.net

Echo
Area code(s): 212, 718
97 Perry Street, Suite 13
New York, NY 10014
Voice: 212-255-3839
URL: http://www.echonyc.com
E-mail: info@echonyc.com

Florida Online
Area Codes: 407, 813, 904
Digital Decisions, Inc.
3815 North US 1, Suite 59
Cocoa, Florida, 32926
Voice: (407) 635-8888
URL: http://www.digital.net
E-mail: info@digital.net

GEMS (Global Electronic Marketing Service) (Server Service)
200 Elmwood Davis Road, Suite 102
Liverpool, NY 13088
Voice: (315) 453-2912
Fax: (315) 453-3052
URL: http://www.gems.com/index.html
E-mail: info@gems.com

Global Connect
497 Queens Creek Road
Williamsburg, Virginia
Voice: (804) 229-4484
Fax: (804) 229-6557
URL: http://www.gc.net
E-mail: info@gc.net

Global Enterprise Services
Area code(s) 201, 202, 203, 338, 541, 212, 215, 401, 510, 516, 609, 708, 809, 908
3 Independence Way
Princeton, NJ 08540
Voice: (800) 358-4437
Voice: (609) 897-7300
Fax: (609) 897-7310
URL: http://www.jvnc.net/
E-mail: info@jvnc.net

HoloNet
Information Access Technologies, Inc.
46 Shattuck Square, Suite 11
Berkeley, CA 94704
Voice: (510) 704-0160
Fax: (510) 704-8019
URL: http://www.holonet.net/
E-mail: info@holonet.net (automated)
E-mail: support@holonet.net

IDS World Network
Area code(s): 401, 305, 407
3 Franklin Road
East Greenwich, RI 02818
Voice: (800) 437-1680
Voice: (401) 884-7856
URL: http://www.ids.net
E-mail: info@ids.net

Infoboard (Server Service)
3 Grant Road
Swampscott, MA 01907
Voice: (617) 592-6675
Fax: (617) 592-3042
URL: http://www.infoboard.com/infoboard
E-mail: infoboard@infoboard.com

Institute for Global Communications/IGC Networks
Area code(s): 415, PDN
18 De Boom Street
San Francisco, CA 94107
Voice: (415) 442-0220
Fax: (415) 546-1794
URL: http://www.igc.apc.org/igc/igcinfo.html
E-mail: igc-info@igc.apc.org

InterAccess Co.
Area code(s): 312, 708, 815
9400 W. Foster Avenue, Suite 111
Chicago, IL 60656
Voice: (800) 967-1580
Voice: (708) 671-0111
Fax: (708) 671-0113
URL: http://www.interaccess.com/
E-mail: info@interaccess.com

Internet Direct, Inc.
Area code: 602
1366 East Thomas, #210
Phoenix, CA 85014
Voice: (602) 274-0100
Fax: (602) 274-8518
URL: http://www.indirect.com
E-mail: info@indirect.com

Internet Express
Area code(s): 206, 303, 505, 602, 719, 800
1155 Kelly Johnson Boulevard, Suite 400
Colorado Springs, CO 80920
Voice: (800) 748-1200
Voice: (719) 592-1240
Fax: (719) 592-1201
URL: http://usa.net, http://www.usa.net
E-mail: service@usa.net

Internet Media Services (Server Service)
644 Emerson Street, Suite 21
Palo Alto, CA 94301
Voice: (415) 328-4638
Fax: (415) 328-4350
URL: http://netmedia.com
E-mail: info@netmedia.com

Internet Presence & Publishing Corp. (Server Service)
World Trade Center, Suite 1700
Norfolk, VA 23510
Voice: (800) 638-6155
Voice: (804) 446-9060
Fax: (804) 446-9061
URL: http://www.shopkeeper.com/cgi-bin/shopkeeper
E-mail: info@tcp.ip.net

InterNex Information Services, Inc. (Server Service)
Area code(s): 408, 415, 510
2302 Walsh Avenue
Santa Clara, CA 95051
Voice: (408) 496-5466
Fax: (408) 496-5485
URL: http://www.internex.net
E-mail: info@internex.net

Kalidospace (Server Service)
P.O. Box 341556
Los Angeles, CA 90034
Voice: (310) 399-4349
Fax: (310) 396-5489
URL: http://kspace.com
E-mail: editors@kspace.com

Liberty Information Network
Area code(s): 213, 310, 408, 415, 510, 619, 708, 714, 805, 818, 909
446 S Anaheim Hills Road, Suite 102
Anaheim, CA 92807
Voice: (800) 218-5157
Voice: (714) 996 9999
Fax: (714) 961 8700
URL: http://www.liberty.com/
E-mail: info@liberty.com

Macro Computer Solutions (MCS Net)
Area code(s): 312, 708, 815
1300 West Belmont, Suite 402
Chicago, IL 60657
Voice: (312) 248-8649
Fax: (312) 248-9865
URL: http://www.mcs.com
E-mail: info@mcs.com

Merit Network/MichNet
Area code(s): 313, 616, 517, 810, 906
2901 Hubbard Pod G
Ann Arbor, MI 48105
Voice: (313) 764-9430
Fax: (313) 747-3185
URL: http://www.merit.edu
E-mail: info@merit.edu

Metasystems Design Group, Inc. (Server Service)
2000 North 15th Street, Suite #103
Arlington, VA 22201
Voice: (703) 243-6622
Fax: (703) 841-9798
URL: http://www.tmn.com
E-mail: info@tmn.com

MIDnet (Server Service)
201 North 8th Street, Suite 421
Lincoln, NE 68508
Voice: (800) 682-5550
Voice: (402) 472-7600
Fax: (402) 472-0240
URL: http://www.mid.net
E-mail: info@mid.net

Mnematics, Incorporated (Sever Service)
Area code(s): 212, 718, 800, 914
P.O. Box 19
Sparkill, NY 10976-0019
Voice: (914) 359-4546
Fax: (914) 359 0361
URL: http://www.mne.com/
E-mail: service@mne.com

Moran Communications
Area code(s): 716
1576 Sweet Home Road
Amherst, NY 14228
Voice: (716) 639-1254
Fax: (716) 636-3630
URL: http://www.moran.com/
E-mail: info@moran.com

MRNet
Area code(s): 612,507, 218
511 11th Avenue Box 212 South
Minneapolis, MN 55415
Voice: (612) 342-2570
Fax: (612) 344-1716
URL: http://www.mr.net
E-mail: info@mr.net

MSEN, Inc.
Area code(s): 313, 810, 800
628 Brooks Street
Ann Arbor, MI 48103
Voice: (313) 998-4562
Fax: (313) 998-4563
URL: http://www.msen.com
E-mail: info-request@msen.com

Mulitmedia Ink Designs (Server Service)
14544 High Pine Street
Poway, CA 92064
Voice: (619) 679-8317
URL: http://mmink.cts.com/mmink/mmi.html
E-mail: rdegel@ctsnet.cts.com

MV Communications, Inc.
Area code(s): 603
P.O Box 4963
Manchester, NH 03108
Voice: (603) 429-2223
URL: http://www.mv.com
E-mail: info@mv.com

NEARNET
BBN Technology Services, Inc.
10 Moulton Street
Cambridge, MA 02138
Voice: (800) 632-7638
Voice: (617) 873-8730
Fax: (617) 873-5620
URL: http://www.near.net
E-mail: nearnet-join@near.net

Neosoft
Area code(s): 214, 314, 409, 504, 713, 800, SprintNet
3408 Mangum Street
Houston, TX 77092
Voice: (713) 968-5800
URL: http://www.neosoft.com
E-mail: info@neosoft.com

Netcom On-Line: Communications Services
Area code(s): 206, 212, 214, 303, 310, 312, 404, 408, 415, 503, 510, 512, 617, 619, 703, 714, 818, 916
4000 Moorpark Avenue, Suite 209
San Jose, CA 95117
Voice: (800) 501-8649
Voice: (408) 983-5950
Fax: (408) 241-9145
E-mail: info@netcom.com

netIllinois
Area code(s): 313, 708, 800
1840 Oak Avenue
Evanston, IL 60201
Voice: (708) 866-1825
Fax: (708) 866-1857
URL: http://www.illinois.net
E-mail: info@illinois.net

Net+Effects (Server Service)
Net+Effects
6475 Dwyer Court
San José, CA 95120
Voice: (408) 739-0557
URL: http://www.net.effects.com
E-mail: info@net.effects.com

Netrex, Inc
Areas code(s): 215, 216, 219, 312, 313, 317, 419, 513, 517, 614, 616, 708, 810
3000 Town Center Suite 1100
Southfield, MI 48075
Voice: (800) 363-8739
Fax : (810) 352-2375
URL: http://www.netrex.com/
E-mail: info@netrex.com

North Bay Network
Area code(s): 415, 707
20 Minor Court
San Rafael, CA 94903
Voice: (415) 472-1600
Fax: (415) 472-2461
URL: http://www.nbn.com
E-mail: info@nbn.com

North Shore Access
Area code(s): 617, 508
Voice: (617) 593-3110
URL: http://www.shore.net
E-mail: info@shore.net

NorthWestNet
Area code(s): 206
15400 S.E. 30th Place, Suite 202
Bellvue, WA 98007
Voice: (206) 562-3000
Fax: (206) 562-3791
URL: http://www.nwnet.net
E-mail: info@nwnet.net

Northwest Nexus
Area code(s): 206
10800 NE 8th Street, Suite 802
Bellvue, WA 98004
Voice: (800) 539-3505 (voice only)
(206) 455-3505
URL: http://www.halcyon.com
E-mail: info@halcyon.com

Nuance Network Services
Area code(s): 205
904 Bob Wallace Avenue, Suite 119
Huntsville, AL 35801
Voice: (205) 533-4296
URL: http://www.nuance.com
E-mail: info@nuance.com

OARNet
Area code(s): 614
1224 Kinnear Road
Columbus, OH 43212
Voice: (614) 292-8100
Fax: (614) 292-7168
Voice: (800) 627-8101
URL: http://www.oar.net
E-mail: info@oar.net

Pacific Rim Network, Inc.
Area code(s): 206, 360, 800
PO Box 5006
Bellingham, WA 98227
Voice: (360) 650-0442
Fax: (360) 738-8315
URL: http://www.pacificrim.net/
E-mail: info@pacificrim.net

Panix Public Access UNIX & Internet
Area code(s): 212, 516
Voice: (212) 741-4400
Fax: (212) 741-5311
URL: http://www.panix.com/
E-mail: info@panix.com

Performance Systems International, Inc. (PSI)
Area code(s): Call or send e-mail to numbers-info@psi.com for list
510 Huntmar Park Drive
Herndon, VA 12180
Voice: (800) 827-7482
Voice: (703) 620-6551
Fax: (703) 620-4586
Faxback: (800) 329-7741
URL: http://www.psi.net
E-mail: info@psi.com

Phantom Access
Area code(s): 212, 516, 718, 914
1562 First Avenue, Suite 351
New York, NY 10028
Voice: (212) 989-2418
Fax: (212) 989-8648
URL: www.phantom.com
E-mail: info@phantom.com

Pipeline
Area code(s): 212, 718
150 Broadway
New York, NY 10038
Voice: (212) 267-3636
URL: http://www.pipeline.com
E-mail: infobot@pipeline.com

Portal Communications Company
Area code: 408, SprintNet
20863 Stevens Creek Boulevard, Suite 200
Cupertino, CA 95014
Voice: (408) 973-9111
Fax: (408) 725-1580
URL: http://www.portal.com
E-mail: info@portal.com

PREPnet
305 S Craig Street, 2nd Floor
Pittsburg, PA 15213
Voice: (412) 268-7870
Fax: (412) 268-7875
URL: http://www.cmu.edu/
E-mail: prepnet@cmu.edu

Rocky Mountain Internet
Area code(s): 303, 719, 800
2860 S. Circle Drive, Suite 2202
Colorado Springs, CO 80906
Voice: (800) 900-7644
Fax: (719) 576-0301
URL: http://www.rmii.com/
E-mail: info@rmii.com

South Coast Computing Services, Inc.
Area code(s): 713, 800, 918
1811 Bering, Suite 100
Houston, TX 77057
Voice: (800) 770-8971
Voice: (713) 917-5000
Fax: (713) 917-5005
URL: http://www.sccsi.com/
E-mail: info@sccsi.com

Spry Consulting Group (Server Service)
316 Occidental Avenue South
Seattle, WA 98104
Voice: (206) 447-0800
Fax: (206) 447-9008
URL: http://www.spry.com
E-mail: info@spry.com

StarNet Communications (Winternet)
Area code: 612
9971 Valley View Road Suite 211
Eden Prairie, MN 55344
Voice: (612) 941-9177
Fax: (612) 942-0981
URL: http://www.winternet.com
E-mail: info@winternet.com

Studio X (Server Service)
1270 Calle de Comercio #3
Santa Fe, NM 87505
Voice: (505) 438-0505
Fax: (505) 438-1816
URL: http://www.nets.com
E-mail: webmaster@nets.com

SURAnet
8400 Baltimore Blvd.
College Park, MD 20740
Voice: (800) 787-2638
Voice: (301) 982-4600
Fax: (301) 982-4605
URL: http://www.sura.net
E-mail: marketing@suranet.net

Synergy Communications, Inc.
Area code(s): 402, 800
1941 South 42nd Street, Omaha NE 68105
Voice: (800) 345-9669
Voice: (402) 346-4638
Fax: (402) 346-0208
URL: http://www.synergy.net/channels/synergy/synergy.html
E-mail: info@synergy.net

Systems Solutions Network
Area code: 302
1254 Lorewood Grove Road
Middletown, DL 19709
Voice: (302) 378-1386
Fax: (302) 378-3871
E-mail: sharris@marlin.ssnet.com

Teleport
Area code(s): 503, 206
319 SouthWest Washington #803
Portland, OR 97204
Voice: (503) 223-0076
Fax: (503) 223-4372
URL: http://www.teleport.com
E-mail: info@teleport.com

Telerama Public Access Internet
Area code: 412
P.O. Box 60024
Pittsburg, PA 15211
Voice: (412) 481-3505
Fax: (412) 481-8568
URL: http://www.telerama.com
E-mail: info@telerama.com

Texas Metronet
Area code(s): 214, 817
860 Kinwest Parkway, Suite 179
Irving, TX 75063-3440
Voice: (214) 705-2900
Voice: (817) 543-8756
Fax: (214) 401-2802
URL: http://www.metronet.com
E-mail: info@metronet.com

The ThoughtPort Authority Inc.
Area code(s): 212, 312, 314, 412, 801, 813
2000 E. Broadway Suite 242
Columbia, MO 65201
Voice: (800) 477-6870
Fax: (314) 474 4122
URL: http://www.thoughtport.com/
E-mail: info@thoughtport.com

UUNET Technologies, Inc.
3060 Williams Drive
Fairfax, VA 22031
Voice: (800) 258-4039
Voice: (703) 206-5600
Fax: (703) 206-5601
URL: http://www.uu.net
E-mail: info@uunet.uu.net

VNet Internet Access, Inc.
Area code(s): 704, 919, Public Data Network (PDN)
1206 Kenilwratch Avenue
P.O. Box 31474
Charlotte, SC 28231
Voice: (800) 377-3282
Voice: (704) 334-3282
URL: http://www.vnet.net/
E-mail: info@vnet.net

XMission
Area code(s): 801
Voice: (801) 539-0852
URL: http://www.xmission.com
E-mail: support@xmission.com

XNet Information Systems
Area code(s): 312, 708, 815
3080 East Ogden Avenue, #202
Lisle, IL 60532
Voice: (708) 983-6064
URL: http://www.xnet.com
E-mail: info@xnet.com

Index

A

B

F

G

H

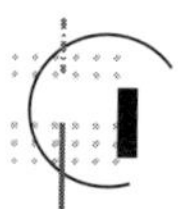

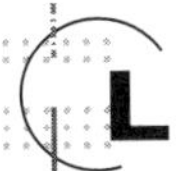

M

N

O

P

Q

R

S

T

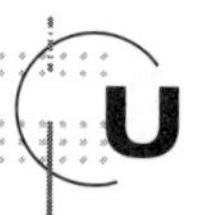

U

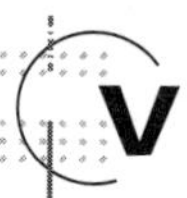

V

W

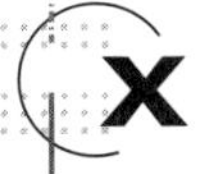

X

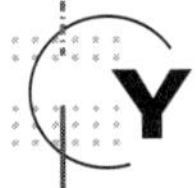

Y

Looking Good in Color 

$29.95

272 pages, illustrated

Like effective design, using color properly is an essential part of a desktop publishing investment. This richly illustrated four-color book addresses basic issues from color theory—through computer technologies, printing processes and budget issues—to final design. Even the graphically challenged can make immediate use of the practical advice in *Looking Good in Color.*

Looking Good in Print, Third Edition

$24.95

462 pages, illustrated

For use with any software or hardware, this desktop design bible has become the standard among novice and experienced desktop publishers alike. With more than 300,000 copies in print, *Looking Good in Print, Third Edition,* is even better—with new sections on photography and scanning. Learn the fundamentals of professional-quality design along with tips on resources and reference materials.

Newsletters From the Desktop, Second Edition

$24.95

392 pages, illustrated

Now the millions of desktop publishers who produce newsletters can learn how to improve the designs of their publications. Filled with helpful tips and illustrations, as well as hands-on tips for building a great-looking publication. Includes an all-new color gallery of professionally designed newsletters, offering desktop publishers at all levels a wealth of ideas and inspiration.

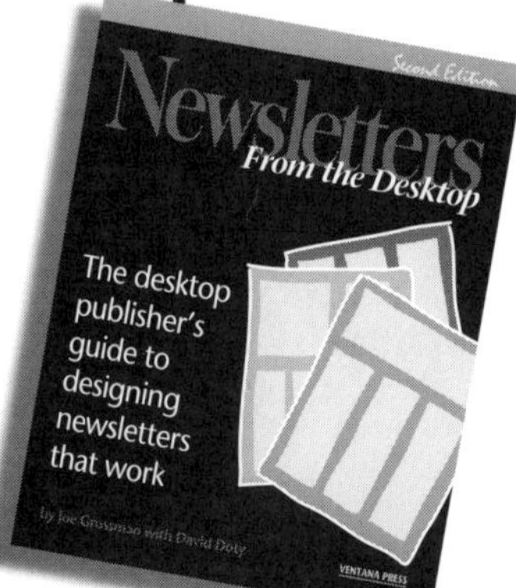

Books marked with this logo include a free Internet *Online Companion*™, featuring archives of free utilities plus a software archive and links to other Internet resources.

Check your local bookstore or software retailer for these and other bestselling titles, or call toll free: 800/743-5369

Walking the World Wide Web 

$29.95
360 pages, illustrated

Enough of lengthy listings! This tour features more than 300 memorable Websites, with in-depth descriptions of what's special about each. Includes international sites, exotic exhibits, entertainment, business and more. The companion CD-ROM contains Ventana Mosaic™ and a hyperlinked version of the book providing live links when you log onto the Internet.

America Online's Internet for Macintosh, Second Edition

$24.95
315 pages, illustrated

Forget about expensive, inscrutable Internet connections! AOL members can slide onto the Infobahn with a mere mouse-click. Same easy, graphical interface, no extra charges. This new edition adds tips on using AOL's new Web browser along with FTP, newsgroups and more.

Internet Roadside Attractions 

$29.95
376 pages, illustrated

Why take the word of one when you can get a quorum? Seven experienced Internauts–teachers and bestselling authors–share their favorite Web sites, Gophers, FTP sites, chats, games, newsgroups and mailing lists. Organized alphabetically by category for easy browsing with in-depth descriptions. The companion CD-ROM contains the entire text of the book, hyperlinked for off-line browsing and online Web-hopping.

Check your local bookstore or software retailer for these and other bestselling titles, or call toll free: 800/743-5369

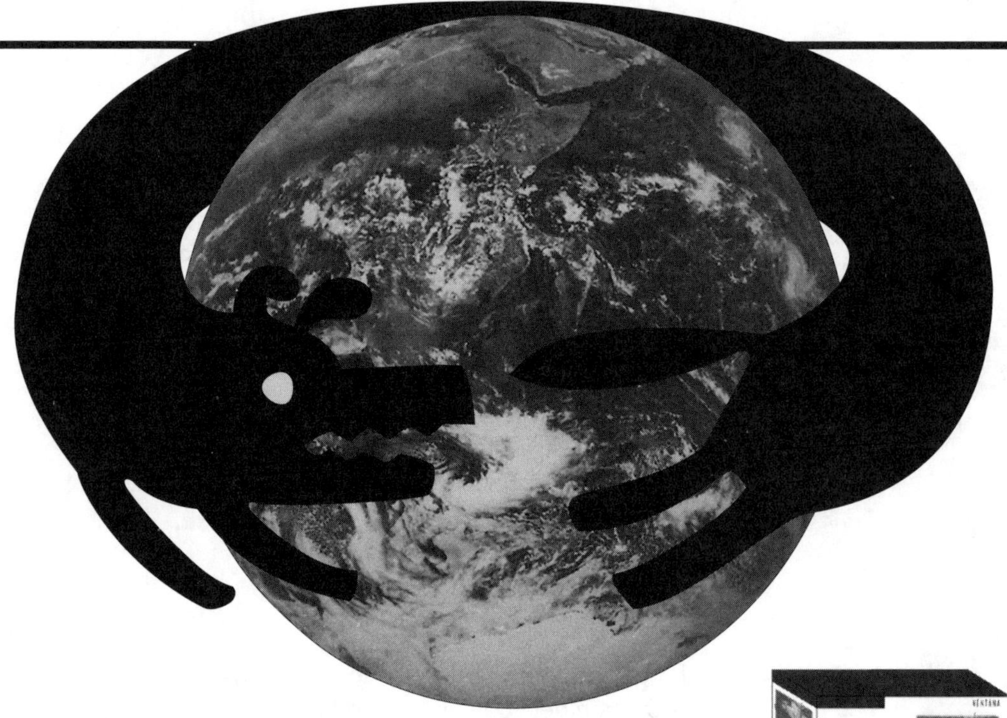

To order any Ventana Press title, complete this order form and mail or fax it to us, with payment, for quick shipment.

TITLE	ISBN	Quantity		Price		Total
Advertising From the Desktop	1-56604-064-7	______	x	$24.95	=	$ ________
America Online's Internet for Mac, 2nd Edition	1-56604-284-4	______	x	$24.95	=	$ ________
HTML Publishing on the Internet for Mac	1-56604-228-3	______	x	$49.95	=	$ ________
Internet Roadside Attractions	1-56604-193-7	______	x	$29.95	=	$ ________
Looking Good in Color	1-56604-219-4	______	x	$29.95	=	$ ________
Looking Good in Print, 3rd Edition	1-56604-047-7	______	x	$24.95	=	$ ________
Looking Good With QuarkXPress	1-56604-148-1	______	x	$34.95	=	$ ________
Mac, Word & Excel Desktop Companion, 2nd Edition	1-56604-130-9	______	x	$24.95	=	$ ________
Newsletters From the Desktop, 2nd Edition	1-56604-133-3	______	x	$24.95	=	$ ________
The Official America Online for Macintosh Membership Kit & Tour Guide, 2nd Edition	1-56604-127-9	______	x	$27.95	=	$ ________
The Official America Online for Windows Membership Kit & Tour Guide, 2nd Edition	1-56604-128-7	______	x	$27.95	=	$ ________
Photoshop f/x	1-56604-179-1	______	x	$39.95	=	$ ________
The System 7.5 Book, 3rd Edition	1-56604-129-5	______	x	$24.95	=	$ ________
Voodoo Mac, 2nd Edition	1-56604-177-5	______	x	$24.95	=	$ ________
Walking the World Wide Web	1-56604-208-9	______	x	$29.95	=	$ ________
World Wide Web Kit—Macintosh, Ventana Mosaic	1-56604-272-0	______	x	$49.95	=	$ ________
World Wide Web Kit—Windows, Ventana Mosaic	1-56604-271-2	______	x	$49.95	=	$ ________
				Subtotal	=	$ ________
				Shipping	=	$ ________
				TOTAL	=	$ ________

SHIPPING:

For all standard orders, please ADD $4.50/first book, $1.35/each additional.
For *World Wide Web Kit* orders, ADD $6.50/first kit, $2.00/each additional.
For "two-day air," ADD $8.25/first book, $2.25/each additional.
For "two-day air," on the kits, ADD $10.50/first book, $4.00 each additional.
For orders to Canada, ADD $6.50/book.
For orders sent C.O.D., ADD $4.50 to your shipping rate.
North Carolina residents must ADD 6% sales tax.
International orders require additional shipping charges.

Name ________________________ Daytime telephone ________________________

Company ____

Address (No PO Box) ____

City ________________________ State______ Zip ____________

Payment enclosed ___VISA ___MC ___ Acc't # ________________________ Exp. date________

Exact name on card ________________________ Signature ________________________

Mail to: Ventana • PO Box 13964 • Research Triangle Park, NC 27709-3964 ☎ 800/743-5369 • Fax 919/544-9472

Check your local bookstore or software retailer for these and other bestselling titles, or call toll free: **800/743-5369**

WWWow

Get On It

with HoTMetaL PRO™

- Import and convert Word, WordPerfect, and many other files
- Easier to use interface, including new toolbar
- Enhanced URL support
- Faster, smaller, more streamlined performance

Available on Windows, Mac and Unix

The best selling HTML publishing tool has just gotten better. Introducing HoTMetaL PRO 2.0, the easy way to create hypertext linked multi-media Web documents for Mosaic, Netscape or any other World Wide Web browser.

Introductory half price offer: **HoTMetaL PRO 2.0 for $99 US***

If you already have HoTMetaL PRO 1.0, upgrade for $59 US*

To order, call 1-800-360-8454

*Limited time offer regular list price $195. Call for details

SoftQuad SoftQuad Inc. 56 Aberfoyle Crescent, Toronto, ON, Canada •email: sales@sq.com Web Site: http://www.sq.com •For european orders, call +1 (416) 239-4801 or fax +1 (416) 239-7105